THE MECHANISM

A CRIME NETWORK SO DEEP IT BROUGHT DOWN A NATION

VLADIMIR NETTO

TRANSLATED BY ROBIN PATTERSON

EBURY
PRESS

1 3 5 7 9 10 8 6 4 2

Ebury Press, an imprint of Ebury Publishing
20 Vauxhall Bridge Road
London SW1V 2SA

Ebury Press is part of the Penguin Random House Group of companies
whose addresses can be found at global.penguinrandomhouse.com

First published by Ebury Press in 2019
First published with the title *Lava Jato* in Brazil in 2016
by Primeira Pessoa, Rio de Janeiro

www.penguin.co.uk

A CIP catalogue record for this book is available from the British Library

ISBN 9781529102895

Typeset in 11/14.3 pt Arno Pro
by Integra Software Services Pvt. Ltd, Pondicherry

Printed and bound in Great Britain by Clays Ltd, Elcograf S.p.A.

The legal status on 1 January 2019 of all individuals connected to this case can be found on p. 527.

Contents

Key Players and Political Parties

POLITICIANS

Luiz Inácio Lula da Silva (Lula), 35th President of Brazil
Dilma Rousseff, 36th President of Brazil
Renan Calheiros, speaker of the Senate
Delcídio do Amaral, Workers' Party leader in the Senate
Eduardo Cunha, speaker of the Chamber of Deputies
João Vaccari Neto, Workers' Party treasurer
José Dirceu, former government minister
Fernando Collor de Mello, senator and 32nd President of Brazil

JUDGES AND PROSECUTORS

Teori Zavascki, Justice of the Federal Supreme Court
Sergio Moro, federal judge in the southern city of Curitiba
Rodrigo Janot, prosecutor general of Brazil
Deltan Dallagnol, federal prosecutor leading the Car Wash task force

PETROBRAS EXECUTIVES

Paulo Roberto Costa, director of Supply Division
Nestor Cerveró, director of International Division

Renato Duque, director of Services Division
Pedro Barusco, executive in Services Division

BUSINESSMEN AND INTERMEDIARIES

Marcelo Odebrecht, chairman of Odebrecht group
Ricardo Pessoa, chairman of UTC Engenharia
Augusto Mendonça, executive at Toyo Setal
Júlio Camargo, consultant
Fernando 'Baiano' Soares, lobbyist
Alberto Youssef, black-market currency trader
José Carlos Bumlai, businessman friend of Lula's

POLITICAL PARTIES

PMDB (*Partido do Movimento Democrático Brasileiro*): Brazilian
Democratic Movement
PP (*Partido Progressista*): Progressive Party
PSDB (*Partido da Social Democracia Brasileira*): Brazilian Social
Democratic Party
PT (*Partido dos Trabalhadores*): Workers' Party
PTB (*Partido Trabalhista Brasileiro*): Brazilian Labour Party
SDD (*Solidariedade*): Solidarity

Introduction

MISHA GLENNY

Brazil matters. Not just to Brazilians but to every inhabitant of this planet. It's by far the biggest country in South America and the number one exporter of iron ore, coffee, orange juice, beef and soya – to name just a few commodities. It is currently the ninth largest economy in the world, but by 2050 analysts are confident that it will be the fourth largest after China, India and the US. But the critical reason we need to understand what's happening in Brazil is the Amazon. This rainforest is the lungs of our planet. Brazil has stewardship over 60 per cent; how it chooses to manage the Amazon will have an impact on all of us.

The book you have in your hands is vital to understanding the country's immediate past, its present and its unpredictable future.

I am writing this introduction in the wake of the inauguration of Brazil's new president, Jair Bolsonaro. The new leader makes no secret of his ideology or his political intentions, as his frequent use of misogynist, racist and homophobic language testifies. He eulogises Brazil's military dictatorship, which lasted for twenty-one years from 1964. During impeachment proceedings against the left-wing president, Dilma Rousseff, he lavished praise upon a former colonel, Carlos Brilhante Ustra, who headed up the torture unit at the time when Rousseff was a political prisoner.

Following the result of the Brexit referendum and the election of Donald Trump in the US, the rise of Bolsonaro is yet another disturbing example of the polarisation of public discourse since the financial crash of 2008. But his success also confirms how right-wing populists around the world have been able to exploit the anger triggered by economic failure and political stagnation much more effectively than liberals, social democrats and the Left.

The implications of Bolsonaro's victory are potentially as far-reaching as the Trump presidency. Like his US counterpart, Bolsonaro is a climate-change denier. During his campaign, he initially said he would take the country out of the Paris Climate Change Agreement, although he later moderated that position. Nonetheless, following the elections in Brazil, illegal forest clearance in the Amazon has jumped by 50 per cent, as developers are convinced that Bolsonaro will support their plans to expand agricultural land and mining sites at the expense of the world's most important natural habitat. If, as is feared, this pattern continues during his presidency, it will be the single biggest setback to the measures put in place by the Paris Agreement to combat climate change.

Yet despite this, Bolsonaro takes office boasting huge domestic popularity. He won the election in the second round with 55 per cent of the vote and, as he prepared to take power, 75 per cent of Brazilians said he was on the right track, with only

15 per cent condemning his extremist policies. *The Mechanism* offers key insights into how and why this happened.

Bolsonaro's election victory came as Brazil was recovering from what, by some estimates, was the largest corruption scandal in history – anywhere in the world. In Brazil it is known by the name of *Lava Jato* or Car Wash. The name comes from a somewhat convoluted reference to a petrol station, which provided the information leading to the first arrests in this scandal. At the time, the detectives and prosecutors involved had no idea that this routine investigation would be lifting the lid on a nation wide cesspit of money laundering and corruption which went right to the very top of Brazilian politics and business. Not only did it engulf the country's superstar politician, former president Luiz Ignácio Lula da Silva, known simply as Lula, it also culled some of Brazil's most powerful oligarchs, notably Marcelo Odebrecht, the erstwhile CEO of South America's largest construction company, Odebrecht. The reverberations were felt not only across Brazil but also much of South America where, it emerged, Odebrecht had been bribing politicians and civil servants left, right and centre.

It is impossible to understand the rise to power of Bolsonaro without pulling back the curtain to reveal the mind-boggling scale of Car Wash. Until the scandal, this former army captain was widely regarded as a ludicrous, isolated figure in the Chamber of Deputies spouting fanatical rhetoric. But much like Trump in America, he recognised the disgust many Brazilians felt regarding mainstream politics, and his assault on power was supercharged by the fallout from Car Wash.

The author of this book, Vladimir Netto, was a well-regarded journalist with Globo TV, the second largest television network in the Americas. In late 2014, he went to the capital of Paraná state, Curitiba, to cover a relatively minor aspect of the Car Wash story. He decided to stay on a few days and quickly submerged himself in the increasingly dark waters of the main investigation. Just over two years later, he finished this book.

Netto is a deft writer with an ability to conjure up the many characters who people Brazilian public life. Some are sinister, others clownish. Some are suave, others desperate. Most are on the take, one way or another, cocking a snook at the public whose taxes they were spending on cars, flats, ranches, private aeroplanes or works of art by the great masters.

One of the more gripping aspects of this story is watching how it slowly dawned on some of the most powerful people in Brazil that they were no longer immune from prosecution and imprisonment. Supported by their legions of lawyers, they indignantly denounced the criminal justice system and the alleged infringement of their liberties. These issues had rarely bothered them in the past. With 700,000 men and women in jail, Brazil has one of the most overcrowded and barbaric prison systems in the world. But almost all those locked up come from miserably poor backgrounds. It was unusual to see their ranks swell with some very rich people, even if many were able to negotiate reduced sentences or home imprisonment through the many plea bargains that took place. The tool of the plea bargain, basically imported from the United States, had not been much used in Brazil until then, but it was used to deadly effect by the Car Wash investigators and the man who led them, Judge Sergio Moro.

Moro became one of the most important public figures in Brazilian history within the space of two years. Like many young, middle-class Brazilians disaffected by the country's venal politicians during the 1990s, Moro eschewed a political career in favour of law. He was deeply influenced by *Mani Pulite*, the landmark anti-corruption campaign launched in Italy during the early 1990s, and became convinced that his home country needed to engage in a similar purging of the political system.

Before Car Wash, Moro had been in charge of two key cases. One led to the conviction of the notorious leader of Rio de Janeiro's biggest crime gang. But before this, he successfully prosecuted a huge financial scandal involving a major bank, Banestado. A key figure in this case was a currency dealer and money launderer called Alberto Youssef. So when Moro learned that Youssef was operating again through the currency-exchange shop at the petrol station, his interest was aroused. What happened next is the detailed subject of this book, meticulously recorded by an author who has succeeded in turning a bafflingly incomprehensible tale into a clear narrative.

There were many phases in the Car Wash investigation, but two are overwhelmingly significant for the light they shine on how deep the roots of institutionalised corruption have grown. The first concerns the bosses of Brazil's major construction companies. Car Wash reveals how they had arranged themselves into cartels that carved up the many lucrative contracts handed out by the semi-state-owned oil company Petrobras. Until just three years ago, Petrobras was the most valuable company in all South America. When its central role in Car Wash became clear, its shares and rating collapsed to junk status (although they have since recovered).

It is hard to fathom how much money swilled through the balance sheets of the construction companies and the hands of their greedy managers. Judge Moro starts by uncovering payments in the hundreds of thousands of pounds before these become millions, and then tens of millions. It is mere months into the investigation when the total embezzled crosses the one-billion-pound mark and keeps growing.

The jail sentences handed out to the construction bosses marked a turning point. Ever since colonial times, when Brazil's resources were greedily extracted by the Portuguese crown, this country's political and economic elite has committed crimes with impunity. This explains in part why Brazil is one of the most unequal countries in the world. The images of men like Marcelo Odebrecht, who received a sentence of almost twenty years, entering correctional facilities left Brazilians open-mouthed.

The second critical phase focused on the country's leading politicians. This was much more controversial and divisive. As Moro was investigating leading members of Lula's left-wing Workers' Party (PT), there was a separate move to impeach his successor and colleague, President Dilma Rousseff. The case against Rousseff was weak. Certainly, she was an ineffective president and earlier, as chairman of Petrobras, she had failed to notice the huge machine of corruption roiling underneath her. But nobody had ever accused her of personal gain, which places her among a small minority of Brazilian politicians. The charges brought against her by Congress were the equivalent of dropping litter, while further down the street other politicians were mugging people in the street at gunpoint.

The PT was not the only party to be caught up in the Car Wash scandal, but its role was critical. It had been the party in power for most of the duration of Car Wash and was therefore key in appointing Petrobras's senior managers who administered the complex system of paybacks. The coincidence of

Rousseff's impeachment with Lula being taken in for police questioning in early spring 2016 looked to the Left in Brazil as though it was an overarching conspiracy.

In some districts, the Left welcomed the consequences of Car Wash, especially in cities like Rio de Janeiro, dominated by the centre-right Brazilian Democratic Movement (PMDB). For years, this party has acted as kingmaker and its leading lights had learned how to monetise the power this conferred on them. The deeply corrupt Governor of Rio was brought down by Car Wash while the speaker of Congress's lower house, Eduardo Cunha, another PMDB member, was the biggest parliamentary fish to be caught in the judicial trawl. Cunha is a man habitually referred to by commentators as having acted like a mafia boss in Congress.

But during the investigation into Lula, the political atmosphere began to sour. Judge Moro's office released the contents of a wiretap that had been put on Lula's phone, including a sensitive conversation with President Rousseff. Netto retells the incident in forensic detail. He leaves readers to make up their minds about the incident, but it certainly confirmed suspicions for many supporters of Lula and Rousseff that Moro was playing fast and loose with evidence that should have remained confidential until it was needed in court.

Since then the polarisation of Brazilian society between the Right and the Left has accelerated, thickening a toxic atmosphere with which people in the United States and Britain have also become familiar in recent years. As so many leading figures in government, Congress and in the legislatures of Brazil's twenty-seven states stood discredited, there were few people prepared to argue the case for urgently needed political reforms. Ultimately, reform can only be introduced by the very politicians who have exploited Brazil's constitutional weaknesses to feather their own nests. And the turkeys are not about to vote for Christmas.

It was this situation that Bolsonaro was able to exploit so successfully and turn his political convictions, which until then had been regarded as liabilities, to his exceptional advantage.

Sergio Moro has always been resolute in denying any party-political affiliation or working on behalf of any particular ideology. Netto quotes him extensively and carefully on this: 'I have absolutely no, zero, zero connection with any party or person connected to a party. The judge works with the facts, the evidence and the law ... Issues of political party, interests or other such matters are not the business of my profession.'

Largely because of the judge's insistence that he was a neutral player, Bolsonaro surprised everyone when he announced after his election victory that Sergio Moro would become his new Minister of Justice, a post which Moro assumed on 1 January 2019. Moro insists that he will be focused on judicial reform, but given the new president's repeated insistence on a tough, militarised response to the profound social and policing challenges facing the country, it will be interesting to see how Moro will avoid being an active participant in Brazil's sharp turn to the right.

Brazil is only at the beginning of an extraordinary and ominous new chapter but to understand what happens henceforth, understanding the origins are essential. That is what Vladimir Netto gives us in this book.

MG

7 January 2019

FROM A PETROL STATION TO THE HEART OF THE REPUBLIC

Thursday 17 March 2016

As fate would have it, the nomination of former president Luiz Inácio Lula da Silva as chief of staff to his successor, Dilma Rousseff, took place on the very day Operation Car Wash celebrated its second anniversary. It was not a happy occasion. Brazil was in a state of political upheaval, with protests both for and against the government taking to the streets. One group called for President Rousseff to resign, chanting: 'Dilma out! Workers' Party out!' From the other group came the reply: 'Down with the coup!' In front of the Palácio do Planalto, where the swearing-in ceremony was to take place, the two groups clashed in a noisy and tense battle of words and insults.

Former president Lula da Silva – universally known by the nickname 'Lula' – was in the very eye of the storm. In recent months, Operation Car Wash had been gradually closing in around him. A fortnight earlier at 6 a.m. on 4 March, the former president, wearing a tracksuit, opened the door of his apartment in São Bernardo do Campo to. There were fifteen men from the Federal Police with a warrant to take him in for questioning.

Downstairs, an unmarked vehicle belonging to the Tactical Operations Unit, the Federal Police's elite squad, was standing by, ready to swing into action should the need arise. From that moment, it became clear that Lula had become the principal focus of the investigation. Despite the ex-president's denials, there were suspicions that he was the owner of a seaside apartment in Guarujá and a country retreat in Atibaia, both registered in other people's names. Federal prosecutors were seeking explanations for the various refurbishments carried out to these properties at the expense of the construction firms OAS and Odebrecht, and José Carlos Bumlai, a cattle-breeder who was also under judicial investigation.

The path that led Operation Car Wash to Lula's door was long, tortuous and full of surprises. The operation's first success was finding information in a humble petrol station – the Posto da Torre in Brasília – about black-market currency dealers involved in money laundering in the southern state of Paraná. Phone taps led to several of the dealers being arrested, including Alberto Youssef, who became key to the whole operation. On 17 March 2014, when the police arrived at the Hotel Luzeiros in São Luís, in the northern state of Maranhão, to take Youssef into custody, no one imagined where it would lead. Except, perhaps, Youssef himself. In the middle of the night, realising that the Federal Police were after him, he was convinced that he would once again be up against Sergio Moro, the judge on the 13th Federal Bench in Curitiba, who had found him guilty years earlier in the Banestado case. He was afraid, but did not attempt to flee, preferring to face his fate. Youssef's arrest revealed his links to Paulo Roberto Costa, the former director of supply at Petrobras. Gently teasing out the threads, the investigators uncovered a gigantic web of corruption within Petrobras, involving senior management of the state-owned company, large corporations and government politicians.

Operation Car Wash detonated the most electrifying series of events in Brazil's recent history. There were moments of high drama, like the day in March 2015 when judicial proceedings were opened against forty-nine people, including forty-seven elected politicians. Or the day when the Federal Police knocked on the door of a hotel room in Brasília where the senator and majority leader Delcídio do Amaral was staying. On hearing that he was being arrested, he asked, 'Can you do that to a serving senator?' It had never happened before. The operation broke all barriers, demolished myths and traditions, and showed that sometimes it is possible to make the changes that are needed.

Two years after it began, Operation Car Wash reached the very heart of the republic. On 13 March 2016, millions of Brazilians had come onto the streets to protest against Rousseff, Lula, the Workers' Party and corruption. It was the biggest demonstration in the country's history. Three days later, Lula was nominated to be chief of staff, provoking a new wave of indignation and protests, this time in front of the Palácio do Planalto, Brasília's strikingly modernist presidential palace. Former president Lula rejoining his successor Rousseff's government was viewed as a desperate attempt to protect him from the jurisdiction of the ordinary courts and thus escape from the rigour and courage of Sergio Moro, the judge who had been conducting the Operation Car Wash trials and upholding the principle that the law is the same for everyone. He wasn't alone; throughout this story, all the main players would try to escape Moro's clutches.

On the very same day that Lula's appointment was announced by the government, Moro took the decision to suspend the wiretap on the former president's telephones and to make public the recordings of his conversations with friends, ministers and even the current president herself. It was the most controversial of all his decisions. One conversation in particular, between Lula and President Rousseff, ignited the country:

'Lula, I just want to tell you something.'

'Go on, love, tell me.'

'Look, I'm sending over "Bessias" with the letter, just so you have it. Now, only use it if you really have to – it's the appointment letter, OK?' says Rousseff.

'Uhuh. OK, OK,' replies Lula.

'That's all – just you wait there, because he's on his way.'

'OK, I'm here, I'll hold on.'

'OK?'

'OK.'

'Bye.'

'Bye-bye, dear,' ended the former president.

To the investigators, the conversation sounded like an attempt to obstruct justice, a means of avoiding the possibility of Lula being arrested. To the government, the recording of the conversation looked like a crime against national security. The release of the conversation, recorded just a few hours earlier, brought crowds of people onto the streets. As evening fell in Brasília, people left work and joined the growing chorus of protest outside the Planalto, calling for Rousseff to resign. Everyone on the political scene was astonished. At that moment no one knew what might happen.

On the next day, 17 March, the president made an uncompromising speech at the packed nomination ceremony, defending Lula, whom she called 'this country's greatest political leader'. She rejected the interpretation of her conversation about the appointment letter as having anything to do with giving immunity to her comrade in arms. Rousseff said she would insist on a full investigation of all the facts. She wanted to know who had authorised the wiretap, why they had done so and why they had permitted the recording to be released.

'Fomenting unrest within Brazilian society, on top of lies, underhand dealings and questionable practices, violates constitutional principles and guarantees, violates citizens' rights and sets very serious precedents. This is how coups start,' declared the president.

A short time later, Lula's nomination as chief of staff was suspended by a preliminary ruling of a federal court, which was later confirmed by Justice Gilmar Mendes of the Supreme Court. Lula would never take up the post. Amid all the upheaval, the speaker of the Chamber of Deputies, Eduardo Cunha, a sworn enemy of Rousseff, decided that the climate was right to start setting up a committee that would analyse whether the president could be removed from office. That afternoon, the Chamber of Deputies appointed its impeachment committee.

The afternoon ended with large demonstrations 'against the coup and in defence of democracy' in every state of the country, including in front of the Congress building in Brasília. The protestors shouted loudly in support of the government, ex-president Lula and the Workers' Party. Lula appeared at the largest demonstration, on Avenida Paulista in São Paulo, where he was loudly applauded after making a speech saying that everything would soon be hunky-dory again. Only days earlier Sergio Moro had been hailed as a hero by the protests against the government; at these protests against impeachment, he was seen as the villain.

On 17 April 2016, the Chamber voted in favour of impeachment by 367 votes to 137, and on 12 May the Senate authorised the opening of proceedings against President Rousseff that resulted in her removal from office. But before this, Eduardo Cunha, the speaker of the Chamber of Deputies, was himself ejected from office. A defendant in the Operation Car Wash trials, the Supreme Court also suspended his mandate as congressman.

During those vertiginous weeks of 2016, Operation Car Wash occupied every corner of public discussion, became the topic of conversation in every bar and every political gathering, mobilised theatre audiences, dominated social media, invaded people's homes and even divided families. The whole country talked about nothing else. Independently of what might happen from now on, for each of the many people involved, the operation has become part of Brazil's history. Between March 2014 and March 2016, it went from the pursuit of a small-time money launderer to defining the very rules for exercising political power in Brazil. It no longer makes any sense to ask whether Operation Car Wash had any effect; it has already brought the country to its most dramatic hour of truth.

Chapter 1

THE HOUSE BEGINS TO FALL

16 March 2014

A TENSE NIGHT

On a Sunday night in 2014, two years before the citizens of Brazil took to the streets in protest, the Federal Police were monitoring Alberto Youssef's movements around São Paulo. The black-market currency dealer was the main target of Operation Car Wash, which was scheduled to begin the following day. From the southern city of Curitiba, where the operation was being coordinated, detective Márcio Anselmo was sorting out the final details of the searches and arrests that would be carried out the following morning. A specialist in financial crime, he had managed, with only two officers and in the midst of a police officers' strike, to tease out the threads that would lead to Operation Car Wash and had brought the investigation to the point where it was now time to put boots on the ground.

Alberto Youssef was living in a large apartment in Vila Nova Conceição, an upmarket neighbourhood of São Paulo. His apartment was valued at R$3.8 million,[1] in a building where the monthly service charge alone was R$3,094 and where the luxury cars in the underground car park attested to the residents' wealth. The four officers sent to arrest Youssef had taken rooms in a nearby hotel. At around 8 p.m., two of them went to the petrol station near the apartment building. They ordered coffee and the team leader, detective Luciano Flores de Lima, laid out their approach strategy: 'That's where we're going tomorrow. One vehicle stays here by the entrance, the other goes straight in as soon as they open the gate. We'll get the security guard as a witness …'

Checking out the location the night before was part of the routine. They knew that their arrival the following morning would need to be fast and decisive so as not to give time for the doorman to warn their target, giving Youssef the chance to destroy evidence or throw a USB memory stick out the window. He was a high-risk and experienced target. He drove several cars and had numerous mobile phones. He was so smart that the police officers did not notice when he left his apartment that night – they had returned to the hotel to rest before getting up early next morning to begin the operation. At 6 a.m., the arrests would begin. But the night would be long and full of surprises. In Curitiba at around 11 p.m., Márcio Anselmo received an alert: a signal from Youssef's mobile phone had been picked

---

[1] Note to English edition: During the events described in this book, the value of one Brazilian real (R$) fluctuated between approximately US$0.25 and US$0.45, and between £0.15 and £0.25. It is not therefore practical to give accurate conversions of every amount mentioned in this book, but as a very rough rule of thumb, dividing by three gives an idea of the equivalent in US dollars, and dividing by five gives an idea of the equivalent in sterling.

up near São Paulo's Congonhas Airport, shortly after 9.30 p.m. Then the signal disappeared. Youssef was on the move. Márcio Anselmo called the team in São Paulo and warned the team that their target was off the radar. In an exclusive interview for this book, Alberto Youssef revealed what happened that night: 'I'd booked the plane the Friday before. Everything was ready to take off at 9.30 p.m. on Sunday evening. I left home at 9 p.m. The guys didn't realise; they messed up. I left home as normal, and kept checking in the rear-view mirror to see if someone was following me. I headed straight to the hangar. When I arrived, there was a short wait before the plane was ready. Everything was fine. It was a clear night. I had a nice flight.'

In the middle of the night, the signal reappeared. Youssef had switched his phone on when he landed. He was in São Luís, capital of the northern state of Maranhão. 'I could easily not have switched my phone on. I hadn't intended to use that mobile. But I'd agreed to call my daughter to let her know I was OK,' he explained.

So, in the early hours of 17 March 2014, the day the Federal Police were scheduled to arrest him and various other suspects, Alberto Youssef strolled out of the airport and got into a taxi. At 2 a.m., he arrived at the Hotel Luzeiros in Ponta do Farol, on the São Luís seafront. He had two large, identical black suitcases. Accompanying him was a man with a smaller suitcase and a case of wine under his arm. The two were filmed by security cameras as they leaned against the hotel check-in desk. Marco Antonio de Campos Ziegert, also known as Marcão ('Big Marco'), was given room 1312. Youssef was in 704. The two of them talked calmly, giving no indication that they might be aware that the police were closing in on them. Youssef, however, had some suspicions and knew that something was in the offing. He had taken extra precautions and was on the lookout. For as long as he was unsure, he carried on as normal. Hours before being arrested, he was in a hotel room with a suitcase full of money – a relatively common situation for him. Beside him on the bed lay R$1.4 million in cash. It was part of a transaction Youssef was carrying out to resolve a problem for his friend and business partner Ricardo Pessoa, chairman of UTC Engenharia.

Pessoa's construction firm, UTC/Constran, had been owed just over R$113 million by the government of the state of Maranhão. The legal battle had been dragging on through the courts for years, but Youssef had told Pessoa he had contacts in the state and promised to lend a hand. It had taken several months, but the matter had been successfully resolved. Youssef held meetings with members of the Maranhão government and managed to put together a deal that was approved by Governor Roseana Sarney in November 2013. The debt was to be paid in twenty-four instalments of R$4.7 million.

UTC was jubilant when the first instalment landed in its bank account. Walmir Pinheiro Santana, the firm's finance director at the time, sent an email to Youssef, copied to Ricardo Pessoa, in which he affectionately called Youssef 'cousin' and praised his dedication to the case: 'I know very well how difficult it was to close this deal, almost six months of comings and goings … Now we just need to cross our fingers that the state keeps up all the remaining instalments.' Youssef replied: 'Thank you Walmir, but everyone deserves congratulations. Without the help of everyone involved, this deal would not have been possible. Let's make sure it goes well right to the end. Warm regards.' Below the message appeared the footer: 'Sent from my BlackBerry 10 smartphone.' He didn't know it, but his BlackBerry was being tapped by the Federal Police. Meanwhile, there were some problems to sort out with the Maranhão state government: February's instalment had been paid on time, but March's was late.

As soon as the team discovered that Youssef was in São Luís, they began to call round the hotels, helped by the fact that Márcio Anselmo knew the city, having participated in a previous operation involving the state. An officer on the team called one of the hotels on the list.

'Hello, Hotel Luzeiros,' answered the receptionist.

'Alberto Youssef, please.'

'Just a moment,' said the receptionist, looking through the list of hotel guests.

The officer had only wanted to check whether Youssef was there, but the receptionist immediately transferred the call to room 704.

Youssef jumped when the telephone rang.

'Hello?'

The officer hung up.

Youssef was worried. It could only be bad news. Something must have happened, he thought. He was carrying a lot of money. He immediately went down to the reception and asked for the number the call had come from. He took the piece of paper; the area code was Curitiba. He went back up to his room and dialled the number.

Someone answered: 'Federal Police.'

'Sorry, wrong number.'

This time he was the one who hung up. One thing was clear: he was going to be arrested. He knew that the Federal Police would arrive at dawn, because Brazilian law only permits night arrests when a suspect is caught actively committing a crime. He still had a few hours. What now? He had money, a chartered plane and the certainty of being arrested. Why didn't he make a run for it? 'Because I always prefer to deal with problems head-on. I knew it was Curitiba, so I knew it was Sergio Moro. It could only be him,' said Youssef.

Still in the hotel, he sat on the edge of the bed and thought. 'My only concern was not to be arrested with all that money; not to be taken with anything on me. But I didn't throw out my mobile phone. As far as I was concerned, by that time everything was being tapped. Getting rid of it would only create another problem – it would count as destroying evidence,' noted Youssef.

The hotel's security cameras filmed Youssef leaving his room at 3.30 a.m., pulling one of his black suitcases. He got into the lift and pushed the button for the thirteenth floor. When the door opened, he went to room 1312, Marcão's room. He came out again ten minutes later, this time without the suitcase. He had left R$1.4 million, in cash, with Marcão.

'I went to Marcão's room, left the money with him and said: "I want you to deliver this if something happens to me." "Is there going to be a problem?" he asked. "I reckon there'll be someone knocking on my door at 6 a.m. I think I'll be arrested in the morning. It'll be the Federal Police, from Curitiba."'

As Youssef said later, the money was to be delivered to João de Abreu, who at that time was Governor Sarney's chief of staff. In his testimony to the Petrobras congressional inquiry in May 2015, Youssef said that 'as far as I know, the money arrived'. Before the delivery of this R$1.4 million, Youssef had already sent two other payments of R$800,000 to the chief of staff. The two men who carried the money for him, Rafael Angulo Lopez and Adarico Negromonte Filho, told police that they took the money to the Palácio dos Leões, the headquarters of the state government in São Luís, taped to their bodies. João de

Abreu's lawyer, Carlos Seabra de Carvalho Coelho, denied that his client had ever received any money from Alberto Youssef. In August 2015, the Maranhão civil police indicted Youssef, Abreu, Marcão, Lopez and Negromonte for corruption and criminal association. On 24 September, the court ordered that João de Abreu be held on remand, but he managed to get this revoked and was released from jail in October. Towards the end of the year, prosecutions were begun on the basis of information provided by Operation Car Wash.

After delivering the money to Marcão, Youssef returned to his room and waited for the police to arrive. By that time, Márcio Anselmo, the detective, had already telephoned the police superintendent in Maranhão. In order to rule out any risk of a leak, the superintendent went personally to make the arrest at 6 a.m. When the officers knocked at the door of his hotel room, Youssef gave himself up without any resistance. It wasn't even necessary to handcuff him. His bag contained seven mobile phones. At the offices of one of his companies, GFD Investimentos, twenty-seven more were found in and around his desk. Youssef used what the police call 'point-to-point phones', different devices to speak to each particular contact, making it difficult for the police to intercept his calls. They would have to start off by examining all thirty-four phones and their various apps, in order to analyse the extent of Youssef's network of contacts.

On checking the footage from the hotel security cameras a few days later, the officers saw the images of Youssef leaving a suitcase with his friend. They also saw that, later that day, when all the police activity had finished, Marcão left the hotel calmly pulling a case behind him, got into a white taxi and disappeared. The police managed to locate the taxi, but the driver said he couldn't remember where he took the passenger.

Marcão returned to the hotel at around 3.30 p.m., without the suitcase. He went up to his room, before coming back down and giving the man at reception the case of wine he had been carrying under his arm when they checked in. The wine was collected a few days later by an aide working for the chief of staff at the Maranhão state government, but the money in the suitcase was never recovered. Marcão settled his bill at 11 p.m. and left the hotel. The following day, 18 March, the state government transferred another instalment of R$4.7 million to UTC/Constran. Some time later, the Maranhão state government released a statement denying they had granted any favours towards the company in relation to the payment of the state's outstanding debts, and said that it had saved R$28.9 million as a result of the transaction.

On being taken into custody, Youssef knew that he would up against federal judge Sergio Moro. This scared him. 'I am the type of guy who has the courage to suckle a leopard, but the only man on this earth that I'm afraid of is that guy Sergio Moro,' Youssef told me. Youssef had already been judged and found guilty by Moro in the past. He knew the severity of the judge's pen. Even worse, this time the police and federal prosecutors had managed to gather a lot of evidence against him.

On that first day of Operation Car Wash, Antonio Figueiredo Basto, Youssef's lawyer, received a call at 6 a.m. 'When the phone rings at that time in the morning, it's because there's a problem, right? I'm used to it. It's when clients call to tell me they've been arrested. Youssef told me he was being arrested in Maranhão, on the orders of Sergio Moro. I was surprised: "Really? Sergio?"' recounted the lawyer. By now already in custody, Youssef told his lawyer he needed his help, and explained why: 'Look, this game is not what you think. It's going to be the biggest trial in the country. It will take down half of Congress. It'll bring down the republic.'

THE BEGINNING OF THE END FOR 'LITTLE PAULO'

In Rio de Janeiro, 2,253 kilometres south of São Luís, it was also a tense start to the day for another important person in this story: Paulo Roberto Costa. The former director of supply for the state-owned oil giant Petrobras had recently received the gift of a car from Alberto Youssef. The police wanted to know the reason for the generous gesture, so they went looking. This was to cause a great deal of trouble for both Youssef and Costa.

Paulo Roberto Costa's name had come up almost by accident. He wasn't included in the first batch of arrests in Operation Car Wash. Over Christmas in 2013, Márcio Anselmo was staying with his family on a remote farm with no internet, and decided to read a report he had printed out about the email accounts Alberto Youssef had been using. Under one of them, paulogoia58@hotmail.com, he found an invoice for a Range Rover Evoque that Youssef had just purchased for R$250,000. The detective thought it strange, because the car was not registered in Youssef's name, but to a Paulo Roberto Costa. Costa seemed to be another of Youssef's clients. Or maybe it was a cover, thought Anselmo. With no means of checking who it was, he noted down the name, and only when he returned to work after the holidays did he discover that Costa was a former Petrobras director.

Anselmo went to see inspector Luciano Flores de Lima and showed him the invoice.

'What do you make of this? Paulo Roberto Costa, former director of Petrobras,' asked Anselmo.

'Youssef and Petrobras ... Do you think there might be some connection? What's Youssef got to do with Petrobras?' Luciano wanted to know.

His suspicions aroused, Márcio Anselmo decided to deepen his investigation into the car purchased by a black-market currency dealer for an ex-director of the company. He requested a warrant to seize the vehicle and to take Costa in for questioning. It was the beginning of the fall from grace of the former director of Brazil's biggest company, not to mention everything else that would follow in the months ahead.

Ironically, the investigators discovered that the car had been purchased on impulse. Paulo Roberto Costa and Alberto Youssef had been stuck in slow-moving traffic in São Paulo, when they passed by a Land Rover dealership. Their various schemes had been running for years and Costa was relaxed and getting careless. In an interview for this book, Paulo Roberto Costa recounted his conversation with Alberto Youssef that day.

'That's a nice Evoque over there. Someday I would like to own one of those cars,' commented Costa.

'Not someday. We'll buy it now. Let's go in,' replied Youssef.

Youssef parked and they got out. Costa took a good look at the Land Rover.

'I'll pay for the car and we'll deduct it from the other money,' said Youssef, decisively.

Costa had been retired from Petrobras for more than a year and genuinely thought that nothing would come of it.

'Youssef bought and paid for it, told them to get it bulletproofed and had it delivered to my house,' recounted Costa. 'My wife never liked that car. The day it arrived she realised, call it a sixth sense, that it would cause trouble. Women know these things.'

Marici, Paulo Roberto's wife, was right. Her husband's life was about to change completely on account of that gift. But first he would need to give a statement to the police. It was a delicate situation. At that moment, having been brought in for questioning, Costa was scared and committed a serious error that helped set the course of everything that followed: he asked one of his daughters, Arianna, to go to the offices of Costa Global, the consulting firm he had set up after leaving Petrobras, and remove some documents.

Arianna immediately called her sister, Shanni. The two of them called their husbands and rushed over to the consultancy's offices in Barra da Tijuca, the glitzy beachfront suburb south of Rio. They took away documents and more than R$100,000 in cash. In other words, they concealed evidence. In doing so, they even came close to running into the Federal Police face to face. In fact the officers arrived at Costa Global's offices first, but they couldn't get in and decided to go to Costa's house, also in Barra da Tijuca, to get a key. Costa's daughters and sons-in-law arrived just after the police had left the building, narrowly missing each other in a scene worthy of a French farce. On returning with the keys for the office, one of the officers asked the building's head of security just as a routine question, if he had noticed any unusual movements around office number 913 that day. The answer was 'Yes'.

The police rushed over to the building's security system control room and watched the recordings from that morning, showing the daughters and sons-in-law arriving and then leaving the premises laden with binbags full of documents. The building's security cameras had recorded the crime of concealing evidence. On the film, at exactly 8.16 a.m., Arianna Azevedo Costa Bachmann parks a black car outside the main

entrance and takes lift No. 3 with her husband, Marcio Lewko-
wicz. He's carrying only one bag. At 8.20 am., Marcio comes
back down in lift No. 1 with a black backpack and bag, which
he leaves in the car. It's the first of four trips. At that point, the
cameras record Paulo Roberto's other daughter, Shanni, and
her husband, Humberto Mesquita, arriving in a white car. The
couple take the lift. Humberto comes straight back down and
stays at the entrance to the building, holding his mobile phone.
All of them appear to be nervous and in a hurry. Marcio comes
down, this time with a white bin bag, which he leaves in the car.
He phones someone and then goes back up. A few minutes later
he returns, this time in lift No. 4, with a clear plastic bin bag. He
speaks to Humberto and his sister-in-law in front of the building, and the couple leave. Once again, he goes up to the office
and comes back down with another black backpack. He leaves
it in the car and, empty-handed, goes up for the last time. He
comes down shortly after with a large bin bag. His wife, beside
him, is carrying two other bags, a brown one and a pink one. At
all times Marcio is holding his phone. The couple load the final
bags into the car and leave, the to-ing and fro-ing having lasted
almost an hour. The cameras recorded them leaving at 9.14 a.m.
The police arrived shortly after and discovered everything.

Ignorant of what was taking place at his office, Paulo Roberto
Costa appeared at Federal Police headquarters downtown, for
his first round of questioning as part of Operation Car Wash.
He was in a bad mood and wanted to get out of there as quickly
as possible. Although now retired, he still had a lot of influence
from the days when powerful politicians in Brasília affectionately referred to him as 'Little Paulo'. The first question asked by
the policewoman conducting the interview was: 'What's your
occupation?'

'I currently work as a consultant in the areas of oil, gas, infrastructure generally and petrochemicals,' replied Costa.

When she asked if he knew Alberto Youssef, he said he did, and had done since his time at Petrobras, but that he hadn't had business dealings with him.

'Who introduced you?'

'I don't remember,' replied Costa, adding that it was only after retiring in 2014 that Youssef had approached him, regarding 'providing consulting services in your future environment'.

'And the car?' asked the policewoman, referring to the Land Rover.

'Paying for the car was because of services I provided after my retirement.'

'This consulting of yours resulted in some type of final report?'

'As far as I remember, the consulting was principally given through meetings in person and verbal conversations,' replied the former Petrobras executive.

The policewoman moved on to a key question: 'Can you confirm that Petrobras sought tenders for works at the Abreu & Lima refinery, for a total value of R$8.9 billion divided between five consortia?'

Costa took a deep breath and replied that yes, he was aware of those tenders. He said that at the time he was Petrobras's director of supply, but explained that his responsibilities did not cover tendering, which came under the Engineering Division. When the policewoman referred to the Camargo Corrêa conglomerate for the first time, Costa informed her that he had not participated in the choice of firms that had tendered for the Abreu & Lima refinery, adding that 'as a result of my work at Petrobras, I know people at all the large construction firms'.

For her penultimate question, the policewoman asked: 'Are you aware of the payment by Alberto Youssef of a commission, to any person or persons, resulting from the tender process involving the Consórcio Nacional Camargo Corrêa or the Abreu & Lima refinery?'

'No,' replied Costa.

Her final question was a precursor of what was to come: 'Have you ever been arrested or prosecuted for a criminal offence?'

'Never.'

That was about to change. But not just yet.

At Paulo Roberto Costa's house, the police found notes detailing the connections between Costa and large building contractors. There was a handwritten table of names, in three columns. In the first column was a list of big construction firms, such as Mendes Júnior, IESA, Engevix, UTC/Constran, Camargo Corrêa and Andrade Gutierrez. In the second column was the name of the boss of each firm. In the last column, entitled 'Observations', were phrases like 'Willing to cooperate', 'Already cooperating, but will do more for the campaign at PR's request' and 'Already spoke to candidate and will cooperate at PR's request'. The investigation had produced the first indication that it would reach all the way up to company bosses and politicians. It would not be long in coming.

However, at that moment the police were dealing with a more urgent situation: they had to arrest Paulo Roberto Costa. As well as the car given by Alberto Youssef, the police had found in the house a large quantity of cash in various currencies: more than US$180,000, €10,000 and R$750,000. The suspicious car, the large amount of cash and his daughters' trip to his office to conceal evidence provided enough reasons for the police to request, and for Moro to grant, a warrant for Paulo Roberto Costa's arrest on 20 March 2014. This constituted phase two of Operation Car Wash.

Costa's detention was initially temporary, because Moro decided to set a time period for the missing evidence to 'reappear' by. When this did not happen, he ordered that the former Petrobras director of supply be held on remand indefinitely. In his ruling he wrote: 'The removal of material, evidence and money from the professional premises of the subject of investigation, Paulo Roberto Costa, on the very same day as the searches, is one of the clearest cases of interference in the gathering of evidence that this judge has ever encountered. There is no lawful justification for these actions and there is no record of the missing evidence having been recovered. I add to this the abrupt withdrawal of financial investments held by the person under investigation with various banks, in an apparent attempt to prevent any eventual action by the judicial authorities to seize them.'

Paulo Roberto Costa's daughters and sons-in-law – Shanni, Arianna, Marcio and Humberto – were then formally charged by federal prosecutors with acting, along with Costa, to destroy documents that could supply evidence of crimes being investigated by Operation Car Wash. The first set of legal proceedings against the Costa family had begun. At that moment, the former director was still the idea of doing a deal with prosecutors. He told everyone, both investigators and others involved in perpetrating the corruption scheme, that he would never talk, even if it meant spending a long time in prison. Nevertheless, Costa's arrest worried a lot of people.

Paulo Roberto Costa had worked at Petrobras for thirty-five years. He joined the company in 1977 through the competitive public examination system and reached the ranks of senior management in 1995. Before becoming director of supply in 2004, he was in charge of the Bolivia–Brazil gas pipeline. Before that he had run Gaspetro and managed Petrobras's natural gas unit. Costa said in his deposition that it was at the beginning of Lula's first term in office that he met José Janene, the federal congressman from Paraná state who was the leader of the Progressive Party in the Chamber of Deputies. Janene called Costa in for a chat and said he would make him a director of Petrobras, but in return Costa would need to take account of the party's requests. Costa accepted, and remained a director of Petrobras until 2013, throughout both of Lula's two terms in office and part of Dilma Rousseff's first term. For eight years he was responsible for various major construction projects at the oil giant. He knew almost all Brazil's major construction firms intimately and was the key to an immense corruption scheme. But the Operation Car Wash investigators had not yet discovered this; they had only just started, and although the Federal Police would soon carry out searches at the premises of businesses connected with Costa, and even at the Petrobras headquarters in Rio de Janeiro, for the time being the investigation was focused solely on Costa.

BIG MONTHLY, 'COUSIN' BETO AND THE ORIGINS OF OPERATION CAR WASH

No one could have imagined that this was the beginning of the biggest and most significant police operation of recent times – not even the operation's command had any idea of what was to come. On Monday 17 March 2014, the day that Operation Car

Wash took to the streets for the first time, it was a bright sunny morning in Curitiba, a somewhat rare event in the rainy capital of Paraná. The investigators thought it was a good omen. The searches were going well, and despite the mishaps overnight, Alberto Youssef was safely in jail.

At that point, they were focused on chasing black-market currency dealers. They had identified four criminal groupings, each of which was the target of a different investigation. There was Operation Car Wash itself and three others named after films: Bidone, Casablanca and Dolce Vita. Bidone, meaning 'swindler' in Italian, was the operation investigating Alberto Youssef, at that time considered by some detectives to be the biggest clandestine financial operator in Brazil. And now he had fallen into their hands.

The chain of events that led to Youssef's downfall began in 2006, eight years before Operation Car Wash burst onto the scene. The 'Big Monthly' corruption scandal (so called because the politicians involved received monthly bribes) from 2005 was still being investigated and the leader of the Progressive Party, José Janene, was battling to hang on to his position in Congress, in the face of claims that he had received more than R$4 million from the scheme. At the federal prosecutors' office in Curitiba, staff received an alert from the Council for Financial Activities Control, the body responsible for monitoring abnormal financial transfers, that they had spotted suspicious movements in bank accounts belonging to some of the congressman's aides: numerous small deposits from the same source and withdrawals of money in cash.

Deltan Dallagnol, the federal prosecutor who would later coordinate the Operation Car Wash task force, asked the

Federal Police in Londrina, Paraná, where Alberto Youssef lived, to investigate. The detective who took on the case, Gerson Machado, had long suspected a connection between Youssef and Janene. Despite receiving threats, Machado tried to find proof, but by 2008 the investigation had still not made much progress. The prosecutors working on the case were on the point of recommending that it be shelved. That's when Operation Car Wash's first lucky break came: the Federal Police received a report that José Janene and some of his relatives were laundering money through a company in Paraná.

A businessman called Hermes Magnus, Janene's former business partner, had gone to the police and given a statement that laid the foundations of Operation Car Wash. Magnus told the investigators that a criminal gang under José Janene's control had infiltrated his company and almost put him out of business, all for the purposes of laundering money. 'When Hermes turned up, everything started to become clearer,' recounts Machado. Dunel Indústria e Comércio, a manufacturer of electronic goods based in Londrina, needed to raise funds for some new projects and equipment, so Magnus was looking for new investors. That was when a colleague mentioned Janene, who owned a business called CSA. What Magnus didn't know was that part of this firm's money had, according to investigators, come from the Big Monthly corruption scheme.

When the 2005 scandal broke, Janene was accused of receiving a bribe of R$4,100,000, to be split between him and the Progressive Party. The investigators suspected that CSA and Hermes Magnus's firm were being used to launder part of this money. Magnus told the investigators that right from their first meeting, Janene promised to invest R$1 million in the business, which he did indeed do, although he charged a high price. In return, Magnus opened Dunel's books to Janene, who became his business partner and took control of the firm's cash flow. Thus, in the words of federal prosecutors, the congressman was able to disguise the illegal source of the money being injected into the business. That's when the bank transfers began. The first deposit was made into Dunel's accounts on 20 June 2008, in cash, at a bank in São Paulo; it was for R$28,804, to pay the employees' salaries. Other deposits followed, always in cash, from São Paulo or Brasília, and at a frenetic pace. Small, fragmented transfers, typical of someone trying to avoid attention since large transactions were automatically notified to the authorities. To the investigators, it was clear that this was a money laundering operation. Janene's investment of more than R$1 million took place between June and November 2008. The larger part, R$618,343 came from Janene's company, CSA. The remaining R$537,252 was transferred in Brasília from accounts controlled by Carlos Habib Chater, a currency dealer who owned the Posto da Torre petrol station that would later inspire the name of Operation Car Wash.

Hermes Magnus recounted that on Saturdays, José Janene and his friends would put on big barbecues. 'It was a ritual every Saturday morning. Janene would pick me up in his car and take me to his mansion, where the parties and barbecues took place. Everyone would be there,' said Magnus. A ferocious man, who knew he was going to die young due a congenital heart problem, José Janene never minced his words. Between the various starters, he would boast that only he and former government minister José Dirceu could bring down the then-president, Lula da Silva. Magnus realised that he and his business were effectively trapped, and decided to inform the police. On the basis of information from Magnus, the police opened a new inquiry, sought the cooperation of the firms involved, and confirmed the movement of money between Dunel in Londrina and the Posto da Torre petrol station in Brasília. The petrol station was also involved in suspicious transactions with other businesses. The investigation looked promising, but the months were passing and there was still no definitive evidence. In September 2010, José Janene died and the case went cold.

At this point the investigation could well have died, too – it would not have been unusual for that to happen in Brazil. Then, in April 2013, a new line of enquiry opened, thanks to the good work of detective Erika Mialik Marena, the person who would later give Operation Car Wash its name. Marena was in Brasília working on another financial crime investigation, Operation Miqueias ('Micah'). One of the main suspects had a lot of contact with Carlos Habib Chater, the owner of the Posto da Torre petrol station, indicating that Chater was still active, somehow. This caught Marena's attention and she reported it to Márcio Anselmo. They decided to request a wiretap on Chater's phone, since he was the connection between the two investigations. 'When I was talking with Márcio about what we should do, he said, "Look, if they're still laundering money, it's a chance to deepen your investigation and take down that gang. If their dirty money ends up here in Paraná, then we'll get them down here,"' recalls Marena. It might not lead anywhere, but there was no harm trying. They filed the request. The birth of Operation Car Wash was approaching.

At Chater's petrol station there was a snack bar, a laundrette and a bureau de change, but no car wash. Even so, Marena, who would later become the head of the Federal Police's financial crimes unit in Paraná, decided to register the investigation in the Federal Police's internal system under the name 'Car Wash'. 'Obviously I thought of Car Wash because of the petrol station, which also had a laundrette, and because I was fully aware that this was not something small. They weren't washing something small, like in a laundrette. They weren't even washing cars by hand. This was on an industrial scale, like an automated car wash,' says Marena. The intercepting of Chater's phones was authorised on 11 July 2013, but the police encountered a difficulty: all the lines were in the name of the petrol station. Which one was used by Chater? Then, listening to the recorded phone conversations, a police officer heard a petrol station employee giving someone another number, registered with a different phone company. Márcio Anselmo decided to investigate: there was clearly something going on. For this line, Chater was using a BlackBerry. The Federal Police knew that money launderers in Brasília often used this type of handset to discuss business, using its message service, BBM. The police started monitoring Chater's BlackBerry on 28 June and, that same day, they uncovered signs of a complex structure of foreign currency operators: four criminal outfits, led by four major dealers. Among them was Alberto Youssef. But it wasn't easy to get his name. In telephone conversations, everyone called him 'cousin'. The very first message the police intercepted from 'cousin' was suspicious: 'I need to buy 10k paper. You got it?' he asked Chater.

But who was this 'cousin'? No one could figure it out, until a newly arrived young police officer, given the job of listening to the hours and hours of telephone recordings, sent a WhatsApp message to his colleagues containing precious new information: one of those under investigation had referred to the 'cousin' as 'Beto' – a common abbreviation of Alberto. It was a moment of carelessness, just a tiny slip, but enough to identify the suspect. Detectives Marena, Anselmo and de Paula rushed to the recording room and turned up the volume to hear better. Igor Romário de Paula had previously been an air traffic controller and recognised Youssef's voice from when he had been a pilot criss-crossing the skies of Paraná with contraband merchandise. It was him. It was Youssef's voice, of that he was certain. The three of them had also worked on the Banestado case (Banco do Estado do Paraná – the state bank of Paraná) and had listened to hundreds of Youssef's phone calls. 'Beto' was Alberto Youssef, who was well known to the Federal Police. Checking one of the addresses mentioned in the messages was the final confirmation. The three police officers could scarcely believe it. They were going to catch Alberto Youssef.

OLD ACQUAINTANCES

Alberto Youssef's involvement further awakened Sergio Moro's interest in the case. At that time, Moro had recently returned to Curitiba, following a stint in Brasília. For the whole of 2012, he had been acting as an auxiliary judge in the offices of Justice Rosa Weber at the Federal Supreme Court. He had been summoned there for two reasons: to assist the Supreme Court judge with the Big Monthly case, and to coordinate a group of judges looking after other criminal trials. Justice Rosa Weber wanted to reduce the pile of pending criminal cases that she had inherited following the retirement of Justice Ellen Gracie. Moro took care of both tasks and helped to prepare judgments for the full court to vote on. He was a fair and efficient boss, and quickly gained the trust of Weber.

Originally from Maringá in Paraná Sergio Fernando Moro's parents had been teachers and he received a Catholic education. He went through primary and secondary education at a private religious school, and then studied law at Maringá State University. He did an internship at a law office specialising in tax law, then passed the exams to become a judge at the age of twenty-four, beginning his judicial career in southern cities like Cascavel and Joinville, where he took a liking to criminal cases. From 2003 onwards, he was attached to a part of the judiciary specialising in combating money laundering. He was the judge in major cases like Operation Farol da Colina ('Beacon on a Hill') and, particularly, the Banestado scandal, the biggest foreign currency scandal ever discovered in Brazil, where the sums involved reached R$30 billion. In that trial alone, Moro found ninety-seven people guilty, among them Alberto Youssef. He also conducted a major trial against the drug trafficker Fernandinho Beira-Mar. The experience he acquired over the years led him to participate actively in initiatives like the National Strategy to Combat Corruption and Money Laundering, a group bringing together investigators and judges. In 2010, Moro even wrote a book on the subject, which became required reading in judicial circles. In his book, *Crime e lavagem de dinheiro* (*Crime and Money Laundering*), he argued for judicial reforms to deal with organised crime: 'The slowness of Brazil's judicial system, with multiple appeals and up to four different levels of trial, has a knack of indefinitely delaying the application of criminal law, undermining both its effectiveness and society's confidence in the rule of law on many occasions.'

He had long studied the running of large operations against organised crime, such as the Italian investigation, Operation Clean Hands. In an article written ten years before the beginning of

Operation Car Wash, Sergio Moro wrote about how a generation of young judges had managed to disrupt a growing wave of corruption in Italy in the 1990s, beginning with Operation Clean Hands. The lesson for Moro was that legal proceedings, which in Italy had also begun with a state-owned oil company and spread to various political parties, could be the beginning of a chain of positive outcomes. In the Italian case, one of the most important lessons was that large-scale action by the judiciary against corruption would only be effective in a democracy if it had the support of the public. That's how it had been with Clean Hands, one of the most important crusades against corruption anywhere in the world.

At the beginning of 2013, back in Curitiba, Moro went to the swearing-in of the new chief superintendent of the Federal Police in Paraná, Rosalvo Franco.

'It's been a while since we've had a financial operation here in the state,' commented the judge to the new police chief.

The previous police administration had not prioritised this type of offence; the financial crimes unit had been drained of staff and its investigations almost completely wound up.

'Let me tell you something. I'm not going to reinvent the wheel. I'll put people into the unit who've already worked in the sector,' replied Franco.

This made all the difference. In no time at all, the newly appointed but experienced detectives, all specialists in financial crime, began to sniff out the trail that would lead them to Alberto Youssef.

Youssef had not yet become well known throughout Brazil, but he was already influential and powerful in Paraná. Moro had known of him for a long time. He had already had Youssef arrested in 2003 during the Banestado case. He was one of the operators of the enormous scheme for evading foreign exchange controls and, after a few months in prison, made one of the first plea bargain agreements in the history of Brazil – ratified by Sergio Moro himself – under which, in return for getting out of jail, Youssef gave evidence against a bunch of black-market currency dealers and promised to turn his back on the world of crime. He had lied. When Moro found out that Youssef had gone back to his old tricks, he felt bitterly disappointed and betrayed. Now they would meet again in court.

In the intervening ten years, Youssef had become stronger than ever. He was no longer just a black-market currency dealer. He was a financial mega-operator specialising in money laundering for businesses and politicians. At the same time, he was also running various criminal organisations. The Federal Police reckon that between 2011 and the day of his arrest, Youssef had knowingly and wilfully carried out more than 3,500 transactions evading Brazil's foreign currency controls. The total amounts involved exceeded US$400 million. He had grown even richer through these dealings. He had bought the apartment where he now lived, in the wealthy Vila Nova Conceição district of São Paulo. He had ten luxury cars registered in other people's names, and took trips on yachts and private jets. His life now was very different to his childhood.

As a little boy, he had begun working when he was only seven, selling snacks at the airport at Londrina. 'I started by selling pastries, but the baker's son shot me in the face with his air rifle. The pellet's still there. After that, my mum told me I wasn't going back there, and she started making snacks for me to sell. So that's what I did. The airport was my school,' Youssef told me. In the 1980s and 1990s, Londrina Airport was frequented by the biggest contraband smugglers in the country, and it was where Youssef took his first steps into the world of crime. He quickly learned to fly a plane so that he could get in and out of neighbouring Paraguay more easily. From smuggling, he moved into foreign currency, where he dealt on the black market. After a few years he'd moved beyond even that.

After José Janene's death in 2010, Alberto Youssef had gradually come to control, almost single-handedly, the scheme to extract kickbacks from Petrobras construction works and pass the money to the Progressive Party – the same scheme that supported Paulo Roberto Costa's position as a director of Petrobras. He became close to construction bosses and powerful politicians, which caused resentment among some former colleagues. João Cláudio Genu, former chief of staff to the Progressive Party leadership in the Chamber of Deputies, who was also investigated in relation to the Big Monthly corruption scandal, went as far as to send him a threatening email calling in an old debt in August 2013:

So what's going on, sir? I've had no success from the things we've done together. I don't really know why, as I always held you in the highest respect and esteem. When JJ was still around, everything was very chummy and it was all sweetness and light. But since he passed away, I'm hearing nothing but a load of hot wind. You've got close to PR – I'm not jealous, but I feel betrayed. You've got close to the right people, powerful people, whom I introduced you to – again, I'm not jealous, but I feel betrayed. You promised to pay me my share for all the things we did together, but nothing's happened for nearly two years. I don't understand. These days you're powerful and courted by everyone, solving everyone's little problems. I don't want anything, only what's owed to me. It's the kind of thing that makes you lose confidence in people. I just wanted to warn you that I'm not giving up what's mine – I'll do what I have to do, no matter what.

Genu added that it wouldn't come cheap because the whole thing was 'a complete balls-up'. At the end of the email was another threat: 'Remember, any problem is very bad news, as much for you as it is for me. I'll do what I have to do, no matter what. Yours expectantly, JC Genu.'

Perhaps as a result of such an intense and pressured lifestyle, Youssef suffered a heart attack in September 2013. He was alone at home having a bath when he began to feel unwell, and he nearly died. He says that if he hadn't lived so close to a hospital, he wouldn't have pulled through. 'No one helped me. I drove myself. I thought to myself that I didn't want to die and that it was up to me to save myself. It was very stressful. I arrived at the hospital almost unable to breathe – for the last two blocks, I don't know where I got the air from. I felt an enormous pain in my chest, couldn't breathe and my jaw was locked,' says Youssef. He was admitted to the Albert Einstein Hospital in São Paulo for ten days. His cardiac capacity was only 37 per cent. The doctor recommended complete rest, but that was not an option for someone like him; the requests for money didn't stop, even when he was in a hospital bed.

One day, Carlos Habib Chater called from a new number in a chatty mood. Chater's phone was clean, but Youssef's was being tapped by the police. In the words of the officer listening to their conversation, 'Habib talked and talked, because he was pretty sure that no one had that phone, which he had just switched. But he hadn't reckoned on the phone at the other end being monitored. Youssef just kept replying, "Uhuh, uhuh, of course, yeah … right … no, I'm recovering, I'm in hospital, it's difficult, I dunno …"' The police officer recalls the incessant demands on Youssef: 'Everyone was calling him asking for money, or for him to sort out something or other. They'd tell him, "Life's a bitch, hope you get better … Now, about that little problem, that money …" as if to say, "Right son, pull yourself together, you've had a heart attack but nobody gives a toss about that, you've got to carry on with the business."'

Youssef needed to keep feeding the scheme with money. He had become a cog in a machine and couldn't stop. In that phone call, his friend Chater – who would also be arrested some six months later – even commented that he suspected the Federal Police were mounting a new operation. During Operation Miqueias in 2013, the Federal Police had busted a scheme to skim off the employee pension funds of various municipalities and arrested some of their acquaintances, but the two of them hadn't been troubled. Chater was very clear in talking about his fears: 'I reckon there's another [investigation] under way, OK? Because it doesn't make sense, and I've seen about these things! I reckon there's something else going on in parallel, OK?' Youssef didn't want to encourage any more discussion on the subject, so just replied 'Uhuh' and hung up. He knew that sooner or later he would be arrested and there would be a high price to pay.

EUROS IN HER UNDERWEAR

Six months later, the police were getting very close to Alberto Youssef. Nelma Kodama, another currency dealer in São Paulo, was arrested at the airport in Cumbica, two days before

Operation Car Wash was launched. She had been Youssef's lover for eight or nine years, and ran one of the criminal cells under investigation. She had €200,000 hidden in her clothing when she was arrested while trying to go to Italy. Her arrest immediately entered police folklore because, according to the detectives, she was carrying all the money hidden in her underwear. The detectives let her go through the X-ray machine and into the departure lounge. She hadn't declared the money to the Federal Revenue and adopted the method often used by drug traffickers of being the last person to join the boarding queue. Kodama claimed that the Revenue's counter had been closed when she arrived at the airport. The police detained her when she reached the steps of the plane. One detective held her arm and asked her to accompany him. 'Fine, sir, but I don't have anything. Will the plane wait for me? Can you ask the pilot?' asked Kodama. The detective went up the steps and told the pilot, out of Kodama's earshot, that he could take off: this passenger would be staying behind.

As she was taken off to be searched, Kodama joked with the detective, 'Are you going to hold me tight like that? I like it.' Her flirtatious manner would become well known within the Federal Police. On the moving escalator, she discreetly adjusted the money in her underwear. The detective noticed and warned the police officer who would be conducting the search. The officer found the €200,000, divided into four wads of €500 notes, hidden in Kodama's underwear. The volume wasn't large and could easily have passed unnoticed. An interesting detail is that when Kodama went to the airport that Friday evening, the Federal Police did not initially want to arrest her. She was due to be arrested on Monday, at the same time as the other suspects, and the officers were afraid that news of her arrest might alert the others. On the other hand, had she got on the flight to Milan, she would have found out about the others being arrested while she was out of the country, and would not have returned to Brazil. The money gave them an excuse to arrest her. Without it, she would have escaped.

Sergio Moro was informed immediately. Kodama and Youssef were in frequent communication at the time of their arrest. On 7 March 2014, ten days before phase one of the operation, Kodama sent a flirty email to Youssef: 'Hey sweetie, are you hungry?' 'Ravenous,' replied Youssef, to which Kodama countered, 'Lying down or standing up?' In the rest of the conversation, she recalled their trip to Puerto Iguazú, the Argentine town at the river crossing where Brazil, Argentina and Paraguay meet, and said that the only man in her life was Youssef. 'Ricardo [Pessoa] thinks you're the only man who managed to harness me,' wrote Kodama. 'Hahahaha,' replied Youssef. In their emails, Kodama called herself Greta Garbo, Angelina Jolie and Cameron Diaz. Months later, at the Petrobras congressional inquiry, speaking about her relationship with Youssef, Kodama said that she had been in a relationship with him for eight or nine years, and then began singing Roberto Carlos's love song 'Amada Amante' to the bemused congressmen.

Their relationship went beyond flirting and financial transactions – they were always there to help each other. On 13 March 2014, Youssef warned Kodama, 'Another thing: there'll be a police operation tomorrow. So you know what to do.' Operation Car Wash was scheduled to begin on 17 March, four days later. Kodama replied that there was a helicopter waiting for them at the Campo de Marte airfield in São Paulo: 'If you want, we have an Agusta ready for us at Marte, OK? It's all in hand.' Youssef thanked her: 'Great, whenever it's needed I'll tell you.' Kodama was arrested the following day and Youssef sent no more messages to her phone.

On the Monday, when the police arrived at Kodama's house, they found signs that some cupboards and drawers had been recently disturbed, but even so they seized documents, along with several expensive paintings by famous artists: Iberê Camargo, Cícero Dias, Antônio Gomide and Heitor dos Prazeres. Even a Di Cavalcanti graced the walls of the money smuggler. The investigators were suspicious of her refined taste in art. It was the first seizure under Operation Car Wash of works of art potentially acquired with criminal money. It would not be the last.

After the arrests under phase one of Operation Car Wash, the police had to assess the material they had gathered and set new objectives for the investigation. It called for especially meticulous analysis, as Sergio Moro was well known for his rigour concerning investigations that came under his jurisdiction. 'That attentive eye of his is our safety blanket. When he needs to pull people's ears, he pulls. He turns down surveillance requests, rejects accusations where he doesn't see sufficient supporting evidence, and refuses to grant arrest warrants. His oversight is needed,' Erika Marena recounted in an interview for this book. In that first phase of the operation, more than 80,000 pages of documents were seized, in addition to various computers, mobile phones and other electronic devices. Detectives Anselmo, Marena and de Paula ploughed their way through the material. They quickly made a preliminary analysis of what had been discovered and divided the tasks between them.

It would be an investigation like no other, and the first signs of this were becoming apparent. In Alberto Youssef's office, the police uncovered a sophisticated operation for laundering money, built around front organisations like MO Consultoria e Laudos Estatísticos and GFD Investimentos.

Breaking banking secrecy, the rules which previously protected the financial dealings of these companies from public scrutiny, revealed what would be one of the most important pieces of evidence in Operation Car Wash: the big Brazilian building contractors had deposited millions with Alberto Youssef. Big companies like Mendes Júnior, Galvão Engenharia and OAS were some of the first names to appear. MO Consultoria alone had moved R$90,000,000 over a period of five years. Something was very, very wrong, the investigators realised.

Meire Poza, an accountant working for Youssef who voluntarily decided to cooperate with the police, said that when her employers asked her to regularise MO Consultoria's accounting position, she looked at the numbers and replied that it was practically impossible. The firm had neither the business activity nor the documentation to justify the quantity of money swilling around it. Poza also knew about GFD, and it was she who had drawn up the firm's first invoice to the construction firm Mendes Júnior. She told the police that she even asked how GFD, with no substance whatsoever, was going to provide any kind of service to a construction firm of that size. From João Procópio, Youssef's business partner, she got the following response: 'Mendes Júnior will deal with everything.' Big names were starting to appear. The police began opening investigations into each of the building contractors that had transferred money to Youssef.

Curiously, when the police asked the reason for the payments, all the firms provided documents of supposed consulting contracts as evidence of the provision of services. The contracts were fraudulent, and this was also something the firms would end up having to answer for in court.

THE TASK FORCE IS BORN

It wasn't long before the police and federal prosecutors' office realised that Operation Car Wash was going to need very close attention. The problem was that the matter was in the hands of José Soares, a prosecutor who did not have much experience in financial crimes and kept raising queries and doubts about the best way of proceeding. He had already written a report saying that the case should be transferred to another state, which deeply worried the investigators. Operation Car Wash had been born in Paraná, and there it would stay. The challenge was that it was now taking on proportions much greater than initially expected; they needed to expand the team.

One day, the group coordinator, Letícia Martello, who worked in the federal prosecutors' criminal unit in Paraná, knocked on the door of fellow prosecutor Deltan Dallagnol to sound him out. Although only thirty-four years old, Deltan Dallagnol – who had joined the federal prosecutors at the age of twenty-two – already had experience of investigations into money laundering, corruption and evasion of foreign currency controls. Having recently returned from completing a master's degree at Harvard Law School, Dallagnol had already taken part in meetings on Operation Car Wash and some of his colleagues were encouraging him to take on the case.

'Deltan, what do you think about you and me setting up a task force for Operation Car Wash?' asked Martello.

'I'm in. I'll support you, but I can't be the one arguing for the creation of a task force. You have my total support, but I don't want to appear to be pleading my own cause,' said Dallagnol.

Everything was sorted. Martello made a phone call to Brasília and, a few days later, the prosecutor general, Rodrigo Janot, nominated a group of prosecutors to work on the case. A problem as large as this needed additional hands and minds – they would need to process all the material they had collected and prepare the first set of formal accusations. Deltan Dallagnol was chosen as team coordinator.

Dallagnol, who throughout the investigation would demonstrate his abilities as a leader and communicator, had to put together his team. The first person he called was Orlando Martello, a specialist in investigations into black-market currency dealers, who was a friend of his as well as being Letítia's husband. Vladimir Aras at the prosecutor general's office in Brasília suggested Carlos Fernando dos Santos Lima and Januário Paludo because of their experience. Dallagnol and these other prosecutors had already worked together on the Banestado case. Now the same group was getting together again, this time with more force, to confront a more powerful enemy. Two new names were chosen to add to the group: Diogo Castor de Mattos and Andrey Borges de Mendonça were chosen for their technical ability and willingness to work in a team. Within a short space of time, the prosecutors brought twelve sets of criminal proceedings against the four criminal groups identified so far. Fifty-five people were accused of crimes against the national financial system, criminal association and money laundering, in addition to corruption and embezzlement. The task force managed to freeze almost all the assets in Brazil belonging to the accused.

The initial meetings took place at the federal prosecutors' offices in Paraná. The rooms, like Dallagnol's on the fourteenth floor, were cramped, the walls lined with books on financial crime and a sofa squeezed in by the door. It quickly became clear that it was impossible to work there. They needed a larger space, so they moved to another building on the opposite side of the road. First, they took a set of offices on the seventh floor, across the hall, ironically, from some offices used by Petrobras, before moving to an even larger space on the eighth floor. Major discoveries would be made in those offices – but first they needed to study the case further. Among the thousands of documents, the names of large construction companies were beginning to appear. At first there were only a few brief references, but later they were everywhere: on bank statements, certificates of deposit and various lists and tables.

Operation Car Wash's first case of corruption in Petrobras concerned construction works at the Abreu & Lima oil refinery, in the northern state of Pernambuco. It involved two of Youssef's firms, GFD Investimentos and MO Consultoria e Laudos Estatísticos, along with the steel firm Sanko Sider and the construction firm Camargo Corrêa. The latter had been responsible for building a coker unit at the refinery. The Federal Audit Office had already drawn attention to signs of overbilling in the construction works, but the firm was continuing to receive money when Operation Car Wash began.

Camargo Corrêa had contracted Sanko Sider to provide tubes and other equipment, and had paid Sanko and another group company R$113 million between 2009 and 2013. Part of this money was a disguised kickback. Documents found in Youssef's office revealed that Sanko had made dozens of payments to the accounts of companies controlled by Alberto

Youssef, in particular MO Consultoria and GFD Investimentos. MO was a front company serving only to issue invoices for consulting services that were never provided, and to launder money, while GFD was used by Youssef to hide his assets. Between 2009 and 2013, Sanko paid R$6 million to GDF and R$26 million to MO. There were seventy payments to MO in total. The money was quickly withdrawn from ATMs in cash or transferred to other accounts that Youssef controlled. Later on, some of it was transferred out of the country via spurious foreign exchange contracts, set up in relation to imports that never existed – a new method of evading foreign currency controls that was little known to the police and prosecutors. When questioned by police, Youssef's employees said that the consulting services described in the contract had never been provided. When the police asked Meire Poza, the accountant for some of Youssef's companies, how she was sure that the contracts were false, her response was clear: 'I was there every day.'

Márcio Bonilho, Sanko Sider's founder, who initially tried to maintain that Youssef's firms really had provided ancillary services in financial administration as described in the signed contract, ended up later admitting, in testimony to Sergio Moro, that it was all a farce. He explained why he had thought it worth his while to enter into contracts with the black-market currency dealer: 'He had good credibility in the sector and knew a lot of decision-makers.' When Moro asked what type of influence Youssef had among the directors of construction firms, Bonilho described it as follows: 'I never knew exactly the degree of influence he had, but I knew he had good contacts and could open doors. If I wanted to meet a director whom he knew, he would introduce me. He'd introduce me, arrange a meeting, and I knew things would go well.'

It was in a phone conversation with Bonilho, intercepted by the police, that Youssef let slip for the first time that Paulo Roberto Costa might be corrupt. Youssef was complaining about an executive at a construction firm:

> No, the worst thing, for fuck's sake, is that the guy's serious. He thinks that he's the one who's out of pocket. Can you believe it? Yeah, there are all sorts of nutters out there. Out of pocket? With the amount of money we've given this idiot? He's got a real nerve saying he's out of pocket. Christ, just do the sums: I got R$9 million gross. I paid 20 per cent, so that leaves seven and a bit. Do the sums and see how much he got, see how much his sidekick got, see how much Paulo Roberto got, and the other fella, and then see how much was left over. Then he comes and tells me he's out of pocket? For fuck's sake, no one knows how to count – if you ask me, no one knows how to count in this fucking business ... They only think of themselves.

THE REUNION

The reunion between Moro and Youssef took place on 22 July 2014, in a federal courtroom in Paraná. It wasn't Youssef himself giving evidence that day, but Hermes Magnus, giving evidence about José Janene and others taking over his company to launder money. The named suspects and their lawyers were in the courtroom. Youssef listened in silence, as the federal prosecutor asked Magnus to establish a timeline and explain his accusations in detail.

'Yes, in detail, but also concisely,' interrupted Moro, who was sitting as judge.

Each time Magnus lost himself in twists and turns, Moro would remind him of the need to be concise. At one point, a surly-looking Alberto Youssef reacted by accusing Magnus of lying. Moro interrupted him, but he carried on: 'He's lying! He's a liar!'

The tension in the courtroom rose and the judge called for order: 'Mr Youssef, I will not have that type of remark in my court.'

Youssef tried to object and the judge responded firmly: 'If you continue, I will have you removed from the room. Do you understand?'

Their next encounter was just over a week later, and this time Youssef was contradicting Moro himself. In a hearing on 1 August 2014, the judge had said that the plea bargain agreement from the Banestado case – requiring Youssef to abandon his life of crime – was now deemed to have been breached. Youssef protested, saying he hadn't even been given the opportunity to argue his case and hadn't even been notified, even though he was already back in prison.

'In my opinion, I'm absolutely certain that I've complied 100 per cent with that agreement. I ought to have had the right to argue my case. You only allowed me to give my side of it after notifying me of your decision here in court. So I asked Your Honour if you would reconsider the agreement, as well as in relation to me being held on remand, and Your Honour said you wouldn't. Or only partially. On that basis, I don't intend to answer questions here because, with all due respect, Your Honour, I believe that Your Honour is conflicted when it comes to hearing these accusations against me,' said Youssef.

'I understand your concerns, but I have already made my position clear,' responded Moro, without further discussion.

Since Youssef was not prepared to answer questions, the judge terminated the hearing immediately.

'IT'LL BE HELL'

By that time, those under investigation had realised that the legal battle in Curitiba would not be easy. The evidence was strong, the case against them solid and the judge rigorous. Things would be easier for them if the trial were to take place in Brasília or another city, out of Sergio Moro's hands – or, even better, if Operation Car Wash were to be wound up completely, as other such operations in the past had been. Around that time, Youssef discovered a listening device in his cell, hidden in the gap between the ceiling panel and the concrete floor above. He disconnected it and showed it to his lawyers when they came to visit him. The story ended up in the papers – illegal surveillance was suspected and the matter was investigated. It turned out that the device wasn't working; it could well have been there for a long time, possibly since the drug trafficker Fernandinho Beira-Mar had been held in the same cell some years earlier. The episode, however, like later ones, would be used to try to discredit the operation and the investigators. 'It was a war situation. I was trying to bring them down and get the investigation terminated, and they were trying to screw me, and my family, as much as possible,' Youssef later admitted.

It was indeed war. At that point, the Federal Police asked for Youssef to be transferred to the Catanduvas Federal Penitentiary, a maximum-security prison in Paraná, much to the irritation of Youssef's defence. 'I told Márcio Anselmo to stop persecuting my client,' said Antonio Figueiredo Basto, Youssef's lawyer. Moro decided to keep Youssef in police custody. But what really annoyed Youssef was the investigation publicly disclosing details of his personal life, including more than 10,000 telephone calls with one of his lovers, Taiana Camargo, between 2010 and 2013. This was how Youssef's wife, the lawyer Joana D'Arc, found out about her husband's latest extramarital affair. The story quickly reached the internet, and Taiana appeared the cover of *Playboy*, her modesty covered by only a fistful of US dollars. A disgusted Joana filed for judicial separation soon after.

In the courts, the defence teams were attacking various formal aspects of the investigation – procedural matters which, if not properly followed, might eventually lead to the case being thrown out. One of the lawyers' first arguments was Sergio Moro's lack of jurisdiction to conduct the case. Under their analysis, it was up to the courts in Rio de Janeiro or São Paulo to try the cases, since the alleged offences had been committed in those two states. The lawyers repeatedly deployed the argument that 'none of the alleged events took place in Paraná', and filed requests asking that 'Your Honour declines jurisdiction for the hearing and judging of criminal charges and transfers these proceedings to the constitutionally competent judicial authority'. Moro replied within the text of his formal ruling, stating that the first crime discovered was committed in offices in Londrina, in the north of Paraná, where Alberto Youssef was accused of carrying out money laundering. Furthermore, there were allegations of corruption and embezzlement at the Presidente Getúlio Vargas refinery, within the Curitiba metropolitan area.

Another matter raised was the legality of intercepting messages sent via BlackBerry. The defence lawyers alleged that the Federal Police's initial interception of messages on Alberto

Youssef's BlackBerry had been illegal. Their recordings revealed conversations with Youssef that were considered fundamental to the police's ability to extend their investigations and discover new names. The lawyers said that the interception request had been sent by the Federal Police's Department for Combating Organised Crime in Brasília to the Canadian company RIM (Research in Motion). However, in their opinion, the international cooperation request should have been passed through the central Brazilian authorities, in this case the ministry of justice. Since Brazil did not have an international cooperation agreement with Canada, where BlackBerry's headquarters was situated, they applied for the evidence to be set aside, but Sergio Moro rejected their requests. The issue was debated back and forth for many months. In May 2015, for example, OAS's defence team once again filed for the evidence to be deemed inadmissible. The lawyers also recalled that Sergio Moro had been declared conflicted in a previous investigation involving Alberto Youssef. This had been a few years after the Banestado case, when accusations surfaced that Youssef had broken his plea bargain agreement and was continuing with his criminal activities. In one of these accusations, a detective informed the judge that Youssef had hidden R$25 million offshore. Moro declared himself to be conflicted in relation to the supervision of that particular investigation, but not to the others that targeted Youssef. In an official report, Moro explained that he had recused himself from that investigation because, in that particular case, the Federal Police's investigations had been instigated by a detective who disagreed with Youssef having been granted a plea bargain. Moro considered that the argument in favour of investigating the allegation of offshore assets went against the terms of the plea bargain agreement that he himself had officially authorised at this time, and it was this conflict which motivated his recusal.

At the time, in a meeting held in a cigar shop in Curitiba, some of the defence lawyers provoked Antonio Figueiredo Basto, Alberto Youssef's lawyer. They said that the investigation would end up in Brasília.

'The only guy here who's going to work is you. We're going to get rich without working,' they joked.

'You're wrong,' replied Basto. 'This shit is going to be hell for everyone, and none of you are prepared for that. I know this guy. I know Sergio Moro.'

FIRM HAND

So who is this man whom all the suspects were so eager to get away from? Born in 1972, Sergio Moro is one of a new genera- tion of judges who graduated after the introduction of the new constitution in 1988. Moro is visibly uncomfortable with the notoriety he has gained. Before Operation Car Wash, almost no one took any notice of him, but as the investigations went on, Moro had to change his routine. These days, he goes nowhere without a bodyguard.

In the early days of his career as a judge, he received a proposal to set up a group of judges specialising in money laundering offences. It would be hard work, but just the type of challenge he needed. If it was work that Moro wanted, that was what he got, especially when documents relating to the Banestado case began to arrive from the city of Foz do Iguaçu, down on the border with Argentina and Paraguay. Back then it seemed a monumental task, but seen in perspective it was merely a trial run for for what he would face years later with Operation

Car Wash. Once the Banestado trial was over, Moro took on another case that was dangerous as well as complex, against the drug gang run by Fernandinho Beira-Mar. During cross-examination, the drug dealer who had long reigned in Rio de Janeiro remained silent, under the advice of his lawyers. On the last day, however, he requested a 'one-to-one' with the judge.

'The thing is, mister, I have some businesses that are legal, like the distribution of gas canisters, for example, even if the source of the money is drug dealing,' admitted Fernandinho.

In effect, this was a confession, but the judge preferred to do everything according to the proper procedures. 'Mr Beira-Mar, if this is what you wish to declare to the court, go and get your lawyer and formally write down what you're telling me.'

Beira-Mar didn't do it. The trial was a difficult one and there were worries relating to the security of the judge and his family. It was decided that the Moro family would have security twenty-four hours a day from both the Civil Police and the Federal Police. The couple couldn't even drive their own cars. The children found it very strange and Rosângela, Moro's wife, made up an explanation that wouldn't scare them: 'It's because daddy has been a very good judge and he's won a prize. Now we're going to have a driver.'

It was a difficult six months, full of restrictions and some unusual situations. The Moro family learned to deal with moments of stress as naturally as they could, but this became more difficult during the period when the judge went to live in Brasília as an assistant to the Supreme Court judge Rosa Weber. However, his wife supported him: 'Is this what you want? If it's going to make you happy, you should go.' The opportunity to play a small part in the Big Monthly corruption trial was also very important for Moro. It was as if he were following a route on a map that began with the Banestado case and Alberto Youssef's plea bargain, passing through the tense drug-trafficking trial, then continuing with the behind-the-scenes work on a major corruption case at the Supreme Court, before reaching Operation Car Wash itself.

Sergio Moro tries to lead an ordinary life, despite his office being at the epicentre of the biggest juridical-political-corporate earthquake in Brazil. He lives with the dilemma of wanting the case to be known about, aware that public opinion plays an important part in reaching a successful outcome, but at the same time preferring by temperament not to be at the centre of attention. 'The important thing is the case,' he says, whenever asked for his opinion or for details of his personal life. 'Everything I have to say is in the official reports of the case.' He does not usually give interviews, preferring to speak through his judicial decisions and in a handful of public appearances, such as lectures and conferences. In his judgments, Moro is detailed, diligent and precise in his arguments. He doesn't let the pace of a trial slow down and he takes a firm hand when necessary. 'He's one of the good ones,' says his office manager, who coordinates the team of assistants at the 13th Federal Bench in Curitiba. 'It's a pleasure to watch him at work.' An experienced strategist with immense technical knowledge and a huge willingness to work, Moro also won the respect of the prosecutors involved in the operation. Like most judges', his desk is covered in papers, but he doesn't let the dust gather. He follows everything and reads every detail of the trial process, which he keeps organised into hundreds of separate files and folders on his computer.

Sergio Moro saw in Operation Car Wash a once-in-a-lifetime opportunity to defeat corruption on a battlefield where other operations had failed. The case, which had consequences for powerful people nationwide, began with a relatively obscure black-market currency dealer, and developed into something much bigger, involving a former Petrobras director in Rio, money launderers in São Paulo and politicians in Brasília. Fearing precisely this outcome, at the beginning of the operation those under investigation tried at all costs to escape from Sergio Moro and the tentacles of Operation Car Wash.

But one by one, the defence's requests were being thrown out by the federal court in Paraná and also, when they appealed, by the Regional Federal Court for the 4th district, in Porto Alegre. These defeats confirmed for the lawyers that the best solution was to escape Moro's grasp completely. In the meantime, however, they had one more shot. The names of two federal congressmen, André Vargas from the Workers' Party and Luiz Argôlo from Bahia Solidarity, and that of Senator Fernando Collor de Mello, at that time with the Brazilian Labour Party and himself a former president of Brazil, had surfaced in the investigation. Paulo Roberto Costa's defence lawyers argued that, because of the involvement of two members of the legislature, the whole investigation should be moved to another forum: the Federal Supreme Court. So the case reached Brasília for the first time; would this mean that Sergio Moro was now out of the picture? The answer would be given by the Supreme Court. Operation Car Wash hung by a thread.

Chapter 2

PLEA BARGAINS CLEAR THE WAY

19 May 2014

THE DAY THE CAR WASH STOPPED

There were just eight pages, sent by fax. When they arrived at the 13th Federal Bench in Curitiba that Monday morning, a buzz quickly spread around the office, which was soon replaced by solemnity. The office manager handed the fax to Sergio Moro apprehensively, almost shaking. Teori Zavascki, the Supreme Court judge with overall responsibility for the Operation Car Wash trials, had taken a decision that could have completely changed the course of the story: he had suspended all proceedings relating to the operation and ordered the release of the twelve detainees suspected of having taken part in the criminal scheme. Was this the death of Operation Car Wash?

The operation was little more than two months old when Justice Teori Zavascki made the decision, in response to an application by Paulo Roberto Costa's defence team. The lawyers were arguing that the case should be transferred to the Supreme Court because the names of federal Congressmen André Vargas and Luiz Argôlo had come up in the investigation, when

Youssef's conversations with them had been intercepted by the Federal Police. In Youssef's office, they had also found evidence of deposits into Senator Fernando Collor's bank account. According to the Brazilian constitution, it falls to the Supreme Court, not the courts of first instance, to investigate and try federal congressmen and senators.

The defence were complaining that Sergio Moro had sent only a brief report informing the Supreme Court that André Vargas's name had come up in the investigation, which was not enough. 'Such a precaution, as well as being insufficient, is clearly illegal. Once the presence has been established of a person entitled to privileged forum by virtue of their status as federal legislators – in this case persons, plural – it is not for the judge at first instance to decide whether the case should be split or not,' wrote Paulo Roberto Costa's senior lawyer, Fernando Fernandes. In his view, Moro should have sent all the Operation Car Wash proceedings to the Supreme Court, whose job it was to decide what should or should not be investigated by the lower court.

In response to the Supreme Court's intervention, Sergio Moro explained that 'during the investigation, specifically during the interception of Alberto Youssef's phone calls, evidence was unintentionally gathered in the form of messages exchanged with persons identified simply as "Vargas". It was only more recently, following the various searches and arrests, that the Federal Police concluded that the "Vargas" in question was the federal congressman André Vargas, and that there was a potential criminal character to the messages.' These elements had been separated from the trial documentation and sent to the Supreme Court. Moro said that he had decided not to transfer all the proceedings to the Supreme Court because there was no record or indication of André Vargas's involvement in the other facts being investigated. 'Federal Congressman André Vargas has never been investigated as part of the proceedings. The alleged evidence relating to him arose purely by chance from the interception of Alberto Youssef's phone,' he added. But it was no use.

In his ruling, Justice Teori Zavascki ordered: '(a) the suspension of all inquiries and related criminal proceedings by the authority in question, together with the suspension of all arrest warrants, including that of the claimant, thereby resulting in immediate release where such persons have not been detained on other grounds, and (b) the immediate transfer of all related proceedings to this Supreme Court.'

The Supreme Court judge granted the ruling because he found that Moro had split the proceedings himself, transferring only the part relating to legislators to the Supreme Court. Teori Zavascki recalled that in the past a Supreme Court hearing had already decided that it was an affront to the jurisdiction of the court for a judge of first instance to split an investigation of his own accord.

The defence lawyers were euphoric. It was their first victory. With a wide grin on his face, Paulo Roberto Costa left the police cells in Curitiba that very afternoon. He was the first person arrested under Operation Car Wash to be freed through the direct intervention of the Supreme Court. The news spread rapidly. In the jail there were celebrations – the other prisoners thought that they would be released next. Youssef's defence even said they were expecting his release the following morning. When he received the Supreme Court's ruling, Sergio Moro asked to be left alone, saying that no one was to interrupt him, and locked the door. Alone in his office, he began to write a formal response: 'I have late this morning received Your Honour's decision ...'

Tension was running high at the 13th Federal Bench. Outside the locked door, everyone held their breath.

'... As a consequence, I have ordered that a release warrant for the claimant, Paulo Roberto Costa, be issued ...'

At this point, a sense of disquiet was spreading through the corridors of the Federal Police and the public prosecutors' office. The fear was that the entire investigation would be transferred from Paraná to Brasília. While the Supreme Court was reaching its final decision, their work would have to be put on hold. They were horrified. The most pessimistic among them thought that Operation Car Wash might be shelved entirely because of a matter of jurisdiction. 'I reckoned there was no chance; the trial was moving to the Supreme Court,' recounts one of the assistants. The defence lawyers had been attempting this since the beginning of the operation. There had been long meetings in São Paulo between the various defence lawyers to develop a strategy to transfer the investigation to the Supreme Court, and hopefully get it stopped altogether.

Away from all the others, Sergio Moro remained locked in his office. The security camera in the corner of the room recorded his silent work at the computer. Soon the text was ready. Moro was extremely cautious in his response; it is not normal for a judge at first instance to question the decisions of the court of final appeal. What Moro did was request guidance from the Supreme Court judge regarding the full extent of his decision. He needed to query it without being disrespectful, finding the right balance between a wish to keep the operation in Paraná and his respect for judicial hierarchy. It was an unusual course of action that many judges would never have attempted.

'I am sending this request respectfully seeking guidance as to the ambit of your decision, given that those accused who should be released have not been named in it, nor have those proceedings which should be transferred to the Federal Supreme Court been specified,' he wrote. He noted that among the Operation Car Wash proceedings, there were actions relating to drug trafficking and money laundering. 'I therefore respectfully enquire of Your Honour whether these actions relating to drug trafficking and money laundering should be transferred to the Federal Supreme Court, and whether prisoners accused of those offences should be released.' Moro also pointed to the flight risk of two prisoners, Alberto Youssef and Nelma Kodama, whose offshore bank accounts containing millions had already been identified. 'My objective is simply to clarify the entire scope of the decision communicated to me, in order to ensure that the trials, public order and the due application of criminal law are not put at risk through an interpretation on my part that may turn out to be mistaken. Evidently, in the event of clarification that all the trials should be transferred and all prisoners released, such decision will be immediately implemented,' concluded Moro, and ordered that his response be sent immediately to the Supreme Court, also by fax.

Moro did not know what would happen next. 'It is very difficult for a Supreme Court judge to backtrack,' he thought. The next day, he read in a newspaper that some lawyers had made fun of his response. 'Only the judge failed to understand that the decision affected all of them. Even my intern understood,' said one. But this would not be the end of the story.

In fact, Sergio Moro's boldness ended up saving Operation Car Wash. On studying Moro's arguments, Zavascki changed his mind, deciding to uphold the detention of the other defendants and releasing only Paulo Roberto Costa. 'In the light of the arguments made and facts disclosed in the additional information provided, I authorise, as a precautionary measure, that the rulings be maintained, including those relating to orders for arrest and detention,' wrote Zavascki. It was very frustrating for Youssef and the others. 'Without detailed knowledge of the proceedings, I do not wish to take hasty decisions,' Zavascki confirmed to the journalists on duty at the Supreme Court that day, recognising that it would be difficult at that point to decide who should be released and who should remain in custody.

In Curitiba, the judge, the police and the prosecutors all breathed a sigh of relief. If all those on remand had been released, it could have been the beginning of the end for the operation. Zavascki's decision to suspend the proceedings, however, still stood. The matter would be referred to the Supreme Court, which would give its final word on whether the trial could continue in Paraná. Zavascki's decision was merely preliminary and would be further analysed by the rest of the Supreme Court. For this reason, the initial sense of relief in Moro's office was quickly replaced by a new concern. Zavascki had ruled that all the files be sent to Brasília. There was no choice but to comply, and Moro gave instructions for all the documents to be printed. The annexes relating to each separate line of investigation could be sent digitally, but the actual transcripts of interviews couldn't be. Several boxes of documents were sent to Brasília, and the investigation in Paraná was put on hold. Every line of enquiry ground to a halt – they just had to wait. Moro's victory had been important, but partial; he had avoided all the prisoners being released, but the doubt about whether the trial itself would be transferred to the Supreme Court remained.

That day, Moro reflected on events as he cycled home. Years earlier, the Supreme Court judges had fought among themselves over the Big Monthly corruption case. Some of them had felt that the trial should be split according to the various categories of defendants, but the president of the Supreme Court, Joaquim Barbosa, had convinced his fellow judges that it shouldn't. This time, the situation had arisen in a slightly different manner, since the trial had already begun in a lower court. It would not be easy to decide.

THE DEFENCE DRAWS UP STRATEGIES

After Paulo Roberto Costa's release, the press interest in Operation Car Wash began to cool. After all, the only people now in prison were black-market currency dealers. The defence lawyers were confident that the former Petrobras director would not be returning to jail. The lawyers of various other defendants coordinated their actions and the number of requests for release increased each week. All of them hoped to be as lucky as Costa. After a few weeks out of jail, the former director started to sketch out the usual Brazilian defence strategy: deny everything and keep repeating that he was innocent. No one wanted the case to proceed, especially the politicians.

Costa's first move on leaving jail, where he had been for fifty-nine days, was to give an interview to the newspaper *Folha de S.Paulo*. He decided to speak to the reporter at the home of his new lawyer, Nelio Machado, in Rio de Janeiro. Before the interview, Machado quietly asked Costa if he had an offshore bank account. 'Absolutely not,' his client replied. To the newspaper, he said almost the same thing: that he had never made illegal transfers abroad. 'My involvement in money laundering and illegal foreign transactions is zero,' he stated. He confirmed that he knew Youssef, but when asked why suppliers to his former employer had made deposits with Youssef's companies, he replied: 'I couldn't say.'

He gave the same speech when he appeared in front of Congress to talk about the scandal. It would be the first of several visits, each time with an appearance and demeanour different from the one before. On this occasion he gave an impassive performance. His beard neatly trimmed, hair combed and his expression somewhere between sincere and weary, Paulo Roberto Costa walked slowly into the room where the Senate inquiry into Petrobras was being held. The session looked likely to be a gentle one, and so it proved to be. With no fewer than five friendly senators taking part and an opposition that was not in the mood for a fight, there was little pressure on him. He said what he wanted to say, denied taking part in any kind of money laundering scheme involving Alberto Youssef and even stated brazenly: 'I don't know where they got that story.'

Courteous towards the legislators, he paused to think before speaking and said that the purchase of the Pasadena refinery had been a 'good deal' for Petrobras and that he deplored having been 'massacred by baseless accusations'. Costa's testimony was a complete farce, but it also contained a message which at that point was sincere: 'I'm no suicide bomber.' Not yet. In his testimony, the former director made it clear that he knew many politicians and confirmed that he had travelled with Dilma Rousseff to Venezuela; at the time she was leading a Brazilian government delegation and he was representing Petrobras, but it was nothing more than that. He even confidently complained about the seizure of cash in three currencies – US$180,000, €10,000 and R$750,000 – that the Federal Police had found in his house.

'I don't see any problem with having that amount of money at home,' he railed. According to the version he gave the senators that day, the Brazilian reais were to be used for payments by his consulting firm, Costa Global. He admitted that the dollars and euros had not been declared to the tax authorities, which sounded like a clever strategy to the senators present that day: confessing to the minor offence of not paying some taxes. Some months later, he would tell Sergio Moro that the dollars and euros were genuinely his, but that having the reais 'wasn't right'.

On leaving the hearing, the leader of the Workers' Party in the Senate, Humberto Costa (no relation of Paulo Roberto Costa), who would also be investigated by Operation Car Wash several months later, on suspicion of having received R$1 million for his 2010 campaign, said that the testimony was 'satisfactory'. Paulo Roberto Costa was very happy when the session ended. He'd succeeded in getting out of jail and had got off to a good start with the congressional inquiry; he imagined that from then on, things could only get better. But this feeling would not last long.

While Paulo Roberto Costa was at Congress, the Supreme Court was meeting on the other side of the road to consider whether it should bring all the Operation Car Wash proceedings before the Supreme Court itself, thereby slowing them down, or leave them to the federal courts in Paraná. No date had yet been set for a ruling, but on the basis of other evidence federal prosecutors had filed a new request for Costa's arrest, and Teori Zavascki of the Supreme Court decided to raise a question of order. Now the destiny of Operation Car Wash would be decided.

This decision captured everyone's attention more than Paulo Roberto Costa's little performance at the congressional inquiry.

The defence lawyers were sure that the investigation would be transferred to Brasília. The prosecutor general, Rodrigo Janot, was heavily involved in the case, detailing the initial steps taken in the investigation and arguing that it should be split and that the part involving defendants not entitled to parliamentary privilege should remain in Curitiba. The court decided that Sergio Moro's actions had been correct and implied no disrespect whatsoever to the Supreme Court, by five votes to zero. They therefore sent the eight criminal actions back to the federal court in Paraná, along with the investigations relating to Operation Car Wash that were currently before the Supreme Court. They left it to Sergio Moro to decide the matter of Costa's detention. Victory was complete; the case was firmly in Moro's hands once again. The judge cancelled his planned holiday and set to work on the case once again. Paulo Roberto Costa heard the news on television and went to bed a worried man, with good reason.

The next day, the police knocked on the door of his house, not at dawn, as was the usual practice, but at 4 p.m. The judge had made an express request that the arrest be made that same day, as there was a 'real and immediate danger' of flight. Paulo Roberto Costa had a Portuguese passport that he had not disclosed to the Supreme Court. Furthermore, federal prosecutors had received information that the former director had US\$23 million in an account in Switzerland, an amount of money incompatible with his earnings. The money was in the name of offshore companies. Costa's lawyer was attending the funeral of the former governor of Rio de Janeiro, Marcello Alencar, when he received news of his client's arrest. He rushed over to the Federal Police headquarters.

Costa's bank account had been discovered by Swiss public prosecutors, who got in touch with their Brazilian colleagues as soon as they became aware that the former Petrobras director was being investigated in Brazil. The two sides exchanged information: the Swiss were also conducting an investigation and had frozen Costa's bank account. One of the Brazilian prosecutors recalled the day the news arrived: 'Deltan received an email from Switzerland. When he read it, he exclaimed: "Oh, it looks like they've found something of Paulo Roberto's! Twenty-three million things, to be exact!"'

Deltan Dallagnol sought permission to use this information for a new arrest warrant. To help the investigation, the Swiss authorities officially informed Brazil that they had found indications that Paulo Roberto Costa had received millions in kickbacks in 2011 and 2012 from firms involved in the construction of the Abreu & Lima refinery in Pernambuco. Furthermore, in an unusual move, they authorised that this information could be used for the purposes of a Brazilian arrest warrant. So less than thirty days after being released, Costa returned to police custody. When his lawyer arrived, he finally told him the truth: 'I have an account,' he whispered in Nelio Machado's ear.

Paulo Roberto Costa's situation had just become much more complicated, but it would be another two months before he took the decision that would change the course of the whole story yet again. Between now and then, there would be a lot of pressure behind the scenes. Many powerful people were involved and there was much at stake.

EXPLICIT THREATS

Meire Poza, Youssef's accountant, was feeling the heat. A representative from the construction firms was insisting on talking to her. Poza arranged a meeting in a public place – the food court at a São Paulo shopping centre – and recorded the conversation on her mobile phone:

'Hello Edson, how are you?'

'Hey there, Meire. I'm fine. How are you?' replies Edson.

After a few more pleasantries, Poza cuts to the chase: 'So, what brings you all this way?'

'Well now, Meire … We're rather worried about you, that's all,' says the representative.

'About me? Why would you be worried about me?'

'We don't understand why you're refusing our help,' he says bluntly.

'Well, to be honest, I don't understand why you're insisting on helping me so much,' replies Poza, laughing nervously.

'We're worried about you, and your situation. After all, you're the only woman involved in this whole thing. We know you have a daughter, and that there's only the two of you … That's why we're insisting on helping you,' says Edson, leaving little to the imagination.

Without changing his tone of voice, the representative identified only as Edson continues, despite Poza's objections. He tells Poza that she is part of a 'closed group' of 'privileged' persons who can help each other, and that she can neither leave the group nor refuse their help.

'I'm starting to dislike this conversation,' says Poza.

'It's true, very true. Suddenly, one word out of place can be dangerous, harmful. So Meire, the important thing is to not talk too much!' he says, clarifying the purpose of the conversation further.

'I think you're threatening me,' reacts Poza.

'It's just a matter of warning you of the kind of care that needs to be taken. You might, without meaning to, say something that contradicts large businesses, politicians, construction firms – the biggest in the country, you understand. This is why we want to help you, just to guide you ...' says Edson, reaching out to touch her arm.

'Don't touch me, please. I don't like it. Let me tell you something ...'

'Sorry.'

'Apology accepted.'

At this point, Poza gets up and says goodbye, and Meire asks him not to come looking for her again. Before leaving, she says one last thing: 'You can do me one more favour. You'll probably be there with your clients, with Camargo, with UTC, Constran ...'

'Yes, yes,' says Edson hurriedly.

'With OAS ...'

'OK.'

'Well tell them all to go to hell!' she says, and walks off.

Like Poza, Costa was also subject to all kinds of pressure. But for him there was one force that spoke louder than any of the others.

IN THE BACK OF A POLICE VAN

He had to speak quickly. The two of them were being taken to a hearing, and the police van would soon be arriving at the federal court building in Curitiba. It was an opportunity to talk. Squeezed into the back of the vehicle, in the so-called 'bird-cage' used for transporting prisoners, the breathing of the once all-powerful director of supply at Petrobras, Paulo Roberto Costa, was clearly audible. He came straight to the point:

'There's nothing else for it, Beto. I'm going to do a deal with the prosecutors.'

'Not yet, Paulo. Wait just a little bit longer. They haven't yet ruled on my habeas corpus,' said Youssef, referring to the provision in the Brazilian constitution against arbitrary or illegal detention.

'I'm not waiting a minute longer, Beto,' said Costa.

'Alright then. You go your way, I'll go mine,' said Youssef.

It was 21 August 2014. Costa was under pressure from his family. Two days earlier, his wife, daughters and sons-in-law had met his lawyer and announced to him that they were negotiating a deal with prosecutors.

'Let me get this straight. You're going to decide this without hearing what Paulo Roberto has to say? He's the one in jail. You might be having a tough time, but I think you owe it to him, at the very least, to wait until I've spoken to him,' Nelio Machado told them.

The lawyer wasn't in favour of plea bargains, but went to Curitiba to speak with his client. Paulo Roberto Costa assured him that under no circumstances would he talk. Machado was confident he would get him out of jail within a couple of days with an application for habeas corpus. At the end of the conversation, Costa mentioned that his wedding anniversary was on 6 September and invited Machado to come and join them for a glass of champagne to toast the occasion. He expected to be home by then. Nelio Machado recalls, 'He said to me: "The only possible scenario [for a plea deal] is if you don't succeed in this habeas corpus application. But other than that, there's no way I'd do it, absolutely no way." And I thought, "Well, it's what he wants that counts, not what his family wants."'

But as Costa says himself, a week is a long time in jail. Only those who've been there know. By then he was on the defensive; he had spent the last seven days in a state penitentiary in Piraquara, on the outskirts of Curitiba, and he was scared. He couldn't bear being behind bars any longer. The possibility of being found guilty and receiving a sentence that could well exceed the forty years handed down to Marcos Valério, the man who had run the Big Monthly corruption scheme, terrified the former Petrobras director.

The lawyer left the meeting with his client and that very night drafted an application for habeas corpus, which he presented to the Regional Federal Court for the 4th district at 5 a.m. on 22 August 2014. However, one hour later, at dawn, the police launched phase six of Operation Car Wash. The investigators ransacked the premises of thirteen consultancy firms linked to Costa's daughter Arianna, his son-in-law Humberto, and a friend of theirs, Marcelo Barboza, all based in Rio de Janeiro. Federal prosecutors had noted a 'vertiginous growth in the assets of these firms' while Costa was a director of Petrobras. It was the last straw. That very day, Costa met with a new lawyer, Beatriz Catta Preta, a specialist in plea bargains, in Curitiba.

Various factors influenced Costa's decision, but none of them weighed heavier than the pressure from his family. He wanted to watch his grandchildren grow up. On realising that he had no chance of escaping a prison sentence and that his daughters were also being investigated, he pursued a path that would lead him to reveal everything he knew about Brazil's largest ever corruption scheme. He dispensed with the services of Nelio Machado and signed a retainer with Beatriz Catta Preta, who would negotiate a plea bargain for him and many others investigated under Operation Car Wash. Catta

Preta had previously been the lawyer of one of those accused in the Big Monthly scandal, a black-market currency dealer called Lúcio Bolonha Funaro. She issued a press release after her meeting with Costa: 'A settlement is one possible route. I will analyse all possibilities.'

The investigators waited expectantly. Catta Preta, who was holding parallel talks with her new client's family, had already got in contact with the investigators the previous week. First she called one of the prosecutors on the task force and told him that Paulo Roberto Costa was going to cooperate. Then she called back to say that he had changed his mind, after being put under pressure. The expression she used to explain the cause of the setback was 'dark forces'. After another meeting with her client, she called once again: Costa had decided, finally, to cooperate. The prosecutors were jubilant. They knew that some divisions at Petrobras, such as the one headed by Costa, had budgets that exceeded those of many government departments. They were also aware of the scale of the corruption in which Costa was involved; the scheme was bigger than they had initially thought. As director of Petrobras, Costa frequently dealt with contractors and politicians; if he told them everything he knew, they could discover much more than they might ever have imagined at the beginning of the investigation. They started negotiating. Paulo Roberto Costa was in a very tricky situation, in custody and accused of many crimes, but he had been a skilful negotiator for decades and it was one of the things he was best at. In the long discussions with the prosecutors, it was he, rather than his lawyer, who took the lead role. He complained that they were asking too much from him, that he had already provided them with everything and that he needed his wealth to support himself and his family.

'He "cried" quite frequently, using arguments like: "Ah, but these are my assets, accrued from my salary over so many years. You're asking too much, it's just not on, I need something to live on afterwards. I'm already giving you everything and you're crying over the crumbs; you want one or two million more here in Brazil, when I'm handing over seventy million overseas,"' recounts one of the negotiators. Throughout the process, the two sides tried to strengthen their respective positions. There were long hours of detailed negotiation and by the end it was agreed that Costa would tell them everything he knew. On 27 August 2014, he signed the plea bargain agreement with federal prosecutors.

At that point, the prosecutors decided to do something new: to divide the various subjects of investigation into different annexes. It was Deltan Dallagnol's idea. Dividing it this way solved a potential problem: if the names of any politicians were to come up, some of the annexes could be sent to the Supreme Court without prejudicing other parts of the investigation; one annex could be disclosed without disclosing the others. The list was drawn up. Paulo Roberto Costa listed the annexes one by one; there were eighty in total. He had a lot to reveal.

In the cooperation agreement, the former director promised to return the kickbacks that he'd received, including the millions frozen offshore, to disclose all the crimes committed and to give names of the other criminals. If it was proved that he had lied or withheld information at any point, he would lose all benefits, including the right, as envisaged, to serve his prison sentence under house arrest, with an electronic ankle tag. Since he had indicated that legislators were involved – federal congressmen and senators, whose investigations would be subject to the Supreme Court – the prosecutor general Rodrigo Janot, who had jurisdiction over such matters, needed to authorise the negotiation. He approved the cooperation agreement, guaranteeing a more lenient sentence in the future and authorising the Federal Police to hear Paulo Roberto Costa's deposition. It was time for him to start talking.

THE FIRST PLEA BARGAIN

Paulo Roberto Costa began giving evidence on 29 August 2014, at the headquarters of the Federal Police in Paraná. The officer leading the interview was detective Erika Marena. Beside her was Felipe Hayashi, one of the other detectives who had been involved with Operation Car Wash from the beginning. Diogo Castor de Mattos, a federal prosecutor who had written his Master's thesis on white-collar crime, was also chosen to attend. Paulo Roberto Costa was accompanied by his lawyer Beatriz Catta Preta and his friend Luiz Henrique Vieira.

The testimony began with the customary declarations, which would be repeated at all future meetings, for example the witness stating that he 'intends to cooperate in an effective and voluntary manner', and that he 'has given a solemn undertaking to tell the truth'. In these preliminaries, Costa also confirmed that he was aware that the plea bargain depended on the results, such as the identification of the participants in the criminal undertaking, its structure and allocation of tasks and responsibilities. Furthermore, he acknowledged that any concessions would take into consideration the 'personality of the cooperating suspect, the seriousness and consequences of their criminal actions and the effectiveness of their co-operation'. Among these concessions were the right to have his name and public image preserved, the right to be held in his own cell separate to the other detainees, and the right not to have eye contact with the accused during court hearings.

After these preliminary declarations, the actual questioning began. The initial questions were about 'political elements', and more specifically what Costa called the 'politicians–government–contractors triangle'. Costa quickly named twenty-seven politicians who were 'implicated in criminal offences': three governors, ten senators and fourteen congressmen. He indicated that he might well come up with more names after checking his diary and papers further. For each name, he gave the number of times that the person had committed a crime, and when. It was a bombshell.

The mood in the room was tense; the investigators did not take their eyes off Costa and watched his every movement. It was a rare opportunity to understand the nuts and bolts of a gigantic corruption scheme. 'We already knew of the existence of the scheme Costa was describing, but the moment when somebody comes and confirms it, well, it's quite impressive,' said one of the detectives. 'We'd never had someone of his weight coming and telling us, "Look, I did this, then this happened." The guy was a director of the company, he was very powerful, maybe that's why it made such an impression.'

Costa began by talking about his own life. He had been with the company since 1977 and was in charge of Petrobras's Supply Division from May 2004 to April 2012. Before that, he had held a variety of technical and managerial posts within the company, always earned on merit and he was always hard-working, but he had then reached a point when mere ability was not enough to progress further. To be promoted to director he needed political patronage, as is the case with all companies linked to the government. Costa drew a comparison with the Armed Forces:

an officer, no matter how well qualified, will at most reach the rank of colonel; to become a general requires personal recommendation. In the case of Paulo Roberto Costa, his patron came from the Progressive Party: José Janene. The then-leader of the Progressive Party in the Chamber of Deputies invited him to be a director of Petrobras. Janene promised his support and nominated Costa for the job – it was what he needed to achieve his ambitions. He knew that the party would ask for something in return, but he claimed he had no idea at the time what it meant to 'join the scheme'.

'It's a complete fallacy to say that genuine campaign donations exist in Brazil. In reality, they are loans to be repaid at high interest once the candidate is in office. No one gets elected in Brazil with only official donations. The declared amount of election expenses corresponds on average to one third of the sum that is actually spent. The rest comes from illicit or undeclared sources,' vented Costa. Costa revealed that after being nominated by the Progressive Party, he had been asked to provide funds not only to the Progressive Party, but also at various times to the centre-right Brazilian Democratic Movement (PMDB), and the left-wing Workers' Party, using money from the Petrobras coffers. If he didn't meet their requests, this would mean leaving his job to be replaced by someone else. He was most frequently approached by the Progressive Party and the PMDB, and more sporadically by the Workers' Party. But he had also suffered the attentions of members of the centre-left Brazilian Social Democratic Party (PSDB), who asked him for money to help stop a congressional inquiry into Petrobras being set up in 2010. All the parties denied Costa's accusations, but he described everything down to the smallest detail.

According to Costa, the scheme also functioned in divisions beyond his own: Petrobras had been divvied up between the parties. The chairman's office and four other divisions (Services, Gas and Energy, Exploration and Production, and Finance) were the fiefdom of the ruling Workers' Party, the Supply Division was run by the Progressive Party and the International Division by the PMDB. The Services Division, which was responsible for Petrobras's largest contracts, was headed by Renato Duque, who had been recommended for the post by the Workers' Party.

That wasn't all. According to Costa, the small number of firms with the size and technical capacity to take on large-scale engineering projects in Brazil, the so-called 'Club of Sixteen', had created a cartel to defraud Petrobras's multi-billion tendering processes. They would meet in São Paulo or Rio and decide who would get each project or contract, and what percentage of the fee the kickback would be. Only after agreeing this among themselves did they present their bids to Petrobras, coming in just below the maximum amount that its tendering committee would accept. Then there would be the inevitable additional items that inflated the cost further, almost always necessary because of mistakes in the initial projections.

Paulo Roberto Costa explained that in any quotation, whether initial or final, the contractor providing such services to Petrobras would expect a profit margin of 10 to 20 per cent. On top of this amount, the contractor would charge a further 1 to 3 per cent on the final price (thus, given the scale of these projects, inflating the cost by millions), and would then pass this money to the political party that controlled that particular division of Petrobras. The rules were clear. Without the over-invoicing and the kickback, the firm would not be called to participate in the next tender and the director would cause problems in the contract itself, such as non-payment, delaying payment and not approving additional amounts – the kind of thing that could choke the contractor.

This is how the scheme was set up to siphon off Petrobras's publicly owned assets. Since everyone involved in the scheme gained, the corruption became institutionalised and was present in all of the oil firm's contracts and engineering projects. The contractors grabbed as much as they could from the state-owned firm, and the kickback demanded by politicians was deducted from this money. Costa talked and talked, as the investigators listened in silence, astonished.

Of the 3 per cent that was siphoned off, one third went to the Progressive Party (the party that had nominated him for the job) and two thirds went to the Workers' Party. Costa said that from time to time he would have to share the money destined for Progressive Party politicians with those of the Workers' Party, the PMDB and, on one occasion, the PSDB. He was talking about millions of reais. If there were no external parties to be paid, the Progressive Party's 1 per cent was divided as follows: 60 per cent for the party, 20 per cent to launder the money and 20 per cent for Paulo Roberto Costa and Alberto Youssef. Of this latter 20 per cent, 70 per cent went to Costa. Youssef was responsible for the financial operations, which included receiving the money from the contractors through his front companies, sending part of the money offshore and delivering the other part in cash within Brazil, got 30 per cent.

This was only Costa's first deposition. The days rolled on through the end of August and into September, and one by one all the annexes were dealt with. In an interview for this book, he recalled those days and the investigators' reaction to his revelations about corruption in Petrobras. 'When I started naming names, they saw that it wasn't just me. It was everyone,' he told me. 'I can't say I'm proud of having agreed to a plea bargain. That kind of deal does no good to anyone. But if it hadn't been for what I told them, Operation Car Wash wouldn't be where it is today.' Costa appeared conflicted about his role as informant: 'Being human is a curious thing. It's a relief to talk, but deep down you don't feel good. You're talking about other people, and other people's families, irrespective of whether what the guy did was right or wrong.'

From the very beginning, Costa talked about politicians. Much of what he said was, quite frankly, terrifying. Governors, ministers, senators, congressmen: there were politicians of every level and political hue, principally from the Workers' Party and the PMDB (the two main parties in government at the time), but also from the Progressive Party, the Brazilian Socialist Party and the PSDB. All had benefited in some way from the corruption scheme at Petrobras. All of Brazil's major contractors and their bosses, whom he named one by one, had set up a cartel within Petrobras with the help of its directors, and 3 per cent of the value of each contract was being diverted into the pockets and parties of those involved. The same went for the other divisions involved, such as the Services Division headed by Renato Duque and the International Division led by Nestor Cerveró and later by Jorge Zelada, all of whom were arrested under Operation Car Wash.

In these other divisions, explained Costa, other intermediaries were involved, rather than Alberto Youssef. Fernando Antonio Falcão Soares, also known as Fernando Baiano, was responsible for the laundering and distribution of assets to politicians and officials connected to the PMDB. For the

Workers' Party, the middleman was João Vaccari Neto, who was the party's national treasurer at the time. Costa provided all the details. Names that would provide the leads for future phases of Operation Car Wash were pouring out.

After several weeks of giving evidence to the police, Paulo Roberto Costa was again summoned to appear before the congressional inquiry into Petrobras, for his second visit to the Senate since the scandal broke. On his first visit, he had been well treated – this time he was not so lucky. He walked through the Congress building, unhandcuffed but guarded by federal agents and Senate security personnel. Feeling hungry, he asked to have lunch before his testimony. The hot food in the Senate's famous restaurant – beef in a red wine jus with puréed potatoes – reminded him of better times.

At the inquiry hearing, his appearance greatly changed and sporting a new moustache, he sat beside his lawyer, Beatriz Catta Preta, and found himself in a much more hostile environment than on the previous occasion. No one greeted him, with the exception of Humberto Costa, the Workers' Party's leader in the Senate. Right at the start, Paulo Roberto Costa announced his intention to remain silent; for as long as he was providing information to the judicial authorities, he could not say anything. The inquiry turned into a platform for grandstanding congressmen and senators. During the two hours and forty minutes he was present, the parliamentarians hurled merciless insults and abuse at him, calling him a crook and a coward, a liar and a cheat, and a criminal gang leader who had pillaged Petrobras.

Costa sat through all this without reacting. He occasionally exchanged a few words with his lawyer, drank some water or coffee, endured the insults and, when someone asked an objective question, replied that he 'reserved the right to remain silent'. He said this phrase some seventeen times during the hearing. Even in the face of grave provocation, such as when the congressional leader of the PSDB held up a photo of Costa evidently enjoying himself and writing something on President Rousseff's overalls at a formal Petrobras event, he merely stared back in silence. When another congressman said that Costa would only talk under torture, he shot a revealing glance at his lawyer. On the contrary, he was talking a great deal, and of his own free will – but he would not reveal anything on this particular day. The truth would be kept for another occasion.

Costa returned to Curitiba and finished giving evidence. Once this part of his cooperation was concluded, he was released on house arrest. He arrived back in Rio de Janeiro on 1 October 2014 and his car was followed by helicopters from TV stations from the airport to his home in Barra da Tijuca. 'It was like something from Hollywood. As I went into the house and hugged my wife and daughters, there were two helicopters filming, one stacked above the other, almost colliding,' he recounted.

ALBERTO YOUSSEF'S NEW DEAL

At the same time, another important collaboration under Operation Car Wash was about to take place in Curitiba. Following Paulo Roberto Costa's capitulation, it was Alberto Youssef's turn. His negotiations entered a decisive phase once Costa had made his decision; the currency dealer knew that if the former director talked, he would have no other option. So at the end of September, just over a month after his accomplice, Youssef made a deal with the federal prosecutors.

It was Youssef's lawyer, Antonio Figueiredo Basto, who announced that his client was going to make a 'full confession'. Youssef's defence reckoned they had negotiated a very good deal, and that it was his best chance of not passing the rest of his days behind bars. 'He will answer everything they ask him. He will cooperate fully with the courts,' confirmed Basto. The public declaration was well-pitched, as at that point there was still some fear within the task force around any cooperation agreement with Youssef. He had made a similar agreement in the Banestado case and, upon his release had gone straight back to the world of crime. Why should they trust him again? The debate lasted for weeks, but in the end the view prevailed that it was better to do a deal. He had a lot to say. At the last minute, however, Youssef's lawyer almost scuppered the whole thing: 'I don't want the agreement, at least not until I've had a serious discussion with the prosecutors. I've told Beto not to sign: "Don't sign this shit. They're going to shaft us," I said.'

The meeting at the federal prosecutors' office had started at 8 a.m. There were around ten people in what felt like an abandoned office; the task force was moving to a larger room in another building and the furniture had already been removed. There were just a few sections of desks left, which they pushed together to form a makeshift table in the middle of the room, with chairs arranged around it. By now it was already midday. Antonio Figueiredo Basto raised his hand and protested.

'I'm not going to sign this agreement. Look, if the rest of you want to sign,' he said, pointing to the three other lawyers, 'then be my guest, but I think this deal's no good. Three years in prison is too much.'

Reducing the jail sentence was one of Antonio Figueiredo Basto's principal demands. To Youssef, he gave a very direct piece of advice: 'I'm telling you not to sign.'

He knew that it was much more difficult to abandon a negotiation after everything else had already been argued and agreed. He wanted to gain time, so he decided to go and have lunch with the other lawyers before closing the deal with the federal prosecutors.

'We won't sign before lunch. We'll go and get something to eat, and then we'll come back for the signature,' Basto announced. He got up and left with the other lawyers. The prosecutors, still sitting, speculated about what might happen.

'He'll come back and sign,' said one of them.

'But he just said he wouldn't,' replied another.

'He'll come back quietly and sign the agreement.'

'How do you know?'

'It's just a negotiating tactic.'

And so it was. Figueiredo Basto returned and signed the deal, without any further questions. One prosecutor looked at another and smiled silently. One of the assistants of the prosecutor general, the person responsible for investigating elected politicians, was present at the signature.

Alberto Youssef's plea bargain agreement required, of course, that he tell the truth and not commit any more offences. Beyond that, he had various other obligations: to reveal all the crimes he knew of; to name those involved, including and especially politicians; and to provide proof. Youssef would also have to surrender assets such as real estate, luxury cars and money held offshore – R$50 million in total. 'I'm not going to incriminate anyone who was not involved, and nor am I going to shield anyone. The information I provide will be ethical and truthful,' declared Youssef. His lawyer was seeking judicial pardon and immediate release for his client, or house arrest, but the agreement fixed a sentence of a minimum of three years and maximum of five, in a closed prison.

Youssef began answering questions at the beginning of October, just before the first round of the presidential elections. Overall, the sessions lasted for over one hundred hours. They took place on consecutive days, except when Youssef was admitted to a Curitiba hospital due to his weak heart. At a speed dictated by Youssef's health, his evidence grew to fifty-eight annexes, each one related to a specific incident, a specific accusation or a line of enquiry to be followed. Dozens of investigations were opened on the basis of what Youssef revealed. He also brought documents to back up what he was saying and explained how the embezzlement was carried out and how the whole kickback scheme worked.

The curious thing is that in the first line of his very first statement, Youssef cites the name of José Janene: 'In order to clarify events, the witness declares that in 1997 he met Congressman José Janene, with whom he developed a personal friendship.' Youssef had decided to begin with the very genesis of the scheme – one of its initial creators, and indeed the very person who had brought him into it. Youssef recounted that in 2002, Janene had come to him in dire straits. He was campaigning and needed money. Youssef helped his friend by giving him US$12 million, money that he had made from illegal currency transactions in São Paulo, Londrina and on the Brazil–Paraguay border.

Janene was extremely grateful. He was elected as a federal congressman; the doors of the Chamber of Deputies opened up, and Alberto Youssef went in with him. But then a problem arose, when Youssef was arrested as part of the Banestado scandal and was out of action. When he came out of prison, the Big Monthly scandal had erupted. José Janene's involvement in it had made him a household name throughout Brazil, but he still owed money from that 2002 campaign, and Youssef went to find him. That was when he discovered that Janene was working with Paulo Roberto Costa and that there was a big scheme operating within Petrobras.

Youssef joined the gang. He started by making payments and deliveries of cash for Janene, charging him a commission as a means of recovering the 2002 loan. The money came from contracts with Petrobras's Supply Division, run by the Progressive Party. Janene, now an ex-congressman, controlled everything with an iron fist. He checked all the numbers personally.

João Ricardo Auler, a former chairman of the board of Camargo Corrêa and a defendant in the Operation Car Wash proceedings, told Sergio Moro that Janene was a ferocious man to deal with. One day in 2009, he had 'charged into' the construction firm's headquarters in São Paulo, demanding payment of kickbacks relating to engineering work at the Presidente Getúlio Vargas oil refinery in Paraná. Auler, who was arrested in November 2014, explained at his trial how the two of them had met:

I met Janene sometime in 2005, when we were examining an oil pipeline. He was a federal congressman then. As he had an interest in projects relating to mines and energy, he came looking for me. I had a couple of meetings with Janene. We discussed that pipeline project in 2005. In 2006, he came to me with Paulo Roberto Costa, who by then was director of supply at Petrobras and whom I already knew.

He presented Costa as being one of his guys, nominated by his party, the Progressive Party. On that occasion, he asked me for campaign donations. I said: 'I don't see a problem. We'll look into whether we can do it or not, according to the law.'

After that, Auler didn't see Janene for a while. Sometime around 2008, Janene came to see him again. Auler described the meeting: 'He was with Alberto Youssef. He presented Youssef as his right-hand man. He said they were setting up projects with the Supply Division at Petrobras. He said we would be obliged to pay a commission, in reality a bribe, for a project at the Getúlio Vargas refinery. I said, "Mr Janene, I haven't agreed anything with you. I have absolutely no knowledge of this. I'm not involved in the firm's day-to-day activities, the operational part, and I don't agree with this."'

But Janene was not to be beaten. He arranged another meeting and once again insisted on a kickback for the works at the Getúlio Vargas refinery. In his deposition, Auler recalled this meeting:

It was a tense meeting and he told me that if we didn't fall into line, we would be punished in relation to other contracts with the Supply Division. He came looking for me again, and I stopped seeing him. Then, one day in 2009, he arrived at our offices unannounced. My secretary informed me that he was there. I told her that I would not see him. I had nothing to say to him. That's when he charged into my office. Janene was a ferocious man and I wanted nothing more to do with him. I said I would not discuss Petrobras any further with him, and that he should speak to Eduardo

Leite [an executive with the firm who had been in charge of Camargo Corrêa's Oil and Gas Division since 2008]. I left the two of them discussing it in the room. It was a critical moment for me.

At that time, the scheme was running at full steam ahead. Youssef was being presented to construction bosses as Janene's right-hand man. When Janene's heart problems began, Youssef took on more responsibilities: he accompanied Costa to meetings at the construction firms and set up payments and transfers. Soon he was dealing directly with the contractors. 'These guys had problems with Petrobras every day, without exception. No doubt about it, the company needed someone as their point of contact to help things go more smoothly,' recalls Youssef.

In these meetings, he realised from various comments that it was the large contractors that decided who would win the big Petrobras tenders and then decided what would be left over for the smaller contractors. When the investigators asked him who was participating in the scheme, Youssef recited the same list as Costa had, the one that named the sixteen largest building contractors in Brazil. He also gave the names of all the directors of these companies who participated in the cartel. He described in great detail how the corruption scheme worked, how he received money through the accounts of either MO Consultoria e Laudos Estatísticos or GFD Investimentos and how money was transferred overseas. He said that he used various offshore companies and businessmen, like Leonardo Meirelles from a company called Labogen.

On 3 October, Youssef's second day of providing evidence to the federal prosecutors, he asked to make an addition to his previous evidence relating to politicians, and went straight to the top: he said that former president Lula da Silva knew about the scheme, that President Dilma Rousseff knew and that powerful former ministers like Antonio Palocci and José Dirceu also knew. One of the detectives from the Federal Police recalls what happened: 'He came in with this story all prepared. When we asked, "But how do you know that? Did you participate in anything directly?" he responded that he hadn't. Youssef's a complicated guy ... You have to be very careful ...'

Youssef's sensational declaration did not become public knowledge at that time. His plea bargain, as well as being protected by judicial secrecy, had not yet been officially approved. In a few days, however, when three key people would sit face to face in a room at the court building, this story would be revealed.

THE JUDGE, THE MONEY LAUNDERER AND THE DIRECTOR

Thursday 8 October 2014. The height of the Brazilian presidential election campaign. The first round of voting had been three days earlier and the country was split between the Workers' Party and the PSDB. President Dilma Rousseff, standing for re-election, and her opponent Senator Aécio Neves were preparing for the final battle in the race for the presidency, the second-round run-off that would take place in just over two weeks' time. Operation Car Wash, which had kicked off almost seven months earlier, was already the subject of newspaper headlines and political debate, but this was a historic day. The two informants who had revealed the scandal at Petrobras, Alberto Youssef and Paulo Roberto Costa, were going to give their first public testimony about the corruption scheme that had been bleeding Brazil's biggest company dry for a decade.

In the proceedings regarding the engineering contracts at the Abreu & Lima refinery in Pernambuco, Sergio Moro had already heard statements from the prosecution and defence lawyers. Now it was time to hear the two key witnesses. Moro began with Paulo Roberto Costa.

'Mr Costa, you are accused by federal prosecutors of committing an offence and therefore, in your capacity as a defendant, you have the right to remain silent. You are not obliged to answer any questions. Nevertheless, as has already been recorded in the court transcript, you have entered into a plea bargain agreement with federal prosecutors and, under those circumstances, in accordance with our legislation, having entered into that agreement and undertaken to disclose what you know, you are giving up your right to silence by giving your testimony,' Sergio Moro informed him. 'That agreement has been entered into by you, your defence lawyers and federal prosecutors. It is merely brought before the court. The court will always err on the side of respecting the agreement, irrespective of the choices made by the federal prosecutors. Nevertheless, in order to receive the benefits envisaged in the agreement, you must necessarily fulfil your obligations under it. Above all else, what matters to the criminal justice system is that you say only the truth.'

'Indeed, Your Honour.'

'It doesn't matter whether the truth is good for your defence. It doesn't matter whether the truth is good for the prosecution. The only thing that matters to the criminal justice system is the truth. Understood?'

'Yes.'

With these preliminaries out of the way, Sergio Moro began to ask his questions. He had a rough idea of what Costa was going to say, but he had not read the transcripts of his previous statements, which at that point were being reviewed by the Supreme Court. Moro first wanted to know about Costa's qualifications and training, and the background of his career at Petrobras. Then he asked about how he had been nominated to join the company's senior management team.

'In the written submissions by the prosecution, there is a reference to the fact that you obtained the position of director of supply by virtue of a political recommendation from former federal congressman José Janene. What can you tell me in relation to that?'

'Yes, that is correct. At Petrobras, for as long as I have known, the directorships and chairmanship have always been political appointments,' replied Costa. 'I was appointed, in reality, by the Progressive Party, to take on the post of director of supply.'

'And specifically by Congressman José Janene?'

'By the party. At the time, he was the party leader.'

'The fact that you were the political nominee of that particular grouping, and the influence of Congressman José Janene in your appointment, was that common knowledge within the company?' asked Moro.

'Yes, yes. Within the company's senior management, yes.'

'Including the other directors and the chairman of Petrobras?' continued Sergio Moro.

'Yes, that is correct.'

Moro then asked about the cartel between the contractors. Costa confirmed the existence of an agreement between the construction firms, the sharing out of building contracts and the payment of kickbacks to the directors of Petrobras. Moro wanted to know which companies participated in the cartel, to which the former director replied firmly: 'Odebrecht, Camargo Corrêa, Andrade Gutierrez, IESA, Engevix, Mendes Júnior, UTC. I've listed them all in the statement I gave; there might be others there.'

Paulo Roberto Costa made it clear that he spoke only to the bosses of the various companies: 'My contact, Your Honour, was always at the level of chairman or CEO; I never had contact with, let's say, operational staff.'

Moro asked if these directors knew about the remuneration, and Costa replied that they did. He went on to tell the judge that all the firms paid kickbacks in return for contracts. The money went to the Workers' Party, the PMDB and the Progressive Party. The former director explained how the overpricing for the building contracts was calculated and how the money from the projects was divided between the politicians, the intermediaries and himself. He said that a contractor had never refused to pay and added, by way of justification: 'They are the same contractors who take part in various other infrastructure projects throughout Brazil, whether rail, road, airports, ports, hydroelectric power stations, sewage works or social housing projects. If they caused problems on one area, they might face problems in others.'

Everything was interconnected: projects, contracts, payments to politicians and employees. Moro asked why Costa continued to receive kickbacks even after he had left Petrobras in April 2012. He replied that there had been disagreements over 'services' provided during his time as director, which had therefore been paid for after his departure.

At the beginning of the hearing, the judge had clearly explained to Paulo Roberto Costa that he could not mention the names of elected politicians involved in the scheme, because they fell within the jurisdiction of the Supreme Court. For this reason, the former director was careful to refer only to having periodic meetings with a 'political group'. At another point, he said that a diary seized at his house contained amounts and account entries relating to 'political agents of various parties who benefited in relation to the 2010 election'.

When he had finished his questioning, Sergio Moro allowed the various parties' lawyers present in the room to ask their own questions.

The lawyers had set a trap for Moro. They began by asking questions that would force Costa to say the names of the politicians involved. Moro was alert to this. The lawyer for one of the accused then asked Costa directly for the names of the politicians involved.

'No, madam counsel. You are entering into the subject that we have just discussed,' said the judge.

The defence counsel persisted and Moro replied more firmly, 'I have just stated that that is the jurisdiction of the Supreme Court.'

The learned counsel tried once more, again Moro stopped her. She returned once more to the issue and Moro was categorical, 'Madam counsel, that question is inadmissible. Must I explain, yet again?'

Then Youssef's lawyer, Antonio Figueiredo Basto, tried the same trick and asked if the scheme had financed the campaigns of the majority parties, including the 2010 ones. Experienced and well respected in Curitiba, Basto knew Sergio Moro very well, having acted in various cases before him. Moro rejected his question too, and Basto complained that his client was being prejudiced.

'Is your client a politician or Mr Alberto Youssef?' asked Sergio Moro.

That is was what Moro was up against then – and still is, to this day. He had to remain alert to every trick and strategy, seeking the maximum amount of information within the strict confines of his jurisdiction. If he allowed the witness to mention the names of politicians, it could subsequently have been used by the lawyers to contest the proceedings.

After Paulo Roberto Costa, it was Alberto Youssef's turn to give evidence. Sergio Moro was about to begin his questioning, when Youssef's lawyer interrupted him.

'What is the matter, counsel? Can we begin?' enquired Moro.

'I would like to explain that we don't have an officially approved agreement, and yet there has been a request from federal prosecutors for my client's cooperation to begin today. Therefore, Your Honour, the issue is whether today's evidence will count as part of the cooperation agreement which is currently being dealt with by the prosecutor general and the Supreme Court. If my client receives such an assurance, he will speak. If not, then he cannot give evidence,' stated Figueiredo Basto.

The prosecutors agreed and the judge confirmed that the day's evidence would count as part of Albert Youssef's cooperation. He could speak. The judge turned to Youssef: 'Are you prepared to renounce your right to silence for the purposes of your cooperation with the judicial authorities?'

'I will cooperate,' replied Youssef.

The judge asked Youssef about his participation in the scheme and what information he could provide.

'Well, first of all I want to make it clear to Your Honour and the federal prosecutors that I am neither the instigator nor the leader of this scheme. I'm just a small cog in what happened at Petrobras. There are people much higher up, even higher up than Paulo Roberto Costa; by that I mean public officials. This whole thing happened within Petrobras's construction contracts, and I was one of the intermediaries,' began Youssef.

'Can you clarify for me how it all worked, this misappropriation of funds from Petrobras, or from contracts entered into between these building contractors and Petrobras? How did it actually work?'

'Well, according to what I know, every company that had an engineering contract with Petrobras, every single one of them, had to pay 1 per cent to the Supply Division and 1 per cent to the Services Division.'

'And these amounts were intended to be distributed to public officials?'

'Yes, to public officials, and also to Paulo Roberto Costa, who was the director of supply.'

'And also to the Services Division?'

'Yes, but it wasn't me who dealt with the Services Division. There was someone else working with them, a Mr João Vaccari, if I'm not mistaken. That money went to another party.'

And so, little by little, Alberto Youssef began detailing what he knew about Brazil's biggest ever corruption scheme. He confirmed all the information given by Paulo Roberto Costa and added some more. Asked by his own lawyer, Youssef said that he attended meetings with 'political figures', contractors and Costa, and recalled that minutes had been taken.

'Sorry, but you're telling me that formal minutes were taken of this?' asked Moro in surprise.

'Written minutes were taken.'

'But did they record all these details?'

'Yes they did, Your Honour.'

Youssef said that he could provide the minutes, but that at that moment they were in the hands of a 'third party'.

Since the testimony was public, the story made the front pages of the national newspapers. Paulo Roberto Costa's and Alberto Youssef's revelations had an immediate effect on the presidential election campaign. The opposition candidate Aécio Neves made much of the widening scope of the investigations: 'We are now seeing how corruption has become institution- alised at the heart of our biggest company. These investigations must proceed further.'

Dilma Rousseff said she had always fought corruption and questioned the public release of the evidence in the middle of an election campaign: 'We were very surprised, the whole country was very surprised, by the release of statements provided to the judicial authorities by two individuals arrested by the Federal Police. I find it very strange and very disturbing that this type of material should be released during an election campaign. This kind of thing should not be used lightly during electoral periods.'

Sergio Moro responded the very same day, releasing an offi- cial press release regarding Operation Car Wash. It was signed by Nivaldo Brunoni, head of the federal judiciary in Paraná, as a show of support for Moro's work. The press release recalled that: 'The examination of the witnesses had been carried out at a public hearing, which anyone could attend. Furthermore, the evidence given had been immediately added to the electronic records of the proceedings, which are available on the internet. The terms of the plea bargain agreement remain confidential, but this should not be confused with the evidence given or to be given in criminal proceedings, which is public. The sole concern of the judicial authorities in Paraná is with the speed and effectiveness of the judicial process.'

The system of electronic document disclosure, called 'e-proc', used by the Paraná federal courts, would become well known throughout Operation Car Wash as one of the principal instruments of transparency and effectiveness in the legal proceedings. As many of the hearings were public, information was transmitted directly from the federal courtroom to the court of public opinion. It also provided an effective means of promptly summonsing witnesses and defendants.

PRE-ELECTORAL TENSION

Two days before the second round of the presidential election, the temperature rose even further, when the front cover of the weekly news magazine *Veja* published the statements that Youssef had secretly given to federal prosecutors, that Dilma Rousseff and Lula da Silva had known about everything. This stoked arguments that had been circulating on the internet for months and brought the level of tension between the candidates and their respective supporters to a new peak. Demonstrators protested in front of the headquarters of Editora Abril, the magazine's publishers. They daubed the pavement, walls and nameplate outside the publisher's building with slogans such as VEJA LIES. They ripped up copies of the magazine and scattered the pieces around the entrance to the building, mixed up with toilet paper and rubbish bags.

Aécio Neves's campaign filed a criminal complaint with federal prosecutors, requesting an investigation into Rousseff and Lula. In her final election broadcast, Rousseff lambasted the magazine's actions: 'I cannot remain silent in the face of this act of electoral terrorism orchestrated by *Veja* magazine and its shadowy partners. It is behaviour that puts the press to shame and is an affront to our democratic traditions. Without providing any concrete proof and based solely on supposed statements of people from the criminal underworld, the magazine is attempting to involve me and former president Lula directly in the events at Petrobras, which are subject to judicial investigation.' Showing opinion polls placing her in first position in the presidential race, she said that this was 'an attempt to intervene dishonestly in the election results'. The Workers' Party announced that it would sue the magazine for damages.

On election day, Alberto Youssef was urgently admitted to the Santa Cruz Hospital in Curitiba, having suffered a sharp fall in blood pressure. 'His blood pressure almost collapsed ... I remember people coming to treat him here in prison. If help hadn't come, he would have died,' recalls a prison officer. Youssef had been lying on the top bunk in the cell. 'When I tried to get down, my leg went all wobbly and I fainted and fell. I was in a cell with three drug dealers. They resuscitated me,' he recalls. The Federal Police called the emergency services. Their initial examination revealed a significant variation in his heartbeat, and he was rushed to the hospital in an ambulance, with police escort. The sight of him being rushed through the corridors of the Accident & Emergency unit on a stretcher provoked rumours that shook the nation: that Alberto Youssef had been poisoned.

The Federal Police's head of operations in Paraná, Newton Ishii, began receiving an endless stream of phone calls. 'They didn't stop calling: "Is the guy dead, Newton?" I'd reply: "No."

I asked Youssef, who was lying on a bed beside me: "So, when's your funeral?" And he said: "My what?"' recalls the policeman. The false reports raced across the internet like wildfire. Hours later, the investigators were still calling the hospital room where Youssef had been admitted. 'Is he really OK?' detective Igor Romário de Paula asked the team accompanying the prisoner. The doctors assured them that he wasn't going to die, but the police presence was reinforced, just in case. Military police were stationed outside the hospital, guarding the entrances. Plain-clothed officers patrolled the corridors of the wing where Youssef was being treated. It was election day and they could not be too careful. The minister of justice, José Eduardo Cardozo, had to appear in public in order to give assurances that Youssef's 'death' was just a rumour.

That night, under proper medical supervision, Youssef watched the vote counting on television from his hospital bed. It would be the closest ever election in Brazil. When the result was announced, confirming Dilma Rousseff's re-election, Youssef exclaimed: 'Holy shit, I'm fucked. Fucked. I told Paulo Roberto to wait. Now they'll come after us.'

But there was no way out of it. And so, over several months of giving evidence, Youssef told the investigators everything he knew about the politicans, the contractors and the scheme. It was he, for example, who introduced another of the important people in this plot: Júlio Camargo. Camargo was a consultant who had previously worked for the engineering firm Toyo Setal, and now operated as a kind of middleman with Petrobras and had a close connection to the former minister José Dirceu, even lending him his private jet so he could travel around Brazil without the inconvenience of flying with commercial airlines, given that there were people who hurled insults at Dirceu in public places, such as airports. As well as being the friend of powerful people, Júlio Camargo also knew Fernando Baiano, the PMDB's middleman in the scheme, doing a number of business deals with him, of varying legality.

In his deposition of 13 October, Youssef revealed for the first time the name of federal Congressman Eduardo Cunha, from the PMDB. He said that the congressman had received kickbacks from Fernando Baiano when signing a contract to lease drilling vessels from Samsung.

On one aspect, however, he left a lot to be desired. In the plea bargain agreement, Youssef was also required to identify where the missing money was hidden and help to recover it, but it needed to be money that had not already been detected by other regulatory authorities. No secret bank accounts belonging to Youssef or his relatives were ever uncovered. Even Janene's widow was questioned about a joint offshore account, in vain. Even so, the plea bargain agreement was officially approved by the Supreme Court in December 2014. After so many months on remand, Youssef could think of only one thing: getting out of jail. He thought it was the least he could expect – after all, he had revealed the whole scheme. His heart problems were another reason: Youssef filed a request to spend several months under house arrest, on account of his medical treatment. His lawyer contended that his client's cooperation had been fundamental to the investigation. 'He has helped Operation Car Wash more than anyone. Without him, it would never have reached its current scale. He deserves it,' repeated Antonia Figueiredo Basto to anyone who would listen. To reinforce their arguments, the defence team sent medical reports to the federal prosecutors, but the prosecutors were against it and the judge refused the request. The prosecutors knew that the plea bargain agreement had enabled Youssef to avoid serving a sentence that could have stretched to hundreds of years in prison; he would remain on remand for the good of the investigation.

THE FLOODGATES OPEN

News that Paulo Roberto Costa and Alberto Youssef had done deals with the prosecutors started a chain reaction. Two other informants quickly surfaced. Júlio Camargo and Augusto Ribeiro de Mendonça Neto, both linked to the Toyo Setal group, offered further information and evidence to support the investigations. After them, Pedro Barusco, a former executive at Petrobras who had reported to Renato Duque in the Services Division, would expose yet more aspects of the scheme and put on the table nearly US$100 million that he had hidden in Switzerland, the proceeds of embezzlement at Petrobras. It was a time of much negotiation and strategy for the investigators. They remarked that each of the informants had a specific role in the investigation. 'Some are bricks and others are mortar. Both are important,' says Eduardo Mauat, one of the first detectives to work on Operation Car Wash.

Each of these new plea bargain agreements were negotiated between the various individuals and the prosecutors working for the Operation Car Wash task force, before being submitted to Sergio Moro for approval. The prosecutors were excellent negotiators specialising in plea bargains. Some of them had helped to create this form of judicial cooperation. Plea bargains, although recognised by the law since 1990, had only been fully implemented in 2013 by a new law on organised crime. It was a new instrument for combating crime that was producing many results. In addition to information and evidence, the prosecutors demanded that those under investigation undertake to do something not often seen before: return the stolen money. They succeeded, but it was not easy.

When Beatriz Catta Preta phoned to say she had two more clients, Júlio Camargo and Augusto Mendonça, who were interested in doing a deal, four prosecutors immediately got on a plane to São Paulo. At the first meeting, however, the two men were apprehensive, not telling everything and keeping their cards close to their chest. The problem was that the prosecutors already knew some of what they had to tell. Deltan Dallagnol was tough with them: 'If you have made us come all the way here to tell us only half the story, you should go back and think harder about what you want to do. If this is what you have to show, we're not interested in a deal.' Júlio Camargo was fuming. The meeting was over.

The following week, the two of them came back with a lot more information. In their depositions, Júlio Camargo and Augusto Mendonça confirmed that in order to sign a contract with Petrobras, it was necessary to pay a kickback on every project. More than that: step-by-step, they provided evidence that led the investigation ever closer to the large contractors who had been acting as a cartel to defraud Petrobras's tendering process.

The agreement setting out the terms of the two men's plea bargains was signed on 22 October. Augusto Mendonça was the first to talk, on 29 October. In his deposition, Mendonça revealed something that was critical to understanding the logic of this aspect of political corruption. He said that he had made official donations to the Workers' Party, but with money that came from kickbacks arising from contracts with Petrobras.

In a long statement, Mendonça detailed how this 'club' of companies operated with Petrobras. The large contractors met together regularly to decide who would get each building project. Their meetings were recorded in tables and diagrams with suggestive names like 'Rio Bingo' when referring to, for example, a contract for the Rio de Janeiro Petrochemical Complex (known as Comperj). Mendonça provided a document which he described as the 'club rules', which had been drawn up and circulated by Ricardo Pessoa of UTC, at a meeting of the club in 2011. The document describes how the 'sporting championship [...] has become an annual competition with the participation of sixteen teams, structured as a league, who will play against themselves and with others, with the winner receiving a prize at the end of each round'. The main objective was the 'preparation of the teams for national and international competitions, always aiming to break new records and win greater prizes'. The rules detailed the number of teams who should participate and what should be done in the event of rounds that were cancelled or lost. At a certain point, it even expressed its concern at the need to organise 'competitions at lower levels'.

This is what the investigators had wanted to know. Costa and Youssef had spoken about the cartel, but they had never attended its meetings. The investigators needed somebody who could say what happened inside the cartel, which is exactly what Augusto Mendonça was doing. Moreover, for the federal prosecutors, it was good news that the first company to seek a plea bargain was one of the smallest in the scheme. If it had been one of the very powerful construction firms, the prosecutors might not have been able to negotiate a good agreement. They would have had to make big concessions because they did not yet have all the information. It was also a good result for Júlio Camargo and Augusto Mendonça.

In parallel with the plea bargain agreement, Toyo Setal reached a leniency agreement with the Brazilian antitrust authorities in February 2015, denouncing twenty-three companies as participants in the Petrobras cartel. This opened the door to reduced antitrust fines which, in the absence of a leniency agreement, could have reached 20 per cent of the company's gross sales.

Mendonça described how the transfers were made to Renato Duque, former director of services at Petrobras and the Workers' Party's middleman in the scheme. He said that it was Duque who made contact with the contractors, accused the former director of receiving more than R$60 million in kickbacks and alleged that some of the money for the Workers' Party was also made through official campaign donations. Under the terms of the plea bargain agreement, Augusto Mendonça still paid a fine of R$10 million, but was able to avoid prison.

While Augusto was giving his series of statements, Júlio Camargo also began to talk. The interviews took place at the offices of the prosecutor general in São Paulo. Camargo was the owner of three companies – Treviso Empreendimentos, Piemonte and Auguri – which made payments to Youssef's front companies, and also to another company, Jamp Engenheiros, which was controlled by yet another middleman, Milton Pascowitch. Pascowitch would occupy the front pages in the following months on account of his links to the former minister, José Dirceu. The connections between the two were one of the factors that led to the former minister's arrest.

Júlio Camargo was working for Toyo Setal, but the investigators had information that he was also a kind of middleman in the scheme himself, in that his firms were used to transfer funds to political parties and politicians. In the 2010 campaign, he was one of the largest individual donors, donating a total of R$1.12 million to ten candidates for the Senate, the Chamber of Deputies and the state legislatures in São Paulo and Mato Grosso do Sul.

In his plea bargain, which began on 31 October, Júlio Camargo confirmed that the construction firms who had contracts with Petrobras acted as a club: they agreed prices and shared out building projects for the state-owned company. He admitted having paid around US$30 million to the lobbyist Fernando Soares, more commonly known as 'Fernando Baiano', who was the PMDB's middleman at Petrobras's International Division. He also admitted having bank accounts in Switzerland, New York and Uruguay, through which he had moved at least US$74 million between 2005 and 2012, and he identified the contracts which had been used to move the money to the slush funds controlled by the Workers' Party, the PMDB and the Progressive Party. He denied, however, paying kickbacks to politicians, a declaration he would later revise and which would shake Congress to its foundations by implicating the speaker of the Chamber of Deputies, Eduardo Cunha.

Júlio Camargo agreed to pay a fine of R$40 million and, like Mendonça, managed to avoid prison. Once his plea bargain was concluded, he was allowed to participate in the legal proceedings as a free man, and his assets were not frozen. He retained, for example, the 'Old Friends' stud farm, set up in 1994 in Bagé, Rio Grande do Sul. The stud farm was the result of a long-standing love of animals that had been passed down the generations. His father had been a well-known biologist and Júlio had already served as director and president of the São

Paulo Jockey Club, becoming one of the leading breeders of racehorses in the country.

Sometime after Júlio Camargo and Augusto Mendonça, Operation Car Wash delivered yet another bombshell: Pedro Barusco. Following in the footsteps of Paulo Roberto Costa, Alberto Youssef and the two building contractor executives, the former manager at the Services Division at Petrobras decided to turn himself in voluntarily, rather than face possible arrest. Also represented by Beatriz Catta Preta, he entered into a plea bargain agreement on 19 November 2014 and started giving evidence the following day. The speed of arranging Pedro Barusco's cooperation was not the general rule when it comes to plea bargains. Alberto Youssef's agreement, for example, took months of negotiation between his lawyers and federal prosecutors.

Occupying the position just below that of Renato Duque in the Petrobras hierarchy, Barusco was in an ideal position to witness the looting. Indeed he had taken full advantage of it himself. In his plea bargain agreement, Barusco said that he dealt with operational matters at the Services Division, while Duque was keener on dinners and social contacts. With all his offshore money, Barusco also enjoyed the good things in life: drinking expensive wine, smoking cigars, sailing around on yachts and frequenting the famous Gávea Golf & Country Club, which had been founded by a group of Englishmen in Rio de Janeiro in 1920. At that point, however, suffering from serious bone cancer and wanting to avoid jail, he decided to talk. He provided lengthy and devastating evidence to the prosecutors. The ease with which he talked about the amounts paid in kickbacks left the detectives aghast. Felipe Hayashi described Barusco's first deposition as surreal and beyond imagination:

'At the beginning it made us feel ill; it's difficult to believe that it really happened.'

Barusco agreed to return around US$100 million to the public purse and provided information on middlemen, building contractors and senior personnel at Petrobras. He had spent almost none of the fortune he had acquired. He saw that he was about to be put on trial and that the money would not save him. Furthermore, Augusto Mendonça had cited his name to the investigators and then telephoned him to let him know. Barusco felt under pressure and saw that there was no way of escaping. He had a lot of money, and they would soon get to him. In the first part of his deposition, Barusco talked about Duque, admitted receiving around R$50 million in kickbacks over the years and estimated that the Workers' Party had received, solely through contracts managed by him, somewhere between US$150 million and US$250 million. He even spoke about João Vaccari Neto, the former treasurer of the Workers' Party, who also acted as one of the scheme's middlemen and whom he called 'Ruck', because he always went around with a rucksack on his back, just in case it was needed to carry money.

The former manager had methodically recorded in his personal files the dates and amounts of kickbacks, as well as the relationship of the beneficiaries and the posts they held at Petrobras. He liked to use nicknames. In his records, Renato Duque was identified as 'MW', a reference to the song 'My Way', immortalised by Frank Sinatra. Barusco referred to himself as 'Sabrina', on account of a former girlfriend. The people who delivered the money were referred to as 'Big Tiger', 'Watermelon' and 'Eucalyptus'. The investigators were impressed with Barusco's degree of organisation and discipline, and said that his records were a 'treasure chest' of evidence about the scheme. His revelations were considered just as devastating as those of Paulo Roberto Costa and Alberto Youssef, and perhaps even more so. He provided the prosecutors with the names of all the beneficiaries, the bank account numbers of those receiving payments and stated that he had shared kickbacks with Renato Duque from 'more than seventy contracts' with Petrobras between 2005 and 2010. Barusco had previously destroyed some documents for fear of being arrested, but was able to reconstruct all the details of the payments through offshore accounts – he had memorised everything.

Renato Duque's former right-hand man also controlled the payment of kickbacks to his boss, as Duque was not very adept at that sort of thing. At times, Barusco would receive the money on Duque's behalf and later transfer the money to him offshore. Always offshore. He and Duque preferred it like that. There was one important detail: Duque wanted cash every fortnight, so Barusco would put together packages of R$50,000 and hand them over personally. Barusco kept a large amount of cash in his house for this purpose. When Operation Car Wash began, he got in touch with Bernardo Freiburghaus, one of the scheme's middlemen in Switzerland, and sent all the cash he had at home out of the country.

As part of his plea bargain, Barusco also told the investigators what he knew about the connections between Petrobras and SBM Offshore, a Dutch firm that constructed and operated deep-sea oil exploration platforms. The SBM Offshore case was a huge scandal in the Netherlands. Under pressure from the authorities, the firm had already admitted to offences relating to corruption and reached a US$240 million settlement agreement with the Dutch prosecutors, in order to be released from accusations regarding the payment of kickbacks in Equatorial

Guinea, Angola and Brazil between 2007 and 2011. Despite accusations from a former SBM employee and the settlement agreement between the company and the Dutch prosecutors, Petrobras announced at the time that it had investigated the matter and did not find any indications that its managers were receiving kickbacks.

SBM's commercial representative in Brazil was Julio Faerman. The investigators believed that he might be the conduit for kickbacks to former employees of Petrobras. Faerman was believed to have received more than US$123 million in commission from the Dutch firm between 2005 and 2011, and to have shared some of this with Petrobras employees in exchange for leasing contracts on floating oil platforms. Faerman, who had known Barusco for years and had visited his house with his family, had little choice but to follow his friend's example by also cutting a deal with prosecutors, that was officially approved in June 2015. In his deposition, Faerman related in detail how kickbacks were paid in order to obtain contracts for SBM. As of the beginning of 2016, the firm was still negotiating a leniency agreement with the Brazilian comptroller general.

Lastly, Barusco told how the scheme had also reached Sete Brasil, a half-state, half-private sector company set up to build the major exploration and drilling rigs that would explore the riches of Brazil's newly discovered 'pre-salt' offshore oil deposits. In 2011, he left Petrobras to become director of Sete Brasil. The company started with orders of US$22 billion from Petrobras. The aim was to create a major Brazilian marine engineering company, but it was also infected with corruption, and the dream ran aground on Operation Car Wash.

As for Barusco, since his deal guaranteed that he would not serve a prison sentence, he carried on with life undisturbed.

Despite being ill and no longer able to attend the Gávea Golf & Country Club, he could at least go to the beach. In July 2015, after refusing to give evidence to a congressional investigation into the scandal on grounds of his worsening health, the former Petrobras manager was photographed sipping a beer and enjoying a sunny Sunday afternoon on a beach at Angra dos Reis. For him, talking undoubtedly provided the best outcome.

By that point, even though many businessmen and others had already lost a great deal of sleep on account of the first set of plea bargains, only the tip of the iceberg of the enormous corruption scheme at Petrobras had come to light. But the cordon was tightening, and news was beginning to circulate that Sergio Moro was coming under pressure for not sending senior businessmen and politicians to jail. At the same time, police investigators were beginning to suspect that they were being spied on.

The day before phase seven of Operation Car Wash began, a news report came out that shook the team at the Federal Police, in what the police themselves viewed as an attempt to intimidate them. The newspaper *O Estado de S. Paulo* published an article saying that the Operation Car Wash detectives had made comments on Facebook during the election campaign that were highly critical of President Dilma Rousseff and former president Lula da Silva. The police officers' error in expressing political views gave rise to one of the first attacks on Operation Car Wash. Its aim was to raise doubts about the impartiality of the team of investigators. The director general of the Federal Police, Leandro Daiello, had advance notice that the material would be published and called to warn the detectives, who decided to open an internal inquiry into the matter. It was yet another indication that there might be people within the Federal Police working against Operation Car Wash. The episode could have greatly weakened the operation, but it ended up being overtaken by something much more important: Sergio Moro had issued new arrest warrants. The following day a new phase would begin – and it would be one of the most fundamental of the whole investigation.

Chapter 3

DOOMSDAY

14 November 2014

WHAT SORT OF COUNTRY IS THIS?

Dawn was approaching as teams of police officers headed out into the streets at various locations throughout Brazil, ready to execute search and arrest warrants that would form phase seven of Operation Car Wash, code-named 'Doomsday'. At 6.20 a.m. in São Paulo, reporters from the *Folha de S.Paulo* watched as a dozen police officers and federal tax inspectors arrived at the Camargo Corrêa building on Avenida Brigadeiro Faria Lima. Five police cars entered the underground car park, while three officers stayed at the gate controlling the entrance to the construction firm's headquarters. The police left several hours later, laden with crates of documents. The long-established construction firm had been leading the consortium responsible for building the Abreu & Lima oil refinery in Pernambuco, which at that time was the most expensive engineering project under construction anywhere in the country, worth R\$24 billion. It was the start of a day that would shock the nation.

At dawn, the Federal Police also knocked at the door of one of the three luxury apartments owned by Petrobras's former director of services, Renato Duque, in a building in Barra da Tijuca, on the coastal fringes of Rio de Janeiro. Duque immediately called his lawyer, Renato de Moraes, for help. Towards the end of the police search, he called him again.

'From what I understand, they're almost finished,' said Duque.

'Is it search and seizure only?' asked the lawyer.

'Search and seizure,' confirmed Duque.

'Only?' persisted the lawyer. 'They don't have a warrant to take you in for questioning?'

'No, they don't,' said Duque, not entirely sure.

'Nor arrest?' continued the lawyer.

'Do you want to talk to him?' asked Duque, referring to the detective leading the search.

'Yes, of course I'll talk to him.'

'Do you want to speak to my lawyer?' Duque asked the detective. 'Hold on a second ...'

The line went silent for over ten seconds while the detective said something to Duque. When Duque returned to the phone, he had some bad news.

'They have a warrant for temporary detention.'

'Is the warrant from Curitiba?' the lawyer asked.

'Yes.'

'OK.'

'What do I do? Wait here?' asked Duque.

'No. What's the procedure they're following?' asked the lawyer.

Duque asked the detective, who told him that first they were going to the Federal Police headquarters on Praça Mauá in downtown Rio de Janeiro. On hearing that, the lawyer gave his first instructions to his client. 'Don't say anything. We'll sort it out from this end,' he advised, and quickly began to explain what temporary detention was.

'Should I take clothes? How does all that work?' Duque interrupted.

'Take clothes, medication ... We need to find out whether you're staying in Rio de Janeiro or ...'

'Right ...' Duque turned and spoke to the detective once more. 'He says I'm going to Paraná. What's all this, man? What sort of country is this?' he said to his lawyer.

'Just keep calm. You arguing with him won't achieve anything – they're just following orders,' replied the lawyer, reassuring his client that he would meet him at the Federal Police headquarters downtown.

Duque was arrested, among other reasons, because two executives connected to the engineering firm Toyo Setal had accused him of receiving kickbacks in Switzerland via an off-shore company called Drenos. To the Federal Police, his position looked similar to Paulo Roberto Costa's. On leaving Petrobras, the former director had set up his own firm and entered into consultancy contracts with the building contractors who were supplying services to the state-owned oil company. This was how, the argument ran, he had pocketed the rest of the kick-backs owed to him. According to Renato Duque's defence team, his arrest was 'unjustified and unnecessary'. In court sub-missions, his lawyer Alexandre Lopes categorised it as illegal confinement and said that in cases such as this, the normal rule was to remain at liberty while responding to such accusations.

A career employee at Petrobras, Duque was first recruited through the public competition system in 1978, one year after

Paulo Roberto Costa. By 2003, he had risen to the position of director of services. It was said around the company that his elevation had been politically motivated. Discreet and attentive, Duque was, according to the Operation Car Wash investigators, nominated by the all-powerful José Dirceu, who was chief of staff to President Lula da Silva at the time. He ran the Services Division for nine years, from 2003 to 2012, and knew a lot about the scheme.

The morning television channels were quick to report the news: the Federal Police were in the process of arresting yet another former Petrobras director, as well as the owners and directors of some of the largest building contractors in Brazil. Three hundred federal police officers and fifty tax inspectors had been mobilised in five states – São Paulo, Paraná, Rio de Janeiro, Pernambuco and Minas Gerais – as well as the Federal District of Brasília, to carry out eighty-five judicial warrants. There were forty-nine warrants of search and seizure and twenty-five warrants of arrest, of which nineteen were temporary and six were preventative, that is to say indefinite. Among those detained were some of the richest men in the country. Their day had begun in the worst possible manner, with the police searching their homes and taking them to jail. There were also orders to freeze up to R$20 million in the accounts of sixteen individuals and three companies. Twenty executives from eight large building contractors that employed hundreds of thousands of workers, were arrested. The accusations: corruption, money laundering, criminal association, operating a cartel and fraudulent tendering.

New information was coming in every minute: Marice Corrêa de Lima, sister-in-law of João Vaccari Neto, the Workers' Party's treasurer, was also being brought in for questioning.

And Fernando Baiano, named as the PMDB's middleman at Petrobras, was still being sought by the police.

From his office, Sergio Moro followed every step of the operation: he was kept informed by detectives and prosecutors about how the searches and arrests were proceeding; he had analysed every piece of evidence, every accusation and every deposition; he had asked some of his assistants to postpone training courses and travel. This was a decisive phase and he would need all the help he could get. New and important people had come up in the investigation. Baiano's name, for example, had become public in the deposition given by Paulo Roberto Costa in October, around one month before phase seven began.

'What other parties, other than the Progressive Party, ran a scheme involving Petrobras management?' the judge asked Costa.

The response was unambiguous: 'As for the Workers' Party, the link that the director of the Services Division had was with the treasurer of the Workers' Party, Mr João Vaccari. Directly with him. With the PMDB, which involved the International Division, the person who dealt with all of that was a guy called Fernando Soares ...'

'Also known as Fernando Baiano?' Sergio Moro asked.

'Exactly,' replied Costa.

On the day of the operation, Baiano could not be found: he'd disappeared. The detectives suspected there'd been a leak. Some of the targets they had already arrested had given them the impression that they were expecting the arrest; some of them had gone abroad, especially in August when the news first broke that Paulo Roberto Costa had made a confession, while others had emptied their bank accounts. Many of them slept in hotels, moving to a different place every night, and on the day of the arrests were found far away from their homes. The chairman of Queiroz Galvão, Ildefonso Colares Filho, for example, was arrested in Rio de Janeiro. The police suspected he'd been sleeping at the Fasano, a luxury hotel on the Ipanema beachfront where the normal room rate is more than R$2,000 per night. The chairman of OAS, José Aldemário Pinheiro Filho, usually known as Léo Pinheiro, was also not at home, having travelled by private jet to Salvador, the capital of Bahia. He was arrested at the airport. On locating him, detective Márcio Anselmo informed the head of the secretariat of the 13th Federal Bench that he would be sending them an urgent request. From his home, he got in touch directly with Sergio Moro, who immediately authorised a search of the aeroplane as well.

The previous night, one lawyer sent a message to a client warning him, 'Gerson, there are rumours that tomorrow there'll be a Federal Police operation on the Operation Car Wash case.' Gerson Almada, who was vice chairman of Engevix, was arrested the following morning. At some of the places searched, the police found nothing. At others, there were even press photographers waiting for them. But the incident that most caught their attention took place at the headquarters of OAS. When the team of sixteen investigators arrived at the main entrance at 6.30 a.m., they were met by three lawyers who introduced themselves as representing the company. The police officers asked what they were doing there at that time in the morning. They replied that they made a habit of arriving early. At that point, a photographer from the *Folha de S.Paulo* began taking photographs. Detective Felipe Hayashi ordered him to leave immediately and asked the lawyers if they knew him. They said they didn't, but the detective was suspicious about the whole situation. The fear was that the operation was itself being monitored. Sergio Moro was informed accordingly.

At the 13th Federal Bench in Curitiba, the team had arrived very early that morning, as they always did when large-scale operations were under way. The telephones were ringing constantly, with calls from lawyers wanting to know the reasons for the searches and arrests of their clients. The explanations were only released after midday.

Towards the end of the morning, Ricardo Pessoa, chairman of UTC Engenharia, handed himself over to police. Officers continued carrying out searches at his company and the other construction firms. Thought to be the coordinator of the club of building contractors, Pessoa had a special relationship with Alberto Youssef. The two were business partners, owning a hotel in Bahia, and very close. Pessoa had even visited the building in São Paulo where Alberto Youssef's office was located, and they also communicated frequently by text message. Between September and December 2013, the police tracked thirty-five messages between them. The investigators intercepted a New Year's Eve message sent on 31 December 2013 in which Youssef wrote: 'Heartfelt greetings from your cousin.' Ricardo Pessoa replied: 'My friend and cousin. I want to thank you for your partnership and loyalty. Warm regards. Ricardo.' As well as Pessoa, other employees of UTC who were arrested during phase seven had visited Youssef's offices. The director Walmir Pinheiro Santana and employee Ednaldo Alves da Silva, for example, had been photographed in the building's reception area, according to material collected by the police. Between February 2011 and December 2013, Ednaldo da Silva alone had gone to Youssef's office building dozens of times.

'WE ARE ALL EQUAL'

Although it had not been without problems, the team that had set up the latest phase of Operation Car Wash was satisfied with the results. So far, the work had advanced very quickly, and the detectives were motivated and saw the chance of producing a real result that would be symbolically important for the country. It was not the first time that building contractors had been arrested in Brazil, but never before had so many executives been taken to jail in a single police operation, particularly bearing in mind the size and importance of the companies and the personal wealth of those detained. In order to inform the press about this new phase of Operation Car Wash, a joint press conference was set up for 10.40 a.m. on the morning of the arrests, a little later than usual on account of the scale of the operation. At the arranged time, detectives, federal prosecutors and auditors from the Federal Revenue entered the auditorium at the Federal Police headquarters in Paraná.

The prosecutor chosen to sit at the table along with the detectives was Carlos Fernando dos Santos Lima, an experienced investigator and one of the coordinators of the group. The other prosecutors sat in the third row of the audience, in order to evaluate the questions and answers. The assistant director of the Federal Police in Paraná, José Washington, opened the press conference and handed over to detective Igor Romário de Paula, who started by giving a quick breakdown of the number of arrest warrants that had not yet been carried out. And he issued a warning: those who had not yet been found were still on the wanted list and were therefore prevented from leaving the country.

The police had made searches and seized evidence at eight large construction firms and arrested executives from seven of them. But why had the arrests only happened at seven companies if the investigation involved a supposed cartel formed by sixteen contractors? At that point, the firms OAS, Camargo Corrêa, UTC, Mendes Júnior, Queiroz Galvão, IESA and Engevix had contracts of almost R$60 billion with Petrobras. In the words of the detective, 'In relation to these firms, we have collected robust indications of involvement in the formation of a cartel and the misappropriation of funds for the corruption of public officials.' He emphasised that the operation had not been based only on the plea bargain information provided by Alberto Youssef and Paulo Roberto Costa – they had other evidence, too.

Gerson Schaan, head of the Operation Car Wash investigation at the Federal Revenue, explained that the construction firms had been entering into contracts with front companies which pretended to provide consulting services. They issued false invoices and received millions in payment. These 'consultancies' were one of the main mechanisms for the payment of kickbacks. The language used in the contracts found by police in their searches of the offices was always generic, so as to hide the real purpose of the transactions. The value of the services provided was determined without any apparent criteria, accounting documentation or demonstrable results; all was down to the mutual understanding of the parties. This is how millions of reais were paid in kickbacks, although it was still not possible to know the exact amount for certain.

'We estimate the fraud to be in the region of R$1 billion,' said Gerson Schaan. By then, they had already identified payments of more than R$50 million made between 2009 and 2013 by construction firms to front companies used by the scheme. 'This figure will increase,' warned Schaan. As chief coordinator of research and intelligence at the Federal Revenue, he knew what he was talking about: 'This is one of the most complex investigations I have ever participated in.'

When it was his turn to speak, the prosecutor Carlos Fernando dos Santos Lima used rather symbolic language, the strongest of the press conference and carefully chosen for the occasion, which was the eve of the anniversary of the proclamation of the republic: 'Today is a republican day. Federal prosecutors stand shoulder to shoulder with the Federal Police and the Federal Revenue in saying that there is neither fear nor favour in this republic. We are all equal. Anyone who commits any kind of illegality will face equal consequences.'

It was almost midday in Curitiba. The Federal Police were still deployed in various locations around Brazil, looking for suspects. In São Paulo, the building contractors' executives were being taken to the airport. On the way, motorcyclists shouted 'thief' in the direction of the police van carrying the prisoners, without even knowing who was inside. The police officers were accustomed to this kind of behaviour, the executives were not. Even so, they remained relatively calm throughout the journey and seemed confident they would soon be released.

The first shock came as they prepared to board the aircraft. One by one, the prisoners had to go into a room and undergo a more detailed search, to ensure that they were not carrying anything prohibited onto the plane. The procedure, which included removing all their clothing and squatting, shocked those who were accustomed simply to going through the metal detector before boarding. The fourteen prisoners waited for the police aircraft to take off from São Paulo: next stop, Rio de Janeiro. Once there, under police escort, the former director of services at Petrobras, Renato Duque, and three more prisoners, among them Ildefonso Colares Filho, chairman of Queiroz Galvão, joined the group as the plane took off for its final destination: the Federal Police headquarters in Curitiba, Paraná.

Meanwhile in Curitiba, the task force's main concern was executing the arrest warrants for those who had not yet been located. Sérgio Mendes, vice chairman of Mendes Júnior, was not in his house in Brasília. The operation's command unit had contacted the Federal Police in Belo Horizonte, because the businessman owned several ranches in the state of Minas Gerais. However, his properties were so large that it would take days for the police to search them. He could stay hidden for a long time, or even flee the country – he had the means: aeroplanes, money abroad and long-standing loyal employees. However, he preferred to face whatever his fate might be. His lawyer phoned detective Márcio Anselmo halfway through the afternoon.

'Sir, my client is not in Brasília and wants to know what the procedure is. He has decided to turn himself in,' announced the lawyer Marcelo Leonardo, who had defended Marcos Valério in the Big Monthly scandal.

'That's good,' replied the detective. 'But the Federal Police's aeroplane has already left São Paulo heading for Rio. From there, it will come here to Curitiba.'

'No, I'll bring him straight to Curitiba, if you can assure me that he won't be arrested on the way. My client will turn himself in today,' the lawyer assured.

At the airport in Belo Horizonte, Sérgio Mendes boarded a company jet and told the pilot to plot a course for Curitiba. It was better like this. It would be embarrassing for a member of the mighty Mendes Júnior dynasty to flee the country. Ensconced in the comfortable upholstery of the private jet, Sérgio passed the time discussing the case with his lawyer, Leonardo. At a certain point he closed his eyes and thought about what was awaiting him. By the time he handed himself in to the Curitiba police, darkness had already fallen in the capital of Paraná.

A HARSH REMEDY AGAINST CORRUPTION

After a long day's work, Sergio Moro was getting ready to go home. Sticking to his belief that a judge must speak only through official documents, he allowed himself to reflect on the country and on the current moment in Operation Car Wash in the final paragraph of his decision ordering the arrest of the building contractors:

> Operation Car Wash, the product of the effective investigative and prosecutorial work of both police and public prosecutors, has received a lot of attention from civil society, including intense scrutiny in the media. The magnitude of events has provoked protests, including those at the highest levels of authority in the country, in relation to the operation. These protests have drawn the attention of this court to recent statements about the operation by Her Excellency President Dilma Rousseff, and by Senator Aécio Neves. Despite being opponents in the recent presidential elections, both of them have unanimously, in my interpretation, affirmed the necessity of this trial continuing, and its importance for the nation's institutional framework. The senator, in a strongly worded intervention in the Upper Chamber, called for the 'investigations to be deepened and exemplary punishments handed out to those at the centre of the biggest corruption scandal in the history of this country'. As for Her Excellency the President, she has stated in a newspaper

interview that the Operation Car Wash investigations have created an 'opportunity' to curb impunity in the country. Evidently it falls to the judiciary to apply the laws in an impartial manner, independently of political statements of whatever nature. Nevertheless, these statements coming from two of the most senior politicians in the country, and from opposite sides of the political debate, reinforce the need for an immediate institutional response so as to bring to an end the cycle of criminal behaviour uncovered by these investigations, thereby rendering inevitable the use of robust remedies such as precautionary arrest.

Sergio Moro now also lifted reporting restrictions on the investigations, asserting the public interest in doing so: 'I understand that, considering the nature and scale of the offences being investigated, the public interest and constitutional requirements for public justice prevents the continuing imposition of secrecy surrounding the court proceedings. The lifting of reporting restrictions will further not only the wide-ranging exercise of their defence rights by those being investigated, but also the healthy public scrutiny of the conduct of public authorities and the criminal justice system itself.'

In his decision, the judge explained how the executives had made vast payments to front companies controlled by Alberto Youssef, that these companies did not provide any services and that there were strong indications that kickbacks had been paid. It was revealed that the Consórcio Nacional Camargo Corrêa alone, which was involved in the Abreu & Lima refinery in Pernambuco, paid R\$113 million into the bank accounts of Sanko Sider between 2009 and 2013. During the same period, Sanko transferred R\$29 million to accounts controlled

by Youssef, mainly MO Consultoria. According to Moro, there
was further evidence:

> More recently a manager from one of the companies in
> the cartel, together with another intermediary in these
> transactions, entered into a plea bargain agreement with
> federal prosecutors. Augusto Ribeiro de Mendonça Neto
> from Toyo Setal Empreendimentos and Júlio Camargo
> have each confirmed the existence of the cartel, the
> defrauding of Petrobras's tendering process, the laundering
> of money through the bank accounts of Alberto Youssef
> and other intermediaries, and the payment of kickbacks to
> public agents, among them Paulo Roberto Costa. In their
> testimony they describe the entire scheme of cartel for-
> mation, money laundering and payment of undue benefits
> to public agents, confirming the participation of not only
> Youssef and Paulo Roberto Costa, but also of building
> contractors and even that of Renato Duque, Petrobras's
> director of services, and Fernando Soares, commonly
> known as Fernando Baiano, another intermediary charged
> with the laundering and distribution of money to public
> agents.

The judge also drew attention to the fact that Júlio Camargo and
Augusto Mendonça were not merely describing events. They
were providing details of bank accounts, dates of transactions,
locations of meetings, detailing the methods used, contact telephone numbers and documents, some of them fictitious, used
to 'cover up the crimes perpetrated'. In other words, 'they are
demonstrating, proving and documenting all the events described in their testimony, and confessing their own involvement',

said Moro in his fifty-two-page judgment upholding the arrest of the executives from the construction firms. The two men had revealed the trail of corruption at Petrobras. 'The deposition transcripts are very detailed, revealing payments of kickbacks from various Petrobras construction projects such as Repav, Cabiúnas, Comperj, Repar [the Presidente Getúlio Vargas refinery], the Urucu–Manaus pipeline and the Paulínia refinery, paid to Renato Duque and to a Petrobras manager named Pedro Barusco, with details of the method of payment and the overseas bank accounts used,' said Moro, before continuing: 'Júlio Camargo further describes, in detail, the payment of kickbacks through Fernando Soares to Petrobras's International Division linked to Petrobras's acquisition of drilling platforms, including revealing the form of payment and the use by Fernando Soares of the accounts of two companies, Techinis Engenharia e Consultoria S/C Ltda and Hawk Eyes Administração de Bens Ltda, for the receipt of US$8 million in kickbacks.'

By that time, the defence lawyers were already attacking the plea bargains, worried about the new avenues of enquiry they were opening up. Sergio Moro defended the plea bargains and denied any form of coercion on the part of the authorities:

These witnesses are equally criminal in their conduct. The criminal is not illegally coerced to cooperate. Their cooperation is always voluntary, even if not at their own instigation. There has never been any illegal coercion against anyone involved in Operation Car Wash on the part of this court, the prosecuting authorities or the Federal Police. The precautionary arrests were requested and granted because there was sufficient evidence that offences had been committed and reasonable grounds to believe, given the indication of serious and habitual criminal activity, that there was a risk of such criminal activity being repeated. No person has been arrested in order to obtain their confession or cooperation. It is certainly true that cooperation does not, as a rule, result from sincere remorse, but rather from the criminal's expectation of receiving a reduction in sentence. If the trial, the prospect of conviction and the precautionary arrests are themselves in accordance with the law, it is impossible to conceive of any form of 'illegal coercion' on behalf of the Federal Police, prosecutors or judiciary. Those who come criticising plea bargains are, it would appear, in favour of the rule of silence, the *omertà* of criminal organisations, and it is this that is reprehensible.

The use of the word *omertà* was not a random choice by Sergio Moro. It comes from Italian and literally means 'a conspiracy', but in the south of Italy, where the Mafia is strongest, it is also understood to mean a vow of silence between mafiosi, a consensus among criminals never to cooperate with the authorities. In the document, Sergio Moro also cited Operation Clean Hands, the source of inspiration for Operation Car Wash:

Piercamillo Davigo, one of the members of the team in Milan conducting the famous *Mani Pulite* (Clean Hands) Operation, said: 'Corruption involves someone who pays and someone who receives. If they both remain silent, we will never discover anything.' It is certainly true that a plea bargain is not entered into without rules and precautions, one of the most important being that the word of the cooperating criminal must always be corroborated by independent evidence and, furthermore, if found to be untruthful, the cooperating criminal loses the benefits of the agreement. In the present case, it should be added that as a condition of the agreement, federal prosecutors required the repayment by the collaborating criminals of very substantial sums of money, running to tens of millions of reais. Many of the statements provided by Alberto Youssef, Paulo Roberto Costa and others who cooperated still need to be assessed in depth, so as to verify whether or not they have the required corroborating evidence.

Regarding the culpability of the building contractors specifically, the judge said that substantial proof existed:

Meanwhile, regarding the building contractors and their managers, there is already a significant body of evidence. First of all, it is appropriate to recall that there are statements, not only from the cooperating criminals but also from other defendants who have not entered into plea bargain agreements, confirming the use of MO Consultoria, Empreiteira Rigidez, RCI Software and GFD Investimentos by Alberto Youssef for criminal purposes. There are also witness statements of a similar nature. All of them are unanimous in alleging that the companies did not, in fact, provide any kind of expertise or services to the building contractors, and indeed did not have the means to do so. The most significant evidence of all is in the form of documents. The large payments made by the building contractors to bank accounts controlled by Alberto Youssef give rise to documentary evidence that pre-exists the plea bargain agreements, and this evidence is not prone to any form of manipulation.

The payments, according to the investigation, were made during the same period in which the building contractors were carrying out vast engineering projects for Petrobras:

> The contracts entered into between the building contractors and the companies used by Alberto Youssef, or the invoices issued, explicitly refer to the Petrobras projects. It is difficult to envisage any possible legitimate economic reason for the payment of millions of reais from the building contractors to accounts controlled by Youssef. Finally, it is worth repeating that three of the companies, MO Consultoria, Empreiteira Rigidez and RCI Software, do not in fact exist, did not provide any form of expertise or services, and were used merely for the purposes of providing fraudulent consulting contracts and invoices. The fourth, GFD Investimentos, while a genuine company, exists for the purpose of managing Alberto Youssef's assets, and has similarly provided no form of expertise or services to the building contractors.

Moro recalled that he gave the construction companies the opportunity to defend themselves, but they did not do so.

> If there were legitimate economic reasons, the contractors failed to clarify and explain them. A series of linked investigations were set up, one for each contractor. In each of them, at the request of the police, this court granted the

contractors, by means of subpoena, the opportunity to clarify events that justify the legality of the transactions and provide relevant documentation. The results have so far been disappointing,' wrote the judge. 'In addition, when investigations specifically set up by this court offered this opportunity to clarify the facts regarding the payments made to accounts controlled by Alberto Youssef, to this court's surprise, some of the contractors declined to do so, but even more seriously, some of them simply presented to these investigations the same fraudulent contracts and invoices as before, behaviour which can be characterised, in theory at least, as committing new offences of providing false documents.

The executives ended up also facing charges for this additional crime of presenting false documentation to the judicial authorities.

After concluding the official document, Sergio Moro left his office and went home, but continued to receive messages about the progress of the operation. He needed to rest because the next day would be a long one. The police were still hard at work.

PRISON CAN CHANGE A MAN

The final group of detainees from phase seven of Operation Car Wash finally arrived in Curitiba at 5.30 a.m. the following morning. They had waited hours for the Federal Police's Embraer 145 to be fixed, after suffering a technical problem at the airport in Rio de Janeiro. The businessmen were exhausted after their long day; it was almost twenty-four hours since the police had come knocking at their doors early the previous morning. They had been arrested and their houses searched, all in front of the TV camera crews, and had then faced a tense and tiring flight. Seated next to the windows, they had each travelled handcuffed and accompanied by a police officer.

Once the plane was on its way to Curitiba, Newton Ishii, the Federal Police's head of operations in Paraná, mobilised his team and headed out to the airport. But when they got there, he found the runway closed for overnight repair. He had to insist on getting the runway reopened so they could receive the prisoners in the dark and deserted airport.

It was already morning when they arrived at the police headquarters; the businessmen were taken to a waiting room on the ground floor of the building, where members of the public normally wait for passports to be issued. While police officers took down details from the prisoners' identity cards, their luggage was searched. Before being taken to the cells, each one of them was given a kit with a toothbrush, toothpaste, soap and a T-shirt, along with any medication their lawyers had brought for them. The police allowed them to keep their own clothing but they had to hand over jewellery, belts and shoelaces – it was normal practice to remove the last two items as a precaution. Everything was carefully recorded and sealed in plastic bags.

To enter the police cells in Curitiba, the prisoner first has to go through a door with a magnetic locking device into a small waiting area and a corridor leading to a gate made of thick steel bars that run from floor to ceiling. On the other side of the gate are two wings, each with three cells. With the arrival of the new prisoners the jail was now full, and eight suspected drug traffickers had to be hurriedly taken to a nearby state penitentiary during the night. Alberto Youssef was already being held in one of the wings. The new prisoners were put in the other wing, to avoid any difficulties. They were divided into groups of four prisoners per cell, which each measured twelve square metres. The remaining nine prisoners would have to sleep on foam mattresses in the corridor.

Each cell had a bunk bed and a concrete table. It was a desolating sight for those more accustomed to the best that money could buy. There weren't even enough beds for everyone, so the older prisoners would sleep in the bunk beds while the others spread out on foam mattresses on the floor. They had gone from extreme luxury to a cold cell with white-painted walls, a tiny sink and a stainless-steel WC with only a low wall for privacy. Any food or cleaning products brought by visitors were kept on a low shelf near the floor. Each of the cells had various improvisations for hanging clothes, which took a long time to dry because of the damp. At the end of the wing, another barred gate led to a space where the prisoners could exercise for short periods of time. On their arrival, there was a moment of complete silence among the prisoners.

That day, the only comfort they received was a mug of milky coffee and some bread and cheese. The first round of interviews was scheduled to begin at 10 a.m. the following day, but this ended up being postponed. The prisoners needed to sleep – and the detectives did, too.

On 15 November, the front page of the national newspaper *O Globo* featured the faces of those being investigated in Operation Car Wash with the headline ARRESTED or FUGITIVE. In the jail, after a brief rest, they faced another shock: a queue for the bathroom. There were only two showers between all the prisoners. It would be a difficult day. One of the prisoners suffered from high blood pressure; two were crying in their cell; two others had gone completely silent, not speaking to anyone. All of them were in low spirits and couldn't believe what was happening. Since it was forbidden to smoke in their cells, Ricardo Pessoa, a heavy smoker, was one of the most restless.

Soon the visits from their lawyers began. They brought expensive sheets and blankets, purchased in Curitiba's best shops, and large parcels of clothing sent by relatives. Each one of the bags piled up at reception had the name of the prisoner written on it in blue marker. The lawyers also brought juice, fresh fruit, biscuits, cereal bars and chocolate. The senior detective commented jokingly to the lawyers, 'Today I'll let it through, but not tomorrow.' The prisoners asked for books – they read a lot to pass the time and gradually built up a decent library in the jail.

At lunchtime, the police handed out hot meals of rice, beans, chicken, salad and macaroni. Some of the prisoners spoke as they ate. Hanging over them was the risk of being transferred to a prison run by the Paraná state authorities, a possibility that the newspapers were already discussing. They were very afraid of the state prison system, having heard many horror stories. They would prefer to stay in the police cells and sent increasingly desperate requests to the detectives. At that point, the authorities preferred to keep them in police custody a little longer. It was better to keep them waiting. This strategy would prove to be a good tactic.

The detectives began questioning the prisoners that afternoon, Saturday 15 November; it was a task that would take some time. According to the schedule, all the prisoners would be interviewed over the course of the next four days. That same Saturday, Dalton Avancini, chairman of Camargo Corrêa, and

João Auler, chairman of the company's board of directors, handed themselves over to a detective in a hotel next to the Federal Police's headquarters in São Paulo; they were taken by car to Curitiba. And so there were twenty-three prisoners by the end of the second day of phase seven. Two more were still on the run: Fernando Baiano and Adarico Negromonte Filho, the elder brother of Mário Negromonte who was the former minister for cities in Dilma Rousseff's coalition government and one of the leading figures in the Progressive Party. According to the investigators, Adarico was one of Youssef's 'mules' carrying money overseas, especially for politicians.

During that time, the name of João Vaccari Neto began to come up more frequently in the investigation. The treasurer of the Workers' Party had not been arrested or called in for questioning during phase seven of Operation Car Wash. However, someone very close to him was named and asked to give evidence to the Federal Police: his sister-in-law, Marice Corrêa de Lima. This was an unexpected bonus for the police. They had tapped Alberto Youssef's phone and monitored his text messages, which were his preferred method for arranging deliveries of cash throughout Brazil and abroad. In one of these text messages, sent to an executive at OAS, José Ricardo Breghirolli, he arranged the delivery of cash to Marice's home in the Cerqueira César neighbourhood of São Paulo. The investigation alleged that she had received R$110,000 from OAS in December 2013, in addition to a further R$244,000 from her brother-in-law. On being called to give evidence, Marice denied receiving the money, but confirmed that she had been living at that address for many years. It was just what the police needed at that moment. At the end of that month, João Vaccari, still treasurer of the Workers' Party, was applauded at a meeting of the party's National Executive and declared that he had done nothing wrong.

The holiday celebrating the proclamation of the republic was marked by the first protests against the Rousseff government in several Brazilian cities. According to the Military Police, 10,000 people gathered on Avenida Paulista in São Paulo, shouting 'Workers' Party Out' and 'Lula and Dilma ran Car Wash'. Many wore the football shirts of the national team, and a minority called for the return of the military regime.

President Dilma Rousseff was on an official visit to Australia for a meeting of the G20. She had been warned of what was happening over the telephone by the minister of justice, José Eduardo Cardozo, who in turn had been woken by the director general of the Federal Police, Leandro Daiello, with the news that Operation Car Wash was on the move once again. Far from Brazil, Rousseff first instructed her minister to appear in public and state the government's position in relation to the operation. 'The opposition cannot turn Operation Car Wash into the third round of the elections. The investigation will continue, whomever it may hurt,' Cardozo told the main national newspapers.

Upon leaving the meeting in Australia, Rousseff spoke about the subject for the first time: 'It's no good demonising all the building contractors. They're big companies and if A, B, C or D are doing things that are wrong, they will pay the price. Now this doesn't mean we're giving these companies a seal of approval.' Despite defending the companies, Rousseff recognised the importance of the investigation: 'The Petrobras scandal will change forever the relationship between Brazilian society, the Brazilian state and private business. It will change Brazil forever.'

Meanwhile, back in the overcrowded police cells in Curitiba, the businessmen's lawyers were trying to pass optimistic messages to their clients. They said they had already gathered sufficient material to demand the complete cessation of Operation Car Wash, on the grounds of errors committed by prosecutors and by the judge, Sergio Moro. The executives, however, were afraid that they would suffer the same fate as the businessmen involved in the Big Monthly scandal, who had received much harsher sentences than the politicians.

The lawyers filed their first applications for the prisoners to be released. Over the following three days, ten writs of habeas corpus were lodged. All of them were rejected, despite relating to some of the most powerful businessmen in the country. On the Sunday morning, it was decided that the prisoners should undergo a full body examination. The streets would be quieter on a Sunday – at least there would be less traffic. A large convoy left the Federal Police headquarters in Curitiba towards the end of the morning, followed by the entire press corps. All the commotion, unusual in that neighbourhood on a Sunday, was watched by the bemused inhabitants. One of them, Teresa Kulik Czepaniki, watched the cars passing by and said, with the wisdom of many years living close to the police station, 'This is something big. The only people who get to be held here are very educated and very rich.' She knew that it was related to Petrobras and Operation Car Wash, after seeing all the comings and goings the previous day and watching the news on TV.

Many journalists were already waiting for the police convoy when it stopped in front of the Curitiba Institute of Forensic

Medicine. Because of the layout of the building, the prisoners had to get out of the car and enter the institute from the street, in front of all the onlookers. It was therefore an excellent opportunity for the photographers and TV cameras to get pictures of the arrested businessmen. Some covered their faces, others held their heads high. None of them showed any sign of injury. As soon as he finished the examination, Ricardo Pessoa seized the opportunity and turned to detective Newton Ishii (who would become known to the public as the Federal Police's 'Japanese guy', on account of his Japanese surname and heritage) and asked for a cigarette. Ishii handed him one. To the police officer's surprise, the chairman of UTC appeared to smoke the entire cigarette in one drag. Prison abstinence is tough.

Meanwhile, the police were still looking for Fernando Baiano. They went to three addresses in Barra da Tijuca but found nothing. Suspicions grew that he had fled the country. The officers had monitored a series of international flights Baiano had taken in October, the month before the arrests. To the police, these movements were a sign of fear. 'He knew he was going to be arrested,' said a veteran police officer in Curitiba. Named as the PMDB's middleman in the scheme, the lobbyist Fernando Baiano was accused of having distributed millions of dollars in kickbacks to Petrobras's International Division. In his plea bargain agreement, Júlio Camargo described in detail the payment methods and the receipt of US$8 million in kickbacks through Baiano. For this reason, in addition to the issuing of his arrest warrant, the assets of two companies controlled by him were frozen: Techinis Engenharia e Consultoria S/C Ltda, and Hawk Eyes Administração de Bens Ltda.

The strategy of criminal lawyer Mário de Oliveira Filho, who was defending Fernando Baiano, was to gain time by filing a writ of habeas corpus to try and overturn the arrest warrant issued by the federal court in Curitiba. 'The arrest of Fernando Soares is absolutely unnecessary. On two previous occasions he has volunteered to provide clarification. He has even agreed to receive a summons by telephone,' said the lawyer, who gave assurances that his client would present himself to give evidence on 18 November.

Mário de Oliveira Filho gave a statement about Operation Car Wash that caused fury in the press: 'If by chance a businessman comes to an arrangement, legal or otherwise, with some politician to pay something, or rather if he doesn't do that – and anyone who says they know nothing about that knows nothing about the history of this country – well, he doesn't get any business. Take any local municipality anywhere in the country, and any small contractor with four employees. If he doesn't come to an arrangement, he won't put so much as a spade in the ground.' According to the lawyer, nothing gets done in Brazil without the payment kickbacks.

For some time, the police had been monitoring Fernando Soares's habits. Living in a penthouse in one of the most expensive apartment buildings in Rio on the seafront at Barra da Tijuca, his routine included a morning run along the beach, working out at the gym and a strictly controlled diet. He owned luxury cars and took business and networking meetings over meals in expensive restaurants. He knew a lot of important people, among them Otávio Azevedo, the chairman of Andrade Gutierrez, who was also investigated under Operation Car Wash. From Gutierrez he bought the motorboat *Cruela I*, in which he liked to sail up and down the coast near Rio de Janeiro.

Fernando usually spoke softly and always tried to be discreet. For some time he gave the impression that he might not reappear. There were suspicions that he was in Spain and had no intention of returning to Brazil. Rumours also circulated that he had met with a lawyer in Paris and told him that if he was arrested, he would do a deal with prosecutors. The threat sounded more like a call for help. After all, the PMDB was the party that had been propping up first Lula's and then Rousseff's coalition governments for some time. Without news on Baiano's whereabouts, the Federal Police requested Interpol to issue a Red Notice, putting him on the list of the world's most wanted criminals.

The game of hide and seek ended on 18 November, when Baiano handed himself in after long negotiations between the police and his lawyer. As soon as he arrived in custody, the police officers realised that he had come determined to resist and was prepared to stay in prison for as long as it took. But prison can change a man.

TRAIL OF GUNPOWDER

That night, 18 November, Sergio Moro was working late. The time limit for the temporary detention of the fifteen suspects was running out. Some of the most eminent lawyers in Brazil had come to Curitiba, expecting that their clients would soon be released, but a local lawyer, Marlus Arns, made a prediction: 'In the last fifteen years, I have witnessed all the Federal Police's operations here in this state, and they always follow the same script. If this operation sticks to the script, by the end of today they will all be held on remand. The judge won't release anyone.' The police and federal prosecutors had indeed requested that various executives remain in prison on a preventative basis, indefinitely. The judge examined each case on its merits and released his decision after 8 p.m. Moro decided to release nine people, on the grounds that the evidence so far indicated that their involvement was relatively minor. But he kept six prisoners on remand: Renato Duque, Dalton Avancini, João Auler, José Aldemário Pinheiro Filho, Mateus Coutinho de Sá Oliveira and Ricardo Pessoa.

The defence lawyers went off for a rather downcast dinner. Renato Duque and the five titans of Brazilian civil engineering would be joining the other six executives who were already in the same situation, including Sérgio Mendes and Gerson Almada. This group would be spending quite a lot of time together. Adarico Negromonte, the last of the fugitives, gave himself up a few days later. According to his lawyer, he had been at his country home in a remote part of São Paulo state ever since the arrest warrant was issued and had not been contacted by the Federal Police.

As time passed in jail, routine set in. The once busy executives now had two hours of sunbathing per day, in a small space only a couple of metres across and covered by bars that let through the rather insipid Curitiba sunshine. They had to clean their own cells, toilets and the corridors of the jail. They took turns to wash their socks and underpants. One of the prisoners organised exercise classes for the others. Almost all of them lost weight. Alberto Zacharias Toron, one of the defence lawyers, described how he found them when he visited: 'They couldn't wear watches, so one of the first questions they asked us was what time it was. They were very anxious about the time, which they said went very, very slowly.'

During these first few days in jail, the prisoners' behaviour varied. One of them never left his cell; another was unusually agitated. Renato Duque barely spoke, according to the prison guards. Other reports at the time said that at one point he actually sang, to cheer up his companions in misfortune. Since cigarettes were prohibited, some of them had to use nicotine patches for the first few days. After that they stop smoking. To try and provide at least some privacy, they wedged one of the mattresses upright between the bunk beds and the toilet, and agreed that whenever anyone was using it they would hang a towel on the mattress to let the others know. One day, the toilet got blocked and one of the executives was appointed to sort out the problem. 'They were using too much toilet paper. That's what blocked it. I even had to ask the lawyers to buy more,' said one of the prison guards. Eduardo Leite, vice chairman of Camargo Corrêa, became unwell several times with high blood pressure. A week after being arrested, he had to be taken to a private hospital in Curitiba for treatment. His blood pressure had reached 170/90, according to the prison guards.

Following phase seven of the operation, the Curitiba Federal Police's daily routine, already far from tranquil, became frenetic. There were journalists at the door day and night, and TV broadcasting vans were always on standby to provide the latest live update. The neighbours had already got used to the disruption.

The lawyers continued trying to get their clients out of jail, but the writs of habeas corpus continued to be rejected by the courts. During this time, the police interviewed the suspects being held under five-day temporary detention orders. Most of them remained silent during the detectives' questioning, on the advice of their lawyers. Gerson Almada, from Engevix, was one of them. In his first interview, he was recorded saying 110 times that he would 'use his constitutional right to remain silent'. Nor did Eduardo Leite, from Camargo Corrêa, answer the detectives' questions. His lawyers denied the accusations on his behalf. 'There's no corruption whatsoever concerning him. He doesn't get involved in corruption. He's a director, a technical director. He will deny any form of corruption,' said his lawyer.

Nevertheless, despite the resistance of some prisoners, the interview process did reveal some new information. Othon Zanoide de Moraes Filho, from the Queiroz Galvão group, for example, said that Youssef was the person who directed the contractors' contributions to the Progressive Party. The Mendes Júnior executive, Rogério Cunha de Oliveira, said that Paulo Roberto Costa had complete freedom on which companies to invite to tender for Petrobras projects. For the Operation Car Wash investigators, this seemed to be a recurring feature: companies paying to be invited to participate in the tendering process. It was yet another indication that strengthened suspicions of a cartel.

Erton Medeiros Fonseca of Galvão Engenharia was the first to pursue another strategy. He told the police that he had agreed to pay kickbacks to Paulo Roberto Costa and Alberto Youssef, but only under duress. He also said that the money was intended for the Progressive Party. Medeiros also confirmed the payment of kickbacks in contracts with the Services Division at the time it was led by Renato Duque. His lawyer, José Luís de Oliveira Lima, commonly known as 'Mister Juca', gave interviews following his client's questioning by police. As Medeiros was getting into the lift reserved for prisoners, his lawyer explained to waiting journalists, 'My client has made it clear that he and the company he works for were the victims of an extortion racket run by a public-sector employee. All of the contracts entered into by the company with Petrobras were legitimately obtained. If he had not given into the extortion by this public-sector employee, the contracts would not have gone ahead. The company would have had difficulties receiving what was owing to it, including the money needed for performance of the contract itself.' When asked about who had carried out the extortion, the lawyer did not dodge the question: 'Initially, he met with former congressman José Janene; he then spoke with Alberto Youssef and also with Paulo Roberto Costa.'

Sérgio Mendes, vice chairman of Mendes Júnior, also took the same line. He admitted a single payment of R$8 million to Alberto Youssef's companies, but said that he had done this under duress and to preserve current and future contracts for the company. His defence lawyers then asked the courts for him to be released on remand. In return, he undertook not to make donations to political parties or participate in tendering consortia. In the application presented by his lawyer Marcelo Leonardo, Mendes agreed to these conditions, including that he should 'refrain from having any contact with any of the business leaders under investigation' and to 'provide, via Mendes Júnior, accounting records and documents requested by the Federal Police'. His defence argued that Mendes had turned himself in to the police, had a young family and was cooperating with the investigations. He had even voluntarily provided the code to the safe in his office in Belo Horizonte. By doing this, Sérgio Mendes was trying to go home and face trial from the relative comfort of house arrest. But no one would be leaving jail yet.

Wednesdays were visiting day at the police holding cells in Curitiba. The wives, children and mothers of the executives would come to see them, trying not to attract attention. The women usually wore black tailored outfits, or jeans, high heels and blazers. They always arrived in the midst of a group of law-yers, but little details gave them away: the large dark glasses from luxury brands and the designer shoulder bags. Inside the bags were basic necessities and whatever else they could bring for the prisoners. They gave their names to the staff at reception, took a ticket and waited tensely for their turn to pass through the barrier and take the lift up to the holding cells. Next to the entrance was the room for people waiting to get their passports. The women waited in there, hoping to shake off the journalists. Sometimes they managed to pass unnoticed, sometimes not. Whenever they were spotted, most of them looked down and walked straight on, ignoring questions. Only once did the wife of an OAS employee, arrested on suspicion of having received and passed on bundles of cash in kickbacks, lose her composure. On leaving the jail, her nose still a little red, she was recognised and quickened her pace. Faced with the mêlée of reporters, photographers and TV cameras, she put her head down, showed them the finger, and burst out: 'Vultures! Failures, the lot of you. That's what you are. If you'd studied, you wouldn't be journalists.' As she got into the car, a lawyer tried to justify her actions: 'She's desperate. She's the wife of one of my humbler clients.'

José Ricardo Breghirolli, the desperate lady's husband, was not exactly 'humble'. Breghirolli, who would later be sentenced to eleven years in jail by Sergio Moro, had been involved in transferring money within the scheme and had exchanged text messages with Youssef. It was he who gave Youssef the home address of Marice Corrêa de Lima, Vaccari's sister-in-law, in São Paulo, with the message: 'Ask for Marice around 2.30 p.m.' On one of Youssef's lists entitled 'Money delivery' (in English, curi-ously) and dated the same day as that text message, he had noted two amounts, R$44,240 and R$200,000, with the reference 'SP'.

A recurring subject of discussion in the Curitiba jail during that period were the plea bargains. Rodrigo Janot, the prosecutor general, who had been following Operation Car Wash closely, explained in an interview how the negotiations between the criminals and federal prosecutors worked: 'It's like a trail of gunpowder. When one begins to talk, the others think: "Will I be the only one left?" and that's when they really open their mouths. They'll all negotiate. One asked me: "And what if I've got no one to give you?" And I replied: "Oh, you'll always have someone to give us. At least give us your own confession. The only thing I won't accept is full judicial pardon. If it's an offence that qualifies for semi-open prison, I'll push for open. You'll serve your sentence at home, no problem at all."'

Janot was sending a warning to those under investigation: it would be possible to negotiate their sentence, but only if there was cooperation. This was a new and so-far unexplored path for the defence teams – it was not traditionally a feature of Brazilian criminal law. Many of the lawyers were radically opposed to the whole notion of plea bargains and they still had many cards up their sleeve. The battle was only just beginning.

Chapter 4

THE DEFENCE COUNTER-ATTACKS

3 December 2014

SERGIO MORO AND RODRIGO JANOT UNDER PRESSURE

Renato Duque left the holding cells on the first floor of the Federal Police building in Curitiba shortly after 12.30 p.m. He was wearing a dark blue polo shirt and jeans. Accompanied by his lawyers and the custody officer, he took the prisoners' lift down to the ground floor. 'Thank you for everything,' he said graciously. As he passed through the turnstiles in the entrance lobby, he was immediately surrounded by journalists with microphones and recording devices.

His lawyers tried and failed to form a cordon around him. The reporters bombarded Duque with questions, in an attempt to get him to make a statement. The former Petrobras director carried on walking without saying a word. He tried to show calmness. They persisted. Duque quickened his pace, almost running. He needed to get out of there. 'I want to see my family, that's all,' he said, his voice almost a whisper. The lenses in his glasses darkened as they caught the sun. Flanked by his lawyers, he made it to the waiting car. The hordes of journalists followed,

their cameras filming. A motorist driving past shouted: 'Thief!
Crook! Bandit!' The photographers didn't stop until the car had
disappeared down the street. Duque headed to the airport and
took a plane to Rio de Janeiro.

From the window of the second floor of the Federal Police
building, one of the investigators watched the scene. 'At
the beginning of Operation Car Wash, we all worked on the
basis that the suspects would be held for only a week. No one
expected the arrests to last more than a week. That's what we all
said,' explained the detective.

Duque had been in jail for twenty days, but was getting out in
time to spend Christmas at home. Others would not be so lucky.
The Supreme Court judge Teori Zavascki freed him following
an application from his defence claiming that the prosecutors'
justification for him being held on remand – risk of flight – did
not apply. Zavascki agreed, but highlighted the amount of evidence against the former director at that point: 'While there are
ample elements of both the act and the intent to commit serious
offences, there has been no indication of concrete facts demonstrating his intention to evade justice.' For Zavascki, the fact that
Duque had money abroad was not a sufficient reason for keeping
him in prison. He did, however, prohibit him from leaving the
country and required him to hand in his passport.

The defence team celebrated the decision to free Duque.
'It undoubtedly represents a return to proper procedure. Due
legal process, without premature punishment and unwarranted
arrests, has always been upheld by the Supreme Court,' said
the lawyer Renato de Moraes. In its application to the Supreme
Court, Duque's defence used the argument that remand is an
exceptional measure and that the federal court in Paraná – Sergio Moro – was 'turning the normal rule on its head in order

to psychologically torture persons who are presumed innocent, with the threat or imposition of illegal detention'.

In the lawyer's view, Moro was issuing arrest warrants on the basis of 'conjecture'. It was the first moment of relief for the lawyers since the beginning of phase seven, and their biggest victory since the entire operation began. Their job had not been an easy one; they had filed numerous writs of habeas corpus trying to get their clients out of jail and trying to shift the case to another court, without success.

They tried at all costs to move the investigation from Curitiba because of Moro's implacable reputation. The lawyers tried every type of argument. They said that since Petrobras was headquartered in Rio, the case should go to Rio. Or that the building contractors were based in São Paulo and therefore the investigation should go to São Paulo. Others said it should be in Brasília, because of the alleged involvement of politicians. But the higher courts upheld Moro's decisions and the investigation stayed in Paraná. Even worse, in the midst of this judicial battle, the defence lost a major ally.

On 20 November 2014, less than a week after phase seven was launched, Márcio Thomaz Bastos, a former minister of justice in Lula's government and at that point, the principal coordinator of the various defence teams involved in Operation Car Wash, died. It was a major blow.

Even in hospital, Thomaz Bastos had been following the case until a few days before he died. He had held meetings with other lawyers from his hospital bed, giving them guidance and deciding their next moves. Former president Lula da Silva was one of those who had visited him in hospital. Experienced and respected, Bastos was accustomed to dealing with moments of crisis. He had been minister of justice at the beginning of the

Big Monthly corruption scandal and had been responsible for choosing a number of the current Supreme Court judges. His experience and affability made him the defence lawyers' most effective representative in dealing with the government and the Supreme Court. He had worked for Odebrecht and for Camargo Corrêa, but his influence and natural leadership would in any case have guaranteed him a strong presence among the group of defence lawyers. With his death, a lot would change.

'Márcio was working to put together an alternative that would protect the economy,' one of the lawyers told me. It was a good strategy at that point. The country's economic crisis was going to deepen anyway in the following months because of the increase in unemployment and fall in GDP. The crisis was caused by other mistakes in economic policy, but the argument deployed by the defence was that the economy was slowing down as a result of the uncertainty created by Operation Car Wash. The implicit threat was that if Operation Car Wash continued then jobs would be lost and infrastructure projects put on hold – after all, these companies were some of the biggest investors in Brazil. Even with Márcio Thomaz Bastos gone, the defence would continue to rely on this argument, for they had no alternative. Duque was already out of prison, but they needed to find a way out for the contractors and their executives.

On 24 November, the lawyer Alberto Toron, who followed Márcio Thomaz Bastos's line of thinking, gave an aggressive interview to the *Folha de S.Paulo* newspaper, saying that 'when it comes to the evidence, Operation Car Wash looks like Guantánamo', referring to what he viewed as its basis on 'secret' depositions. Toron also said that it was a serious irregularity for the judge, Sergio Moro, not to let the defendants give the names of politicians in their depositions, and that the whole case should be tried by the Supreme Court: 'In my view, there is an unmistakable element of coercion in obtaining the cooperation, or at least confessions, of informants.' There were further harsh words from the eminent lawyer: 'What gives me enormous cause for concern is that the appeal court has given its blessing to all the actions of the judge at first instance, without undertaking the necessary analysis,' asserted Toron, and added, 'I wouldn't go as far as to say that the Supreme Court is a hostage of Moro, but up until now it has been conniving in a complete farce.'

Toron was deeply critical of Sergio Moro's actions: 'We lawyers with experience of dealing with Judge Moro have deep reservations about the way in which he conducts investigations. You will tell me that a judge does not conduct investigations, but in this case the judge is often ahead of the public prosecutors. We do not want an accusatorial judge. We want a judge who is equidistant from the police and prosecutors.' When the reporter asked whether Moro had taken sides, Toron went even further: 'It saddens me to say this, but he has lost all impartiality. I think that beyond the rhetoric, he has already decided the case and we are just going through the motions. That's why he ordered them to be held on remand, as a way of prejudging the executives.'

Moro did not respond through the press. He preferred to do so in the proceedings themselves. The day after Toron's interview, Moro wrote in one of his official reports that the allegations of the defence lawyers were fantasy. 'Contrary to what has been alleged by some of the defence lawyers, including, strangely, statements made to the press rather than in court proceedings, this trial judge is not usurping the competence of the Supreme Court,' wrote Moro. Nevertheless, the lawyers' arguments continue to be repeated in newspaper articles and interviews.

The attacks on the judge were all part of the defence's strategy to extricate the construction companies from their predicament. In his interview to the *Folha de S.Paulo*, Toron began sowing the seeds of their economic argument: 'The prosecutors are handling this simply as a police matter and are not taking into account the economic dimension.' And he defended the idea of the businessmen paying fines rather than serving prison sentences: 'Anyone who talks of a fine of R$1 billion is talking about a very big amount that hurts anyone's pocket.'

He then threw in the name of Rodrigo Janot. 'There are more than a million jobs at risk because of Operation Car Wash. Is it a matter for the police? Of course. But there is also an economic side. If the prosecutor general were leading the investigations, perhaps we would have a more conducive atmosphere. Federal prosecutors lack a strategic vision of the case, beyond simply punishments and arrests.' Toron was preparing the ground to press on with the strategy that Márcio Thomaz Bastos had been working on before his death, a few days earlier.

Bastos had quickly realised that this case was going to require a certain creativity on the part of the defence lawyers. At a meeting in his office with some of the other lawyers, he had been the first to support the idea that the best outcome would be some kind of settlement. In fact, for him there was no other route. Several months before he died, Thomaz Bastos went to see the prosecutor-general. He was accompanied by José Gerardo Grossi, a lawyer and old friend. His objective was to sound out the possibilities of starting negotiations between the prosecution and defence. Bastos had a friendly conversation with Janot, beginning with all the usual pleasantries, despite the gravity of what was to come. The lawyers then came to the point.

'We are thinking about the possibility of studying various solutions to this case, and wondering whether some of them might in due course be approved,' said Márcio Thomaz Bastos.

'I think that's a good idea. Let's look for something that works for us both,' replied Janot.

'Could we come to some sort of understanding or agreement?' asked Bastos.

'It depends,' replied the prosecutor general.

'Well, I'm thinking of something we could do to resolve this situation, something that might work going forward ...'

'Well that's all very well, but without punishment for past events, it won't fly. It just won't fly. It's not going to be possible.'

The conversation carried on a little longer and ended with a promise that it would be continued.

'Yes of course, let's arrange another meeting and keep on talking,' said Janot, as he stood up and shook hands with the two lawyers. 'Let's turn these lemons into lemonade.'

When they had left, Janot commented, 'If that's what they think, this isn't going anywhere.'

Reports of Márcio Thomaz Bastos's conversation with the prosecutor general circulated among the defence lawyers. Various meetings were held over the following months. The plan was well under way.

A clear indication that this was the case is that the police later found detailed notes of these meetings at the headquarters of Engevix and at Ricardo Pessoa's house. The papers at Engevix revealed a certain confidence that the judiciary and federal prosecutors would be lenient. 'Janot and Teori know they can't make the decision themselves. It could bring the country to a standstill,' was written on one page. Further down, another note: 'Concede. 1bn. Confess cartel.' The investigators understood this to mean that the companies would agree to pay hefty fines of around R$1 billion and admit liability for the relatively minor offence of forming a cartel. The notes from another meeting, which took place at the end of May 2014, criticised Supreme Court Justice Zavascki's ruling on certain aspects of the case. The paperwork seized by the police indicated that there really was a coordinated plan of action between the defence teams. The documents also indicated that OAS had been charged with the task of gathering material and hearing the views of 'Márcio', presumably referring to Márcio Thomaz Bastos.

At Ricardo Pessoa's home, the police found six pages of handwritten notes of a similar nature. On one page was written: 'Press campaign to change public opinion.' On another page was a scribbled diagram linking the words: 'agreement', 'companies' and 'antitrust authorities'. Another line linked the word 'companies' to 'cooperate TF' (which could mean task force) and to 'crimes by individuals'. To one side was written 'suspend criminal proceedings'. Beneath what might have been a reference to a law firm, were listed five points:

1. Transfer investigation to Supreme Court
2. Study main agreement (best form of)
3. Undermine accusations
4. Get rid of accusations / archived accusations
5. Actions on improbity

Notes at the bottom of the page indicated the fees to be paid for the lawyer's services: 'R$2 million upfront', '5 x 400,000' and 'R$1,500,000 success'. Dated 20 October 2014, another note from what seemed to be a meeting with a lawyer listed four points:

1. Júlio Camargo: Júlio turned informant – it's serious
2. Deal by MTB[2] : meeting with prosecutor – good

Then further below, beneath the names of two lawyers:

   X said prosecutors wouldn't be against
3. Continue talking to MTB
4. Dealings with prosecutor general's office: plea bargain – forget it

Eleven days later, on 31 October, notes from another conversation were jotted down on paper: 'Plan B. None. Nothing. Plan A. Join MTB deal with PG.' Two lines below was written: 'Deal on its way', with an arrow pointing to 'admit minor offence (cartel) and heavy fine', all underlined and circled. Further down the page: 'PG. If there's resistance he'll call in the proceedings.' The final note, dated 4 November 2014, was apparently made by Ricardo Pessoa ten days before his arrest and began: 'Plan A no corruption.' After that appeared the words 'negotiation of deal with PG' and the following three points:

1. No lack of capacity
2. No cond. individuals
3. No plea bargain

---

2   Presumably Márcio Thomaz Bastos.

Beneath the list was an expected timetable: 'Within 30 days – establish general outline.'

These rough notes left little doubt as to the strategy the defence would use for its counter-attack. Their whole plan of action was built around, and could be summarised in, the conviction set out in the papers found in Ricardo Pessoa's house: 'Deal on its way.'

A week or so after the final note was written, a group of defence lawyers went to Curitiba to talk with the task-force prosecutors. It was 13 November 2014, the day before phase seven began. Not knowing that they would be arrested the following day, one of the executives asked, 'So could we set up a channel of dialogue between us?'

'Sure, no problem,' replied prosecutor Carlos Fernando dos Santos Lima.

'Can you assure us that while we're in these negotiations, we won't get arrested or anything like that?'

'We can't guarantee that,' replied one of the prosecutors.

This answer worried the lawyers. In legal matters, when someone says they can't guarantee, something's amiss, thought one of them. They left the meeting suspicious, and became even more so when they encountered Alberto Youssef's lawyer coming out of the lift. On their way to the airport, they began to hear initial reports that there might be a police operation the following day. Phase seven was on its way. Shortly after that came the death of Márcio Thomaz Bastos. But despite losing their principal spokesman, the plan stayed the same: pay billions in fines in return for reducing or even eliminating the sentences to be served by their bosses, creating the impression that the problem was merely one of forming a cartel, which should be punished with severe fines, then arguing that the case should be set aside so as to avoid damaging the wider economy. Following Thomaz Bastos's death, the lawyers asked for a meeting with Rodrigo Janot, which was granted. They explained what they were planning in terms of a deal, but made it clear that they would not agree to discuss plea bargains.

The following day, press reports suggested that Janot had told the lawyers that he would speak to the prosecutors in Curitiba; he did not want to be known as the 'jailer-general'. Even so, when Duque was released at the beginning of December, the Curitiba prosecutors feared the worst. Articles in the press hinted that a deal was being stitched together to save the construction companies and their executives from the harshest penalties. On 29 November, the Radar column in *Veja* magazine, written at the time by the journalist Lauro Jardim, published a piece saying that Rodrigo Janot was holding meetings with 'construction companies implicated in Operation Car Wash'. According to the journalist's sources, Janot had recommended they admit the offence of forming a cartel, which would be more 'defendable', and would not involve the government. He had also apparently promised that the contractors would not be declared ineligible for public contracts and could therefore continue working for the public sector.

That same day, Senator Aloysio Nunes Ferreira accused the prosecutor general of trying to shield the government. Through his secretariat, Janot stated that the information published in *Veja* was wide of the mark and that 'in a plea bargain everything is negotiable, except for judicial pardon'.

A few days later, however, Rodrigo Janot learned that a lawyer was going to present the Curitiba prosecutors with the outline of an agreement containing the defence's initial proposal. This document would detail the terms and conditions of a deal between the parties and, according to that lawyer, had Janot's blessing – which was not, in fact, the case. It was called a 'Plea Bargain and Change of Conduct Agreement' and began by saying that its objective was to 'set out measures to prevent future breaches, remedy damage caused, enable the recovery of the proceeds from breaches of criminal and administrative law, and comply with measures of a punitive nature'. The cooperating parties, whether individuals or companies, were required to confess only to the offence of forming a cartel, to set out their participation in the scheme, to provide evidence and to name public officials who had received payments, especially Petrobras employees. The companies would pay fines, undertake not to commit further offences, not to participate in public tenders for a period of six months and not to make donations to political parties for seven years. If they agreed to this, the case would go away. Once the agreement was signed, the police and federal prosecutors would be required to request both the release of the prisoners and the imposition of lighter penalties. The agreement would also apply to new incidents that might come to light during the investigation. The document accurately reflected what the construction companies wanted at that stage.

The Curitiba prosecutors were very suspicious: they thought that this was a scheme to smother the case at birth. An envoy from the defence teams said that the prosecutors would be called to a meeting with Janot, and the following day, there was indeed a summons for them to go to Brasília. The atmosphere was terrible. As night fell in Curitiba, the nine prosecutors decided to travel together. Early the following morning they met in the departure lounge at the airport. As they boarded the plane, they discussed their commitment to the task and promised each other that they wouldn't give up. If necessary, they would all resign together. 'At that point, the fear was even that the prosecutor general might give in and go along with the idea of a deal. There was a lot of pressure from the lawyers. But he didn't give in,' relates one of those present at Janot's meeting with the task force.

Rodrigo Janot was very skilful. He said he was counting on the prosecutors to press on with the investigation and assured them that there would be no deal. He confirmed that he had met with the defence lawyers, but made clear to them that those under investigation needed to own up to their crimes. He told the prosecutors that he would not falter and would push the investigation right to the end. Janot was conciliatory with the prosecutors, but asked them to trust him: 'It's a two-way street. If I trust you, you have to trust me.' They all left the meeting feeling reassured. The card they were holding up their sleeves, collective resignation, was set to one side. Janot went straight from that meeting into another, already scheduled, with the defence lawyers. In this second meeting, he complained bitterly about the behaviour of the defence lawyers. The atmosphere soured. After that, Janot stopped meeting with the defence lawyers and the possibility of a deal evaporated. At the end of the following week, the prosecutor general was forced to state his position publicly. When the magazine *IstoÉ* published his photo on the front cover and said that a deal letting the government off the hook was imminent, Janot reacted. In an interview with TV Globo's national news programme, he was unambiguous in his choice of words: 'There is no possibility of me agreeing to a deal of that type.' He was committing himself publicly.

The message reached its intended audience. The defence lawyers listened attentively, read the signs and modified their strategy. They weren't giving up, though. Their next step was to go to the government. After a tense election and months of work for those involved in Operation Car Wash, 2014 was drawing to a close. The courts were going into recess and the businessmen implicated in the Petrobras scandal would spend a Christmas they could never have imagined: in jail and far from their families.

DEFENCE LAWYERS APPROACH THE MINISTRY OF JUSTICE

Shortly after the New Year festivities, while many Brazilians were still enjoying their seaside holidays, Operation Car Wash began to heat up once again, displaying its remarkable capacity to remain in the public eye month after month.

Nestor Cerveró, former director of Petrobras's International Division and already accused by the federal prosecutors of offences of corruption, money laundering and criminal association, had gone to spend New Year in London. On his return, he was arrested at Rio de Janeiro's Galeão Airport. The investigators had discovered that on 16 December 2014, one day before becoming a defendant in one of the Operation Car Wash criminal proceedings, Cerveró had requested that a private pension fund of R$463,000 be redeemed and the money transferred to an account in his daughter's name. The Council for Financial Activities Control reported to the Operation Car Wash investigators that the manager of the bank had warned Cerveró he would lose 20 per cent of the value of the fund – almost R$100,000 – if he cashed in the pension fund before the maturity date. Even so, according to the bank manager, Cerveró wanted to go ahead. Cerveró's lawyer later denied this, contending that his client had merely made an enquiry but had decided not to withdraw the money in view of the cost that would be incurred.

Cerveró's arrest warrant was issued on 1 January 2015. The judge who issued it was not Sergio Moro – during the year-end holiday, Judge Marcos Josegrei da Silva was dealing with the most urgent matters. And, according to federal prosecutors, this was urgent. They alleged that the former Petrobras director needed to be arrested because he was continuing in his 'criminal mindset' and seemed to know no ethical or legal bounds in trying to ensure that he would not suffer the consequences of his actions. The prosecutors named Cerveró as a member of the 'most important criminal organisation embedded within the Brazilian state in history'. According to the federal prosecutors, the corruption within Petrobras had still not been stopped. There were reports of kickbacks being paid even in 2014, after the beginning of Operation Car Wash.

Arrest warrant in hand, the police waited in the early morning for Cerveró's plane to land at Galeão Airport. So that he would have no chance of escaping, the police officers waited for him in the walkway linking the aircraft door to the terminal building. When they approached him, his reaction was, 'But I'm not fleeing. I'm coming home. I'm entering the country, not leaving.' Despite his protests, Cerveró was arrested. 'You can argue over the arrest warrant in court later. For now, we're going to carry out the order,' said the police officer leading the operation.

This was phase eight of Operation Car Wash. Cerveró was taken to one of the Federal Police's rooms at the airport, where he waited for his lawyer to arrive as his baggage was examined. Then he was taken to a cell at the police station within the airport, where he had to wait several hours for the next scheduled flight to Curitiba. On the floor of the tiny cell there was only a thin foam mattress with a pillow but no sheet. He complained. 'How am I going to sleep?' he complained It was too dirty. 'Well, then stand,' replied the police officer.

Half an hour later, he was fast asleep on the mattress. On arriving in Curitiba, he kept his head down on his way into the police station. For the first few days he remained sullen. On the outside, his defence lawyers continued trying to find a solution. It was time to return to Brasília.

Influential lawyers in the capital publicly supported the necessity of negotiating a deal in the interests of the economy. This was the view of criminal lawyer Antônio Carlos de Almeida Castro, nicknamed Kakay, who was defending former governor Roseana Sarney (PMDB), former minister and Senator Edison Lobão (PMDB), and Senators Ciro Nogueira (Progressive Party) and Romero Jucá (PMDB) in the Operation Car Wash proceedings. In an interview with *Época* magazine in January 2015, he relaunched the idea of a deal: 'Federal prosecutors are doing their job and the Federal Police are carrying out their constitutional role, but it would be more interesting for lawyers, prosecutors and judiciary to sit down together and think not about how to bury the investigation, but how to prevent these companies from collapsing. It's a huge wasted opportunity. Many of these companies are multinationals that also have activities outside Brazil and are a source of national pride.' Kakay also used the opportunity to make a fierce attack on Sergio Moro, although carefully preceded with praise. 'In the courts of first instance, when you take a judge who is serious and competent, but also stubborn and who thinks he's a national saviour, you can end up with someone who does a variety of things that are completely unnecessary and harsh, but ends up as man of the year in every magazine. If an appeal court overturns the decision, it's seen as being lenient.'

The government was sensitive to the defence's arguments and tried to help the construction firms under investigation. Luís Inácio Adams, attorney general at the time, was given the task of persuading public opinion that the comptroller general's office could validly enter into leniency agreements with the companies, and that this would not in any way prejudice the investigations being undertaken by the federal prosecutors.

In fact, when the comptroller general enters into a leniency agreement, this prevents another investigation, for example by federal prosecutors, from getting the courts to impose a more severe punishment on the firm in question. The Anti-corruption Law also provides that when there is a leniency agreement with the comptroller general, the courts cannot prevent guilty firms from receiving financial incentives or loans from the public sector, usually a crucial factor for such companies. It was one of the government's main levers to try and reduce the impact of the Curitiba investigations.

Luís Adams therefore gave interviews to one newspaper after another, repeating again and again that the construction firms were being pressurised with threats of heavy fines and that this could render their whole business unviable: 'Apparently, some people want to threaten closing the whole firm down, in order to get them to cooperate. That doesn't seem right to me. Now, with all due respect to the investigation, while it has enormous merit, this doesn't justify everything; it doesn't justify forcing the closure of companies which are ready to make amends, to cooperate fully with the investigation and to adopt new practices to prevent corruption.'

The attorney general was directly attacking the federal prosecutors, who had criticised the government's moves to facilitate leniency agreements through the comptroller general: 'It's absurd that one branch of the state wishes to interfere in the conduct of an investigation by another branch, that is to say the comptroller general, by using such a highly political and ideological argument as claiming that the government wants to "smother" an investigation. This is simply not happening!' Adams defended his position firmly: 'The government wants to rescue economic activity, which means jobs, investors, banks who have lent money, the whole supply chain. If we can combine boosting the investigations with maintaining economic activity, why would we choose instead to close down the companies?' The federal prosecutors reacted quickly. Their representative at the Federal Audit Office was alerted and filed a motion with the court, asking it to prevent the comptroller general from signing any kind of agreement with the companies under investigation without the knowledge and agreement of the federal prosecutors. At the same time, individual prosecutors held separate conversations with officials at the Federal Audit Office. The president of the Federal Audit Office, Aroldo Cedraz, decided to call a meeting between his officials and three prosecutors from the Operation Car Wash task force in Curitiba. The prosecutor general, Rodrigo Janot, was also invited, but preferred not to attend.

The audit officials asked whether the companies had the means to pay the heavy fines they might receive and recalled the case of SBM Offshore. The Dutch company had admitted in its own country that it had paid kickbacks to the Brazilian authorities, had reached an agreement with the Dutch public prosecutors and had paid US$240 million in fines. Here in Brazil, when SBM began talking with the comptroller general about a leniency agreement, it was proposed that they pay a fine of R$1 billion (equivalent to approximately US$270 million). The prosecutors were sincere in their reply to the officials' question: they did not know whether the firms had the means to pay the fines, but they, the prosecutors, still had to impose them. The firms had committed deliberate wrongdoing and would have to pay the price. The prosecutors also feared that the companies might abandon negotiations with them and go off to do a deal with the comptroller general, who could stop them being declared ineligible for public contracts.

After the meeting, the audit officials agreed with the prosecutors' main argument, which was that the comptroller general entering into leniency agreements would do nothing to further the investigations; on the contrary, it could inhibit them. The government did not have access to various pieces of evidence that had not yet been made publicly available by the Curitiba prosecutors, and which could extend the scope of Operation Car Wash beyond Petrobras. There seemed to be a movement under way to contain the investigation within the confines of the state-owned oil giant. One of those present at the meeting commented in private that, whether the government liked it or not, these young prosecutors were the masters of the investigation.

Lawyers for the firms under investigation arranged a meeting in Brasília with the minister of justice, José Eduardo Cardozo. Rumours circulated that they were seeking some kind of help from the government to release the executives, who by now had been held on remand for several months. Accompanied by former congressman Sigmaringa Seixas, Sérgio Renault, UTC's lawyer, met Cardozo in his office. At the time it was reported that Cardozo had advised the lawyer not to sign any plea bargain agreement because Operation Car Wash would change course after carnival, in February. The minister denied this, but the reaction was immediate. Joaquim Barbosa, a former president of the Supreme Court, sternly criticised the minister of justice on Twitter and said that honest Brazilians should call for his resignation. The opposition in Congress demanded an investigation into the episode by the ethics committee. For Sergio Moro, the meeting was reprehensible and intolerable. This is what he recorded in his decision ordering the renewal of Ricardo Pessoa's detention on remand:

> There is the proper sphere of the courts and the proper sphere of politics. They should be like oil and water, never mixing. The holding on remand of the construction firms' leaders should be argued in legal proceedings in court. It is intolerable that representatives of the arrested executives and their firms should attempt to call into question the judicial process and judicial decisions in holding discussions with political authorities, in complete disregard for due legal process and thereby risking the integrity of the judicial system and the application of criminal law. It is even stranger that politicians and lawyers who are not involved in the criminal proceedings are participating in these meetings. The minister of justice is not responsible for the actions undertaken by the investigations. It amounts to an unwelcome, albeit unsuccessful, attempt on the part of the accused individuals and companies to procure political interference on their behalf in the judicial process.

Moro considered the episode yet further proof that the construction firms' executives, imprisoned since November, were trying to interfere in the investigations: 'Certainly in the present case, the courts will not be easily influenced by political or economic interference. Any attempt at improper interference from economic forces, whether directly by co-opting witnesses, or indirectly by seeking undue political influence in the judicial process, must be severely reprimanded. This in itself justifies, by virtue of the risk to the integrity of the proceedings and the judicial system, the imposition of detention on remand.'

Independently of the pressure from the lawyers, layoffs at the construction firms investigated under Operation Car Wash really did accelerate after phase seven of the operation, and all the companies involved suffered. Those who were already in financial difficulties found their situation worsening. The more prudent, being less indebted, dealt better with these turbulent times. Of course, the first to pay for their misdeeds were the executives who had been arrested in November, but the consequences of their criminal behaviour would soon be felt by many innocent people. As soon as the firms began to run into difficulties, and out of credit, they began to lay off workers. In a period of two months, at the end of 2014 and the beginning of 2015, the companies under investigation made 12,000 people redundant throughout the country, according to a trade union survey.

The wave of layoffs, which would worsen during the first half of 2015, had been predicted by economists as resulting from a series of mistakes in economic policy. It spread, and halfway through 2015 the government announced that a million jobs had disappeared from the formal economy. For many economists the crisis, which would have happened irrespective of Operation Car Wash, had been masked by artificial measures that had exhausted the public coffers, such as tax exemptions granted to some groups and subsidised loans that increased public debt. The bill for years of mistakes had now arrived. But for those defending the firms, whether in the political or legal sphere, it was very useful for the problems to be seen as a consequence of the investigation.

As a result of Operation Car Wash, the construction firms' contracts with Petrobras had been suspended and all engineering work halted at the two principal oil refineries under construction in Brazil, the Rio de Janeiro Petrochemical Complex (Comperj), and the Abreu & Lima refinery in Pernambuco. Unable to borrow money from the financial markets because of the investigations, and with delays in payments owing from Petrobras – which was no longer recognising additional payments due under the contracts and had begun questioning increases in costs – the construction firms were beginning to show real signs of difficulty. First they delayed paying salaries, and then they laid off workers. At these two refineries alone, 63,200 workers were sacked between December 2014 and November 2015. The biggest problems were in Pernambuco: of the 38,000 workers employed at the Abreu & Lima site, 37,200 were laid off after 2014, according to the construction workers' trade union.

Alumini, one of the smallest members of the once powerful club of building contractors, was one of the first to fall to its knees: it sacked more than 5,000 employees and had difficulty paying them their entitled severance pay. The company's bank account was frozen by a judge in Pernambuco, on allegations that it had not fulfilled its obligations to its workers. Within a very short time, the firm filed for insolvency administration. Practically all the companies involved in the Car Wash scandal, whose contracts with Petrobras had been suspended, needed to lay off workers. At the Rio de Janeiro Petrochemical Complex in

Itaboraí, where 30,000 workers had been employed, only 4,000 remained at the end of 2015, according to the construction workers' trade union. The industry's trade body reported that the sector was suffering from the freezing of major infrastructure projects, especially those for Petrobras, and that as a result it was having difficulties maintaining levels of employment: 85,000 jobs were lost in the sector in 2014 and 88,000 were lost in 2015. One of the reasons, according to the industry's trade body, was Operation Car Wash's impact on the building contractors, but it is not possible to be specific about how many workers were laid off solely because of the investigation. All of this happened at a time when no other jobs were being created in the wider economy. Many of these workers, out of work through no fault of their own, ended up at home with no other alternative but to watch the crisis unfold on television, while struggling for their own survival.

THE RISE AND FALL OF PETROBRAS

For Petrobras, things had gone from bad to worse since the beginning of Operation Car Wash. In December 2014, an article by Juliano Basile in the newspaper *Valor Econômico* introduced a new key character in the public's understanding of the corruption scheme. Venina Velosa da Fonseca had trained as a geologist and was a former managing executive in the Supply Division at Petrobras, working for Paulo Roberto Costa. She had occupied a post directly below Costa and had seen everything at close quarters. For example, she gave testimony on decisions about cost increases at the Abreu & Lima refinery in Pernambuco. One day, Costa had asked her to draw up a plan for the refinery to become operational at an earlier date than planned. It was not a simple task: the director was asking to accelerate an enormous industrial process. It would have an extremely high cost – R$4 billion, according to the report by Petrobras's internal audit committee – but the order came from above that the project was a government priority and was being followed closely by the president's staff at the Palácio do Planalto. The plan was duly approved by Petrobras's management and board of directors.

Venina Velosa da Fonseca says that as time went on, she realised that something was amiss within the Supply Division and, probably, the company as a whole. She even sent an email to Costa in which she set out her thoughts. In her email, marked confidential, she praised her boss and thanked him for the opportunity of working with him. 'I came from a background of extreme poverty and a difficult childhood to become an executive manager within the Supply Division at Petrobras,' wrote Fonseca, before expressing her concerns: 'In more recent times, I have had some difficult moments ... I am faced daily with situations that make me feel very conflicted. I won't go into details, because I know you know what I'm talking about.' Her email then continued: 'When I faced the possibility of having to do things that appeared contrary to the company's rules and procedures, against the ethics code and against the management model we have put in place, I was unable to summon up the creativity required. It was the first time I couldn't convince myself to do something. I just could not accept the way of doing things. In the middle of a heated and tense conversation, I heard words like "coward", "jump overboard" and "trying to pressurise me". I have to confess that I was expecting more support and a little more discussion.'

At a certain point in her email, Fonseca also acknowledged her awareness of the 'political context' in which they found themselves. 'It was never my intention to force the adoption of alternatives in an irresponsible manner, without understanding the context or the full extent of consequences that might place you in a difficult position. During the period I worked in the Supply Division, I "grew up", and I understand perfectly the political context of our work. At the time when I set out my point of view, I felt that we were doing things in a way that could place us in a risky situation and cause unnecessary exposure.'

The former manager also sent warning letters to the then-director of gas and energy at the company, Graça Foster, who would later become chairwoman of Petrobras. They were friends and, to a certain extent, confidantes. Fonseca decided to ask for help. In her letters, she talked about having doubts about what to do and regretted that 'the enormous pride I used to have in the company has given way to shame'. Graça warned Paulo Roberto Costa of his subordinate's actions. A few months later, Fonseca was transferred to Singapore, far from what was happening within the company. At her leaving party, the then-director Renato Duque proposed a toast, and joked that it was a pity they couldn't exile her for life. Indeed they could not. Out in Singapore, Fonseca discovered another corruption scheme. Then she returned to Brazil, just as the crisis was beginning to reach Graça Foster, who was by now chairwoman of Petrobras.

The release of Venina Fonseca's letters was just one more problem for Graça, at the time when there was a growing clamour for her to step down from the chairmanship. At a public hearing in Congress, Graça Foster had said that she was not aware of whistleblowing within the company, but faced with Fonseca's letters, it was difficult to sustain this position. To complete the situation, Fernando de Castro Sá, who was head of the legal department at Petrobras and a friend of Fonseca's, also went public with the wrongdoing he had seen at the company. He told the Operation Car Wash prosecutors that the standard form of their service contracts, previously approved directly by management, had now begun to be sent for prior approval by ABEMI, the association of building contractors. Fernando de Castro Sá had noticed one of the few visible signs that a cartel was running things within the state-owned company; the crisis at Petrobras was only getting worse.

During the entire period of the Operation Car Wash investigations into wrongdoing at Petrobras, the company saw the value of its shares plummet. The relationship between cause and effect was complex. The share price fell because of mistakes in projects where the return on investment became evermore difficult due to the government's policy of keeping fuel prices artificially low, as well as failures of management that were now becoming evident to the stock market. But for many, it was more convenient to stick to the idea that it was necessary to 'defend' Petrobras against its 'enemies'. During the election campaign President Dilma Rousseff herself and former president Lula da Silva both said this. They didn't say that Operation Car Wash was the enemy, but part of the supposed 'defence' of the company consisted of proposing that the company hang on to investments that by then were already the subject of reasonable doubts.

The stock market's suspicions in relation to the state-owned company had preceded Operation Car Wash. Petrobras's finest hour had been 21 May 2008, when the company reached a valuation of R$510 billion. Its preference shares sold for R$42.76 and its ordinary shares for R$53.88. It was a time of euphoria over the discovery of Brazil's deep-sea 'pre-salt' oil reserves. Brazil's sovereign debt had finally attained the long dreamt-of investment grade, after much effort. Instead of beginning to develop the pre-salt oilfields, the government decided to change Petrobras's modus operandi from a concession model to a co-exploration regime. For years this froze out foreign investors and caused the country to lose the opportunity to become a new centre of oil exploration. The company took on a lot of debt to pay for all the investments in areas where the government wanted it to take a leading role, many of which served political goals. Infrastructure costs soared through overpricing, as did the cost of the contracts entered into with the cartel of building contractors. A barrel of crude oil was now selling for US$132 on the international markets, but the price of fuel on the domestic market was not allowed to rise correspondingly, so as not to affect the official inflation rate – a key measure of the government's economic credibility. The value of Petrobras began to reflect this, and its share price fell sharply. Meanwhile the government wanted to accelerate Petrobras's investment programme, so as to generate the economic growth needed for the election campaign of President Lula's chosen successor, Dilma Rousseff.

When President Rousseff took office, the company's value had already fallen to R$383 billion. On 3 January 2011, the preference shares were trading at R$24.39 and the ordinary shares at R$28.63. At the beginning of 2010, the company had raised a huge amount of capital; the government's share of this had been notionally paid for in barrels of future production. This was all done in order to reduce the level of debt and allow the state-owned company to carry on with the various projects it had already started. On 17 March 2014, when Operation Car Wash officially began, the market value of Petrobras had already slumped to R$160 billion, with the preference shares quoted at R$11.84 and the ordinary shares at R$11.62. The company had lost 68 per cent of its market value. At the same time, the Federal Audit Office was estimating the loss incurred in purchasing the Pasadena oil refinery in Texas at US$792 million. President Rousseff, who had been chairwoman of Petrobras's board of directors at the time the Pasadena deal was approved, defended herself by saying that she had not received all the information about Pasadena. During the 2014 election campaign, the company's share price fluctuated in line with the opinion polls. Every time an alternative candidate's showing strengthened, suggesting an alternative to Dilma Rousseff's re-election, the share price rose; Petrobras's value rose to R$300 billion on 2 September when the Brazilian Socialist Party's candidate, Marina Silva, took the lead in the opinion polls.

Operation Car Wash's work continued with new revelations and arrests, but Petrobras's stock market value rose or fell depending on market perceptions of the harm caused by its management strategy and government interference. The government was maintaining its policy of freezing fuel prices, so as to prevent the domestic price of petrol and diesel from rising, despite pressure from Petrobras senior management and the international price of oil remaining above US$100 per barrel.

In November, after the president's re-election, the company was forced to reveal that it was having difficulties getting its accounts audited, confirming rumours that were already worrying the market. The company announced that it would not release its third-quarter balance sheet because its auditors PricewaterhouseCoopers (PwC) had said that they would not sign it off. PwC wanted to analyse the results of the company's three internal investigations prompted by revelations from Operation Car Wash, which had been investigating irregularities in the purchase of the Pasadena refinery, the construction works at the Abreu & Lima refinery and the Comperj project. Like any company with publicly quoted shares, international bank loans, and bonds issued to both domestic and international investors, Petrobras needed to have its balance sheet audited, but the company was unable to do this: it needed to account for losses incurred as a result of serious management errors, including its numerous political appointments. On 31 October, PwC refused to validate Petrobras's internal accounts for as long as Sérgio Machado continued running its Transpetro subsidiary. Named by Paulo Roberto Costa as one of those involved in the corruption scheme, Machado had to be placed on leave of absence. Costa said he had personally received R$500,000 from Machado and, under American law, persons suspected of corruption cannot sign off company accounts. At the request of PwC, Petrobras appointed two independent auditing firms – the Brazilian firm Trench Rossi Watanabe Advogados and the American firm Gibson, Dunn & Crutcher LLP – to analyse its financial situation, including the cost of corruption and overpricing.

At the end of 2014, the government prevented twenty-three companies from entering into contracts with Petrobras, due to the allegations and suspicions of corruption. The company was forced to admit, in an announcement published in widely circulated newspapers, that Operation Car Wash could impact the company's financial results if Paulo Roberto Costa's claims proved to be true. Foreign investors filed a class action in New York, alleging that Petrobras had violated regulations of the Securities and Exchange Commission (SEC) in relation to the US listing of Petrobras's shares. In those proceedings, the investors claimed that Petrobras had provided false information and misleading statements, and had not disclosed a culture of corruption within the company.

Despite all this, President Dilma Rousseff emphatically defended Petrobras and its management. She said that she had no intention of replacing management and that the government was working to ensure the company maintained its credit rating. The president also said that she considered the amount embezzled by some public officials to be absurd, and that the investigation would not destroy Petrobras. 'No way,' she said. But the company was already seriously weakened, and by that point words did not mean much. Events meant that a change of management at Petrobras was inevitable shortly after the start of the new year.

On 20 January 2015, the company revealed a number that shocked the markets and caused great consternation within both the company and government. Petrobras released a set of financial statements, not yet approved by their auditors, in which it tried to extricate itself from its limbo status of being a publicly quoted company without a published balance sheet. This partial set of figures said that the preliminary calculation of Petrobras's losses in 2014 was the astronomical amount of R$88.6 billion, as a result of embezzlement, overpricing, poor investment and government interference. There was a struggle within the board of directors, with Guido Mantega and Miriam Belchior resisting disclosing this figure. The two of them were no longer government ministers, but they remained on the board of Petrobras. The chairwoman, Graça Foster, said that the calculation had been provided to the company by the consultants appointed by company and, as material information, needed to be disclosed. The number appeared almost hidden in an explanatory note, but the news still made the front pages.

Graça Foster's decision put her on a collision course with the government, and she travelled to Brasília on a journey that would end with her removal from the chairmanship of the state-owned company. She was sacked not for her mistakes or omissions, but for wanting to reveal what could no longer be hidden from public view. The market value of Petrobras fell once again, this time to R$120 billion.

When Foster reached the capital, everything was already arranged. She didn't go straight to the Palácio do Planalto, the president's office; instead, she went first to see Joaquim Levy, the minister of finance, to discuss the names of suitable replacements. Then she went to Petrobras's offices in Brasília, to consult with her board of directors in Rio de Janeiro by video-conference. President Rousseff agreed with the argument that it would be better to have someone with good market experience managing the company, which was a positive sign, but no one seemed to want to accept the thorny challenge. With this in mind, the government wanted to make the management changes at Petrobras smoothly, over the course of several days. However, an unexpected decision changed all of that. Upon officially giving her own resignation to the Petrobras board of directors, Graça Foster was in turn presented with the collective resignation of the entire board. President Rousseff had to react quickly. Some names had already been sounded out, while others had support from various officials at the Palácio do Planalto. The presidential chief of staff, Aloizio Mercadante, was in favour of appointing Murilo Ferreira, then chairman of Vale, the mining conglomerate. But Ferreira indicated that he would not accept the appointment, since he was already in the midst of a major restructuring at the mining giant due to a fall in the price of iron ore. Other potential candidates faced similar obstacles, or simply did not want the job. Within forty-eight hours, Aldemir Bendine, then chairman of Banco do Brasil, was announced as the new chairman of Petrobras.

Chosen for his loyalty to the government and willingness to take on the job, Bendine had the difficult task of sorting out the accounting mess that had hit the company following the numerous allegations of corruption and embezzlement. He also needed to deal with its dangerous level of debt. On 22 April, the official balance sheet was finally released. Unable to arrive at an exact amount of the company's losses from corruption, a percentage was calculated of each project approved by the divisions in which embezzlement had occurred. This percentage produced a figure of R$6.19 billion in losses simply from corruption. The balance sheet also recorded a fall of R$44 billion in the value of assets, attributed to management errors. In total, Petrobras had lost R$50 billion through errors and corruption. The overall annual loss, taking into account its operating profits, was R$21.6 billion, the largest ever recorded by Petrobras.

The company's troubles did not end there. There was still much to be calculated, between the payments of kickbacks, the actions of the cartel, political decisions, manipulation of prices and the use of the company for party political purposes. In total, Petrobras lost 90 per cent of its market value between its stock market flotation in 2008 and 26 January 2016, when the share price closed at R$4.20. It would continue to fluctuate, but that day was a milestone. Several factors contributed to the fall in value of the shares, such as the loss of the company's investment grade status in September 2015, shortly after Brazil itself was downgraded.

THE DAY THE TREASURER TREMBLED

On 5 February 2015, the day following Graça Foster's fall from office, Operation Car Wash took to the streets again. Phase nine of the operation was code-named 'My Way', in reference to Pedro Barusco's nickname for his boss, Renato Duque and was focused on the middlemen. Barusco, the former manager in Petrobras's Services Division, was the linchpin of this part of the investigation, which was focused on discovering how the kickbacks were paid, and would reveal names that would become important for the future of Operation Car Wash, such as Mario Goes, Milton Pascowitch and Zwi Skornicki.

On that hot summer's morning in Rio de Janeiro, luxury homes in wealthy neighbourhoods of the city were ransacked by the police, with many works of art seized. A few days later, the Oscar Niemeyer Museum in Curitiba would receive yet another delivery of paintings, the fourth since Operation Car Wash began. They were already putting on a public exhibition of seized paintings, but there would now be another; the quality of the art was exceptional.

That same day, the treasurer of the Workers' Party, João Vaccari Neto, was taken to the Federal Police building in São Paulo to clarify some issues. The investigators said they had been to Vaccari's house and he had refused to let them in. He delayed so long that the police officers had climbed over the gate to get in. Vaccari must have been frightened. He appeared tense and, according to one of the police officers, was trembling and barely able to control himself. He only calmed down when the investigators explained that they had not come to arrest him – they merely needed to take him in for questioning. When they told him that, he stopped trembling. At this point, however, the police, made a mistake. They requested an arrest warrant for Vaccari's sister-in-law, on the basis of CCTV images showing a woman withdrawing money from Vaccari's bank account. The images were, in fact, not of her but of her sister, Vaccari's wife.

At this stage, three months after their arrest on 14 November 2014, twelve of the twenty-three businessmen and executives arrested were still in prison, their lawyers still unable to get them released. The situation was becoming tenser, and the pressure was enormous. Stories were circulating about the supposedly degrading treatment of the executives in police custody. At the end of the week following carnival, with samba dancers still entertaining the lingering crowds in Rio de Janeiro, the *Folha de S.Paulo* published a report saying that the executives were spending the whole day locked in their cells, had to use a shared bathroom with no privacy and at times had to eat with their fingers.

Rumours also circulated that Ricardo Pessoa was talking to the federal prosecutors. Indeed he was, but it was the executives from Camargo Corrêa, the construction firm which Márcio Thomaz Bastos had been defending, who were closer to doing a deal. Advised and accompanied by their very competent lawyers, they had accepted the prosecutors' most important demand: to provide information on offences the police didn't already know about. Negotiations were advancing. If one construction firm reached a deal, the others feared the worst: being left isolated with nothing to offer the prosecutors. The prosecutors dangled their promise of reduced sentences, but with one important detail: whoever talked first would reap the greatest reward. Those who followed would have to provide new information, or they would get nothing. It was good old-fashioned bartering that was motivating the executives in that chilly police jail in Curitiba.

Some of the prisoners, however, wanted nothing to do with it and didn't participate in those conversations. They seemed comfortable with the prison routine and were determined not to speak. Fernando Baiano appeared to be one of these. The police officers, trained to identify criminals and their crimes, suspected he was keeping much bigger secrets – the kind that pay fortunes and that serve to hide much more important persons and much more serious crimes. Baiano didn't give anything away. The names of more suspects were appearing all the time, more names that were linked to him. In statement No. 53, Paulo Roberto Costa briefly mentioned the name of the cattle-breeder José Carlos Bumlai, without giving any details other than that he was very close to Fernando Baiano. There was still much to be investigated about the shady middleman.

The appearance of Bumlai's name, however, attracted the press's attention. The magazine *Veja* reported that during Lula da Silva's presidency, Bumlai had been accorded such special treatment at the Palácio do Planalto that the security guards had even put up a special notice in the guardhouse, guaranteeing him access to the president at any time. It was an unprecedented honour. The notice read: 'Senhor José Carlos BUMLAI is to have priority treatment at the Palácio do Planalto main security desk, and should be directed to his destination, after prior telephone contact, at all times and in all circumstances.' Below this were three photographs of him, to assist with identification. The date of the notice: 12 August 2006.

Businessman and cattle-breeder, Bumlai was introduced to Lula before he was elected president, and the two became very close. Bumlai may well have solved problems for his powerful friend, but he also caused some. In an interview with Fausto Macedo, a reporter from *O Estado de S. Paulo*, Bumlai said that he hadn't known know about the security instructions: 'I open the newspaper and see that security pass saying I have unrestricted access to the Palácio any time I want. I had no idea I had it, that pass. Anyway, surely I should have the pass on me, shouldn't I? So there you are, I never knew about the security pass.' Regarding his friendship with President Lula, Bumlai said he thought it had all been rather exaggerated: 'Well, it's been blown out of all proportion. Am I friends with him? Yes, I'm friends with him, I'm friends with the whole family, but that doesn't justify all this fuss.'

It was just one example of the effects of conducting the proceedings so publicly, which Sergio Moro always defended. In February 2015, when he decided to release Alberto Youssef and Paulo Roberto Costa's depositions, except for those which might hinder the investigation, the judge once again made his position on the subject clear: 'In accordance with constitutional requirements, the conduct of public affairs, including legal proceedings relating to alleged offences against the public administration, must be carried out transparently and publicly. It is not appropriate for the judiciary to be the keeper of dark secrets.' Despite all the turmoil, the proceedings were sticking to the script set by Moro; they would continue to produce new revelations.

At that point, two of the three executives from Camargo Corrêa, who had been imprisoned since November, decided, after weeks of negotiations, to sign plea bargains with the federal prosecutors. The first to talk was Eduardo Leite, the company's vice chairman. Then it was the turn of the chairman,

Dalton Avancini. Both gave details about how the cartel worked. Avancini confirmed that the permanent members of the cartel included Odebrecht, Camargo Corrêa, UTC, OAS, Andrade Gutierrez and Queiroz Galvão, and said that Odebrecht was the firm that 'captained the organisation' and had the biggest influence on decisions, because of its sheer size. The meetings were held at UTC's offices on an ad hoc basis, depending on the timing of Petrobras's tendering process. The meetings were arranged by email or text message, always with the utmost discretion. The headings used were things like 'Petrobras meeting', 'G6 meeting' and 'meeting re Comperj'. All the participants knew that the cartel operated within a context of the payment of kickbacks to politicians and public servants, payments that were made precisely so that the decisions taken by the cartel would in fact be implemented in their contracts with Petrobras.

Once the plea bargains had been officially approved, the executives were given electronic tags and released. Eduardo Leite left the Curitiba jail by the front door without being recognised and, once on an aeroplane, told his family in an emotional phone call. Dalton Avancini, however, was not so lucky: to escape the media siege, the chairman of Camargo Corrêa had to hide in the boot of his lawyer's car.

Things were becoming ever more difficult for the defence lawyers. They had already done everything they could to release their clients from jail. First they had questioned Sergio Moro's professional conduct, using the argument that he was restricting the defence of those being investigated. Then they had contested the reasons given by the judge for their detention. Moro had rejected all the lawyers' requests, prompting appeals to the higher courts. In little over a year, of the 111 appeals presented to the regional federal appeal court, only four were granted. The appeal cases were heard by João Pedro Gebran Neto, a career judge specialising in constitutional and criminal law, who was highly critical in his rulings of the executives' requests to be released: 'I have always understood that, in the case of complex and large-scale criminal organisations, holding on remand should be reserved for those under investigation who, according to the evidence available, are ultimately responsible for the actions taken – such as the senior management of companies involved in a cartel.'

During the same period, the Superior Court of Justice heard sixty-seven appeals against detention on remand, none of which were granted. In the Supreme Court, twenty-six appeals were made and only two were granted. In total, between March 2014 and April 2015, 205 appeals were lodged in the various higher courts, but only six were granted. It was a gruelling battle.

The defence teams had mounted a coordinated plan of attack on Operation Car Wash designed to weaken its underlying foundations; they had tried to shift the proceedings from Curitiba, then sought to do a deal by arguing the necessity of protecting the economy. While the construction firms' role in the scheme was becoming ever clearer, Operation Car Wash was now reaching a decisive moment: it was time to name the politicians who would be investigated.

Chapter 5

JANOT'S LIST

6 March 2015

'THOSE WHO SHOULD PAY, WILL PAY'

The new year got off to a nervous start. In the corridors of Congress, the suspense was almost palpable: who would be on the list that Rodrigo Janot, the prosecutor general, was drawing up of politicians to be investigated for corruption? 'Who knows who's next?' one congressman joked. Bets were being placed. At a certain point, news spread that Janot's envoys would be coming right into the Congress chamber itself to break the bad news to those being investigated in person. Many broke out in a cold sweat; others called their offices discreetly, from a corner of the chamber. Any staff member from the federal prosecutors who was seen in the Congress building with an envelope under their arm attracted everyone's attention. 'If anyone plays a prank on me, I might have a seizure,' said a congressman, with a nervous smile. Many were afraid.

It had been well known since 2014 that Paulo Roberto Costa and Alberto Youssef had talked a lot. Various rumours had circulated for weeks, naming politicians who may have participated in or benefited from the Petrobras scheme, which all added to the expectation of a major revelation. How many would be investigated? The Supreme Court judge Teori Zavascki had approved Costa and Youssef's plea bargain at the end of December 2014 and passed the dossier to the federal prosecutors. According to the constitution, it now fell to the prosecutor general to decide whether to request the opening of judicial proceedings into any politicians suspected of corruption.

The headquarters of the federal prosecutors in Brasília – two circular buildings of mirrored glass, situated directly behind the main esplanade of government ministries – was located less than two kilometres from the Congress building. It was there that the fate of many politicians would be sealed. The depositions of Costa and Youssef had been divided into a series of separate annexes for each individual case, each contained in a light green folder of recycled paper carefully placed in a pile on the prosecutor general's desk.

In Rodrigo Janot's top-floor office, prosecutor Eduardo Pellela was concerned about the amount of work that lay ahead. There were many depositions to assess, and at that point there were only three prosecutors and seven assistants to deal with criminal matters. It was not enough. They needed to decide on a strategy, so Pellela went to see the boss.

'We have three options. One, we could deal with this ourselves, but we don't have enough staff. Two, we could bring in people and set up a working group here. Or three, we could send it to Curitiba. The first option is terrible, and the third even worse. How will they be able to deal with it there?' asked Pellela.

'Hold on,' replied Janot. 'I'm the prosecutor for these cases, and I want to have daily supervision. There's no way it's leaving here.'

'Then let's set up the group,' said Pellela.

'Yes,' agreed Janot.

And so the Operation Car Wash working group within the prosecutor general's office was born, alongside the federal prosecutors' working group in Curitiba. It followed more or less the same model. There were a lot of people cooperating together, but there was one fundamental difference: in Curitiba the decisions were taken collectively, while in Brasília the prosecutor general had the final word.

Consisting of prosecutors experienced in financial crime and combating criminal organisations, the working group was set up by Janot, in accordance with a decree dated 19 January 2015. It included some of the best investigators in the country. The head of the criminal section, Douglas Fischer, was chosen as coordinator. Working with him over the following months would be, among others, Janot's chief of staff Eduardo Pellela, Vladimir Aras, head of international cooperation, and Daniel Salgado, head of research and analysis. Janot also called on two young and two more experienced prosecutors from the Federal District's prosecutors' office to complete the team. They would have the difficult task of investigating and prosecuting the politicians who had benefited from corruption at Petrobras. There were many of them – never had so many politicians been investigated at the same time in Brazil, and with such a short deadline. Rodrigo Janot wanted to send the list to the Supreme Court quickly – he had in mind the end of February or the beginning of March. They would have little more than a month.

The atmosphere on the top floor of the prosecutor general's office was chaotically busy, with prosecutors rushing from one meeting to another. There was a lot to do: the first step was to study in detail all Paulo Roberto Costa's statements, which came to more than eighty hours of recordings, along with Alberto Youssef's, which ran to more than one hundred hours. The prosecutors then cross-checked this against tax declarations, electoral declarations and other information already gathered by Operation Car Wash. Everything was carefully indexed electronically. Prosecutors came from Curitiba to help, and informants were interviewed again to provide more details.

'We were rushing around all over the place. We split up the group, with some going to Rio de Janeiro and others to Curitiba. We listened to what they reported back and kept pushing every time another name came up. Sometimes the people in Curitiba hadn't paid enough attention or were afraid to follow a line of enquiry because they didn't have authorisation. We kept pushing,' recounts one of the prosecutors.

It was a challenge, because the existing material was all they had to work with. Any further investigations could only be done with the Supreme Court's authorisation, so the information the prosecutor general could take into consideration in deciding whether or not to open proceedings was, in theory, already available. It was time to seal the fates of the more than fifty well-known politicians. Gradually the team set up a series of secret proceedings, actions that did not even appear in the Supreme Court's electronic system and that were subject to an even higher level of confidentiality than normal. In all, the information from Costa and Youssef gave rise to forty-two secret proceedings in the Supreme Court, some of which had more than one name. Three other cases went to the Superior Court of Justice, which had jurisdiction to hear cases against state governors. The work of checking all the claims was several weeks behind schedule. As time went by, the pace accelerated. The prosecutors practically lived at the office and almost never went home. Janot kept an eye on everything; staff members report that he read all the documents and corrected the prosecutors' mistakes whenever necessary. Their work was quickly taking shape.

'The prosecutor general would tell them: "We need to have a single standard, and that ruler is the criteria by which I measure my own conduct. It doesn't matter who it is. We're going to use my ruler, my standard,"' recounts one of the prosecutors in the team.

The standard was that if an accuser said that he knew, saw, or had proof that a politician had directly received a benefit, then the prosecutor would request the opening of judicial proceedings, even if it might be closed soon after. If the accuser had merely heard that the politician had received a benefit but did not have some sort of direct information, the prosecutor would request that the matter be closed.

'And no squeezing things through,' advised Janot. The prosecutor general knew they had to play by the rules; the accusations had to be completely watertight, in order to withstand close scrutiny by the defence. As a precaution, one of the group's first decisions was not to press charges immediately but simply to open judicial proceedings, even when there was a strong indication of wrongdoing. According to the law, when faced with indications of an offence committed by a member of the legislature, the prosecutor general has three options: to ask for judicial proceedings to be opened, to close the matter completely, or if there is already sufficient evidence, to press charges. In the latter case, the Supreme Court then decides whether to initiate prosecutions against the politicians, or to dismiss the charges. Janot thought it was unwise to press charges immediately. Some of his assistants also drew attention to the fact that any charges would, in practice, be based almost entirely on the word of informants. Evidence resulting from a plea bargain, although important, is always viewed with a certain degree of distrust, because it is ultimately the word of a criminal. When pressing charges, a prosecutor does not want them to be rejected, so they would stick to opening judicial proceedings. But the question was: against how many?

Some cases were already more advanced and supported by more evidence. This was the case with Senator Fernando Collor, himself a former president of Brazil. Early in phase one of Operation Car Wash, the Federal Police had found documents relating to deposits made by Alberto Youssef into a personal account of the former president. The investigations indicated that he controlled a division of BR Distribuidora, one of Petrobras's subsidiaries. New evidence from Youssef now gave more information about Collor's involvement in the Petrobras scheme. According to Youssef, Collor had received R\$6 million in a transaction with an independent chain of petrol stations that was interested in doing a deal with Petrobras. Youssef claimed that half of this amount had been wired to secret bank accounts abroad and the other half delivered in cash, in Brazil.

A week before the list was published, the Federal Police's intelligence department had picked up information on new risks to Janot's personal safety. He had received death threats, and now began to pay more attention to the fact that his house had been broken into a month earlier. 'These people were in my house for at least eight minutes. They took a remote control that opens the garage door. Inside the house there was a .40 pistol with three cartridges and fourteen bullets in each one, a camera and many items of value, but the only thing they took was the remote control for the garage door. Since then, I have received several intelligence reports, the most recent of which points to an increased level of risk,' the prosecutor general said at the time.

None of the threats materialised, but everyone became a lot tenser. The list was about to be finalised. 'We hadn't fixed a date, but somehow the press had decided upon a date and this created a feverish sense of expectation,' recalls one of the assistants working directly with Janot. 'We said to ourselves: "One way or the other, we have to make a decision." It was one of the tensest days of my career as a prosecutor.'

Work was centred around a large table in the prosecutor general's office, next to a big wall-mounted TV screen. Sitting surrounded by several prosecutors, Janot checked everything, and when he was finished he checked it again, paying attention to the smallest details, to ensure there would be no glitches. People rushed around the room and there was a constant hum of people coming and going, rustling papers and talking in hushed tones. In the midst of the bustle, Rodrigo Janot, Douglas Fischer and Eduardo Pellela remained seated, concentrating on finalising all the documentation. Janot needed to read everything again before signing. There could be no errors. None. 'It was the beginning of an unprecedented series of proceedings at the Supreme Court. We could not make mistakes,' explains Fischer.

That night, with the list nearly ready, a group of civil servants held a prayer vigil outside the building. Janot decided that it would be good to go out and meet them, and was given a rapturous reception. Visibly moved, he told them: 'Those who should pay, will pay. We're going to get to the bottom of this. It's a long process, and it starts now. But we will get to the bottom of this investigation.' The civil servants cheered.

In the heat of the moment, he held up a poster with a slogan referring to himself: JANOT, YOU'RE THE HOPE OF BRAZIL. A photo of him with the poster found its way onto the internet and ended up in all the newspapers, and he was severely criticised for it. Politicians, anxious at the possibility of being on the list, used it to attack him. Later on, even his assistants recognised that it had been a public relations mistake. But at that moment, there was no time to think about it: there were decisions to be made. The whole team carried on working through the night, without a break. The following day, Tuesday 3 March 2015, Janot wanted to sign the formal documents and send everything to the Supreme Court. Along with everything else, he would make one further request: to lift the reporting restrictions on the entire proceedings.

In Congress, the politicians' expectations reached fever pitch.

'There's that quiet tension, that suspense, isn't there? What you're really hoping for, what you really want, is the truth,' said one congressman.

'Truth? Not a bit of it – what everyone wants is not to be on the list,' whispered another.

On arriving at work, the speaker of the Senate, Renan Calheiros, was the target of a clear and direct question.

'Would you say that Congress is anxious about Janot's list?' asked an experienced radio reporter.

'We'll talk soon,' replied Calheiros, walking briskly.

Eduardo Cunha, speaker of the Chamber, almost ran past the journalists on his way into the building.

'What's the atmosphere like, Mr Speaker? A lot of tension backstage?' a reporter asked, walking quickly beside him.

'The usual. I've been in a meeting of party leaders, choosing committees. The House is doing its job, working as normal,' replied Cunha before entering the chamber.

The list arrived at the Supreme Court. Receipt was registered at Justice Teori Zavascki's office at exactly 8.11 p.m., some seventy-two hours before the names would be officially disclosed. That day, even with the press monitoring any unusual movement at the court, no one witnessed the list's delivery. 'So we went in, came out, no one saw,' said one of the prosecutors with a smile. In order to get past the duty reporters, they needed to plan their entrance with military precision. The prosecutors covered the short distance between the prosecutor general's building and the Supreme Court in an 'undercover' vehicle. In the car park of the prosecutor general's building, they chose a white delivery van with no logo. They then arranged with the Supreme Court security guards that they would use the back entrance. They crossed the parking lot and took the judges' private lift, which was the only way inside that the journalists could not monitor. They were carrying four crates of documents. In the lift, the prosecutors were accompanied by an armed bodyguard. The door of Teori Zavascki's office opened. After greeting the judge, who was sitting at his computer, they went into the other room and delivered the documents to his staff. They left by the same route, without speaking to anyone.

The mission had been accomplished, or at least this stage of it. After weeks of working almost nonstop and eating most of their meals in the office canteen, the prosecutor general's team went out for dinner together. The next day would be a little calmer; they had to wait for Justice Zavascki's decisions. Even so, they ate only a light meal at a Japanese restaurant and went home to rest. They still wanted to get into work early – they couldn't relax just yet. Meanwhile the press had virtually set up camp outside the Supreme Court.

FORTY-SEVEN POLITICIANS UNDER INVESTIGATION

The following day, the journalists were waiting for Justice Teori Zavascki on the red carpet outside the Supreme Court. Zavascki walked past at a brisk pace.

'Will there be any news this week?' called out one of the journalists.

Zavascki merely turned his head, made a gesture that meant 'OK' and carried on walking. The 'Dungeon Master', the affectionate nickname from Dungeons & Dragons that journalists had given him, carried on inscrutably. He was known for his discretion, and wasn't going to give anything away.

At that point, the speaker of the Chamber, Eduardo Cunha, had already appointed an excellent lawyer: the retired former prosecutor general, Antonio Fernando Sousa. It was Sousa who had filed the charges against the Big Monthly corruption scheme, and he knew better than almost anyone else how federal prosecutors and the Supreme Court worked.

'I asked him so that if it were necessary, if what was being reported were true, then he would deal with it. I also asked him to file a request so he could find out if there really was something going on. It's only normal. If all the newspapers are publishing stories saying I'm facing some sort of investigation, then it's only natural that I get myself a lawyer to find out more,' Cunha told the journalists.

Over at the Senate, Renan Calheiros was still saying that he knew nothing about the possible inclusion of his name on the list: 'We still don't know anything, anything at all. No one has told us anything.' The speaker of the Senate said he was ready to provide any clarification he could give. 'One of the great things about democracy is that public figures are held to account,' he said on his way into his office.

Janot's list continued to be the dominant subject of discussion in Congress. The minister of international relations, Pepe Vargas, was fed up of talking about it: 'The important thing is that the list comes out quickly and reporting restrictions are lifted, so everything becomes clear and transparent, and we get rid of this atmosphere of anxiety and speculation.'

That afternoon, Teori Zavascki went down to the Supreme Court hearing, accompanied by two bodyguards. His staff did not want him to be accosted by journalists. 'They're following me,' commented the judge, smiling. In fact, the whole of Brazil was following Zavascki. In his office, under orders of absolute secrecy, everyone was working frenetically, late into the night. The time had almost come.

Some politicians already knew that their names were on the list. Rodrigo Janot had sent warnings to the most senior politicians, in a gesture of courtesy to those soon to be investigated. Janot had met with the minister of justice, José Eduardo Cardozo, and had spoken about the list and who would be on it.

In a meeting with the then-vice president, Michel Temer, Janot said that he would be presenting a number of requests to open judicial proceedings to the Supreme Court, and that among those being investigated was the speaker of the Chamber, Eduardo Cunha. Janot explained that these were not formal charges and that this was normal procedure, common even, resulting from information that had arisen in the Curitiba plea bargains. He said that was he simply doing his job as prosecutor general, and that he did not want to create a political incident.

Michel Temer listened in silence and thanked Janot for coming to see him. As soon as Janot left, the vice president postponed the trip he was due to make to São Paulo and called Eduardo Cunha in for a conversation. Cunha turned pale on hearing Temer's confirmation of what he already suspected. Temer said that Janot had not revealed exactly who the suspects were, but he had assured him that there would be no formal charges, merely the opening of a judicial investigation. Cunha exploded with rage, saying that he was being persecuted by the prosecutor general and the government. It was a rehearsal for what he would later say publicly.

The speaker of the Senate, Renan Calheiros, heard the news from Senator Eunício Oliveira, who had received a message from Janot. He too was very annoyed with the government. During the days preceding the publication of the list, Calheiros made criticisms of economic policy, cancelled his attendance at a dinner scheduled between the leadership of his party, the PMDB, and President Dilma Rousseff, and even decided to send back to the executive a piece of draft legislation dealing with tax exemptions on various sectors, something the Brazilian legislature rarely did.

Senator Aécio Neves of the PSDB also knew in advance. Faced with early indications that he was on the list, he sought further information. He asked a lawyer friend of his to get in touch with Antonio Figueiredo Basto, Alberto Youssef's lawyer. His envoy went to Curitiba and came back with an official letter signed by Basto: 'It is important to note that Youssef never himself raised issues relating to Senator Aécio Neves, since he did not know him and had never had any kind of relationship or business dealings with him. When questioned about events involving former congressman José Janene, Youssef clarified that he had never met either Senator Neves or his sister, and that he had only "heard it said" that Neves had "business interests" or influence at Furnas, the state-owned energy company, without however indicating any concrete fact that would justify such suspicion.' Shortly after, Neves managed to confirm that his case would be shelved, but for the majority of politicians on the list, the suspense continued.

That night, the only light burning at the Supreme Court was in Teori Zavascki's office. The following day, Friday 6 March, work began again early in the morning. Zavascki had lunch in his office with his team, settling the final details about publishing the list. The telephone of Débora Santos, the Supreme Court's press secretary, didn't stop ringing. More and more journalists were arriving outside. Zavascki's team had set up a WhatsApp group to deal with all the press enquiries. The judge was adamant that everyone must be informed at the same time. The hours went by. As the end of the day approached, the pressure increased. The whole country was awaiting the news.

Inside Teori Zavascki's office, the atmosphere was one of concentration. At around 7 p.m., sitting at his desk in an open-necked shirt, the judge was waiting for some of the documents to be corrected. He wanted to give everything one last check before signing the decisions. The apparent calm in the office contrasted with the commotion outside. A judge with many years of experience in the highest courts in the land, Zavascki showed no sign of nerves, despite the responsibility he shouldered at that moment.

The list finally came out shortly after 8 p.m. Zavascki approved all the requests from the prosecutor general to open judicial proceedings, and closed all the cases in which the prosecutors did not consider there to be enough evidence to proceed.

Forty-nine people would be investigated, of whom forty-seven were politicians. In addition, he lifted reporting restrictions on the investigations, including all information provided by Alberto Youssef and Paulo Roberto Costa under their plea bargains. Normally very careful with the confidentiality of legal proceedings so as to protect ongoing investigations, the judge held that he was lifting reporting restrictions in this instance in the wider interests of Brazilian society: 'At this moment, there is no social justification for maintaining reporting restrictions. On the contrary, it is important to the values of our republic that Brazilian society is made aware of the events described.' The judge said that while the law provided for restrictions to stay in place until formal charges are made, there was no further justification for the informants' accusations to remain secret once a successful investigation has been assured. 'There is therefore no legal reason to justify the maintaining of reporting restrictions.'

Standing in front of a packed press conference, the Supreme Court's press secretary read out the names, one by one. The news was broadcast live on the TV Globo evening news programme and reached the front pages of all the newspapers. The following day, over forty minutes of the hour-long TV national news bulletin were dedicated to the story. Journalists from the Globo TV network spent the whole day hunched over thousands of pages of court documents, eating their lunch of beef parmigiana around the meeting table. No one was allowed to leave the room.

Janot's list came as a major blow to the Progressive Party. It was the party with the largest number of politicians under investigation at that point: thirty-one. A large proportion of the Progressive Party's federal congressmen were cited in the accusations of the two informants. After all, Costa was the Petrobras director appointed by the party, and Youssef its most important middleman. There were six politicians alone from the southern state of Rio Grande do Sul. But the Progressive Party was not the only one, members of the Workers' Party and the PMDB were also on the list, along with some names from the Brazilian Socialist Party and the PSDB. The split between parties was a natural consequence of Costa and Youssef's roles within the scheme. Both of them were originally connected to the Progressive Party, but as time went by each had developed links with other parties. The Petrobras divisions under investigation were in the hands of the Progressive Party, the PMDB and the Workers' Party. The cases that involved politicians not from these parties – such as Senator Antonio Anastasia from the PSDB and Eduardo Campos, the Brazilian Socialist Party presidential candidate who had died in a plane crash during the election campaign – were seen as isolated cases.

Paulo Roberto Costa and Alberto Youssef had said that part of the money siphoned off from Petrobras had been handed over to politicians on a regular basis. But they had also received extra payments, principally during election campaigns and when party leaders were being chosen. In exchange, the politicians kept the Petrobras directors in their jobs and did not interfere in the building contracts cartel. Alberto Youssef detailed the distribution of kickbacks within the Progressive Party over the years – it was a stable arrangement that carried on even after changes in party leadership, but not everyone received the same amount. When the scheme was set up, José Janene kept the largest part and other leading figures like João Pizzolatti, Pedro Corrêa, Mário Negromonte and Nelson Meurer received amounts varying between R$250,000 and R$500,000 per month. Other Progressive Party politicians involved in the scheme received between R$10,000 and R$150,000 per month, depending on the political influence each had within the party.

It was Youssef and his employees who made all this possible. The money was delivered weekly or fortnightly, depending on the 'customer's' preference, in packages left at the politicians' apartments in Brasília. In the case of the leaders, an additional service was provided: the money would be delivered to their residences in their home states. Wads of cash travelled around Brazil hidden in suitcases or underneath clothing, taped to the body of whoever had been tasked with making the delivery. Youssef could hide as much as R$500,000 in his clothing. For the larger amounts, he would hire a private jet. In his deposition, Youssef stated that Janene would usually receive the money at his condo in Londrina, Paraná; João Pizzolatti, at his apartment in Balneário Camboriú, Santa Catarina; Pedro Corrêa, at his house in the Boa Viagem neighbourhood of Recife, Pernambuco; Mário Negromonte, at an apartment in Salvador, Bahia; Nelson Meurer, at a hotel in the centre of Curitiba, Paraná. There was a lot of travelling involved.

Back then everything went like clockwork. Youssef said that when Janene controlled the flow of money from Petrobras, he dealt with every request from the party's congressmen and never missed a payment; in this way, he built up enormous loyalty and concentrated his power within the party. In 2010, an election year, the scheme was at its height. This was surprising, because only four years earlier, in March 2006, the prosecutor general had started proceedings against those implicated in the Big Monthly corruption scandal. At the end of August 2007, the Supreme Court had accepted the charges against all of the accused. It was expected that this would deter future wrongdoing, but that is not what happened: on the contrary, Paulo Roberto Costa was being constantly pestered by politicians for money. He went to Alberto Youssef's office in São Paulo, wanting to get an idea of how much had already been paid and to whom. Youssef showed him a table with a list of numbers and initials in his diary: '2010 (pp 28.5)', which meant, according to the investigators, that R$28.5 million had gone from Petrobras's coffers to the Progressive Party; '5.5 Piz – 5.0 Ma – 5.3 Pe – 4.0 Nel', indicating the amounts, in millions, allegedly distributed to four leading figures: João Pizzolatti, Mário Negromonte, Pedro Corrêa and Nelson Meurer.

This group ran the party until mid-2011, but according to Youssef, lost influence after Janene's death, thanks to their greed. The four began to keep most of the money and give less to the rest of the party. This quickly became a source of conflict. Another group within the Progressive Party, made up of legislators like Ciro Nogueira, Arthur Lira, Benedito de Lira, Eduardo da Fonte and Aguinaldo Ribeiro, rebelled and took over. Mário Negromonte, minister for cities at the time, was replaced by Aguinaldo Ribeiro. The new leaders went to settle accounts at Petrobras. Paulo Roberto Costa recounted in his deposition that he was asked to attend a meeting with the new group at a hotel in Rio de Janeiro. He was informed that from then on, all payments should be made directly to Arthur Lira, leader of the Progressive Party at the time. They also asked that Alberto Youssef be removed as middleman, but this did not happen in the end, because the construction firms knew and trusted him. 'The businessmen had a different view of me because I always treated them right. They knew that whatever went through my hands would arrive at its destination intact, with no nonsense,' explained Youssef in an interview.

Costa quickly adapted to the new situation, so much so that
as early as 2011, old and new leaders of the Progressive Party
arranged a thank-you dinner for him at an expensive restaurant
in Brasília. He was given a Rolex watch and toasted as 'the PP's
man at Petrobras'. He was dancing to their tune, but he had no
other option. He knew that if he didn't serve his new masters,
he would lose his job. When he became seriously ill in 2006, at
the time of the Big Monthly scandal, he was almost removed
from the Supply Division. He had contracted malaria on a
trip to India and developed pneumonia. According to Costa,
when they heard that he was very ill, with little chance of
surviving, the Workers' Party met with some Petrobras officials
and tried to convince the government to replace him with someone more closely connected with their own party. Even after his
recovery and return to work, they continued trying.

During the same period, Costa became close to Fernando
Baiano, a lobbyist who worked on behalf of the PMDB. Baiano
recounted in his deposition that he had spoken to the PMDB's
leadership in the Senate and explained what was going on.
Costa said in his deposition that congressmen Aníbal Gomes
had been sent by Senator Renan Calheiros to see him. He then
spoke to Calheiros directly and to Senator Romero Jucá at
Calheiros's official residence in Brasília. Costa says that he also
visited Romero Jucá's home and both their offices at the Senate.
Other senators also put in helpful appearances, such as Valdir
Raupp and Edison Lobão, who would later become minister
of mines and energy. On all these occasions, the subject under
discussion was the same: the PMDB's support for keeping him
in his job. So he began to pay kickbacks from Petrobras contracts to PMDB politicians, as well. The middleman for these
payments was Fernando Baiano. In his evidence, Baiano stated

that between 2007 and 2011 he had received more than twenty offshore deposits for Paulo Roberto Costa. This began to annoy the Progressive Party. So much so that one day in 2010, Baiano ran into Youssef having lunch in Rio de Janeiro with Pedro Corrêa, leader of the Progressive Party, who complained: 'So, you're the Fernando Baiano who's giving our money to the PMDB?'

But it wasn't only Progressive Party and PMDB politicians who were knocking at Paulo Roberto Costa's door. In the Supply Division, the kickbacks were 2 per cent of the contract value, and only half of that, 1 per cent, was administered by Paulo Roberto. The other 1 per cent was for the Workers' Party, whose middleman was João Vaccari Neto, the party treasurer. In Costa's diary there are notes of payments to Workers' Party members jotted down in numbers and initials, for example '1.0 PB', which, according to Costa and Youssef, meant a payment of R$1 million to Senator Gleisi Hoffmann's election campaign, routed through her husband, the former minister Paulo Bernardo. Vaccari, the Workers' Party treasurer, was named in the deposition of Pedro Barusco, former manager at Petrobras's Services Division. Barusco estimated that between US$150 and US$200 million was paid to the Workers' Party between 2003 and 2013 with the involvement of João Vaccari Neto. Even PSDB politicians came looking for Paulo Roberto Costa. He said that in 2010 he had met with the PSDB's then-president, Sérgio Guerra. In that meeting, they agreed a payment of R$10 million to the PSDB, in order to block the setting up of a congressional investigation into Petrobras contracts.

The full list of serving congressmen to be investigated was: Aguinaldo Ribeiro (PP), Aníbal Gomes (PMDB), Arthur Lira (PP), Dilceu Sperafico (PP), Eduardo Cunha (PMDB), Eduardo da Fonte (PP), Jerônimo Goergen (PP), Sandes

Júnior (PP), Afonso Hamm (PP), José Mentor (PT), José Otávio Germano (PP), Lázaro Botelho Martins (PP), Renato Molling (PP), Roberto Britto (PP), Roberto Egídio Balestra (PP), Missionário José Olímpio (PP), Nelson Meurer (PP), Luis Carlos Heinze (PP), Luiz Fernando Faria (PP), Simão Sessim (PP), Vander Loubet (PT) and Waldir Maranhão Cardoso (PP). The serving senators on the list were: Antonio Anastasia (PSDB), Benedito de Lira (PP), Ciro Nogueira (PP), Fernando Collor (PTB), Gladson Cameli (PP), Gleisi Hoffmann (PT), Humberto Costa (PT), Lindbergh Farias (PT), Valdir Raupp (PMDB), Renan Calheiros (PMDB) and Romero Jucá (PMDB). Their status under Operation Car Wash is detailed at the end of this book. The investigation into Collor had already begun, because evidence of deposits by Youssef into his personal bank account had come to light as early as phase one of Operation Car Wash.

Along with these serving congressmen and senators, the Supreme Court also decided to open inquiries into the following former members of Congress: Cândido Vaccarezza (PT), Carlos Magno (PP), Luiz Argôlo (SDD), Aline Corrêa (PP), Pedro Corrêa (PP), Pedro Henry (PP), João Pizzolatti (PP), José Linhares Ponte (PP), Vilson Covatti (PP) and Roberto Teixeira (PP). The former minister of mines and energy, Edison Lobão (PMDB), and the former minister for cities, Mário Negromonte (PP), were also to be investigated, along with the former governor of Maranhão state, Roseana Sarney (PMDB), and João Leão (PP), vice governor of Bahia.

Two other individuals, not elected politicians, were to face investigation by the Supreme Court for their alleged involvement: Fernando Baiano and João Vaccari Neto – this was because the prosecutors wanted to investigate whether the scheme set up within the Progressive Party had been repeated within the PMDB and the Workers' Party. For them, the investigations into Fernando Baiano and João Vaccari Neto would be an opportunity to expose the workings of the scheme in these other two parties. Furthermore, the former minister Antonio Palocci was named by Paulo Roberto Costa as having received R$2 million for Dilma Rousseff's presidential campaign from him, through the scheme. Since his political rank did not entitle him to privileged forum, that is the right to be tried by the Supreme Court rather than the ordinary courts, Palocci's case was sent to be dealt with by Sergio Moro in Curitiba.

Justice Teori Zavascki also authorised federal prosecutors to investigate suspicions of criminal organisation. The politicians were accused of setting up a large and sophisticated criminal organisation, to divert money and assets from Petrobras. This was the prosecutors' most important request. The prosecutor general referred to it in his letter to the Supreme Court:

> The main investigation relates to the scheme for payment of kickbacks to politicians named by persons employed within three divisions of Petrobras. According to the depositions given, the politicians named by Paulo Roberto Costa at Petrobras's Supply Division received, every month, a percentage of the value of every contract signed by that division. Another part of the contract value was allegedly destined for members of the Workers' Party, named by Renato Duque at the Services Division. It was this division that selected which construction firm would win the contract, in line with what had been previously agreed between the companies forming the cartel.

Thirty-nine people would now be investigated in a single judicial investigation, which was referred to in the corridors of the court as the 'Big Gang' or the 'End of the World' trial. The majority were Progressive Party politicians – seventeen congressmen and three senators – but there were many from other parties as well, such as the speaker of the Senate, Renan Calheiros, and Senator Romero Jucá, both from the PMDB, and the Workers' Party's former treasurer, João Vaccari Neto. In his formal request to open the judicial proceedings, the prosecutor general wrote that the objective was 'the thorough investigation of the systematic process of illicitly distributing funds to political entities, notably though the use of party organisations, within the scope of the criminal scheme perpetrated at Petrobras.'

In explaining the scheme, the federal prosecutors divided the structure of the alleged criminal organisation into four groups. The first three of these were: the administrative element, consisting of the Petrobras directors; the economic element, that is to say the construction firms; and the financial element, the middlemen. The investigations were now reaching the fourth group, the political element of the scheme, the politicians responsible for appointing the senior management of Petrobras, and in particular its directors. This is what completed the criminal cycle – Paulo Roberto Costa had been nominated by the Progressive Party, Renato Duque by the Workers' Party and Nestor Cerveró by the PMDB. According to the investigators, these directors received kickbacks from the building contractors forming the cartel. The building contractors also paid money to the middlemen, who transferred it to the politicians and Petrobras directors. According to the investigation, Alberto Youssef handled these payments for the Progressive Party, Fernando Baiano for the PMDB and João Vaccari Neto for the Workers'

Party. Teori Zavascki was careful to note, however, that 'the opening of judicial proceedings does not constitute a prejudging of the responsibility for, or material nature of, any offence'.

On the basis that there was no evidence of an offence having been committed, federal prosecutors requested, and the Supreme Court accepted, the closing of investigations against Congressman Alexandre Santos (PMDB), former congressman Henrique Eduardo Alves (PMDB) and Senator Delcídio do Amaral (PT). They also closed a further two sets of proceedings against Senators Ciro Nogueira and Romero Jucá. The latter two, however, would be investigated as part of other investigations, and Senator Delcídio do Amaral would be arrested at the end of 2015 on the dual counts of attempting to interfere with the Operation Car Wash investigations and attempting to help Nestor Cerveró to flee the country.

'We always stressed that our request to close any file was without prejudice to our ability, in accordance with the law and jurisprudence, to reopen the investigation if any new facts arose,' explains one of the prosecutors involved in the Supreme Court hearings. 'We included this rider in all the documents. All of them. I could have requested the closure saying "he didn't do it and it isn't a crime". But in none of these cases did we say that.' The investigators also warned that further names might yet be revealed.

THE POLITICIANS' WRATH

The list did not include the name of Aécio Neves, the former PSDB presidential candidate, nor that of President Dilma Rousseff. The prosecutor general asked for the file on Senator Neves to be closed because he considered the information provided by Alberto Youssef to be insufficient. Youssef said that Neves had received a kickback from a corruption scheme at Furnas, and that the money had been delivered to him through his sister. But there was no proof, and Janot discarded it as hearsay. Senator Neves was immediately approached for comment. Ironically, he said that he took the news as a tribute. He then released a statement in which he attacked the government, without naming names: 'The attempts by elements within the government to implicate the opposition in this investigation have been unsuccessful.'

The investigation against President Rousseff had also been rejected. Janot did not say whether or not there was sufficient basis to investigate the president's involvement, merely stating that paragraph four of article eighty-six of the constitution did not permit the head of the Executive to be investigated for any action relating to the exercise of their position during their term in office. The events mentioned in the various depositions had occurred prior to her inauguration as president.

The speakers of the Senate, Renan Calheiros, and the Chamber of Deputies, Eduardo Cunha, were on the list. It was the first time that the Supreme Court had authorised an investigation into the leaders of both houses of the legislature at the same time and for the same alleged crime.

On the day the list was published, Calheiros had spent a good part of the previous night and that morning preparing an application to the Supreme Court in which he sought access to the accusations against him. He took a brief nap towards the end of the afternoon and when he awoke, the TV evening news was confirming that his name was on the list, suspected of corruption, money laundering and criminal association. He was furious. The accusation referred to meetings having taken place at his house for the purpose of discussing the scheme

and 'receiving money'. As he watched the rest of the news programme, he made trenchant criticisms of Rodrigo Janot to
those around him, accusing the prosecutor general of stirring
up suspicions about him. He spoke by telephone with friends
and allies, repeating to all and sundry that he was perfectly
calm and that he had been through difficult patches before.
He recalled that when he was accused in 2007 of paying child
maintenance for one of his daughters with the assistance of, yes,
a construction firm, he had become a target for the press. Even
so, he had managed to turn things around, had been entirely
absolved by the Senate and had returned to his role of speaker.

That night at the speaker of the Senate's official residence,
a large and airy mansion with a view of Lake Paranoá on the
outskirts of Brasília, Calheiros knocked back several slugs of
Johnnie Walker Black Label and gave an interview to the UOL
columnist Fernando Rodrigues while the two of them tucked
into plates of beef with okra and rice.

'Do you think I don't know what pressure is? The last time
round, the TV news was running reports about me for at least
ten minutes every night. I dealt with all of that on my own, and
I'm still here. I know what pressure is,' he said across the dining
table, in apparently good humour.

Calheiros spoke to the journalist about his name being
included among those under investigation: 'The Palácio do
Planalto has no interest in anyone's name being removed. The
government's game is that the more people being investigated,
the better, especially if it includes Aécio. That's the way the
Planalto sees things.'

And he didn't stop there. In a tone markedly more pointed
than his usual one, the experienced politician let rip to the UOL
columnist: 'The government told everyone that Aécio Neves

would be on the list. Janot said to around ten people that he was being pressured. That Michel[3] was applying pressure to remove Henrique,[4] and that he was going to do so. And that there was pressure to remove Eduardo Cunha from the list. Michel talked to Janot three times.'

The journalist was surprised that the senator was expressing his views so forcefully. 'Renan doesn't normally talk like that. But this time it was war,' wrote Fernando, well accustomed to reporting on scandals at the heart of government.

As well as laying into the government, Calheiros had plenty to say about Rodrigo Janot and his list:

The problem about this list is that it has no clear criteria. I'm not talking about whether the criteria are right or wrong. Just about whether there are any criteria at all. He ordered investigations into some people for exactly the same things that other people have done whom he left out. There are just no criteria. Yesterday he sent someone to say that the whole of my case concerned legal donations. He's campaigning to be reappointed. That's what explains it. But even if the president herself said that when it comes to campaigns 'anything goes', the prosecutor general is taking this to extremes. He's openly campaigning to get reappointed. He took that photo with the protestor's poster saying he was the hope of the whole nation!

Calheiros even attacked a Supreme Court judge, saying that 'Teori ordered Duque's release when there was material evidence

---

[3] Michel Temer, the vice president.
[4] Henrique Eduardo Alves, former speaker of the Chamber of Deputies, who in the end did not appear on the list and became minister of tourism.

against him, and kept others in jail when there was the same level of proof.' He finished the interview promising all-out war: 'Everything must be investigated. There must be a congressional inquiry into the federal prosecutors' office. There are cases of improper conduct among the prosecutors. There is misspending of public money. All these things must be investigated and nobody should fear the investigation.' Calheiros didn't go to bed until after 2 a.m.

Behind the scenes, Calheiros was betting that Janot would not manage to get himself reappointed. His period of office was running out, and even if the president nominated him for another two years, his appointment would still need to be approved by the Senate.

In the house next door, the official residence of the speaker of the Chamber of Deputies, Congressman Eduardo Cunha was equally irritated that night. He had already been battling every mention of his name in relation to Operation Car Wash for several weeks. When one of Alberto Youssef's assistants, a police officer called Jayme de Oliveira Filho who had the job of distributing money for the scheme, had named him in his deposition – saying that he had gone to the congressman's house to deliver cash – Cunha was not bashful about coming forwards. He gave a series of press interviews denying that he knew Jayme, gave his assurance that he had never received any money and stated that the house the policeman had been to was not his. That day, the name of PSDB Senator Antonio Anastasia also appeared in the newspapers. In a testimony given to Operation Car Wash, the same police officer said he had delivered cash to the senator, who denied the accusation vehemently. More than seven months after the beginning of the investigations, the case against Anastasia would be the first to be closed for lack of evidence.

When the list came out, Cunha went on the attack. In an interview he gave in the journalists' lobby at Congress, he accused the prosecutor general of acting as a political arm of the government: 'I won't allow this, and I will defend myself. The prosecutor general is in cahoots with the government. It's yet another piece of nonsense that I will answer and take apart with relative ease.'

Cunha also went to the Petrobras congressional inquiry – which he had played an influential role in setting up and in choosing its chairman – and said what he had to say. He told them that Janot's list was a 'joke', assured them that that he was innocent, that the accusations were false and that there was absolutely no basis on which to open judicial proceedings into his conduct: 'To call someone's reputation into question and then say that requesting the opening of judicial proceedings is nothing to worry about, is in itself something to worry about! Particularly for those who hold positions of power. Randomly naming someone, in an irresponsible and flippant way and as a matter of political expediency, is a way of transferring the crisis from the streets to Congress, and we are not going to allow it,' he said, then added: 'Federal prosecutors chose who to investigate; they did not investigate everyone, and for reasons of a political nature they chose who would be targets of the investigation.'

On being asked by one of the congressmen if he had an offshore account, he said something that would cause him headaches in the future, but which he would continue to repeat, even in the face of strong evidence to the contrary: 'I don't have any accounts anywhere that aren't listed in my tax declaration.'

As he left the Petrobras inquiry, Cunha gave another interview to the press: 'I didn't come here looking for insults or applause; I came in relation to our investigation into the largest corruption scheme in this country.' Later, in his office, he took a copy of the statement he had just given and gave instructions for it to be annexed to the application he had sent to the Supreme Court. He did not want to be interviewed by the Federal Police. The investigators, who had watched the entire session of the congressional hearing on the parliamentary TV channel, would later ask him about things he had denied during the congressional hearing, such as whether he had received any form of 'undue benefit' or had a close relationship with the lobbyist Fernando Baiano.

By then, Eduardo Cunha was already deeply enmeshed in the Operation Car Wash investigation. Federal prosecutors had first heard the speaker's name mentioned in the statements given by Alberto Youssef. Youssef had said that he had become aware of Cunha putting pressure on Júlio Camargo using information requests from one of the Chamber of Deputies' committees. He had wanted a kickback, said Youssef. It was this that sounded the alarm. The information request had to be found. An initial search didn't find any information requests from him. But there was one from Solange Almeida: in 2011, the congresswoman had filed an information request regarding the Brazilian subsidiary of Mitsui, in which Júlio Camargo had been involved. The text of the information request was very firm and contained the following justification: 'Various contracts entered into with the Mitsui Group involving the construction, operation and financing of Petrobras platforms and drilling rigs include what could be seen as indications of impropriety, over-invoicing, high rates of interest, absence of tendering process and undue favours granted to this group, in which Mr Júlio Camargo, known to be a middleman, is a shareholder.' At the time, there was no

investigation or accusation against Mitsui or even Júlio Camargo, who only began to appear in the press after Operation Car
Wash began. In her testimony, the congresswoman herself confirmed that she did not know the Mitsui Group and had known
nothing about them when she filed the information request.

The strange tale of this information request reached the
press, which deeply annoyed Cunha. The speaker of the Chamber ended up sacking the head of its IT department. Cunha told
journalists that it was not he who had instigated the dismissal,
and yet he justified it on the grounds of making an example. On
hearing the news, the prosecutors rushed to Janot's office and
told him: 'We need to speak to this guy right now.' And so, three
hours after his dismissal, the head of the Chamber's IT department was giving evidence to federal prosecutors. He was given
a guarantee of confidentiality to allay his concerns. 'He didn't
hand over any documents, but he provided us with technical
information and showed us on the website how things worked,'
relates one of the prosecutors. The former head of IT confirmed
that the real author of the information request had been Eduardo Cunha, and he provided a technical explanation of how
Cunha's digital fingerprints could still be seen on the request.

'He's able to wipe that information from Congress's IT system?' asked one of those present.

'Yes. There's a record of who deleted it, but the information
itself is lost and can't be recovered afterwards,' he replied.

'If we went there, would you be able to see and extract this
information from the system?' asked a prosecutor.

'Yes,' said the former head of IT.

The prosecutors decided to carry out an immediate search
at the Chamber of Deputies. They sought and were granted
authorisation from the Supreme Court. Eduardo Pellela, Janot's

chief of staff, immediately instructed members of the working group to carry out the order. The difference was that, since it applied to the Chamber of Deputies, this was not the normal type of search and seizure warrant they were all accustomed to. It was a request for information, but one that needed to be complied with immediately. 'It's a less invasive measure than a search and seizure. It's just a request for information and there's no need for police involvement or anything like that,' explained one of the prosecutors.

When the order was issued, on a Monday evening, Janot's chief of staff, two prosecutors and two IT assistants left the federal prosecutors' building and went to meet an official from the Supreme Court, who was carrying Justice Zavascki's order. They held a preparatory meeting in the Supreme Court's car park.

'What's your name?' asked Pellela.

'Antonio,' replied the official.

'Right then, Antonio, don't unseal the order until we're in the director general's office, OK? Not for love nor money. We've got two guys here with badges, two federal prosecutors. They'll go into the Chamber without identifying themselves, take you up to the director general's office, right into the room and that's where you unseal the order. OK?' explained the chief of staff, clearly and succinctly.

'That's fine with me, sir. You can rely on me, I've been doing this for ten years,' replied the official confidently.

The prosecutors then called the office of the director general, Sérgio Sampaio, saying that they wanted to have a meeting with him and asking if he would wait for them in his office. The group took an unmarked car and headed over towards Congress. Meanwhile, Pellela returned to the prosecutor general's office, where he kept in touch with everyone by text message. When the prosecutors arrived at the Chamber of Deputies, shortly before 8 p.m., Sampaio said he needed to inform the speaker of the nature of their request, citing an internal regulation of the Chamber, which was already sitting on his desk. But the prosecutors were prepared for this. They interrupted the director general, somewhat brusquely.

'I don't think you understand. This document says that it is addressed to you, and it's stamped "Strictly Confidential". If you inform Congressman Eduardo Cunha, you will be informing the person under investigation, thereby disobeying a judicial order. You'll be infringing an order of a Supreme Court judge,' said the prosecutor gravely, looking straight at the director general. 'You can tell him if you like, it's up to you. But the document is marked "Confidential". It's up to you – your call.'

After around forty minutes of discussion, Sampaio carried out the order and they went down to the IT department, with Sampaio appearing visibly uncomfortable. Then, once the IT searches were already under way, the director general went to Eduardo Cunha's office and told him what had happened. The prosecutors didn't leave the building until 2.30 a.m. As they left, one of them noticed that the lights in the speaker's office were still on. That same night, a lawyer called Rodrigo Janot's personal mobile phone, but he was suspicious and didn't answer. The politicians were on the alert.

During the search, the prosecutors went through the Chamber of Deputies' records, identified the information they were looking for and then went to find the digital audio tapes used to store data, which were kept in storerooms near one of the car parks within the Congress precinct. They put the tapes into the machines and started to extract the data. Since it would take hours to complete, they had to go home for the night, returning the next day just after lunch. They finally left at 7.30 p.m.: mission accomplished. The operation had been a success, and all without attracting any attention; the press only found out later.

The other politicians under investigation reacted in a variety of ways to the opening of judicial proceedings. Some filed applications for summary dismissal, others wanted to give evidence straightaway so they could come out saying there was no proof against them. One of the more unusual reactions came from the vice governor of Bahia, João Leão, who was at the time under investigation for suspected corruption and criminal association (but later acquitted). One afternoon, he released a statement not very different from those of other politicians, taking the line that he was saddened and surprised, but innocent. 'I will carry on working with my head held high in defence of Bahia and Brazil,' he wrote. Later that night, however, he released a much less formal statement saying: 'I don't know why my name's come out. I didn't know these people. I think it might be because I received support in 2010 from companies involved in the scheme. But dragging my name through a mess like this? I just don't get it. Only thing I can do is wait till they send me a summons and then defend myself.' At this point, Leão rather lost the plot: 'To put it politely, I couldn't give a toss about all these shysters. Frankly, I wouldn't wipe my boots on them. I'm a serious guy and, hand on heart, I've done nothing wrong. On Monday I'm going to Brasília to find out why I've been dragged into this.'

The publication of the list caused great consternation to many politicians. Congressman Jerônimo Goergen, for example, was in Ireland with his wife. When he learned that his name had appeared on the list, he wanted to come home immediately. On Facebook and Twitter, his constituents were demanding explanations. 'It cost me R$6,000 in phone charges just giving press interviews to say I had nothing to do with this. Then quite a bit more to change my flight. I was in no mood to stay there. I remember sitting in Charles de Gaulle Airport in Paris, crying, talking on the phone to my lawyer and watching the news on the TV screens. My photo on TV, in that airport. No one understood why I was crying so much. As I walked around, I felt as if people were staring at me and calling me a thief,' said the congressman. Some of these reactions surprised the investigators. 'One thing is very clear: our job is technical, not political. There may be political consequences, but that isn't our problem,' said a prosecutor.

CLASH BETWEEN FEDERAL POLICE AND PROSECUTORS

Shortly after the publication of the list, the investigators pulled back from the public eye. It was time to work in silence. With the Supreme Court's authorisation, they would be deepening their investigations into suspected corruption, money laundering and criminal organisation. The federal prosecutors had their working group set up and, at the Federal Police, Detective Thiago Machado Delabary was chosen to coordinate the Operation Car Wash task force in Brasília. Known for his discretion, he was given the autonomy to set up his own team and develop his own line of investigation. The work was immense and challenging: the most immediate issue was to define their strategy for the next steps. They would need to coordinate their efforts.

However, at the beginning of April, a misunderstanding between police and prosecutors almost got in the way of the investigations. In the working group's early meetings, the prosecutors gave the detectives a fixed sequence of actions to be carried out, such as the gathering of documents and depositions. But the Federal Police feared that this approach would slow down the investigation. In the detectives' opinion, it was better to carry out all these procedures as quickly as possible, and simultaneously if necessary. So without warning, the Federal Police took six depositions which the federal prosecutors would have preferred to leave until later, after they had gathered evidence that could be used to surprise the suspects during interview. The Federal Police's decision irritated the prosecutors. They informally asked the detectives to suspend taking depositions, but the Federal Police refused. At one point, the detectives told the prosecutors that they had a court order to interview the politicians and that only another court order could stop them from doing so.

The prosecutor general then went to inform Teori Zavascki of the disagreement and officially requested that the Supreme Court suspend police interviews in seven proceedings. This was enough for the matter to reach the newspapers, causing a crisis: the Federal Police were under pressure to take statements quickly and release the politicians under investigation; the federal prosecutors were being prevented from taking decisions in the best interests of the investigation. At that point, the prosecutors began to invite politicians to give evidence at the prosecutor general's office, rather than to the police. The detectives were very put out. There were even rumours that the Federal Police were slipping questions to the politicians before they were interviewed. This was the last straw – the detectives were furious at the rumours. 'There were moves to take the interviews away from us. It was a way of trying to undermine our work,' said one of them. A tense meeting was called:

the police officers complained; the prosecutors insisted. They recalled that on opening the judicial proceedings, Justice Teori Zavascki had said that the federal prosecutors were responsible for the criminal proceedings.

'We have a problem,' argued one of the prosecutors. 'The Supreme Court has already said that Janot is in charge of the criminal proceedings. If the politicians want to give evidence to him, then he's minded to let them be interviewed at his office. Is there anything wrong with that? Of course there isn't. He's in charge. Zavascki's already said this, and there's a ruling of his confirming it.'

'But it's the police's prerogative to run a police inquiry,' replied a detective, quoting a clause in the internal regulations of the Supreme Court that says, 'It is for the police authorities to bring together all the elements necessary for the conclusion of investigations.'

The detectives would not give way. They said to each other that the Federal Police could not simply turn itself into a unit of Janot's operations. There was already a movement on social media with the slogan LET THE POLICE DO THEIR WORK. On both sides people were spoiling for a fight. The argument carried on until one of those present decided to find a consensus.

'Let's try to find a way to resolve the problem. We're just going to cause more stress here,' said one of the prosecutors. 'So here goes. Those congressmen or senators who want to give evidence at the prosecutor general's office will be interviewed there, the rest will come here. And the interviews at the prosecutor general's office will be done with your participation.'

This soothed nerves a little, and the meeting carried on more peacefully. But the problem only really ended when, in a procedural decision, Justice Teori Zavascki wrote that there must be harmony between the two institutions: 'It is of the utmost public interest and essential for the efficient provision of justice that the joint actions of federal prosecutors and police authorities develop in a harmonious manner, in accordance with the appropriate methods, working routines and investigative practices designed by those two entities in accordance with the law, and with the aim, above all other objectives, of seeking the truth in relation to the facts being investigated and using the safest and most efficient methods within the shortest possible timeframe.' Zavascki stated that it was not the function of the judiciary to define the scope of police activity, and explained that when he said at the opening of the inquiries that his judicial authorisation was addressed to federal prosecutors, he did not wish to 'prejudice the proper function of the police'.

In the end, the majority of politicians were interviewed by the Federal Police. 'It was an unnecessary source of stress. And one thing I can tell you, now that this is strictly for the history books: one or two minor details aside, we always work closely with the police. This kind of work is a partnership,' acknowledges one of the prosecutors. The police detectives say the same thing.

In fact, these two institutions, which have the same objective at heart, fought less in this investigation than on many other occasions. Janot's list caused a moment of tension that was quickly resolved. Between the prosecutor general's office and Congress, however, the stress would only increase in the following months. The whole country found itself in the unusual situation of having the speakers of both houses of the legislature being investigated by federal prosecutors – not to mention many other politicians. There would be yet more tremors and the political crisis would get worse. But the battle of Janot's list had been won.

Chapter 6

A YEAR ON THE ROAD

17 March 2015

PERSONALITY OF THE YEAR

By the time Operation Car Wash's first anniversary approached, Sergio Moro's fame had spread throughout Brazil. For months, both the investigation and the judge had been cheered in spontaneous street demonstrations. One of the first times Moro's name appeared at such an event was on 15 November 2014, the day after phase seven began, when executives from the major construction firms were arrested. The protestors carried posters with slogans like MORO FOR SUPREME COURT and THRASH 'EM, MORO!, and banners demanding PUNISH THE CAR WASH. Admiration for the judge was shown in different ways. In one city, a group of women decorated the square in front of the federal court building with yellow ribbons. In another, local residents stood outside the police station with posters saying SERGIO MORO, HONOUR AND JUSTICE and SERGIO MORO, BRAZIL NEEDS HELP and FEDERAL POLICE, PRIDE OF BRAZIL. A former police officer on his way to lunch stopped his car in front of the demonstrators and wept. 'I worked with the police for thirty-five years and I never thought I would see something like this,' he recounted.

On 15 March 2013, the protests against corruption and the government reached their peak, with more than 2.4 million people taking to the streets throughout Brazil. It was a historic day. Demonstrations took place in more than 250 cities, and at most of them there were posters supporting Operation Car Wash and Sergio Moro. In Olinda, a larger-than-life figure of Moro was carried through the streets. In Curitiba, pictures of the judge were paraded alongside the demonstrators. WE ARE ALL MORO, said a poster in São Paulo.

The judge began to be approached by people wherever he went. Stopping to buy some groceries in the supermarket on his way home, he heard his presence being announced by loudspeaker as he stood at the checkout. The other customers applauded. After meeting him, the singer Raimundo Fagner made a video praising him: 'Sergio Moro, pleasure to have spoken to you. We Brazilians are with you. Well done for being here. The country's a mess, but at least you're here. Go for it, big guy!'

On arriving at a book launch in São Paulo, the judge was not only recognised but followed around the shopping centre by more than a dozen people shouting things like 'This guy's the pride of Brazil!', 'My children thank you!', 'Ohhh Sergioo Moroooo!' and 'Justice, justice!'

Sergio Moro was named Personality of the Year at the *O Globo* 'Make a Difference' awards ceremony for his actions in Operation Car Wash, thereby joining a select group of Brazilians that includes Zilda Arns, José Mindlin, Sebastião Salgado and Joaquim Barbosa.

To receive their awards, the newspaper invited the winners of the various categories of prizes to Rio de Janeiro and put them up at the world-famous Copacabana Palace Hotel, where the award ceremony was being held. A suite with a sea view was reserved for Moro. He politely refused. He bought flights for himself and his wife Rosângela, and the two left Curitiba shortly after lunch. He booked a cheaper hotel nearby and paid for it himself. The only thing he requested from the organisers was to be picked up from his hotel and taken back at the end of the night. He got ready quickly, because he wanted to arrive early and speak to the other prize winners.

When he arrived at the Copacabana Palace with his wife, at the designated time and wearing his black suit, black shirt and black tie – clothing that had become his trademark – they were directed to the staircase leading to the ballroom on the floor above. As the waiters poured champagne and the guests chatted while waiting for the ceremony to begin, the cameras suddenly began to flash. Everyone turned at once. Sergio Moro was here. 'When I reached the top step, there was no time to adjust my dress,' Sergio Moro's wife recounted later, laughing.

The judge was now a celebrity. Journalists rushed over towards him. He wasn't used to being surrounded by the press. Reporters asked several questions at once, to which Moro listened carefully, giving brief and concise answers. No matter how helpful he tried to be, the media scrum only became worse. The questions just kept coming and he wasn't able to answer all of them. One of the event organisers tried to usher him away into another room. 'Can the other guests also use that room?' asked Moro. He wasn't just defending the principle that all citizens are equal; the judge really wanted to talk to the other award winners. In the room at the end of the corridor, Moro ended up surrounded by journalists from *O Globo*. Sergio and Rosângela Moro knew the columnists and writers Merval Pereira and Zuenir Ventura, both distinguished members of the Brazilian Academy of Letters, the columnist Miriam Leitão and João Roberto Marinho, vice chairman of the Globo media conglomerate. They stayed talking for some time before the ceremony began. Inspired by this encounter, Zuenir Ventura, known as 'Master Zu', wrote an article that was published in *O Globo* on 21 March 2015, under the title 'An Optimistic Judge': 'A curious thing to find myself in front of this young man of forty-two who has the face of a recent graduate, and who is today the public figure carrying the greatest burden of ethical hopes and dreams in the country. Maybe the success will go to his head, I don't know. But for now, it seems not. No trace of arrogance in his words or gestures, no bragging or omnipotence, no salvationist moralising. Up close, Sergio Moro is normal.'

In his article, Zuenir also described how that night also offered those present, as a contrast to the general sense of moral deterioration in politics, 'the spectacle of a kind of Brazil that works'. The symbol was Sergio Moro, winner of the night's main award for his actions in Operation Car Wash, but other figures from culture, sport, science and music were also being honoured. All of them, like Moro, had made a difference to Brazil in 2014. Sergio and Rosângela sat in their reserved seats in the front row and listened to the speeches of all the other award winners. One of them said it was an honour to be receiving an award alongside the judge.

When his turn came, Moro paid careful attention to what was said about him and projected onto the giant screens. As the judge's favourite photo of his wife appeared on the screens, the person presenting the prize, the columnist Ancelmo Gois, said: 'Remember this name: Sergio Fernando Moro. For he occupies a prominent position in the search for this collective dream of ours: a country where everyone is equal.'

When they called him up to the stage, Moro quickly kissed his wife's cheek and stood up. The packed Golden Room in the Copacabana Palace gave him a standing ovation for several minutes. Moro stood with his head bowed waiting for the applause to end. He accepted the trophy and gave a speech without notes. There were several topics he had planned to talk about. He smiled as he began, but his mouth was rather dry and he sounded nervous. He thanked the organisers for the award, said he was proud to be among the other award winners with their incredibly moving stories and deeds, and then surprised his audience by saying that he felt awkward about receiving the award, because it was for work that was still in progress. He said he would feel more comfortable if the recognition was for a job that had been completed, and he reminded them that Operation Car Wash was not the achievement of just one person.

As judge in an ongoing case, I cannot promise that I will try the case in a certain way or come to a certain result. What I can promise, for this is the duty of all judges, is that I will do my very best to try the case according to the law and according to the evidence presented, respecting the rights of those accused and also taking into account – and I think this is important, for tonight has given us a lesson in this – the rights of the victims and of society at large in seeing this case properly resolved. The objective is always to uphold the rule of law and ensure the application of justice in an impartial and equal manner according to the law, giving judgment according to the evidence. This is nothing to do with the award; it is the commitment of every judge.

He showed in his words and gestures that he would not allow himself to be affected either by tributes or celebrity. He also talked about the demonstrations that a few days earlier had brought more than two million people onto the streets. One of the main themes in all the protests, both for and against the government, was the fight against corruption. Everyone could agree on this:

I was very moved by the recent demonstrations. Clearly there were many groups that took to the streets and their ideas were not all the same, for it is possible to disagree on many aspects, but it is very good within a democracy to see people on the streets. There was at least a common theme, for within our democracy, no matter how disparate it may be, there is a consensus: we are all against corruption. We are all against crime. And we understand, whether we're on the left, right or in the centre, that when corruption is identified and proven, it must be adequately punished.

In finishing his speech, he defended the public nature of the legal proceedings – required by the constitution and not of his choosing – that gave civil society the possibility of being well informed, both about the content of the accusations and also his own conduct in the proceedings.

I am confident that with the support of public opinion, with the support of the population, we can move forward with these proceedings. As has already been mentioned, Brazilian democracy has faced much bigger challenges in the past. We overcame a brutal dictatorship. We also managed to bring hyperinflation under control. We have made significant social advances in recent decades. Corruption is simply one more problem. Within a democratic system, I don't see any problem as insurmountable. With the support of our democratic institutions, with the support of society, I believe that we will succeed in overcoming this problem calmly.

Finally, he thanked his family and specifically mentioned his father, Dalton Áureo Moro, who had been professor of geography at Maringá State University, the same place from which he had graduated in law. At that moment, for only a fraction of a second, his voice revealed his emotion: 'Sadly, my father has passed away, but I have fond memories and enormous respect for him; much of what I have learned in life was from him. I'd also like to say a special thank you to my beautiful wife, who is here with me tonight. Thank you.'

The judge was given another lengthy standing ovation. For those present, it was a night filled with stories of hope, which he also symbolised. Sergio Moro and his wife stayed in the room for some time talking to the other award winners and guests, before deciding to leave. They called for their car. It was raining heavily as they made their way back through the streets of Copacabana to their hotel. As Zuenir Ventura was soon to write, Moro was at that moment the person on whom Brazil's ethical hopes and dreams rested. He was forty-two years old and, up close, he was a normal man.

THE PATH ALREADY TRODDEN

The career that brought Sergio Moro to such public prominence began like that of many other Brazilians. Although he was a good university student, he didn't know if he was on the right path until his third year. He discovered a taste for the law when he started working as a trainee at a law firm. At that point he had some liking for criminal law, but was more interested in the tax cases he was working on at the time. However, he was soon attracted by the idea of becoming a judge and making a career on the bench. He passed the judiciary exams with flying colours, despite not studying much because of his work commitments. Then life took him in a different direction. The first federal bench he sat on did not hear criminal cases. Two years later, the young judge was able to fit in a summer course at Harvard. It was an interesting experience, an opportunity to compare the ways in which the two countries practised law, and it opened his mind even further. It was there he realised that the legal world was much wider than what he had learned at university. He returned to Brazil with new ideas, books and contacts.

When he was promoted from substitute to permanent judge in 1999, the first town he was sent to was Cascavel, in a remote part of Paraná. It was there that he gained his initial experience of criminal trials. He got to know good prosecutors, buried himself in his cases and took a liking to the job. He was then appointed to a post in Joinville, a small town in the neighbouring state of Santa Catarina, where he devoted more time to criminal cases. This was the training that formed the meticulous judge Brazil would later get to know. In 2002 the opportunity arose to move to Curitiba, where his wife's family lived, and he seized the chance, choosing once again to specialise in criminal cases. Today, he would not choose anything else. For him, judging a crime and analysing each and every piece of evidence is much more attractive than other types of cases. There is no routine: every case is different.

He had one further step to take. In 2003, a few months after moving to Curitiba with his family, he learned that Judge Gilson Dipp, whom he greatly admired, had recommended setting up a number of specialist groups of judges throughout Brazil dealing specifically with cases of money laundering. A study by the Federal Justice Council, led by Dipp, showed that the 1988 law on money laundering was not working. Almost no one was being prosecuted for the offence anywhere in the country. Each state was now to have a specialist group of judges dealing only with this and related crimes. In Paraná, the section in which Moro worked was chosen to specialise in money laundering. This meant that Moro would be responsible for all trials relating to this type of crime throughout the state.

There quickly came a succession of cases from the city of Foz do Iguaçu on the Paraguay border, where the criminal courts were swamped with smuggling and drug trafficking cases. They did not have the resources to deal with the large-scale case soon landed on them: the Banestado scandal. It was a baptism of fire for Sergio Moro. The case, considered the biggest ever evasion of capital controls to this day, saw the illegal export of more than R$30 billion from Brazil to the United States. It was during this case that Sergio Moro came across the black-market currency trader Alberto Youssef for the first time, and it was in this trial that Youssef made his first plea bargain agreement, a pioneering step in Brazil that was officially sanctioned by Moro.

Moro knows that good results are not always guaranteed. As for the unusual success of Operation Car Wash, he believes that he was often helped by luck, or what others might call divine assistance. 'I had previously had good cases that resulted in arrest and conviction. But nothing on this scale. But incredibly, things worked out,' said Moro.

Throughout his career as a federal judge, Sergio Moro had seen many trials turn to dust because of some small detail that would give rise to an appeal. He realised how imperfect the judicial system was, with shortcomings and gaps through which the guilty could escape with impunity. Moro began to see that for the system to function correctly was the exception rather than the rule. At a certain point in his career, he became somewhat disillusioned with cases relating to financial crime. He took on other types of cases, such as drug trafficking, and was the trial judge in the case against the international drug trafficker Fernandinho Beira-Mar.

Sergio Moro found inspiration in other judges who made their mark in recent times, such as Giovanni Falcone – the Italian judge who ran the huge mafia trial in the 1980s was one of the role models that Moro studied the most, for various reasons. One reason was Falcone's capacity to keep firm control over such a large trial. Another was his ability to get the support of public opinion, the best vaccine against undue political influences. But there was another side to Falcone that Moro admired: after the trial was successful and the Mafia's operatives jailed, Falcone threw himself into supporting draft legislation to help prevent it happening again in future. Just like Falcone, Moro was convinced that the fight against organised crime required constant improvement in judicial procedures. In Italy, this meant legislation granting concessions to those who confessed their crimes and cooperated with investigations. These had been just as important in Italy as they would be in Operation Car Wash. Moro frequently recommended Falcone's book *Cose di cosa nostra* to his friends and people working for him.

Moro also looked to American law for inspiration. In the United States, most legal disputes end in a settlement between the parties, frequently involving an admission of guilt by one side. If this happened in Brazil, the courts would not be so bogged down with cases. Sergio Moro's academic training included significant aspects of American common law; Brazil's legal system is rooted in the continental European civil law tradition, which is very different. A judge he much admires is Earl Warren, who led the United States Supreme Court when it was ending racial segregation in education. At the beginning of his career, Warren, like Moro, frequently saw his controversial decisions confirmed by the higher courts. And Moro, like Warren, thought that other judicial means could be explored, such as settlements.

The American experience also served to show the proper use of a relatively new instrument in Brazil: plea bargains. These were at the epicentre of Operation Car Wash and central to its success. But they have been harshly criticised by well-known and respected lawyers, who reacted sharply to Moro's methods and style.

When Operation Car Wash began and highly paid defence lawyers from São Paulo landed in Curitiba promising to take the case all the way to the Supreme Court, local lawyers commented that they clearly didn't know Sergio Moro. However, the leading lawyers still had a lot of influence and the technical and legal skills to bring down Operation Car Wash. The war was far from over. The investigators would make important advances in the following weeks, but the defence teams promised a tough fight in the courts.

THE ART OF LAUNDERING MONEY

At the Federal Police headquarters, phase ten of the operation, code-named 'What country is this?' was under way. The name was a reference to something Renato Duque, Petrobras's former director of services, had said to his lawyer on being arrested and taken to Curitiba for the first time, in November 2014. Duque was about to be arrested again: federal prosecutors had discovered that Duque had moved €20 million from secret Swiss accounts to a bank in Monaco. To the prosecutors, it looked like he was laundering money; in fact, it was an attempt to escape investigation by ensuring that the money was not discovered, but it didn't work out. So once more, the police cars rolled up at the entrance to his apartment building in Barra da Tijuca, a smart suburb of Rio de Janeiro.

Duque's arrest warrant referred to four addresses, but the police already knew their target. They went straight to his home. As was their custom, they arrived at sunrise. Duque owned the penthouse and had bought two other apartments in the building for his children. He had given the value of the property as R\$1.2 million on his tax declaration.

The police team was made up of a detective, two police officers and a notary. They did not expect to make any major discoveries, since Duque had already been arrested during phase seven and had probably already got rid of any incriminating evidence. They were mistaken. The first surprise came when they reached the entrance hall. There was a fortune hanging on the walls: works by well-known Brazilian and international artists, such as Joan Miró, Alberto Guignard, Chagal, Djanira, Carlos Scliar, Siron Franco, Antônio Poteiro and Heitor dos Prazeres. There were landscapes, still lifes, a landscape of Sugarloaf Mountain, abstract paintings, you name it. In all, the police counted twenty-four works of art in the main living room alone, which also contained a grand piano. And that was before they even began searching the rest of the house. There were paintings on the walls of almost every room, corridor and staircase, even in the wardrobes. Two paintings hung in one of the corridors. Another corridor leading to the bedrooms had three more. In Duque's study there were fifteen. There were six in his eldest daughter's bedroom and another in the wardrobe. In Duque's own bedroom, six more. There were another six on the staircase leading to the second floor of the penthouse apartment. In the corridor leading from the staircase, a further six. The police found yet more paintings in the guest bedroom, the children's room, in two wardrobes, the gym, the TV room and on another staircase leading back down to the main living room. But the room with the most paintings was the games room, embellished by no fewer than thirty-seven works of art hanging on the walls.

The police took their time photographing each item and cataloguing them in their report. They counted 131 paintings in Duque's apartment in total. They needed to obtain authorisation from Sergio Moro to include high-value items in the search warrant. Even so, they had no means of removing everything. They left the paintings in the custody of Duque's wife and returned to collect them the following day, with the assistance of staff from the Oscar Niemeyer Museum in Curitiba and specialised transportation equipment. It was the largest seizure of works of art under Operation Car Wash.

And there was a further surprise in store for the police, thanks to the sharp wits of a young officer called Prado. He was the least experienced among them, but he was the one who discovered something that no one had spotted during the previous police visit: a secret room hidden behind a wardrobe. 'He had to pull everything out of the wardrobe in order to open it,' said one of the officers leading the operation. Behind the wardrobe was a door operated by remote control, which led to a secret room with its own lighting and ventilation. There they found documents such as the certificates of authenticity for the paintings, and family jewellery such as pearl necklaces and earrings. Everything was seized. In the secret room, the police also found works of art, a computer, three USB memory sticks, a CD-ROM and a memory card, as well as a collection of Mont Blanc pens and cufflinks. In one suitcase, Duque had sixteen Mont Blanc pens, half of them black and gold, the other half black and silver, one of which was engraved with his name. On a small table, the police found a silver Louis Vuitton watch. The jewellery, watch and pens were put in a plastic box and kept in a safe at a branch of CaixaBank.

According to the Federal Police, the works of art had been purchased by Duque in order to launder money, and so they were taken, under police escort, to the Oscar Niemeyer Museum, which had the task of gathering, cataloguing and displaying the artistic assets seized by Operation Car Wash. By September 2015, the Federal Police had seized 268 works of art from those being investigated. Buying works of art, a common ploy in organised crime, was frequently used by suspects in Operation Car Wash in order to launder the proceeds of kickbacks, according to the investigators, But no one surpassed Renato Duque. When the artworks found at his house were joined by those from various art studios in Rio, the police found 153 pieces belonging to him. 'The number of works of art surprised us. If they were genuine, we were dealing with a large amount of money,' said detective Igor Romário de Paula.

The Oscar Niemeyer Museum was chosen as safe depository for the works of art because it follows international museum standards and had sufficient space to store the items safely. The museum always follows the same procedure when it receives works of art. On arrival, they are photographed, identified, catalogued and put through a quarantine process to check whether they contain any fungus or termites that could damage other items in storage. After this period, they are cleaned and stored in the museum's vaults at a constant temperature and humidity. Assessing the authenticity and value of the pieces is done by four experts from the Federal Police along with specialists from two universities, one in São Paulo and the other in Minas Gerais. They analyse any certificates of authenticity seized with the works of art and get in touch with the institutes or families of the artists. The total value of Operation Car Wash's art haul has not been divulged by the Federal Police. According to specialists, most of the pieces are of relatively low value. Some, however, are not: *Landscape of Sabará* by Alberto da Veiga Guignard, was recently auctioned for US$380,000. While it has custody of the works, the museum has been authorised to display them to the public. 'I think it's very interesting, I didn't know it was an exhibition of seized paintings. It's a good way to give some of what they stole back to society,' commented one of the first visitors to see the museum's exhibition.

Renato Duque had been out of jail for just over three months. He was released on 6 December 2014 and arrested again on 16 March 2015, this time by federal prosecutors following their tip-off from the Swiss authorities about the transfer of money to Monaco. Some of that had happened in 2014, as Operation Car Wash was already beginning to encircle him. Duque also sent large amounts of money to accounts in Hong Kong, which were duly frozen on behalf of the Monaco authorities. In addition to the financial dealings in Europe and Asia, the evidence provided by Pedro Barusco as part of his plea bargain at the end of 2014 also weighed heavily on Duque. By that time, Barusco's evidence was already considered some of the most interesting in the case.

'He speaks very naturally, and he's funny. He told us everything about Duque,' said one of the prosecutors. Barusco even spoke of how he administered a large amount of money for Duque, because the former director wasn't able to handle all his own kickbacks. 'That, in fact, became a problem for Duque, because he wasn't able to absorb it. It was a lot of money and the guy had no way of hiding all of it,' observed one of the detectives.

THE FIRST POLITICIANS IN JAIL

Operation Car Wash had accelerated and was now going after politicians. On the morning of 10 April 2015, the ex-congressman André Vargas was arrested as part of phase eleven, codenamed 'The Beginning'. The name was a reference to Vargas being the first politician whose name came up in the scandal, when he was still the all-powerful deputy speaker of the Chamber of Deputies. He frequently presided over legislative sessions and had power and influence within Congress – a lot of power. He felt invincible. So much so that he went as far as provoking the president of the Supreme Court, Joaquim Barbosa, during Congress's opening ceremony at the beginning of the legislative year, mimicking the clenched fist gesture given by those found guilty by Barbosa in the Big Monthly corruption scandal. That was at the peak of André Vargas's power.

However, the tide had turned for the congressman. An article on 1 April 2014 by Andréia Sadi in the *Folha de S.Paulo* reported that on 3 January that year, André Vargas and his family had boarded a luxury Learjet 45 belonging to the air taxi firm Elite Aviation, on a dream holiday. They had taken off from Londrina, Paraná, to João Pessoa, capital of the northern state of Paraíba. Everything had been paid for by Youssef. The revelation of the gift – which cost Youssef R$105,000 – was the beginning of Vargas's downfall. At first he tried to deny it, then said that he had paid for the fuel and asked the newspaper for more time to gather supporting documents, but he had nothing to show them. He ended by asking the journalist how devastating the report would be, and made only one request: 'Please leave my family out of it.'

The night before the trip, the congressman had exchanged twenty text messages with Alberto Youssef about the flight, the plane, the hangar, the pilot's contact details, 'Have a good trip', 'Have a great holiday', and so on. The connection between them was much more intense than even those messages showed. According to records held by the Federal Police, Vargas and Youssef exchanged 270 text messages between September 2013 and March 2014. The last was sent five days before Youssef was arrested. There was no way of denying that they were connected. In his defence at the congressional hearing to remove him from office, André Vargas said he had met Youssef twenty years before and now realised it had been unwise to use the private jet. But he hadn't been very smart. Youssef, who was also from Londrina, had even financed Vargas's election campaign in the city.

Within a period of less than a month, Vargas lost all the power he had ever held. First, he stepped down 'temporarily' as deputy speaker; then he was suspended from Congress; a few days later, he resigned from the Workers' Party, in order to avoid being expelled. He had been in the Workers' Party for twenty-four years, but by the end of April 2014, he was merely a suspended congressman, without a party, facing the prospect of being expelled from Congress entirely. No one wanted to be seen near him; he simply disappeared. The Workers' Party attempted to prevent him from being expelled and worked to delay voting in the various committees investigating the matter, but the process reached the plenary session of the Chamber in time to be voted on before the end of the year. On the afternoon of 10 December 2014, André Vargas was expelled from Congress by an overwhelming vote of 359 in favour, one against and six abstentions. The only vote against his expulsion for breach of parliamentary standards was Congressman José Airton Cirilo (Zé Airton) of the Workers' Party. A few months later, Vargas was arrested and taken to Curitiba to answer charges under Operation Car Wash.

Vargas was found at his large home in the Alphaville Condominium in Londrina. Valued by the courts at R\$2 million, it was listed on the declaration of assets of his wife, Edilaira Soares, at a value of R\$500,000. The problem was that the former owner of the property had declared to the tax authorities that he had sold the house for R\$980,000. According to the police, it was a clumsy attempt to launder money, for which Vargas and his wife were duly charged (although she was later acquitted). Vargas said he was the victim of injustice, claiming that his crimes were nothing in comparison to those of others embroiled in the scandal, but he was quickly abandoned by his party at the first sign of trouble.

Another investigation was launched into Vargas's involvement at the ministry of health in ensuring that the firm Labogen, owned by a former partner of Youssef's, was awarded the contract to produce a certain type of medication. Vargas was exposed by messages he had exchanged with Youssef, and also by information provided by erstwhile participants in the scheme. In his evidence to the police, the owner of Labogen, Leonardo Meirelles, confirmed that Vargas had intervened on behalf of his firm. Youssef's own statements detail a meeting in 2013 at Vargas's apartment in Brasília, attended by Meirelles and the minister of health, Alexandre Padilha, among others. Vargas introduced Labogen to Padilha, who promised to pass on the firm's name to one of the coordinators at the ministry of health. In messages intercepted by police, Vargas and Youssef discussed Labogen being awarded the contract as something that could pay them both dividends. 'We are stronger now,' wrote Vargas. 'Mate, I'm working, don't worry. Trust me. You'll see how much this is worth. Your financial independence. And ours as well, of course,' replied Youssef, ending the conversation with a laugh: 'Hahahaha.'

Youssef spoke about André Vargas's help with the Labogen case at a hearing a few days after Vargas's arrest. On 13 April 2015, more than a year after his own arrest, Youssef was once again face to face with Sergio Moro. As usual, the exchange between the two of them was revealing. On one side, Moro's professional polish; on the other side, Alberto Youssef's ability for play-acting.

'This particular case, Mr Youssef, is limited to charges of entering into fraudulent foreign exchange contracts by the firms Bosred, HMAR, Labogen, Piroquímica and RMV, and the transfer of these amounts to GFD. What do you have to say regarding these events?'

'Well, first of all, I want to say I recognise my mistakes.'

Youssef went on to explain how he would issue invoices to the contractors, receive payment and 'with this money in cash, pay whoever was needed, in this case Paulo Roberto Costa and the Progressive Party politicians'. Youssef continued by naming the currency traders he used and the contractors who provided the money: 'I received various payments from OAS.'

At a certain point, Youssef said, in his defence, that he had used some of the money to invest in Brazil. 'I always had my legitimate activity, which was to run a business, provide jobs, pay taxes, and I always did that. I could have kept the money I made from Banestado and stayed at home. But no, I preferred to invest that money in the market and run the risks that any businessman in this country runs when he set up a business, provides jobs and pays taxes.'

It almost seemed a joke for Youssef to be sitting there with a straight face saying that he could have 'kept the money I made from Banestado' in front of the very same judge who had tried the case. It was laughable, but Moro remained serious.

'That may be so, Mr Youssef, but you also became involved in these events at Petrobras as well.'

'Unfortunately yes, Your Honour. Unfortunately.'

'From what I understand, you ceased your activities as a foreign currency dealer?'

'Yes, I did.'

'But you got involved in this Petrobras business?'

'Yes, I got involved in the Petrobras business. As I said, unfortunately.'

In his deposition, Youssef talked at one point about having rented an apartment from GFD Investimentos and emphasised that he paid the rent regularly. Without losing his cool, the judge reminded Youssef that he himself was the owner of GFD. When Moro said he had no more questions, Youssef asked if he could add something. 'Actually, I would like to point out that I am cooperating of my own free and spontaneous will. My family is paying the price for this. I am paying the price for this;

I've already been in prison for a year and twenty days. I don't know how much longer it will go on for. What I want to say is that in reality, I was only a small cog in this machine and the whole operation was put together in order to get people elected. That's all.'

Youssef then returned to the main subject of the hearing and told prosecutors that he was trying to help Leonardo Meirelles restructure his company, Labogen, which was a good business, but badly run. 'So I asked André Vargas for help, since he was a federal congressman and deputy speaker of the Chamber. I asked him to help us with the ministry of health, to open doors for us. Just to open doors. Because it isn't easy to take a company that's been in the doldrums for several years and just knock on the door at the ministry of health and get someone to listen to you.'

Later on, his own lawyer asked in what way André Vargas had intervened on Labogen's behalf at the ministry of health. Youssef replied, 'Simply opening doors. Unfortunately, these days, if you don't lobby, no supplier gets a look in with any part of the public sector. Sadly, that's how this country works.'

Interfering at the ministry of health in favour of Labogen was only one of the accusations against Vargas. He was also investigated for allegedly controlling a scheme to divert advertising money from the ministry of health and Caixa Econômica Federal, a large state-owned bank. Borghi/Lowe, the advertising agency used by both organisations, subcontracted work to independent production companies and advised them to pay a bonus of 10 per cent of their commissions to two front companies run by Vargas: LSI Solução em Serviços Empresariais and Limiar Consultoria e Assessoria em Comunicação. The first was in Vargas's own name and the other belonged to his brother, Leon Vargas. The two firms did not provide any services, but between December 2011 and March 2014 received a total of R$3.1 million from 193 businesses, including Borghi/Lowe, who paid R$1.1 million to Vargas through this illegal scheme. Borghi/Lowe received R$1 billion from the ministry of health and Caixa Econômica Federal between 2008 and 2015.

In his decision ordering Vargas's arrest, Moro said that in addition to the payment to the two Vargas front companies, the bank Caixa had also paid around R$50 million to IT7 Sistemas, a genuine firm owned by Leon Vargas. The contract was later suspended, although IT7 was operating legally in Curitiba. Leon Vargas was also arrested but was released after five days. In his judgment, Moro reiterated the need to deepen the investigations, since there was evidence that in December 2013 Youssef had assisted with the payment of R$2.3 million in cash to Leon Vargas. On being arrested in Londrina, André Vargas repeated the raised arm and clenched fist gesture he had made during Joaquim Barbosa's visit to the Chamber of Deputies in February 2014.

On the same day as Vargas's arrest, the former congressmen Luiz Argôlo and Pedro Corrêa also found themselves in jail on charges of money laundering and corruption. The accusation against Pedro Corrêa, who had previously been found guilty in the Big Monthly corruption trial, was that he had received R$40 million directly from Alberto Youssef, both for his own benefit and to distribute to other politicians in the Progressive Party. The investigation also discovered a strange increase in Corrêa's wealth, which seemed incompatible with his declared income. The investigators discovered that the congressman was employing congressional assistants during both his own period in office and that of his daughter Aline Corrêa, herself a congresswoman, and then forcing the assistants to transfer part of their congressional salaries to him. Corrêa used this money to pay his credit card bills and for airline tickets, among other things.

As for Argôlo, he was accused of being Youssef's associate in running several front companies and of issuing fraudulent invoices. According to the investigators, he was the politician closest to Youssef. He would drop by Youssef's office in São Paulo to pick up monthly payments in cash, and even used his congressional travel allowance to make these trips. Argôlo and his associates were involved in the illegal movement of R$1.6 million. He was hauled in front of the Chamber of Deputies' ethics committee, but his term of office came to an end before he could be expelled. In his defence, he said that he had nothing to do with the siphoning of money from Petrobras. But it was difficult to deny. In a period of a few months, Youssef and Argôlo had exchanged 1,411 text messages on a variety of subjects. The two discussed financial transactions, deliveries of cash and deposits with third parties named by the congressman. Youssef even gave a plane to his friend, according to Meire Poza, Youssef's accountant. The investigations revealed that the two of them were very close. Some of the messages caught the attention of both police and the public. In one of them Corrêa even wrote to Youssef: 'Love you, man.'

The name Luiz Argôlo, or the initials LA, appeared scribbled in the group's accounts. His nickname was Baby Johnson and so he also appeared as 'BJonson' or 'Band Jonson', the 'Band' being an abbreviation of bandit. Rafael Angulo Lopez, who helped Youssef with keeping the accounts and delivering the dirty money, recounted that one day his boss said, 'Write down the bandit's money there,' so he assumed it was fine to refer to politicians like this in the documents he showed Youssef.

Lopez also said that Argôlo was one of the politicians who appeared most frequently at Youssef's office to pick up money. Lopez would often count out wads of banknotes for the congressman, who brought bags and suitcases that he often filled to overflowing, such was the sheer volume of cash. He also made deliveries to the congressman's apartment in a smart neighbourhood of Brasília, paid for at the public's expense.

Lopez once took R$250,000 all the way from São Paulo to Bahia for Argôlo. He boarded a commercial flight with R$200,000 hidden in football socks he was wearing under his trousers, and R$50,000 more in his jacket and trouser pockets. He passed undetected through the airport X-ray machines, but not without breaking into a cold sweat. It was a big risk to carry so much money at once, but he had no choice.

There was one occasion, however, when Lopez refused to do the job. Youssef called him early one Saturday morning, saying that Luiz Argôlo was outside his office, desperate for money. Lopez went to the office but there was no one there; Argôlo arrived shortly after and said he needed R$600,000. Lopez called his boss, worried because when he had left the office the night before, there hadn't been as much as that in the safe, but Youssef assured him he would find the amount needed. He was right. Someone had been to the office during the night and restocked the safe. Lopez counted the money and gave it to Argôlo, but the congressman wanted Lopez to take it to the airport at São José dos Campos, about eighty kilometres out of town, where he would catch a private jet. Lopez thought this was too much: he wasn't prepared to run the risk of driving along the notorious Dutra highway with such a large amount of money, especially in his own car. Youssef had to call a friend's driver, who took two hours to reach the office. The congressman was not at all happy about having to wait. As soon as the driver appeared, Argôlo left with all the money. Lopez had gained one small victory.

At the police jail in Curitiba, the custody officer put André Vargas, Luiz Argôlo and Pedro Corrêa in the same cell, which was quickly nicknamed 'Mini-Congress'. The three politicians spent their time chatting and playing games of rummy or patience. 'Argôlo always lost, I always won and André always came second. Or there was a draw,' joked Pedro Corrêa, some time later.

THE TREASURER'S ARREST

On 15 April, the police initiated phase twelve of Operation Car Wash, which saw the arrest of João Vaccari Neto, treasurer of the Workers' Party. He was accused of using a printing company to raise money illegally for election campaigns, through contractors working for Petrobras. As well as arresting him at his home in São Paulo on the orders of Sergio Moro, the police officers also carried out arrest warrants against his wife, Giselda Rousie de Lima, and his daughter, Nayara de Lima Vaccari, both of whom were under investigation for suspicious financial activity. A warrant was also issued for João Vaccari's sister-in-law, Marice Corrêa de Lima, but could not be carried out because she was attending a trade union conference in Panama. On her return five days later, she handed herself in to the police in Curitiba and was released after five days.

Phase twelve's objective was to dig deeper into the payment of kickbacks at Petrobras's Services Division. According to the four informants, Alberto Youssef, Paulo Roberto Costa, Pedro Barusco and Eduardo Leite, Vaccari was responsible for channelling money from the fraudulent tendering process at Petrobras to the Workers' Party. Vaccari denied receiving money illegally, but the word of the four informants formed part of the federal prosecutors' justification for seeking his arrest. In his decision on issuing the warrant, Moro emphasised that Vaccari's 'power and political influence' was illustrated 'by the fact that he has not been suspended from his post before now, and there are reports that there have been requests of this nature by some members of his party'.

One of the suspicions about Vaccari was that he had sought kickbacks in the form of legal campaign donations. The notion was supported by the evidence of one such donor, Augusto Ribeiro de Mendonça Neto. To Sergio Moro, it appeared that R$4.2 million 'was transferred at the request of Renato Duque through João Vaccari Neto between 23/10/2008 and 08/03/2012, in the form of election donations registered with the Workers' Party. The donations were made through three companies controlled by Augusto Mendonça: PEM, Projetec and SOG.' The theory was corroborated by another informant, Eduardo Leite, the former director of Camargo Corrêa. According to him, in 2010 Vaccari requested that some delayed payments relating to the kickback scheme should be made in the form of an official donation to the Workers' Party.

As well as the donations, Augusto Mendonça informed the investigators that he had made payments to Vaccari via a printing company. In the words of Moro's ruling: 'At the request of João Vaccari Neto, he had also made payments for services that were all or partially faked, to Editora Gráfica Atitude. Federal prosecutors stated that payments totalling R$1,501,600 between 29/06/2010 and 19/08/2013 had been identified in the bank statements of Tipuana and Projetec, two companies controlled by Augusto Mendonça, with monthly transfers varying between R$93,850 and R$187,700.' According to federal prosecutors, there were indications of connections between the printing company Gráfica Attitude and the Workers' Party which seemed to 'explain João Vaccari's request' for payments to the company.

In their request for the arrests of Vaccari and his relatives, federal prosecutors cited their seizure of a diagram in which Alberto Youssef noted two deliveries of cash to an address in São Paulo. 'The Federal Police have confirmed that the above-mentioned address, Apartment 22, 157 Rua Penaforte Mendes, is the home of Marice Corrêa de Lima, who is the sister of Giselda Rousie de Lima, João Vaccari Neto's wife,' read the judge's ruling. This delivery of cash, Moro went on to say, took place 'at the request of OAS, one of the construction companies involved in the criminal scheme at Petrobras'.

In the case of Vaccari's sister-in-law, Marice Corrêa de Lima, the investigators were suspicious that she had purchased two apartments without the necessary financial means. 'When her bank statements were disclosed, it was impossible to identify any inward credit of R$240,000, corresponding to the amount that she claimed to have received as severance pay, voluntary redundancy, compensation for an accident at work or other statutory entitlements. The closest thing to this were monthly receipts between March and November 2011 from the law firm Luis E. G. S/C, which total R$200,000, but without any clarification as to the nature or reason for such payments,' wrote Moro. The law firm mentioned is that of another former Workers' Party congressman, the lawyer Luiz Eduardo Greenhalgh.

As for the treasurer's wife, Giselda, she came to the investigators' attention after her 2008 tax declaration referred to the purchase of an apartment in São Paulo for R$500,000. 'Her bank statements revealed that on 19/11/2008 Giselda received R$400,000 from CRA Comércio de Produtos Agropecuários. On 27/11/2008, R$300,000 left her account in the form of a cheque made out to Fernando Rodrigues Liberado, the vendor of the apartment. The transaction is surprising in that CRA belongs to Carlos Alberto Pereira da Costa, an employee of Albert Youssef,' wrote Moro. Disclosure of the bank statements of Vaccari's daughter Nayara showed that the increase in her wealth derived from gifts of R$131,000 from her father, R$280,000 from her mother and R$345,000 from her aunt. Sergio Moro addressed this in his ruling:

This information resulting from the disclosure of João Vaccari Neto, Marice Corrêa de Lima, Giselda de Lima and Nayara de Lima's banking and tax records requires further investigation, since it is not yet conclusive. Nevertheless, the prosecutors are correct in stating that they show signs of undue enrichment on the part of João Vaccari Neto's relatives, in particular relating to persons and entities involved in the criminal scheme at Petrobras, such as Carlos Alberto Pereira da Costa and OAS.

There is also documentary evidence of a payment of at least R$1,501,600 through companies controlled by Augusto Mendonça to Editora Gráfica Atitude at the request of João Vaccari Neto as a form of off-balance-sheet donation. In relation to these payments to Editora Gráfica Atitude, it seems to me difficult to envisage a lack of deceit by those involved, since they consist not of registered electoral donations, but of payments made at the request of João

Vaccari Neto entirely or partially for fictious services provided by third parties [...] On the other hand, there is independent evidence from the interception of telephone calls of at least one delivery of a large amount of money in cash by Alberto Youssef to Marice Corrêa de Lima, João Vaccari Neto's sister-in-law, at the request of OAS, a construction firm involved in the criminal scheme at Petrobras.

Moro went on to reject accusations of partisanship: 'This is not an arrest warrant against the political grouping he belongs to. Corruption does not have party colours. It is not the monopoly of any particular party or government,' wrote Moro. 'The seriousness of João Vaccari Neto's conduct is even more marked, since the use of funds from a criminal source to finance political parties compromises the integrity of the political system and the proper functioning of democracy. The world of crime must not be allowed to contaminate the party political system,' the judge continued, highlighting the fact that, until the date of his arrest, Vaccari remained in the highly influential and powerful position of treasurer of the Workers' Party. For the judge, it was an indication that he was still in a position to commit crimes and manipulate witnesses. A few days later, Vaccari resigned as treasurer. He remained in custody.

By that point, Operation Car Wash was over a year old and beginning to take on the shape and scale Sergio Moro had envisaged. There were dozens of separate legal proceedings forming part of an enormous and complex investigation into the gigantic corruption scheme. But the defence lawyers were far from beaten. They would carry on battling through the courts to limit the scope of the operation. In fact, they were about to win one of their most important victories.

CONSTRUCTION BOSSES RELEASED

On 28 April 2015, the Supreme Court ruled that the construction company executives held on remand since November 2014 should be released under house arrest. The judges held that remand could not be used as a form of sentence without trial, and that they had already spent a lengthy period in jail. The decision was taken following an application from the defence lawyers of UTC chairman Ricardo Pessoa, and then extended to the other executives. In a submission that was widely praised by his colleagues, the lawyer Alberto Zacharias Toron argued that his client, who had been accused of coordinating the cartel bidding for Petrobras contracts, did not represent a risk to the investigation, since UTC was now barred from tendering for Petrobras contracts, and federal prosecutors had already collected all their evidence.

According to Toron's analysis, Pessoa's detention on remand meant that he was effectively serving a sentence that had not yet been imposed: 'Holding on remand due to flight risk cannot be based on the suspect's financial means. On the contrary, doing so would give rise to a form of procedural detention based on social class.' The lawyer argued that his client was in his seventies, 'had a clean past and close family and professional connections, and had already made himself available to the police and judicial authorities some two months prior to being arrested'. Toron recalled that Pessoa had been arrested at home and assured the court that he presented no risk to society, since he was no longer in charge of UTC, which in any case was prohibited from providing services to Petrobras.

Justice Zavascki considered detention on remand an 'extreme measure' and ordered that it be replaced with other precautionary measures, such as restrictions on an individual's business activities, house curfew, court appearances every two weeks, prohibition on leaving the country and the use of electronic tagging.

As a result of his decision, José Aldemário Pinheiro Filho (the chairman of OAS) and three of his executives, José Ricardo Nogueira Breghirolli, Agenor Franklin and Mateus Coutinho de Sá Oliveira, were released. The investigators had hoped that Pinheiro would become an informant and tell them whether he had helped to renovate the house in Atibaia a couple of hours from São Paulo, visited by former president Lula da Silva and, if so, how he had done it. They also wanted to get some clarification about the Edifício Solaris building works at Praia das Astúrias, Guarujá, on the coast of São Paulo state, where Lula da Silva's wife had admitted buying a share in an apartment. The works being carried out in this building by the Cooperativa Habitacional dos Bancários de São Paulo (Bancoop) had been paralysed following financial problems, until OAS stepped in and completed them.

In addition to the OAS executives, Sérgio Mendes (of Mendes Júnior), Gerson Almada (Engevix), Erton Medeiros Fonseca (Galvão Engenharia) and João Ricardo Auler (Camargo Corrêa) were also released. All of them handed over their passports to the judicial authorities in Paraná. They were ordered to stay at home at all times, and could only leave their residences to appear at hearings determined by Sergio Moro.

Upon granting habeas corpus to the executives, the Supreme Court judges held that, notwithstanding the gravity of the offences alleged, remand could not be applied as a sentence without trial. This argument reinvigorated the defence lawyers.

Justice Cármen Lúcia, however, held that Ricardo Pessoa, chairman of UTC, should remain in prison until all the evidence from witnesses had been heard by the court in Curitiba. She was of the view that simply standing aside voluntarily from management of the company was no guarantee that further offences would not be committed. Federal prosecutors requested that Pessoa remain in jail, insisting that the criminal organisation operating within Petrobras had not yet been completely dismantled and that Pessoa had a leading role in the scheme. The majority of Supreme Court judges did not agree with this view.

The executives, who by that time were being held at a prison hospital unit run by the Paraná state prison system, left their cells and were taken to the federal court building in Curitiba. They were fitted with electronic tags before going home. Each of them signed a copy of the instructions for using the equipment. They were all obliged to remain tagged twenty-four hours a day. They could not remove them even to sleep or shower. Nor could they allow anyone else to open or damage them. It was their responsibility to keep the battery charged and not leave the designated area, usually their home. The monitoring would be done at a distance, from a room in Curitiba.

Many people assumed that once they went home the businessmen would keep quiet. Upon leaving jail, however, Ricardo Pessoa decided to do a deal. He spoke to prosecutors in Brasília between 25 and 29 May; the transcript of his interview was eighty pages long. The first major boss to cooperate with the authorities, Pessoa provided documentary evidence of cash payments to three parties: the Progressive Party, the Workers' Party and the PMDB. In Lula da Silva's 2006 presidential campaign, UTC had officially donated R$1.2 million, and a further R$2.6 million secretly. Pessoa told investigators that Vaccari would refer to kickbacks as 'pixuleco', a term meaning 'dirty money' that gained nationwide notoriety and was later used as the name of an inflatable dummy of Lula da Silva dressed as a prisoner, which was carried by protestors at street demonstrations.

The businessman also gave statements about Dilma Rousseff's 2014 presidential campaign. He said that Edinho Silva, the communications director in the Rousseff government who had also been treasurer of her re-election campaign, had asked him for R$20 million. Pessoa paid a total of R$£7.5 million in two instalments, the first of R$5 million and the second of R$2.5 million. He provided the prosecutors with a diagram entitled 'Slush Fund Payments to PT', in which he listed the names of Workers' Party politicians who had received illegal payments in 2010 and 2014.

The prosecutors were beginning to deepen their investigations into campaign donations, which they said was a way of concealing the payment of ill-gotten gains to political parties and thereby ensuring the continuity of the overall scheme. It was another form of money laundering. They had a lot of work to do to prove this, and their new informant would be critical to their success. The negotiations over his collaboration, however, were very tough and lasted several weeks, but finally, facing the possibility of a heavy sentence, the businessman capitulated.

Ricardo Pessoa signed the plea bargain agreement in front of the prosecutor general, Janot, at the large conference table in his office in Brasília. He was happy, reckoning he had got a good deal with significant benefits. The prosecutors were also satisfied – having the cooperation of the cartel's coordinator would be very important. As Rodrigo Janot reached over to pick up the signed agreement, Pessoa asked an unexpected question.

'I was always very curious to know what this building was like, in terms of construction. Oscar Niemeyer was the architect, wasn't he?' asked the owner of one of the largest construction companies in the country.

'We have a scale model in the other building. I can take you over there to see how it's built, structurally,' replied one of the prosecutors, Douglas Fischer.

Since Pessoa couldn't be left to wander around because of the risk of him being seen, Douglas took him to a private room, crossing the mirrored external walkway that linked Building A with Building B. Looking at the scale model and comparing it to what he saw through the window, the construction boss began to understand the way in which the building, with its two circular drums built on raised columns at ground level, had been constructed.

'Ah yes, I can see what he did,' commented the construction boss.

The two of them remained chatting for ten minutes. On their return to the other building, a journalist saw Ricardo Pessoa passing through the glass walkway and took a photo, which appeared on the evening news that night. It confirmed that Pessoa had done a deal. As a result of that photograph, all further meetings with him took place in other buildings, so as to avoid leaks.

At the same time, invigorated by the Supreme Court's decision to allow the businessmen to return home, the defence lawyers intensified their attacks and became even sharper in their criticism of Sergio Moro. Some of them said that he was a 'dictator' for ordering the executives' imprisonment before they had been found guilty. Others claimed he was a 'torturer' for having them held on remand for such a long period that they would end up doing a deal.

Moro wrote an article published in a São Paulo newspaper, in conjunction with Antônio César Bochenek, president of the Association of Federal Judges of Brazil, defending the principle of keeping in prison defendants who had been found guilty at first instance, irrespective of any appeals that might be made to the higher courts. At present, defendants who do not represent a risk to society have the right to pursue their appeals at liberty. If Moro's idea were to succeed, this would no longer be possible. The article caused quite a stir in legal circles.

'The constitution provides that no one shall be considered guilty until the judgment has become final,' said Thiago Bottino, professor at the Getúlio Vargas Foundation. 'The presumption of innocence is a cornerstone of the constitution,' he added. The Supreme Court would change this interpretation in February 2016. Pierpaolo Bottini, a professor at the University of São Paulo who also represented defendants in Operation Car Wash, said that Moro's proposal would definitively eliminate the presumption of innocence: 'Moro prefers an innocent person in jail to a guilty one going free.'

Another lawyer for one of the Operation Car Wash prisoners, José Luís de Oliveira Lima, said that Sergio Moro assumed everyone was guilty: 'All the prisoners are already convicted, independently of whatever arguments their defence lawyers may present.' Fábio Tofic Simantob, another defence lawyer, complained that Moro was creating the climate of a 'witch hunt', by proposing legislation that would increase the powers of judges in the lower courts.

In this criticism, one voice was always present: Odebrecht's. Whether through its lawyers or in interviews with the press, Brazil's largest construction company trenchantly criticised both the judge and the investigation. One of the aspects it attacked were the plea bargains agreed by federal prosecutors. Lawyers for one of the company's executives forwarded an application to the Supreme Court stating that before verifying the veracity of the informants' statements, federal prosecutors had 'rushed to sign cooperation agreements that, as if by magic, would allow their signatories to avoid detention entirely or at least transform it into house arrest'. Public arguments about Operation Car Wash would continue for weeks, but what the lawyers did not know was the judiciary's next step: the boss of the country's largest construction company was about to be arrested.

Chapter 7

STORMING THE CITADEL

19 June 2015

ODEBRECHT IN THE SIGHTS OF THE FEDERAL POLICE

At around 6.45 a.m., a taxi turned into Rua Lemos Monteiro in São Paulo, where the Odebrecht building is located. Inside the cab was an employee who couldn't sleep and had decided to go to work early. It was drizzling and a mist hung around the building that housed the global headquarters of Brazil's largest construction firm and second largest private-sector company. Founded in Bahia in 1944, the company was now run by the third generation of the Odebrecht family. Just three days earlier, the company's chairman, Marcelo Odebrecht, had told Brazil's biggest business newspaper that he was very 'irritated' to find himself 'in the line of fire of a political shooting match'. And he reminded readers that the company was responsible for tens of thousands of jobs.

There was no traffic at that time in the morning. The taxi pulled up in front of the building and, in an atmosphere almost like a film noir, it finally dawned on the employee that something was seriously amiss. Four enormous jeeps and other police vehicles were pulled up outside the building, but not blocking anyone from going in through the main entrance or into the car park. Inside the building, anyone could go to their offices except those on the seventh floor (where the computer servers were located), the eleventh (the Latin America department) or the fifteenth and sixteenth (senior management). These were where the Federal Police had been working since dawn broke that Friday, which would be known as the day when, as journalist Elio Gaspari put it, Operation Car Wash reached the very top floor. Silence reigned throughout the offices and corridors of the building. Some employees could not do their work because of the police searches and were advised to go home. Those who stayed at work tried to speak to their bosses to find out what was going on. Senior management could not be found. They were either in meetings or their whereabouts were unknown. According to the employee who had arrived by taxi, 'All the services in the building had started to collapse. The email stopped, cut off by police searches. The telephones weren't working properly. The restaurant was closed. The washrooms were only half-cleaned. The chain of command had completely broken down. Without reliable communication and with managers no doubt afraid to use their mobile phones, the company was descending into chaos. People were receiving orders without being sure exactly whom they had come from or why they had been given.'

At each new order, employees rushed around the building looking for the senior manager responsible. 'It was an incredible scene. All the floors housing most of the Odebrecht companies, as well as the group's holding company, were practically empty. Everyone in there, if they weren't police or prosecutors, was from the legal or public relations department,' recounted the employee.

Despite giving orders that no one was to enter the four floors being subjected to search and seizure, the police had forgotten to block them off. That was how one employee trying to find his boss ended up on the fifteenth floor, where the chairman's office was located. No police officer stopped him. The officers had already been through Marcelo Odebrecht's office. It wasn't ransacked, but there were indications that it had been thoroughly searched. At first sight everything looked neat and tidy, but nothing was in its usual place. A policeman was rummaging through the drawers, watched over by a lawyer.

During the rest of that Friday, the employees heard from their superiors that the accusations were weak and that the initial indications were being misinterpreted. But even the bosses eventually stopped saying anything because they realised they were not convincing anyone. Most of the employees had previously heard their bosses saying that Odebrecht had never behaved like the other construction firms. And now people were asking themselves: 'What does that mean? What was it doing differently?'

The police officers had given phase fourteen of Operation Car Wash the Latin name *Erga Omnes* – To All – because, as detective Igor Romário de Paula explained, they wanted to give a 'clear message that the law applied equally to everyone, irrespective of the size of the company, its public prominence, its ability to influence or its economic power'. That day, 220 police officers in four states carried out eight warrants for preventative detention, four warrants for temporary detention and five warrants for compulsory questioning, in addition to fifty-nine warrants for search and seizure of evidence. The police were going after the two final sections of the cartel named by the informants. Getting there had not been easy. First of all, they had had to untangle a web of middlemen and offshore accounts supporting a sophisticated criminal structure, which took months. Then, in the final straight, they encountered further difficulties. They needed to check the address of every person who would be targeted by the operation, go there undercover, photograph the entrance and work out the best approach route. Soon the work was done, save for one detail: Marcelo Odebrecht's residence.

Widely considered one of the richest men in Brazil, with a fortune of nearly R$10 billion, Marcelo Odebrecht lives in a house valued at more than R$30 million in the luxurious Jardim Pignatari condominium, in the Morumbi district of São Paulo. An extremely exclusive gated community, it is often named as the most secure in São Paulo, and is very difficult to get into. Satellite photographs showed around forty-five houses behind its high stone walls. Which one was Odebrecht's? His house number was 319. In order to check the numbering system and work out exactly which house they were going to, the police officers had to get inside the condo. The officer chosen for the task was the detective who, as his colleagues joked, looked the most like a rich guy. So as not to arouse suspicions, he called an estate agent and said he was interested in buying a house that was currently being advertised on the internet at a price of R$19 million. Since it's not every day that a client appears for this type of property, the agent immediately made an appointment to view the house. The detective put on smart clothes, borrowed a BMW and followed the estate agent to the condo. On the way, he mentally rehearsed what he could say to pass himself off as a millionaire. He parked the BMW with the gate security guard, entered the condo in the estate agent's car and began checking the house numbers in the first street they came to. Odebrecht's house wasn't among them. They went to the spacious house that was for sale. He made polite chit-chat with the agent – grumbling about the traffic and saying that he would have preferred an apartment himself, but his wife was adamant – and then on his way out he asked innocently, 'Can we have a look around the rest of the condominium?'

'Of course we can. Let's take this street,' said the agent.

As they passed by the various houses, he carried on drawing the agent into conversation: 'So then, who are my neighbours?'

'Oh, you've got various businessmen around here.'

The indiscreet agent began to say the names of some of the residents, and then pointed to a house in the distance: 'That's where the Odebrechts live.'

The house was bigger than the others, occupying two plots, with a large lawn at the side. The Federal Police had their missing piece of information. Armed with this, they went back to the satellite photographs, worked out the numbering system, counted the houses and found that the address matched. It was indeed the big house with a side lawn. After two or three more checks, they were completely certain. But how would they get into the condo? The security guards might refuse to open the bulletproof gates, and if they tried to scale them, it could well end up in a shoot-out. Also, the condo might have an exit they were unaware of, which the target could use to escape. The solution was to leave a helicopter ready to take off from base and take the officers straight to the house if their colleagues lost too much time at the gates. The first few minutes of a search are critical, and in this case possibly even more so than usual.

'Good morning, Federal Police. We have a search warrant for a property inside,' announced the police officer when the black cars sporting the Federal Police logo arrived at the condo entrance.

'Whose house?'

'You'll find out once we're inside.'

It was 6 a.m. and still dark. Luckily, the police did not have problems at the gate and the helicopter stayed on the ground, but they still wanted to get there quickly and seize Marcelo Odebrecht's mobile phone. The police cars raced through the streets of the condo, while one stayed with the security guards at the gate, to ensure they didn't warn anyone. Within thirty seconds, they were knocking at the door of the house. Odebrecht himself answered the door. As usual, he had been up since 5.30 a.m. doing his exercises. His voice was still a little croaky.

'Come in,' he said, objecting only to the rifle one of the officers was carrying. The gun was duly left in the car. Marcelo Odebrecht held the door open for the officers and stood there waiting. In the double-height entrance hall a sculpture by Frans Krajcberg hung on the wall. Odebrecht asked to see the warrants; they only showed him the search warrant, duly signed by Sergio Moro of the 13th Federal Bench in Paraná. He began to read carefully. He had not expected Operation Car Wash to come so far. In recent months, from what the police knew from intercepted messages and comments made by him, Marcelo Odebrecht had been trying to stymie the work of detectives and prosecutors working on the operation. He had not succeeded.

Odebrecht's wife, Isabela, arrived and told the police that their daughters were still asleep. An officer asked Odebrecht about his mobile phone, one of the most important things they were looking for. The police had found it difficult to locate and monitor the device that was actually being used by him, because all the phones were registered in the name of the company.

'Let's go and find your mobile phone, since we will be needing that, Mr Odebrecht,' said the police officer.

He walked off into the kitchen. The phone wasn't there.

'It's upstairs. I'll go and get it. I'll go up and see my little girl and you can wait here,' Odebrecht suggested.

'No, from now on I'll go with you. I need your phone right now,' the officer said firmly.

Odebrecht carried on walking, the officer following. They went up the stairs. At the bedroom door, Odebrecht stopped once again.

'It's inside the room. Wait here while I get it,' said Odebrecht.

'No, I'll go with you,' said the officer, and he accompanied him into the bedroom and then into the en suite bathroom, not taking his eyes off Odebrecht's hands. The phone was sitting on the counter. The officer picked it up and switched it off. It was now safely in police custody. The IT specialists would find valuable information on that phone.

In another part of the house, the police found a secret room, as in Renato Duque's house. But the room was clean; there was nothing important inside it.

Once the search was finished, Marcelo Odebrecht was informed that he was under arrest. He would be taken to the Federal Police's holding cells in Curitiba to be held on remand – indefinitely. His wife packed a small case with personal items and a few clothes, and tried to hand it to the detectives, but they looked at her in bemusement. They weren't going to carry his case for him. He could do it himself.

In addition to Marcelo, four other Odebrecht directors were arrested that morning: Márcio Faria da Silva, Rogério Araújo,

César Rocha and Alexandrino de Salles Ramos de Alencar. Márcio Faria and Rogério Araújo had been accused by Paulo Roberto Costa in his plea bargain testimony back in September 2014. According to the former Petrobras director, he had received US$23 million in kickbacks from Odebrecht in Switzerland on the instructions of these two directors. They were arrested at daybreak and the news quickly spread among the company's senior management.

At 6.03 a.m., César Rocha, another director who was due to be arrested but who was away from home that morning, received a phone call from Marta Pacheco Kramer, who also worked at Odebrecht.

'Hi, Marta!' said Rocha, answering at the first ring.

'Good morning. How's things?'

'Fine.'

'There's a police raid happening down at the office. There are several police vehicles. I'm heading down there. When I have any news, I'll let you know,' said Kramer, getting straight to the point.

'They're at Márcio's, OK?' replied Rocha.

'Hello? It's a terrible connection. I'll let you know as soon as I have any news, OK?'

'They're at Márcio's!'

'Ah, OK.'

'Bye.'

To the police, it looked like César Rocha was trying to avoid arrest. According to the GPS tracking of his phone, between 6.03 a.m. and 6.21 a.m., Rocha was close to his home address in São Paulo. When the police arrived there in unmarked cars, they were only able to get in because, by chance, they came face to face with Rocha's wife, Márcia da Rocha Tourinho, outside the garage door. Inside the boot of the car was a bag packed with clothes, a passport in the name of César Ramos with a visa for the United States that was valid until 2020, pre-paid travel cards, credit cards and European train passes, all indications that he might be trying to flee. His wife said that the bag was to be taken to her husband at the beach resort of Engenho, several hours away on the coast. But he wasn't there. It wasn't until 12.20 p.m. that Rocha presented himself to the São Paulo Federal Police, accompanied by Dora Cavalcanti, a lawyer acting for the Odebrecht company.

Alexandrino de Alencar, another director of Odebrecht, was awoken at home at 6.06 a.m, not by the police, but by a call from Marta Pacheco Kramer.

'Hello?' answered Alencar.

'Alexandrino?'

'Yes, it's me.'

'Good morning. It's Marta. Sorry to wake you.'

'Yes.'

'I'm calling to find out if everything's OK with you.'

'Why?' asked Alencar, surprised.

'There are some police vehicles outside the office and we think it's a search operation. We're on our way there now. So I'm checking with a few people to see everything's OK,' said Kramer.

Alexandrino de Alencar heard a noise coming from downstairs.

'I think there's someone knocking at my door.'

'Really?'

'ME!'

'What?' asked Kramer.

'WHAT? Just wait a minute, OK, I'm going to check. If I need anything, I'll call you,' said Alencar.

'Are there people there?' asked Kramer.

'I think it's my housekeeper. OK!' finished Alencar, still unsure what was happening.

'OK, call me,' said Kramer, before hanging up.

At 6.48 a.m., Alencar called Kramer and reached her voice-mail. He couldn't call again, so he left a message: 'Hello Marta, there's a search and seizure going on in my house, OK? It's Alexandrino. Bye.'

The police allowed the director to make two more calls. He called his lawyers.

The Federal Police had been monitoring Alencar's phone for several days and, in a report about the surveillance operation, the police informed Sergio Moro that former president Lula da Silva had spoken by phone with Alencar for three minutes on 15 June 2015, four days before the Odebrecht executive's arrest. The call initially came from someone called Moraes on a phone registered in the name of the Lula Institute. It was 8.06 p.m.

'Hello?'

'Good evening, sir. This is Mr Moraes speaking. Are you available to speak with President Lula?' asked Moraes.

'Of course,' replied Alencar. Moraes passed the telephone.

'Hello,' said the ex-president.

'How are you?' asked Alencar.

'Everything OK?' replied Lula.

'Couldn't be better.'

The two of them talked briefly about a seminar being run by the newspaper *Valor Econômico* about the export of services, and Lula commented that the economist Delfim Netto was going to write an article on the subject.

'I spoke to Delfim Netto today. He's going to publish an article tomorrow in *Valor,* rubbishing everything,' Lula told him.[5]

At the end of the phone call, Alencar mentioned Paulo, which the Federal Police thought referred to Paulo Okamotto, chairman of the Lula Institute.

'And I spoke to Paulo today, about us talking sometime this week and aligning ... and aligning our positions on this jointly with you, OK? Agreed?' asked Alencar.

'OK, agreed. Cheers,' replied Lula.

'Likewise. Bye.'

Referring to the part where there was talk about 'aligning our positions', the police wrote the following in their report: 'It causes us uneasiness that the parties are aligning the positions of their respective institutions.' The police already had suspicions about a possible meeting. A few days earlier, on 10 June, Alencar had called the secretariat and asked: 'What's the address I'm going to? What's the name of the street?'

'Rua Pouso Alegre, number 21,' replied Vilma, the secretary.

'OK, thanks. Bye,' said Alencar.

The Lula Institute's address is 21 Rua Pouso Alegre, Ipiranga, São Paulo.

FIRST DAY IN JAIL

When he arrived at the Federal Police station, Marcelo Odebrecht was taken to a room to go through the usual formalities

---

[5]   In the article, Delfim criticised the 'tragic combination of events engineered by the government in 2014 in order to get itself re-elected', but defended the loans given to support the export of engineering services and said that it was a 'serious mistake' to publicise details of the activities of BNDES, the national development bank.

on being taken into custody. Other arrested executives from construction firms had passed through there in previous phases of Operation Car Wash. Odebrecht was restless and seemed very annoyed. His defence lawyers were on their way. They would say that the arrests had been unjust and unnecessary, that the Odebrecht group was cooperating with police and complying with all requests from the judicial authorities. They would also claim that the evidence presented by Sergio Moro as justification for the arrests was already known, having been cited in various other Car Wash proceedings. But Sergio Moro had decided that now there was sufficient evidence for an arrest.

When Marcelo Odebrecht's lawyers arrived, they conferred privately in a corner of the room. Odebrecht took charge, telling them exactly what he wanted and how he wanted it to be done. He was used to giving orders, and that's what he did, telling his lawyers precisely what they should do, even in front of the detectives. His lawyers did not intervene with suggestions, simply listening and taking notes. Odebrecht admitted to the detectives that he had been expecting something to happen, but had thought the police would raid the company rather than his house, and that they would be investigating the group's construction firm rather than the parent company, which owns forty-nine separate businesses.

At a certain point, the police gave him fifteen minutes to finish talking to his lawyers. Twenty minutes passed, then twenty-two. The police asked all the other lawyers to leave. Dora Cavalcanti from the Odebrecht group asked for more time. Five more minutes passed, and there was still no sign of her leaving. She had to be gently removed.

During the search at Marcelo Odebrecht's house, the police found two mobile phones in a bedroom for his own personal use, one in the study, four in the couple's main bedroom, one in another bedroom and three more in the rest of the house: eleven mobile phones in all. The police had already been monitoring some of them for weeks without any success; most of the phones had been switched off during this period or had simply not been used by him. Odebrecht must be using other mobile phones, thought the officers. In searching for his number, the police also monitored his wife's mobile.

On the day of Odebrecht's arrest, there were a number of calls between his wife and their two young daughters. His wife also called her sister-in-law, Monica Odebrecht. Controversially, the contents of these conversations were made public during the preparations for trial.

The disclosure of his wife's conversations provoked protests from Marcelo Odebrecht, who sued the state for damages, accusing Operation Car Wash of unduly making public information of a private and intimate nature relating to him and his family. The Odebrecht group's lawyers demanded an investigation into who had allowed the disclosure, and requested that the judge rule the recordings to be confidential. Their requests were upheld, but by then the recordings had already reached the press. In May 2016, Moro asked the defence lawyers to indicate which of the conversations should be removed from the trial documentation. Nabor Bulhões, Marcelo Odebrecht's personal lawyer, viewed the release of the family's private conversations at a time of distress as a serious error. 'Sergio Moro himself questioned the police and prosecutors over their motives for including them in the court filings when they were no longer of any interest to the investigation,' stated Bulhões.

The evening news that day would show a scene that many thought they would never see: Marcelo Odebrecht arrested.

Bold by nature and groomed for the role from an early age, he had been leading the family's business empire since 2009. Under his management, the Odebrecht group had strengthened its position in petrochemicals through its Braskem subsidiary, which today is the market leader. It had also expanded its horizons to develop projects in twenty-one countries, reducing its dependence on Brazil.

Also in jail was Otávio Azevedo, the powerful chairman and CEO of Andrade Gutierrez, who had led the construction firm's expansion into the telecommunications sector when it put together a consortium to buy Telemar, one of Brazil's largest telecom companies. Azevedo had long sat on Telemar's board of directors both as chairman and shareholder representative. Elton Negrão, another of Andrade Gutierrez's directors, had been arrested the same day, while Paulo Roberto Dalmazzo, the firm's former boss, handed himself over to the police that night.

Andrade Gutierrez and Odebrecht both run vast construction and engineering projects in Brazil and dozens of other countries, building roads, hydroelectric and nuclear power stations, drilling rigs and even building football stadiums. Together they are responsible for more than 400,000 jobs. The two companies carried out the refurbishment of Rio de Janeiro's iconic Maracanã stadium for the 2014 World Cup. In the same year, the Odebrecht group had revenues of R$107 billion, with its construction firm alone earning R$33 billion, while Andrade Gutierrez's construction activities earned it R$7.5 billion. Now the chairmen of both companies were in custody and on their way to chilly Curitiba, their lawyers rushing to take them blankets and warm clothing.

It was already late at night when the businessmen finally arrived at the Federal Police building in the Paraná capital.

It was also very cold: 6°C. The twelve prisoners were divided between three cells in one of the wings of the police jail and were each given a sheet and a blanket. The lawyers brought more blankets, but this did not make the prisoners' first night in jail any cosier. Each cell measured twelve square metres and held four prisoners, though one of them had to sleep on the floor because there were only three beds. These were made of concrete, with merely a thin foam mattress on top. The tap in Marcelo Odebrecht's cell dripped. The next day they woke up early and were given coffee and some bread and butter at around 7 a.m. They didn't have any contact with the other Operation Car Wash prisoners such as Alberto Youssef and Nestor Cerveró, who had been taken to the other wing. Marcelo Odebrecht, who suffers from low blood sugar, was eating cereal bars every two hours. Since it was Saturday and there were no out-of-hours staff at the police station, they could not receive visits, even from their lawyers. During the morning, the twelve prisoners were taken to the Institute of Forensic Medicine for a full body examination. They filed into the institute one by one, arms cuffed behind their backs. Some of them hid their faces. Marcelo Odebrecht and Otávio Azevedo, at the head of the queue, faced the battery of photographers outside with their heads high. Afterwards they returned to their cells.

Sergio Moro was very clear about his reasons for ordering the arrest of the leaders of the country's two largest construction firms: 'Considering how long the criminal scheme has been in operation – since 2004 at least – together with the scale, measured in billions, of the contracts obtained through crimes connected to Petrobras and the size, measured in millions, of the kickbacks paid to Petrobras executives, it seems inconceivable that this was not known to the chairmen of the two companies, Marcelo Bahia Odebrecht and Otávio Marques de Azevedo,' wrote Moro. In his ruling on the arrests, Moro held that 'all the evidential analysis points to the conclusion, as a preliminary finding, of the involvement of the senior management of Odebrecht and Andrade Gutierrez in the criminal cartel, fraud and payment of kickbacks relating to contracts with Petrobras'.

In the eyes of the federal prosecutors, Marcelo Odebrecht and Otávio Azevedo not only actively participated in their respective firms' actions within the 'club', but in fact exercised control over the cartel's actions and knew about the onward payment of illicit rewards to public officials.

Moro explained in his decision that Odebrecht and Andrade Gutierrez had adopted more sophisticated methods than the other construction companies, such as principally paying kickbacks offshore and through secret bank accounts. They would send the money abroad to bank accounts in Switzerland, Monaco and Panama, and would make the payments to executives connected with Petrobras from them. This was how they had operated with Paulo Roberto Costa, as he had confirmed in his evidence: 'The money from Switzerland, the money that had been deposited there, had all been transferred through Odebrecht.' The executives' defence lawyers reacted by saying that there was no justification in ordering an individual's detention based purely on conjectures and presumptions, and drew attention to the fact that the informants who had given evidence so far, including Paulo Roberto Costa, had stated that Marcelo Odebrecht did not participate in the company's alleged illegal activities. Costa had said to the prosecutors: 'I never dealt with him about any of these subjects. Don't put his name down, because he wasn't a part of that.'

In a letter published in the press on 22 June 2015, the Odebrecht group said that, after over a year of investigation, Operation Car Wash had not presented any facts that would justify such a 'use of force'. The letter spoke of an 'affront to the rule of law', refuted every point of the accusations as being the product of the investigators' own confusion, and ended by saying that 'the truth will out' and 'justice will prevail'. By 2016 the situation had completely changed and the letter was viewed as a strategic error. With the police operation against the Odebrecht group and Andrade Gutierrez, the encirclement of the alleged cartel was complete.

'DESTROY OIL RIGS EMAIL'

Marcelo Odebrecht proved to be an extremely disciplined prisoner. He established a routine and followed it rigorously. He ate, read, exercised, wrote, ate, read, exercised and wrote. He tried to keep busy all day, and at no point showed any sign of being depressed. Despite leaving a home surrounded by every luxury, for which he paid R$19,800 per month simply in service charges, for a cold cell with no privacy in the Curitiba police jail, he found a way of adapting to his new environment. Observing his habit of writing, the investigators sensed that his notes could well provide precious new leads.

On one of his first days in prison, Marcelo Odebrecht wrote a letter to his lawyers Dora Cavalcanti and Augusto de Arruda Botelho. When he came out of his cell with something written on a piece of paper, one of the prison guards asked why he was scribbling away. He responded that it was so he wouldn't forget things he needed to do. When he finished that afternoon, Odebrecht asked a police officer to deliver the piece of paper to his lawyers. Alexandre Ribeiro, a federal prison officer who had come from a neighbouring jail to reinforce the team, followed standard practice: he took the piece of paper and read it. His attention was quickly drawn to the part where Odebrecht had written 'Destroy oil rigs email'. The officer made a photocopy before delivering it to one of Odebrecht's numerous lawyers. He then showed the copy to a colleague. Officer Daniel da Silva thought the handwriting was terrible but managed to read 'Destroy oil rigs email'. He showed it to another officer who also managed to read the sentence and thought Odebrecht rather naïve in thinking that they would not find it very odd. The photocopy was then given to a detective, who summoned the Odebrecht lawyers to explain what it meant.

Marcelo Odebrecht was referring to an email that had been seized on one of the Odebrecht group's computers in November 2014, during phase seven of Operation Car Wash. In the email, Roberto Prisco Ramos from the group's Braskem petrochemical subsidiary was discussing with Marcelo Odebrecht the fact that the company was charging between US$20,000 and US$25,000 per day as an 'excess price' in an oil rig contract for Petrobras. And Marcelo Odebrecht gave an instruction along the lines of accelerating negotiations with two competing contractors. According to Sergio Moro, this showed the extent to which Marcelo Odebrecht was participating in the decisions of the contractors' cartel.

Dora Cavalcanti, the Odebrecht group's lawyer, explained to Sergio Moro and the detectives that in writing 'destroy oil rigs email', Marcelo Odebrecht meant 'refute' the argument of over-pricing in connection with the oil rigs contract. According to her, the 'excess price' mentioned in the email was simply the company's profit margin, and not a reference to over-invoicing. The email about the oil rigs had been seized by the police much earlier and, moreover, was already in the hands of the courts. There was no question of the actual email being destroyed. The police wondered whether Marcelo Odebrecht might have been referring to the destruction of other emails relating to the matter in Roberto Prisco Ramos's email account that had not yet been handed over to the judicial authorities when the instruction was given to his lawyers. Dora Cavalcanti said that this was an infringement of client–attorney confidentiality. The tussle lasted for days. Sergio Moro eventually decided that the letter should be withdrawn from the main investigation and looked into separately.

After almost a month in jail, the Federal Police requested Sergio Moro's authorisation to transfer the businessmen from the police jail to a separate hospital unit run by the Paraná state prison system nearby. Marcelo Odebrecht was among those transferred. The move made no change to his routine of exercising, reading and writing.

At around the same time, the police finished their analysis of Marcelo Odebrecht's mobile phones. What the experts discovered surprised Sergio Moro. Marcelo Odebrecht's calendar app contained an item that began 'Subject: CW', underneath which were written a series of annotations that the investigators believed related to Operation Car Wash. One of them read: 'MF/RA: don't move anything and we'll reimburse everything and take care of the family. Hold on to the end. Clean up MF and RA devices. Leak campaign donation. Another letter me to media? GA, FP, AM, MT, Lula? And Cunha?'

Several days after the discovery, Moro wrote about this in a ruling:

MF and RA appear to be references to subordinates of Marcelo Odebrecht who were also under investigation:

Márcio Faria and Rogério Araújo. Apparently, the annotation indicates that both of them were being instructed not to move money held in their accounts and that, in the case of judicial sequestration and confiscation, they would be reimbursed. The reference to 'clean up MF and RA devices' infers the destruction of evidence, with the instruction that the electronic devices used by Márcio Faria and Rogério Araújo should be wiped, or rather, that messages or files that could prove compromising be deleted. The meaning of 'leak campaign donation' remains to be seen, but may indicate a course of action intended to embarrass or constrain the beneficiaries of the scheme.

Another annotation drew Moro's attention: 'Work to stop/ cancel (FP dissenters ...).' Regarding this, he wrote in his ruling: 'The most disturbing extract is the reference to the use of "FP dissenters" combined with "work to stop/cancel" the investigation. Without prejudice to the defence's right to lawfully contest the investigation or criminal prosecution, the mention of "FP [Federal Police] dissenters" casts a dark shadow over the meaning of the annotation.' The judge finished by asking for explanations from the lawyers: 'Considering the apparent gravity of these annotations, and before drawing possible juridical consequences from them, I have decided to seek clarification from the Odebrecht executives' defence lawyers, in particular those of Marcelo Odebrecht, Márcio Faria and Rogério Araújo, in relation to the aforementioned annotations.'

In a press release at the time, the Odebrecht group declared that the Federal Police's interpretation of the messages was mistaken. The information was being taken out of context.

'In relation to Marcelo Odebrecht, the Federal Police's report draws interpretations of his personal notes that are distorted, taken out of context and lacking in logic. The most serious is the attempt to attribute to Marcelo direct blame for the very serious and illegal acts that are now coming to light and in which the leadership of the Federal Police in Paraná may be implicated, such as, inter alia, the placing of recording devices in cells,' said the company.

Odebrecht was referring to the discovery of a recording device in Alberto Youssef's cell during phase one of Operation Car Wash. The case was still being investigated and there had been some further developments a few months earlier.

On 4 May 2015, detective Mário Renato Fanton, a recent arrival to the team, decided to question Dalmey Fernando Werlang, the officer responsible for installing audio and video recording equipment at the Paraná Federal Police building. In the interview, carried out in the hotel where Fanton was staying, Werlang said that in 2014 he had been requested by detective Rosalvo Ferreira, superintendent of the Federal Police in Paraná, and by detectives Igor Romário de Paula and Márcio Anselmo, to install as a matter of urgency an ambient recording device in one of the Federal Police's custody cells. Werlang said that he went to the cell where Youssef was to be held, and installed the equipment before his arrival. Werlang returned some time later to give the recordings to Márcio Anselmo. In the interview, Werlang said that he was travelling when he heard that the prisoner had found the equipment in his cell. He also said that on returning from the trip, he asked Igor Romário de Paula if there was a permit authorising the device in Youssef's cell and that the response had been 'worse than no'. Only at that point, Werlang said in the interview, did he realise that the listening device was illegal.

Werlang's evidence provoked great controversy within the Federal Police, not only because the interview had, unusually, been carried out in a hotel, but also because several days earlier, detective Fanton had come looking for superintendent Ferreira to tell him that he did not trust the Operation Car Wash team and that they should replace them with new detectives.

Superintendent Ferreira did not do this, preferring to keep the original team in place and remove Fanton and Werlang from the operation. He opened an internal inquiry to get to the bottom of the whole debacle. There was contradictory information. Their investigations indicated that the bugging device had been installed back when Fernandinho Beira-Mar was being held at the jail. The investigation ended up being transferred to Brasília and as of April 2016 had not yet been concluded. Some of the investigators suspected that Odebrecht might have been involved in the incident in some way.

In the indictment, the Federal Police alleged that Marcelo Odebrecht and his directors had knowledge and direct participation in the crimes revealed by Operation Car Wash, in addition to having attempted to obstruct the investigations. On being called to give evidence and present their versions of the events, the directors all preferred to remain silent, with the exception of Marcelo Odebrecht. When asked if he would like to say something in his defence, Marcelo Odebrecht asked for it to be recorded that he had always made himself available to the judicial authorities, that he had already given evidence in Brasília and that for this reason he believed that his detention was not necessary and, finally, that he continued to have full confidence in his colleagues, the other executives who were in custody. He said that he believed in the presumption of their innocence.

Upon accepting the indictment against the Odebrecht group executives, Sergio Moro cited six Petrobras contracts in which Odebrecht may have paid kickbacks to directors and managers at the state-owned oil firm. He also mentioned the secret offshore bank accounts discovered by federal prosecutors to which the kickbacks were delivered. The documentation coming from Switzerland, he said, would be material proof of the route that the money had taken from accounts controlled by Odebrecht to the Petrobras managers.

The prosecutors stated that directors Rogério Araújo and Márcio Faria, under the orders of Marcelo Odebrecht, had made around 115 financial transactions suspected of being money laundering, in order to pay kickbacks to directors and managers of Petrobras such as Paulo Roberto Costa, Renato Duque and Pedro Barusco. The scheme lasted from 2006 to 2014. According to the investigators, the Odebrecht group's main middleman for these offshore accounts was Bernardo Freiburghaus. The mechanism of making multiple bank deposits into the accounts of various companies and individuals in order to cover their tracks was first revealed by Paulo Roberto Costa, then by Pedro Barusco. But the final proof came from Switzerland. The Brazilian prosecutors were preparing their formal charges when the documents arrived that they had requested under international judicial cooperation procedures: the bank account statements confirming the route the money had taken. The Swiss had found these documents and needed only a few more details from the Brazilian authorities in order to complete their own investigations. 'It was an important development because the new information arrived only three days before we were due to file the formal charges,' recalled one of the task force prosecutors. 'It provoked quite a stir here and more than one "Thanks be to Switzerland!"'

The first person to talk about bank accounts in Switzerland and other countries was Paulo Roberto Costa, who said in his plea bargain testimony that he had received US$23 million in an offshore account from Odebrecht. The payments from the company were to maintain a 'good relationship' with him. Costa even reproduced a conversation he had with Rogério Araújo, the Odebrecht director, who suggested he open a bank account outside Brazil and gave him the name of Bernardo Freiburghaus to carry out transactions 'without going through any political party'. According to Costa, Rogério Araújo had told him: 'Paulo, you're a fool. You're helping the others more than you're helping yourself. If you ever need any of these politicians you're helping, they'll turn their backs on you.'

Costa also said that the deposits from the Odebrecht group were made 'every two or three months'. When this testimony became public in February 2015, Odebrecht released an official statement vehemently refuting the accusations of their involvement in the scheme, accusations that had already been reinforced by Youssef's testimony. 'The Odebrecht group denies the slanderous allegations made by the former director of Petrobras and by the currency dealer, who are both confessed defendants in the investigation being carried out by the federal judicial authorities in the State of Paraná. In particular, the Odebrecht group denies having made any payment or deposit to any alleged bank account of any politician, executive or former executive at the state-owned company,' read the statement.

The Odebrecht group's defence team maintained a confrontational posture towards the investigation for many months, including after Marcelo Odebrecht's arrest. Part of their strategy was to attack Sergio Moro. In itself this was not a novelty, since throughout the trial all the defence lawyers had tried to accuse him of various excesses. So Odebrecht carried on with this line. In all the public statements by the firm's lawyers, and in their applications for habeas corpus, they criticised Sergio Moro for alleged abuses committed by him.

Four days after the arrests, amid the lawyers' accusations, the Association of Federal Judges came out in defence of Moro: 'The Association will not countenance generic or unfounded allegations that the arrests and detentions ordered under phase fourteen of Operation Car Wash may have violated the rights and privileges of citizens. Nor will the Association countenance personal attacks of any kind, in particular statements that could cast doubt over the honesty, effectiveness and independence of Brazilian federal judges.' The judges' Association also confirmed their view that everything was being done within the due legal process.

The heaviest criticisms came from the Odebrecht group's lawyer, Dora Cavalcanti. In an interview with *O Globo* newspaper, she said that executives were being arrested before charges had been formalised by federal prosecutors and, in particular, without any definitive allegations: 'These detentions are based on a hasty analysis of an allegation that has not been formally put. What seems to me to be going on in Operation Car Wash, and this has already been examined by the Federal Supreme Court, is an erroneous application of detention on remand.'

In the interview, the lawyer went as far as saying that Moro was showing a lack of due respect towards the accused: 'We find that there has been a violation of the most basic human rights of the citizen. We are analysing this from the point of view of

Brazilian and international legislation, with the premise that you go public seeking clarification and a judge sees this as a reason to keep individuals in jail. I am even studying how to bring an international claim for the violation of my clients' human rights. What's happening is very serious.'

Dora Cavalcanti also complained that many of the charges were being brought based on the testimony of informants:

Operation Car Wash will enter the *Guinness Book of Records* as the investigation with the most informants. And it's interesting how each informant keeps adjusting their account of events in order to preserve their own plea bargain. We have a long chain of informants who keep on refreshing their memory as time goes on, remembering more and more things, little by little. And then we have the informant who, faced with what the other has said, has to readjust what they said originally. And there is even a third type of informant who includes in their testimony what they heard another informant say. In my view, plea bargains in criminal cases, in the way in which they are being used in Operation Car Wash, are absolutely an incentive to lie.

After specifically criticising the behaviour of the judge, suggesting that he was penalising individuals for the unspecified acts of a corporate entity, Cavalcanti said, 'You cannot transfer the grudge you may have towards a company on to individuals by restricting their liberty.' The *O Globo* reporter then asked her whether she was saying that the judge had a grudge against the Odebrecht group. Dora Cavalcanti gave an evasive reply: 'I wouldn't put it like that, because I don't want to deepen the conflict with him.'

It was the turn of the Operation Car Wash prosecutors to react. The day after the interview was published, the task force released a statement, saying that when the lawyer stated that she was going to take the matter to the international courts, she was strongly suggesting that 'the ten detectives, nine prosecutors, federal judge, court of first instance, appeal judges of the Regional Federal Court for the 4th district and the justices of the Federal Supreme Court were all in league to violate the rights of her clients'. It was a long statement and cited the comprehensive material that the investigations were uncovering against the company. They clarified that 'contrary to what the lawyer suggests, the plea bargain agreements are the responsibility of federal prosecutors, not the judge'.

As Operation Car Wash advanced, Moro, while maintaining silence himself, became more and more the centre of debate. It was always he whom the defence lawyers, the accused, the suspects and the politicians had in mind when they voiced their criticisms.

In addition to the compromising annotations on his mobile phone, Marcelo Odebrecht gave a statement to the congressional inquiry that went down badly. Despite appeals from his defence lawyers for him to keep silent when members of the congressional inquiry went to Curitiba to hear evidence from some of the prisoners, Odebrecht decided to speak. He said that he had always taught his daughters not to snitch: 'I have more to quarrel about with the person who snitches than with whoever did the deed.' At that point, a lawyer nudged him and he corrected himself: 'To snitch on someone, you need something to snitch about. That's not what happened here.' The impression remained that he had a lot to say but would not do so.

A month later, in October 2015, a former director of Ode-brecht, João Antônio Bernardi Filho, signed a plea bargain agreement for the first time, in which he admitted that he had set up an offshore company called Hayley in Uruguay, with a subsidiary in Brazil, to manage and conceal assets belonging to the former Petrobras director of services, Renato Duque. Bernardi said that in 2009, Duque came to see him and told him that he had 'money to receive abroad' and asked him to manage it. He had accepted and set up Hayley for this purpose. Bernardi also told the investigators about an incident they found amusing: in 2011, just as he was arriving at the Petrobras building to deliver a R$100,000 kickback to Renato Duque, he was mugged and all the money was taken. The mugger struck it lucky: Bernardi could not go to the police. The allegation strengthened the evidence against Duque.

'GANG OF FOUR'

With the chairmen of Brazil's two biggest construction com-panies in jail, Operation Car Wash was closing in on the cartel operating within Petrobras. But a piece of the puzzle was still missing: the fourth director. Then, on the morning of 2 July 2015, Jorge Luiz Zelada, Nestor Cerveró's successor at Petro-bras's International Division, was arrested under phase fifteen of Operation Car Wash, code-named 'Monaco Connection'. During the search, the police found a pair of overalls with the Petrobras logo, autographed by Dilma Rousseff and Petro-bras's former chairman, José Sérgio Gabrielli. One of the police officers commented jokingly: 'Take them away and auction them for a children's charity.' The prisoner arrived in Curi-tiba in the afternoon and was taken straight from the airport to the Institute of Forensic Medicine. He was accused of making suspicious bank transfers abroad, even after the beginning of the investigations. In total, €11 million had been sent to Monaco and US$315 million to China. The money in Monaco had already been frozen.

Carlos Fernándo dos Santos Lima, one of Operation Car Wash's most experienced prosecutors, said that with Zelada's arrest, the investigation was closing the loop around the four directors who at various times had run the Petrobras corruption scheme: Paulo Roberto Costa, Renato Duque, Nestor Cerveró and Jorge Luiz Zelada. The prosecutor called them the 'Gang of Four'.

'All four of them were at various times directors of the state-owned company and formed the main focus of the investigation into the various scams involving misappropriation of public funds from Petrobras,' explained Lima. 'I'm not going to tell you that the investigation is closed, but I can say that the gang who took over the senior management of Petrobras is now in jail.' It was an important moment for Operation Car Wash.

Zelada had replaced Nestor Cerveró at Petrobras's International Division in 2008 and stayed in the job until 2012. He was named by both Paulo Roberto Costa and Pedro Barusco as one of the beneficiaries of the corruption scheme. Barusco said he had personally delivered R$120 million to Zelada in three visits to his home in Rio de Janeiro. The prosecutors suspected that Zelada had also received kickbacks from the drillships operating contracts, which were valued in excess of US$1 billion. 'There are strong indications of this,' said Lima. 'All the directors responsible for these activities received commissions for business dealings they facilitated within Petrobras, whether in the area of refineries and pipelines, or drillships and oil rigs.'

THE INVESTIGATION'S NEW FRONTIERS

If one loop was closing in Operation Car Wash, another was just beginning: the investigation was extending beyond Petrobras. A respected senior officer in the Navy and one of Brazil's leading authorities on nuclear energy, Vice Admiral Othon Pinheiro da Silva, was arrested. This was phase sixteen of Operation Car Wash, code-named 'Radioactivity'. Vice Admiral Silva, chairman of Eletronuclear, the state-owned company building the Angra 3 nuclear power station on the coast near Rio de Janeiro, had stepped down temporarily from managing the company when he became aware that the investigators might come looking for him. Some of the informants began to talk about corruption in the electricity sector, and the vice admiral was soon suspected of having received kickbacks of R\$4.5 million from the construction firms Andrade Gutierrez and Engevix via intermediary companies, some of which appeared to be fronts. The money ended up in Aratac, Silva's own consulting firm. The vice admiral tried to argue that Aratec was owned by his daughter Ana Cristina Toniolo, who had provided translation services to the construction companies. But in statements to the Federal Police, Toniolo contradicted her father. She said that she hadn't provided any services, simply issuing invoices 'on dad's instructions'.

Athayde Ribeiro Costa, another prosecutor on the Operation Car Wash task force, said that the criminal organisation they were investigating was not restricted to Petrobras, but extended to other parts of the public sector. 'Corruption is endemic in Brazil and it is in the process of metastasising,' stated Athayde.

When the Federal Police arrived at the vice admiral's house, he resisted arrest. Silva was asleep and the detective asked the maid to go and wake him. The naval officer became extremely agitated and yelled from inside the locked bedroom that he was a vice admiral of the Navy and must therefore be treated with due respect. The detective kicked the door twice and said they would smash it in. Silva said that if they did that, he would shoot. It was a tense moment. The police officers were armed. Silva then opened the door and threw himself at one of the officers. There was a brief struggle and the policemen had to immobilise and handcuff him. 'Even immobilised and handcuffed, Mr Silva remained agitated, shouting that we could not behave in that manner, that he was a vice admiral of the Navy and that under military regulations, there must therefore be another officer of at least vice admiral rank present,' recounted a police officer.

Gradually, the policemen managed to calm the naval officer. Once he agreed to speak, their first concern was to locate his guns. Silva pointed to the hiding place where he kept a .40 pistol and a .38-calibre revolver, both licensed, along with a Glock 9mm pistol, a Taurus .38 and a 6.35-calibre Bayard pistol, all of which were unlicensed. Silva explained that the Taurus and the Bayard had belonged to his deceased brother-in-law. During their search, the police also found many documents concerning Eletronuclear and other companies, along with material relating to Operation Car Wash itself. Silva had evidently been following the news, as if waiting for his turn. In his study, the police officers also found a bag containing R$45,000 in cash, which Vice Admiral Silva said was for emergencies. The cash ended up being left *in situ*, because the warrant from Sergio Moro only had orders to seize amounts in excess of R$100,000. As a military officer, Silva could not be held in a police jail and was instead taken to a military facility in Curitiba. After being indicted by the Federal Police and formally charged with corruption by federal prosecutors, the vice admiral formally resigned from his position at Eletronuclear.

Dalton Avancini, formerly chairman of Camargo Corrêa, said in his testimony that the firms involved in the construction of the Angra 3 nuclear power station had to pay kickbacks to Vice Admiral Silva and to the PMDB. Avancini said that shortly before the contracts to resume work at Angra 3 were signed in August 2014, there had been a meeting at the headquarters of UTC in São Paulo, arranged by UTC's chairman, Ricardo Pessoa. At the meeting, Pessoa had made clear that the percentage of kickbacks was to be the same: 1 per cent of the contract value for the PMDB and for the directors of Eletronuclear. Avancini did not, however, say which PMDB politicians received the kickbacks from the power station contracts.

Based on the same information that had led to the arrest of Vice Admiral Silva, on 21 September 2015 the police triggered phase nineteen of Operation Car Wash, which came to be known as 'Nessun Dorma' – the name of the famous aria from the final act of *Turandot*, and which means 'No one shall sleep'. Eleven judicial warrants were carried out: one for temporary detention, one for indefinite remand, seven for search and seizure and two for compulsory questioning.

José Antunes Sobrinho, one of the owners of Engevix, a construction firm involved in Angra 3, was among those arrested. He was suspected of having paid more than R\$1 million in kickbacks to Eletronuclear's management, via Aratec, between 2011 and 2013. Antunes Sobrinho was arrested at home in Florianopolis in the state of Santa Catarina, and arrived at the Federal Police headquarters in Curitiba in the early afternoon. Sobrinho had already been charged with offences of corruption and money laundering in other Operation Car

Wash proceedings involving the former presidential chief of staff, José Dirceu.

With the arrest of some of the biggest business leaders in Brazil, Operation Car Wash had theoretically taken down not only the corrupted, but also the corruptors. It had closed the loop around the cartel companies and arrested yet another director of Petrobras. Now it was making advances within other state-owned entities by following the trail of money. It was perhaps the first time in Brazil that the judiciary was attacking a corruption scheme in its full extent and complexity. In concentrating its efforts on the economic side of corruption, Operation Car Wash had gone so deep that some said it could put in danger the entire model of Brazilian capitalism, which has featured the payment of kickbacks in return for government favours for centuries.

What Sergio Moro and the investigators had been saying for months, in both words and actions, was that corruption was not an intrinsic part of the Brazilian soul. Rather, there existed a system that was tilted in favour of the corrupt, and against those who were honest. In other countries it had been possible to change this. The challenge had begun, but the battle was far from over. What was needed was to attack, once and for all, the most powerful part of the problem: the political core of the scheme, from which everything originated. Once again, Operation Car Wash would be making history.

Chapter 8

'WE'RE HERE,' WARNS THE PROSECUTOR GENERAL

14 July 2015

FIFTY-THREE SEARCH WARRANTS AGAINST POLITICIANS

Rodrigo Janot got practically no sleep that night. He had stayed late at work, into the small hours of the morning. The final set of applications from the federal prosecutors' office reached the Supreme Court at 11 p.m. The president of the Supreme Court, Justice Ricardo Lewandowski, complained about the late hour and said he would only make his decision the following day. Rodrigo Janot telephoned and insisted, and the judge unwillingly gave his ruling. Then he went back to bed. But federal prosecutors discovered one more address that needed searching, and so yet another warrant was needed. It fell to the ancillary judge to wake Justice Lewandowski to request yet another ruling. With a bit of persuasion, he managed to get Justice Lewandowski to study the request, which he granted at 2 a.m.

An hour later, the prosecutor general held a meeting with his team. At 4.40 a.m., most of the prosecutors left the building to meet with the detectives. As with any investigation, it was natural that the lead prosecutor should participate in the meeting to decide the final details of the planned operation, but it still came as a shock. The police officers had never expected to see anything like it: the prosecutor general of the republic, Rodrigo Janot, personally attending the briefing that always takes place just before the police cars hit the streets. It was almost 5 a.m. on 14 July 2015.

Janot entered the room and stood waiting patiently for the meeting to begin. A police officer on standby to find out who the targets of the operation would be – a piece of information that is normally only given once the cars are actually moving – recognised Janot, and commented jokingly to a detective: 'Look who's here! I think we're going to arrest Lula and Dilma!'

Janot had gone to the meeting to give the police officers a clear message: 'We are by your side. I will be at my desk until all of this is over, to resolve any problems you may have.' Soon teams of Federal Police officers in seven states would be carrying out searches and seizures at the homes of serving congressmen, at the official apartments of senators and at politicians' offices. And these were no ordinary politicians. They were important names. Among them were a former president of the republic, Senator Fernando Collor de Mello; a former minister in Dilma Rousseff's government, Senator Fernando Bezerra Coelho; and the president of the Progressive Party, Senator Ciro Nogueira. Leaders of the Progressive Party, such as Eduardo da Fonte, Mário Negromonte and João Pizzolatti were also being targetted by the new operation.

Code-named 'Politeia', meaning 'republic' in Greek, a reference to Plato's famous book about a city where virtue and ethics prevail, the operation's purpose was to search for further evidence of the involvement of politicians in the Petrobras corruption scheme. In all, an unprecedented fifty-three search warrants had been issued by the Supreme Court. Since the courts were currently in recess, the requests had been decided by several different Supreme Court judges: in addition to Justice Teori Zavascki, Justice Celso de Mello and Justice Ricardo Lewandowski were also involved.

After the briefing, the teams set out in their police cars with their lights flashing but their sirens switched off. They made their way silently through the dark streets of the capital towards the homes of the legislators. The prosecutor general went back to his office and carried on working until the last team had carried out the final warrant of the day. From his office, Janot followed everything that was happening on a big screen that showed a map of Brazil. The place where each warrant was being executed was marked by a tag with its geo-referencing data. The tag stayed yellow while the operation was in progress. If there were problems, the tag turned red. Once the warrant was successfully executed, the tag turned green.

The prosecutors were also receiving information through an encrypted messaging app. One messaging group included prosecutors in seven states, and each state team also had their own messaging group dealing with details of a more operational nature. In this way, problems could be resolved as soon as they arose. At one of Collor's addresses in his home state of Alagoas, for example, they found that the entrance gate was made of enormous steel slabs like those in a bank vault. 'It'll be easier to knock down the wall,' said the technical expert. Janot would not authorise that, and so the technicians had to dismantle the gate piece by piece. In São Paulo, the police officers discovered that one of the search addresses was wrong, and that they urgently needed a new warrant. The whole day unfolded in this way.

The execution of the last of the search warrants didn't begin until 5.30 p.m, and almost missed the deadline, since the law prohibits these types of operations from taking place during the hours of darkness. Even though it was late, the decision was made to go in.

The tensest moment of the day occurred at an apartment building, Block G, 309 South Wing, Brasília, where several senators have their official apartments. The Federal Police and the Senate Police, who were responsible for the building's security, had a falling out. The misunderstanding was a direct result of the unprecedented nature of the situation. Since an operation like this had never happened before, no one really knew what to do. The Federal Police had agreed to arrive as discreetly as possible. The police officers were wearing suits and in unmarked cars. As always, they wanted to enter immediately on arrival. The senate police officers, who had not been warned of the operation, resisted and asked to see the judicial warrant for the search, claiming that the apartment building was an 'annex of the Senate' and calling for reinforcements. Congressional vehicles pulled up in front of the building. The Federal Police detectives said that they weren't going to show them anything, that they were simply going to fulfil their orders, and refused to provide the document. The impasse lasted several long minutes. Both groups were armed and the argument almost degenerated into a shouting match. The searches finally began but the Senate Police did not give up. The Senate's lawyer, Alberto Cascaes, was summoned and gave press interviews criticising the Federal Police's actions. He said that in such cases the legislature's police force is normally warned in advance and accompanies the searches. 'They brought a locksmith, smashed down the door, took what they wanted and left without giving any explanation,' the lawyer said to journalists.

At Fernando Collor de Mello's official apartment in Brasília, the Federal Police detectives and officers encountered a further stressful situation. The senator was not there, but the senate police officers banged on the door on four separate occasions while the federal officers were inside, wanting to come in and oversee the search. On one of these occasions, a squabble almost broke out between federal and senate police officers. Each time they asked to see the warrant they got the same response. At no point did the federal officers let them in.

'I don't need to show you the warrant. The senator himself is certainly aware of the judicial investigation under way at the Federal Supreme Court in relation to him; ask his lawyer to contact the Supreme Court. I am only carrying out an order,' the federal detective said.

'If I had been informed, if a request had been put in, there would be no problem,' insisted the senate police officer.

'That's not how the Federal Police works. We do not need to inform the Senate Police. The search warrant can only be shown to the senator himself. I understand your point of view, but please try to understand mine. You are not the recipient of the warrant.'

'Is he in there?' asked the senate police officer.

'No, but that's the standard procedure. Just because the senator isn't here, doesn't mean I'm going to show it to anyone else who happens to be around,' replied the detective, beginning to show some irritation at the officer's resistance.

'I just want to know if he's in there, because it's my job to protect him.'

'He isn't. So you're in the wrong place. He's not here,' said the federal detective, in a faintly sarcastic tone.

'I'm in the wrong place?' retorted the senate police officer angrily.

'You're saying that your job is to protect the senator; I'm saying he isn't here and so you're therefore in the wrong place. I understand you're just doing your job, but I have to do mine. Wait until we're finished. You'll have all the time in the world to go in afterwards, if you like. OK? Thank you,' said the detective, firmly closing the door.

The senate police officer tried to say something, but the door closed in his face. When it was time to leave, there was yet another impasse. The Senate Police did not want to let the Federal Police team leave the building. The atmosphere soured further and tempers flared. One of the federal detectives phoned headquarters describing the situation as 'private incarceration', and threatened to arrest the lot of them. It was only the intervention of cooler heads who calmed everything down that kept the situation from spiralling out of control.

Meanwhile on the shores of Lake Paranoá just outside Brasília, a police team arrived at the Casa da Dinda – the Collor family's sumptuous mansion that had become famous at the time of Collor's impeachment while he was president in the 1990s, when it emerged that the cost of maintaining its extensive gardens was being paid for out of illicit funds. The police had no idea whether the senator would be there, or whether he had gone back to his home state of Alagoas.

'Is the senator here?' asked the police officer.

'Yes,' replied one of the soldiers on security duty – one of Collor's privileges as a former president of Brazil. 'Wait here,' said the soldier.

'We're not here to wait. We need to go in,' replied one of the detectives, already stepping over the threshold.

'No, wait here. President Collor is coming,' said the soldier, calling off the guard dogs.

The detectives waited to see what he would do. 'I thought to myself, "This is going to be tricky." I thought he was going to be difficult, but he was just a bit grumpy,' said one of those present. Collor came to the door wearing a sweatshirt and, half yawning, asked what was going on. He had only just woken up. It took some time before he started asking about the police cars and, especially, about the documents that were being seized. A folder full of old documents pointed towards the existence of overseas bank accounts. The senator said they were from a long time ago. The investigators decided it was important – the accounts might still be active or might hold some interesting information – and so the material was taken away. They went into the study and one of the detectives quickly found a promissory note for US$5 million that brought up memories of Operation Uruguay, an old case of suspected evasion of currency controls that lurked in Collor's past. 'Take it to a museum of corruption,' suggested a young officer. They even found Collor's will. He asked them not to take it, saying that there was a copy on file at the notary's office. The investigators gave way, but took photographs of the document and later went to the notary's office to check.

They seized many documents, including contracts, legal opinions, prosecutors' CVs and various other files. One item particularly surprised the investigators – a sheet of paper with the photos of all the members of the National Council of Federal Prosecutors, including one of Rodrigo Janot. The prosecutor general's photo was circled forcibly with a pen. The detectives consulted the prosecutors as to whether they should confiscate this as well, but decided against it, as it did not in itself suggest any crime.

That day, in addition to thousands of documents, more than R$3.5 million in cash and a number of luxury cars were seized, several of them belonging to Fernando Collor. At the Casa da

Dinda, the Federal Police found a red Ferrari, a Porsche and a Lamborghini. The Ferrari model 458 Italia with a 570 horsepower V8 engine, goes from 0 to 100 km/h in 3.4 seconds and can reach 325 km/h, but it was not even the most luxurious of Collor's cars. The Lamborghini Aventador is more sophisticated, and the model owned by Collor had special paintwork and a removable roof, making it more expensive than, for example, the model owned by the serial entrepreneur Eike Batista, seized by the authorities – but later returned – in claims for damages by investors when his oil company OGX collapsed in 2013. Even the tyres on Collor's Lamborghini were not the standard specification but had been changed for more sporty ones. And this car was even faster than the Ferrari: it can go from 0 to 100 km/h in 2.9 seconds and reaches a maximum speed of 350 km/h. However, the police officers faced a dilemma when it came to taking the sports cars to the vehicle pound: none of them knew how, or indeed wanted, to drive such powerful machines. Moreover, they were completely uninsured, on account of their value. The Lamborghini and Ferrari ended up being driven by Collor's security staff, who were more accustomed to driving them, a police officer accompanying them in the passenger's seat.

When it was time to leave for the vehicle pound, the security guards suggested using a side exit in order to avoid the press outside, but warned that the route would take them over a stretch of unpaved road. In order not to damage the cars, the police preferred to leave by the front gate. The photographs of the sports cars passing through the gate, with the elaborate inscription 'Casa da Dinda' clearly visible above, made front pages worldwide. Overhead, helicopters from various TV companies followed the vehicles to the police vehicle pound. The suspicion was that the cars – which were worth more than R$5 million at the time, and on which large amounts of motor vehicle tax were owing – had been purchased as a money-laundering exercise. They were in the name of a company called Água Branca (White Water) owned by Collor and his wife, Caroline which, according to the investigators, may have served to hide assets belonging to the senator.

Operation Car Wash had already uncovered indications that the former president Fernando Collor de Mello may also have benefited from the kickback scheme at Petrobras. Alberto Youssef said that one of his money handlers, Rafael Angulo Lopez, had delivered cash to the senator's home. Lopez confirmed his boss's story. As part of his plea bargain, he stated that he had delivered R$60,000 to Collor at his luxury apartment in the Bela Vista neighbourhood of São Paulo. He described the living room with antique furniture where the senator met him on arrival. Collor then locked the living room door and the meeting continued in another smaller room. The senator asked him what the purpose of his visit was, and Lopez said he had come to deliver 'a document'. Lopez asked if Collor knew how many pages were in the document, to which the senator replied: 'You ought to know.' Lopez then said, 'I brought sixty.' The 'sixty' were R$100 banknotes, tucked into his jacket and trouser pockets. According to the investigators, the scheme involving Collor concerned BR Distribuidora, the Petrobras subsidiary that runs its nationwide network of petrol stations, and the senator may have had a say in nominating directors for the company. As part of the 'Politeia' operation, more than R$3.5 million had been seized from the office of the owner of a chain of independent petrol stations that, according to the investigators, may have paid a kickback to the senator in order to operate under Petrobras's well-known 'BR' trademark.

Congress all but exploded when news of the searches began to emerge. It was the only thing anyone could talk about. By the end of the morning, senators and congressmen were doing nothing but scurrying from one room to another, for meeting after meeting. The widespread view was that if the Supreme Court judges had authorised the federal prosecutors' applications for the fifty-three searches, it was because they must be well founded. There had to be substantial proof. The fear of legislators soon being arrested spread rapidly around Congress.

Before the end of the morning, the prosecutor general released a statement saying that 'the measures are necessary to shed further light on the events being investigated under the auspices of the Federal Supreme Court. Some of the measures are intended to secure the seizure of assets potentially acquired through criminal activity'. The final word of the statement signed and released by Rodrigo Janot that day was in Latin: *Adsumus* – which means 'We're here'. The word, which was nearly used as the operation's code name, ended up becoming a Twitter hashtag, started by prosecutor Vladimir Aras and widely circulated on various tweets praising the operation.

By this stage, Collor had already begun to retaliate. He released a statement on social media, vehemently contesting the 'completely over-the-top' operation. He claimed that he had made himself available to answer questions on two occasions, only for his appointment to be cancelled the night before. 'Such an arbitrary and invasive measure is flagrantly unnecessary, considering that the events under investigation date from at least two years ago, the investigation has been known about since the end of last year and I, a former president, have never even been called upon to provide clarification,' Collor posted on his Facebook page. He then ended with something that caught the investigators' attention: 'If not even members of the Federal Senate are free from such arbitrary actions, what can be said of the ordinary citizen at the mercy of the institutions of the State?'

Lawyers acting for other politicians involved also criticised the operation, principally claiming that it was unnecessary. 'The senator made himself available, offered information and provided evidence. Unfortunately, in Brazil today such invasive actions are becoming the rule,' said Ciro Nogueira's lawyer Antônio Carlos de Almeida Castro, or as he was often known, Kakay. The law firm acting for another individual under investigation, Tiago Cedraz, son of the chairman of the Federal Audit Office, Aroldo Cedraz, said he considered the search methods used against his client to be an 'unprecedented affront'. Tiago Cedraz had been named by the businessman Ricardo Pessoa in his plea bargain testimony as a source of privileged information. 'A plea bargain negotiated by a confessed offender who is lying for his own personal benefit,' countered Tiago in a press release.

Eduardo Cunha, the speaker of the Chamber of Deputies, was not among those targeted by 'Politeia'. The investigation against him was advancing by leaps and bounds, but on that particular day the searches were targeted on other people. For now he could breathe a little easier, but it would not last long. The day that followed Operation Politeia brought another bombshell in the Operation Car Wash drama. And this one exploded in the lap of Eduardo Cunha.

OPERATION CAR WASH ENRAGES CONGRESS

Giving evidence to Sergio Moro at the federal justice building in Curitiba on 15 July 2015, the informant Júlio Camargo, former consultant at Toyo Setal and middleman in the scheme, said in no uncertain terms that he had been pressurised by the speaker of the Chamber, Eduardo Cunha, into paying US$10 million in kickbacks to ensure that the operating contract for two Petrobras drillships went ahead. Camargo stated that Cunha had told him that he, Cunha, 'deserved' US$5 million of the total amount of the bribe. In addition to the payment of this money directly to him, the speaker of the Chamber allegedly demanded payment of the remaining US$5 million to the lobbyist Fernando Baiano, the PMDB's middleman in the Petrobras scheme.

The issue of the drillships went back to 2006 and 2007. Petrobras had paid US$1.2 billion for two ships built by Samsung in Korea. Júlio Camargo was Samsung's representative in Brazil, for which he was due to receive a commission of US$40 million, to be shared with the PMDB and Nestor Cerveró, then director of Petrobras's International Division. But Júlio Camargo delayed the payments, and the 2012 elections were approaching. The PMDB needed the money.

'We had a meeting. Congressman Eduardo Cunha, Fernando [Baiano] Soares and me. Congressman Eduardo Cunha is often known as being aggressive, but I have to confess that with me he was extremely courteous, saying that he had nothing personal against me, but that I owed money to Fernando, out of which he deserved US$5 million. And that this was causing a great deal of inconvenience,' said Júlio Camargo in his testimony to Sergio Moro. 'It was just before an election campaign, the municipal elections if I'm not mistaken, and he had a series of commitments. He said that I had been delaying this payment for quite some time and that he couldn't wait any longer,' stated Camargo.

He went on to say that Eduardo Cunha was Fernando Baiano's 'silent partner': 'Congressman Cunha did not allow me to pay just his share. "Listen, Júlio, I won't let you do a deal to pay just my share. If you want, you can pay Fernando a bit later, but I need my share quickly. I insist that the agreement includes what you owe Fernando." And then came a SMS: "Between 8 and 10 million US$", or something like that.'

Since Camargo had no money to pay the kickback, Cunha threatened him with putting down a motion in the Chamber of Deputies, officially requesting information and proposing that the drillship contracts be sent to the ministry of mines and energy for evaluation and eventual referral to the Federal Audit Office. Feeling threatened by Cunha, Camargo said that he had asked for a meeting with the minister for mines and energy, Edison Lobão, who was also from the PMDB. Paulo Roberto Costa set up the meeting. He called Lobão and then reported back to Júlio Camargo, saying that he was in luck: the minister was in Rio de Janeiro and could meet him at the Galeão air force base, beside the main international airport. Júlio Camargo flew up to Rio meet him.

In his evidence to Sergio Moro, Camargo described the meeting: 'I said to Lobão: "Something unpleasant is happening. There's a motion down about this, concerning a company I represent and which I think brings only benefits to this country – they're bringing in cheap Japanese money." And Lobão's immediate reaction was: "This is all Eduardo's doing."' Camargo said that Lobão then called Cunha immediately: 'He took out his mobile phone and called Congressman Eduardo Cunha right there in front of me. He said: "Eduardo, I'm here with Júlio Camargo. Are you crazy?" I don't know what the congressman's answer was, but Lobão said: "Come and see me early tomorrow in my office in Brasília, because we need to talk." He hung up and said: "Júlio, what is it about the motion that worries you? Are there things in the contract that shouldn't be there?" I replied: "No, Minister, there aren't."' Lobão reassured Camargo, saying there was nothing to worry about and that it would all be sorted out as soon as possible.

When he found out about the new accusation, Eduardo Cunha questioned Júlio Camargo's motives. 'The informant has already made various depositions, at least four depositions, in which he had not made any reference to me. I vehemently deny the informant's lies, and challenge him to prove them,' wrote the speaker in his press release. Later on, at a press conference in the journalists' lobby at Congress, Cunha declared war on the government and said that from that moment on, he was siding with the opposition. Cunha accused the president's office and the prosecutor general of being behind Júlio Camargo's accusations against him, made just one day after Operation Politeia and on the eve of a major speech he was due to give on television and radio: 'The informant was forced to lie. And I find it very strange that these accusations were made the day before my speech and in the same week when part of the Executive Branch had acted with such swaggering excess in carrying out the search and seizure warrants at the homes of politicians being investigated by Operation Car Wash.'

The prosecutor general's office responded with a statement saying that Júlio Camargo's deposition was not connected to the judicial investigations under way at the Supreme Court, including the investigation into Congressman Eduardo Cunha. In fact, Camargo had long since corrected his deposition. The middleman had signed his plea bargain with the federal prosecutors months before, and had provided information about the Petrobras scheme and the construction firms' cartel without mentioning Eduardo Cunha. The investigators found out from other sources that he must know something about Cunha, and this put Camargo in a delicate situation. He risked losing all of his benefits under the plea bargain, such as being one of the few key businessmen who had not been arrested, and quickly finding himself behind bars. Even worse, he could end up serving a long sentence.

Faced with this possibility, Júlio Camargo did once again what he had done at the very outset: he went to the police and told them everything. This time, however, he didn't go down to Curitiba. He gave evidence in Brasília to the prosecutor general's team. 'I remember the day. He came here, gazed out the window and said he had a correction to make – that he had not talked about Eduardo Cunha previously, because he had been afraid. But that now he would talk,' recounts one of the prosecutors who was there. This time he revealed details of Cunha's participation in the Petrobras corruption scheme, details which he was now, on 15 July, merely repeating in the public hearing before Sergio Moro in Curitiba. But few people knew about his revised statement to prosecutors in Brasília, so they were finding out about it for the first time.

The curious thing is that it was not a scheduled hearing. It had been held at the request of Fernando Baiano's defence team. His lawyers requested the hearing not knowing about Júlio Camargo's new revelations, and they left it with yet one more problem on their hands: in addition to seriously implicating Eduardo Cunha, Camargo had complicated Fernando Baiano's life by revealing compromising details of his participation in the episode. Nelio Machado, Fernando Baiano's defence lawyer, said after the hearing that he considered it 'very odd' that an informant should 'change his version of events' ten months after making his first deposition. In Machado's view, this supposed change of story 'undermines the credibility of the informant, the federal prosecutors and the judiciary, who believed in someone who changes his story depending on events'. By revealing the name of Eduardo Cunha and correcting a serious omission in his deposition, Júlio Camargo once again managed to escape prison. But he would remain in the eye of the hurricane. After all, he had also stated, among other things, that he had lent his private jet several times to another important political figure in the story: the former presidential chief of staff, José Dirceu.

JOSÉ DIRCEU'S SECOND DOWNFALL

Almost three weeks after Operation Politeia and Júlio Camargo's testimony about Eduardo Cunha, it was now the turn of José Dirceu, former presidential chief of staff in Lula's government, to fall into the net cast by Operation Car Wash. Under investigation since 2015 for suspected corruption and money laundering linked to Petrobras, he was already being held under house arrest in Brasília as a result of a previous conviction. Dirceu had been found guilty of corruption in the Big Monthly scandal that erupted some ten years earlier, and since November 2014 had been serving a nearly eight-year sentence of detention under house arrest. He could leave his home during the day and had a job as an administrative assistant at a law firm in the central business district of Brasília, for which he received a salary of R$4,000 per month.

José Dirceu was at home when the police arrived on 3 August 2015. The detectives were a little apprehensive because, strangely, the police surveillance operation had picked up his mobile phone being used in an apartment in a different neighbourhood of Brasília during the early hours of the morning. Dirceu greeted the detectives cordially. He was expecting them. For several weeks, he had been trying to provoke Sergio

Moro, with repeated requests relating to reports of his imminent arrest. Now it was happening, he knew what to do. His only worry was for his five-year-old daughter, and he asked that she shouldn't see him being arrested. The police told the family to take the little girl away from the house, wearing simple clothing and without a backpack, just before the end of the search. In the police car, Dirceu said that he was prepared for a long stay in jail. It was a harsh blow for someone who had been planning to clean up his image after serving his sentence for the Big Monthly scandal. Even his political aides were pessimistic: Dirceu's second downfall would, they feared, be the nail in the coffin of the anti-corruption myth that had played such a leading role in bringing the Workers' Party to power.

Phase seventeen of Operation Car Wash became known as Operation 'Pixuleco', the word for dirty money invented by former Workers' Party treasurer João Vaccari Neto. Around 200 Federal Police officers participated in the operation. In January, the judge Gabriela Hardt, standing in for Sergio Moro, lifted the banking and tax confidentiality of Dirceu's consulting firm JD Assessoria e Consultoria, which revealed various payments to the consulting firm from companies linked to the corruption scheme. JD had invoiced R$29 million in consulting contracts with around fifty companies in recent years, of which R$11 million had come from construction firms being investigated by Operation Car Wash. The police believed that in reality, the money came from the coffers of Petrobras and they wanted to know if José Dirceu's firm had genuinely provided consultancy services, or whether the consulting contracts were simply a means of disguising payments under the corruption scheme.

A report from the Federal Revenue revealed that between 2006 and 2013, JD had received money from at least five companies implicated in Operation Car Wash: the major construction firms OAS, Galvão Engenharia, Camargo Corrêa, UTC and Engevix. In addition to payments from these companies, Dirceu's consultancy firm also received payments of millions of reais from the businessman Milton Pascowitch, accused of being one of the Workers' Party's middlemen dealing with Petrobras's Services Division. Milton Pascowitch had been named by the former Petrobras manager Pedro Barusco as the payer of kickbacks from Engevix.

The Federal Police had arrested Pascowitch in an earlier phase of Operation Car Wash targeting the middlemen and, after spending a while in jail, he too made a plea bargain. Pascowitch's evidence was fundamental to the detectives in uncovering proof of José Dirceu's participation in yet another corruption scandal. The prosecutors had strong suspicions that Dirceu was both an 'institutor and beneficiary of the Petrobras scheme', even during and after his Big Monthly trial and conviction. 'José Dirceu received payments under this criminal scheme while being investigated under "Big Monthly", and also following his arrest,' the prosecutor Carlos Fernando dos Santos Lima said, on announcing the former minister's new arrest.

The warrant signed by Sergio Moro was for detention on remand for an indefinite period. The prosecutors pointed to the same root for both of Brazil's two major corruption schemes. The detectives suspected that Dirceu had begun to set up the Petrobras scheme when he was still presidential chief of staff during Lula's first term of office. 'The DNA is the same. We have the DNA of buying legislative support with money from Banco do Brasil in the case of Big Monthly, and from Petrobras in the case of Car Wash,' said the prosecutor. But there was one fundamental difference: 'José Dirceu now appears as a beneficiary, personally – not on behalf of his party. This was for his personal enrichment,' said Carlos Fernando Lima.

The former chief of staff's brother, Luiz Eduardo de Oliveira e Silva, was also arrested, in his hometown of Ribeirão Preto in upstate São Paulo. As Dirceu's business partner in JD Assessoria e Consultoria, Silva was questioned about the firm's accounting and about where the money had gone. The Federal Police already knew that shortly after beginning to receive payments from the construction firms, Dirceu had made a R$400,000 down-payment on the purchase of the building where his firm operated in the Moema district of São Paulo. He had also paid R$500,000 for a house he bought for his daughter Camila and had paid R$1.2 million to a firm of builders called Halambeck for refurbishments to an apartment belonging to his brother Luiz Eduardo, which Dirceu used when visiting São Paulo. Milton Pascowitch had also paid R$1.3 million to the architect Daniela Facchini, for works to one of the two homes Dirceu owned in a gated community in Vinhedo, in upstate São Paulo. JD Assessoria e Consultoria was also being investigated on suspicion of having received kickbacks from Petrobras subcontractors such as a company called Hope, which provided it with human resources services, and another subcontractor called Personal, which provided cleaning services. Both subcontractors had contracts with Petrobras's Services Division, in which Dirceu supposedly had influence through his nomination of Renato Duque as director. Dirceu's brother, however, contributed little – the answers to the most important questions did not come from him.

José Dirceu was taken to the Federal Police headquarters in Brasília and waited there for the Supreme Court to decide his final destination. Sergio Moro had requested his transfer to Curitiba, but since Dirceu had already been convicted and was serving a sentence fixed by the Supreme Court, Justice Luís Roberto Barroso had to be consulted, which took time. In the afternoon, the Supreme Court judge said that he would probably consider the appeal that same day. He then called Justice Gilmar Mendes and commented on Dirceu's arrest: 'The shocking thing is that while we were investigating and judging the "Big Monthly" case, these practices were permeating through every branch of governmental and administrative activity.' The Supreme Court judge said he was impressed with what the Operation Car Wash prosecutors had discovered: 'It seems to me that beneath it all there is the same root for both "Big Monthly" and for what they're now calling "Big Oil" – not to mention "Big Electric", and goodness knows how many more "Bigs" might still be to come. It seems to me that it's the same source, it's a way of governing, a government model.' Mendes recalled that the Big Monthly investigation had left several loose ends. 'The prosecuting authorities did not, in the end, proceed with the investigations that the joint congressional inquiry recommended in relation to Big Monthly. Back then, we were left with that mysterious figure of R\$170 million of missing funds, but now that isn't even worth a Barusco, is it? So now we're seeing the true scale,' he said, adding that Car Wash had spiralled to unimaginable proportions.

José Dirceu's defence claimed that his detention was unjust and unnecessary: 'There is no risk of flight, because José Dirceu is already serving a sentence of house arrest. He is not interfering in the investigations, nor is he destroying evidence,' explained his lawyer Roberto Podval. In addition, his client was not dangerous and had made himself available to the authorities. As for the payments from construction firms, Podval insisted that Dirceu had told the judicial authorities about the transfers himself. That afternoon, the defence lawyers presented an application that he should remain in Brasília, in a suitable unit run by the local prison authorities. The lawyer commented informally to the detectives that Dirceu had undergone a health check the day before that prohibited him from travelling by air. He said he would ask Dirceu's doctor for a medical report explaining this. Shortly after, a police officer went to see Dirceu and told him that they were already arranging bus tickets.

'Your lawyer says you can't go by plane, so we're going to have to go by bus,' said the officer.

'I know exactly where Curitiba is, officer. It's over eleven hours by road from here,' said Dirceu.

'No, I reckon it'll be more than that. I can't find a direct bus, so we're going to have to stop all over the place,' replied the police officer.

Coincidence or not, the medical report from Dirceu's lawyer certified that he was able to travel by plane after all. They just had to wait for the next flight. The Federal Police plane had already taken off from the airport in Brasília earlier that afternoon with some of the other prisoners heading for Curitiba, stopping off in São Paulo; Dirceu would have to go the next day. Justice Luís Roberto Barroso authorised a night transfer and they even considered taking Dirceu on a commercial flight, but in view of the risk of spontaneous demonstrations from other passengers, in the end they decided to wait and use the Federal Police's own plane. Dirceu took off at 2 p.m. on 4 August 2015. Meanwhile, his lawyer Roberto Podval sat in his office hunched over the documents, analysing the evidence against his client.

At that moment, the Workers' Party National Executive, including Rui Falcão, its national chairman, was meeting at the party's headquarters in Brasília. The meeting had begun in the late morning, but officially the subject of the meeting was not José Dirceu, the main items on the agenda were the government's goal of achieving a primary budget surplus and the recent home-made bomb attack on the Lula Institute. Going into the meeting, Rui Falcão commented sparingly on Dirceu's arrest. 'The party is not abandoning any of its comrades,' he declared dryly. In defence of his colleague, Falcão merely said that just like anyone else, Dirceu 'is innocent until proved guilty'. He added that Dirceu's arrest was an attempt to divert public attention away from the attack at the Lula Institute.

In police custody in Curitiba, José Dirceu quickly became accustomed to his new routine. When the prison guard approached, for example, he would quietly move to the back of his cell. If anyone called him, he would come forwards with his hands behind his back. He obeyed orders without causing any trouble. As one of the police officers recounted, 'He asked me: "What can and what can't I do here?" He said he wasn't going to cause any problems, didn't have health issues or a problem with the food, and that he was very disciplined.' In Curitiba, just as in the Papuda jail in Brasília, where he had already served a sentence, Dirceu kept up the habit of reading a lot, to deal with the enormous pressure he was under.

In his ruling on Dirceu's detention, Sergio Moro wrote that the former chief of staff had 'persisted' in receiving kickbacks on Petrobras contracts, even after leaving the government in 2005. The lobbyist Fernando Moura, who was also arrested during Operation Pixuleco, negotiated a plea bargain and told prosecutors that it was he who had suggested Renato Duque's name to Dirceu. The evidence from Moura, a middleman who claimed to represent Dirceu at Petrobras, coincided with that of another middleman, Milton Pascowitch, who was the first to confirm the link between Dirceu and the scheme. Pascowitch, however, went further in his testimony. He said that he had delivered R$10 million in cash to the Workers' Party headquarters in São Paulo. According to the investigators, Pascowitch was also paying kickbacks to João Vaccari Neto. Pascowitch, who was released on house arrest after signing his plea bargain, explained that the payments were either made to Vaccari personally in cash, or as legitimate donations to the Workers' Party. It was up to Gerson Almada, former vice chairman of Engevix, to tell him how each payment was to be made. The kickback paid in relation to just one contract totalled approximately R$14 million, paid between 2009 and 2011, according to the investigators. Of this total, R$10 million was delivered in cash to the Workers' Party headquarters in São Paulo.

THE CONSIST CASE ERUPTS

During this phase, the police also arrested businessmen Pablo Alejandro Kipersmit, chairman of Consist Software. This company had been chosen, without public tendering, to provide IT services in relation to the agreement between the ministry of planning, the Brazilian Banking Association, and the Syndicate of Private Pension Providers. Milton Pascowitch alleged that Consist Software had entered into a fake consultancy contract with Jamp Engenheiros, a company belonging to him and his brother, in order to transfer cash to the Workers' Party via João Vaccari Neto. Consist Software was said to have paid R$10.7 million to Milton Pascowitch between 2011 and 2013, and according to the investigators, the final destination of this money was Vaccari.

Consist Software would become an important part of the Operation Car Wash investigations. Evidence from Consist's chairman resulted in the triggering of phase eighteen of Operation Car Wash, code-named 'Pixuleco II', ten days after José Dirceu's arrest. On 13 August 2015, in an operation designed to prevent the destruction of evidence, the Federal Police set out to arrest Alexandre Romano, a local councillor in the small town of Americana, São Paulo state, who had connections with the Workers' Party and the Democratic Labour Party. Romano may have been one of the middlemen in a contract between Consist Software and the ministry of planning, in which Consist would provide software to calculate payroll deductions for employee loans provided to more than two million federal civil servants. In order to do this, the government needed to give them access to the ministry's IT system. The data, which came under the responsibility of the minister of planning, Paulo Bernardo, allowed Consist to manage the ministry of planning's system of employee loans. The contract was signed without public tendering, and Consist set to work.

Pablo Kipersmit, Consist's chairman, viewed Alexandre Romano as the key person in obtaining the contract, because of his connections with the pension and banking organisations. Kipersmit told the Federal Police that in order to pay the kickback demanded, he issued various invoices to companies named by Romano. All of the invoices were based on fake contracts for services – the same method used by the construction companies investigated under Operation Car Wash. Romano was accused of having collected and distributed kickbacks with a value of R$52 million that had been siphoned off from Consist's contract with the ministry. Part of the money had ended up in the hands of João Vaccari Neto, the Workers' Party treasurer. According to the investigators, Romano had used invoices from eighteen businesses in various sectors to launder the money, including law firms.

In his ruling authorising the temporary detention of Alexandre Romano, Sergio Moro stated that several of these businesses appeared to be mere fronts. To the Federal Police, Romano's actions revealed a shocking new method of laundering money: through law firms. Alexandre Romano was himself a lawyer and partner in a firm that received R$7.9 million from Consist Software between 2010 and July 2015. Consist also made payments to other lawyers, among them Guilherme Gonçalves, who received R$7.2 million, without apparent justification. The payments were ostensibly for representing Consist in court, but the Federal Police could not find any legal proceedings in which any of these lawyers had represented Consist. For this reason, the law firms were served with search and seizure warrants as part of the operation.

The lawyer Guilherme Gonçalves is himself from Curitiba and worked as the legal coordinator of several election campaigns in Paraná state, including the election of Senator Gleisi Hoffmann from the Workers' Party, a former minister in the Rousseff government and wife of another former minister Paulo Bernardo Silva, who had been minister of planning in Lula's government and of communications in Rousseff's. Analysis of documents seized in Guilherme Gonçalves's office gave rise to suspicions relating to Senator Hoffmann: for example, the Federal Police discovered that her personal driver was paid with money from Gonçalves's law firm. Hoffmann justified this by saying that the lawyer was a personal friend and for this reason she used his driver whenever she was in Curitiba.

Guilherme Gonçalves told the police that the payments made by Consist were for services provided by two law firms of his, but the investigators believed they were looking at yet another scheme set up to launder money. 'It's a new model, a new front to be exploited. We've already had to deal with fake advertising and consultancy firms. Now it's law firms,' explained detective Igor Romário de Paula. The detective drew attention to something he considered to be a 'challenge to the country's institutions': the scheme had continued to distribute kickbacks until July 2015 – 'after at least fifteen phases of Operation Car Wash'. Roberson Pozzobon, one of the federal prosecutors, was also of the view that recent events demonstrated that 'the scheme had become more complex, with characteristics of organised crime'.

According to the investigators, Alexandre Romano had said that part of the payments should be made to Milton Pascowitch's company, Jamp Engenheiros. When his turn came, Pascowitch said in his plea bargain testimony that the payments received by Jamp from Consist were kickbacks destined for the Workers' Party. The party's former treasurer, João Vaccari Neto, had allegedly asked Pascowitch and Jamp to handle the payments because he was having problems with the previous middleman, Alexandre Romano.

Sergio Moro wrote in his ruling that, in the light of Pascowitch's confession, all payments made by Consist to Romano had to be treated as suspicious: 'It is possible that unjustified payments from Consist to Milton Pascowitch and to Alexandre Romano may have been related to benefits the company obtained from the ministry of planning.' And the case did not stop there: there were signs that other politicians were involved.

In a document sent to the Supreme Court a few days after Pixuleco II, Sergio Moro said that the investigation had found 'indications that Senator Gleisi Hoffmann may be the recipient of money of a potentially criminal nature'. The investigators had discovered unexplained payments of R$50,000 to the senator and individuals linked to her. Around 10 per cent of Consist's invoicing had been paid to Guilherme Gonçalves's law firm, and the lawyer had apparently consulted Paulo Bernardo, Gleisi Hoffmann's husband, about how he could use the money, which seemed to be intended to pay the expenses of certain individuals linked to Hoffmann. In evidence to the Federal Police, the lawyer alleged that he was using the legal fees he received to pay 'urgent' client expenses. But one detail caught the judge's attention: these amounts were never reimbursed nor charged by him to those clients.

Since the case involved a senator with rights of privileged forum (the right to be tried by the Supreme Court rather than by the ordinary courts), Moro duly sent the case to the Supreme Court. 'In the search and seizure operation carried out at Guilherme Gonçalves's law firm, documents were gathered which indicate that the amounts received from Consist may in part have been used to make payments in favour of the senator,' noted Moro in the submission he sent to Justice Teori Zavascki.

Hoffmann, who was already being investigated by the Supreme Court on suspicion of being connected to the Petrobras scheme, released a statement stating that she had no knowledge of 'any donation or payment from Consist to my campaign'. Nevertheless, the suspicions surrounding her had already grown. The Consist case, as it became known, provoked a great deal of concern in Brasília. In the corridors of the ministry of planning, there were whispers that the investigation could hit all government ministries very hard indeed. The government feared that advances in the investigation could bring the scandal all the way to the Palácio do Planalto itself. Operation Car Wash was now circling one of the government's most important ministries.

Something needed to be done, and fast, said government aides. It would not be easy and they needed a good strategy. The defence lawyers gathered, in search of a way out.

MORO'S REALISM

Between Politeias and Pixulecos, Brazil was now counting on Operation Car Wash to come riding to the rescue, as if one judicial investigation could provide a magical solution to all the country's problems. Once more, it fell to Sergio Moro to tell people to keep a cool head and their feet on the ground. On 20 August 2015, he used a speech at the Symposium of Business Law in São Paulo to convey his message, in much the same manner as he does in his judgments: 'I often meet people who say to me that "this case will change the country". I hope it will, but I confess that I have no powers of premonition in respect to what will happen in the future, or even in the next month.'

While working with Justice Rosa Weber on the Big Monthly trial, Moro had witnessed the same wave of optimism and wanted to rein in the exaggerated expectations of what could be achieved: 'Two or three years ago, I also heard comments that the case then being heard by the Federal Supreme Court, Criminal Action 470 [the Big Monthly trial], was going to change the country. I don't know if it changed things or not. Evidently it was a decision that deserves every praise, but I still find myself wondering if at times we aren't adopting a rather comfortable position in thinking that these cases are going to be a kind of national salvation, a kind of "Sebastianism", by way of judicial decision.'

In what he said there was a criticism of the very people who were now applauding him – and indeed plaguing him with requests for selfies – but who were themselves doing little to look for solutions. He was alerting them against the old tendency, inherited from the Portuguese, of waiting for a 'King Sebastião' – the young king of Portugal who had vanished in battle in Morocco in 1578, giving rise to the centuries-old myth that he had somehow survived and would one day return to save the nation.

THE GLOOMY CONGRESSIONAL INQUIRY

Meanwhile, Operation Car Wash was continuing to produce unusual scenes. At the end of August, Paulo Roberto Costa and Alberto Youssef met once again, this time at the Petrobras congressional inquiry. Summoned to Congress to explain various contradictions in their respective testimonies, they sat facing each other in front of the congressional committee. The lawyers sat behind their respective clients, sufficiently close to be able to whisper advice in their ear should the need arise. Beside them sat the first row of congressmen.

One congressman asked why Costa had made a plea bargain. 'It was my family's decision,' explained the former director, without hesitation. It was indeed – but he had agreed with and was satisfied with their choice. Youssef spoke about Júlio Camargo. The congressmen wanted to know more details of the man who had delivered Eduardo Cunha, the speaker of the Chamber, into the hands of the police. Youssef did not reveal anything very significant, but said that Cunha was good at paying up. On various occasions, Youssef had needed to go personally with Paulo Roberto Costa to collect payments from Júlio Camargo that had been delayed.

At a certain point, Youssef was stung into saying who Eduardo Cunha's 'puppet' was. A few days earlier, Youssef had said at a court hearing that a 'puppet congressman of Eduardo Cunha' was attempting to intimidate his family, by seeking to lift the banking confidentiality in relation to his daughters. The question came from Celso Pansera of the PMDB and received a robust reply.

'You yourself are the puppet, sir,' said Youssef, looking the congressman firmly in the eye.

The discussion carried on, without any further major revelations. At the end of the congressional hearing, Costa and Youssef embraced like old friends, although they no longer were, and left separately. Costa returned home as he was under house arrest, while Youssef went back to jail. Some time later, Celso Pansera became a minister in the Rousseff government. The congressional inquiry continued to be a platform for a lot of hot air and little substance.

Another nebulous incident was the summoning of the lawyer Beatriz Catta Preta to appear before the congressional inquiry. The summons was presented with the ostensible aim of asking the criminal law specialist, who had acted for nine of the defendants and negotiated various plea bargain agreements under Operation Car Wash, where the money to pay her fees had come from. The summons was unanimously approved by the congressional committee, though it provoked an immediate reaction from professional bodies such as the Brazilian Bar Association, who argued that her summons was illegal.

In a story that no one ever quite got to the bottom of, at the end of July Catta Preta told the reporter César Tralli, in an interview on TV Globo's national evening news programme, that she had been threatened. She said that she had stopped acting for her Operation Car Wash clients, because she felt intimidated by members of the congressional inquiry. She added that she had even closed down her law firm and abandoned her career as a lawyer after receiving 'veiled threats' from members of the congressional committee that had voted in favour of her being summoned. She cried while talking about her decision. Some of the congressmen on the inquiry were circulating reports that she had received more than R$20 million in fees. 'I didn't earn even half that,' Catta Preta told the reporter.

In the interview, Catta Preta said that the intimidation of her and her family had begun just after Júlio Camargo accused the speaker of the Chamber, Eduardo Cunha, of receiving US$5 million in kickbacks relating to Petrobras contracts. She explained that Camargo had not named Cunha in his initial depositions because he was afraid, but that he had later provided proof, including documents, against the speaker. Despite Catta Preta's allegations, Hugo Motta, the chairman of the congressional inquiry, said that her summons to appear still stood. 'The summons has been issued in accordance with the law and the internal procedures of the Chamber, and does not constitute a threat of any kind. The inquiry does not threaten. It investigates,' he stated. Motta said he found Catta Preta's statements regarding threats very odd and considered her TV interview to be an attempt at 'playing the victim in order to conceal illegal actions'. According to Motta, the congressional inquiry could not permit this kind of inference: 'The congressional inquiry will continue its work and its investigations. This victimisation is not going to intimidate us. She needs to provide more information about the threats she received, and the congressional inquiry gives her a big platform to say who is threatening her.'

The chairman of the congressional inquiry raised doubts about Catta Preta's real reasons for not wanting to appear before the committee: 'If she received fees legally and declared them to the Revenue, then why is she afraid of appearing before the inquiry? Have you ever seen a lawyer abandoning cases because they were asked about the source of their fees? This merely corroborates the inquiry's doubts. Something's not right here.' To protect Catta Preta, the bar association filed an application for habeas corpus with the Supreme Court, and won. The president of the Supreme Court, Justice Ricardo Lewandowski, granted a preliminary ruling that the lawyer was not obliged to provide clarification to the congressional inquiry. She could even remain silent during the hearing. 'Justice Lewandowski did not absolve her of the obligation to appear, merely of speaking about her fees,' said Hugo Motta. In the end, however, a date was never scheduled for her to give evidence. After giving the TV interview, Catta Preta left the scene. Her friends said she went to live in Miami where she also has a law firm, but she denied this. She then changed her telephone number, and disappeared completely.

Another curious example of the congressional inquiry's behaviour was the contract it entered into, without public tendering, with the international security consulting firm Kroll, to investigate and identify assets siphoned off from Petrobras into secret offshore accounts that had not yet been discovered by Operation Car Wash. Announced with all due pomp and circumstance by the chairman of the committee, the contract, which cost the Chamber more than R$1 million, failed to come up with anything.

According to Congressman Hugo Motta, Kroll's investigation would serve to render invalid any plea bargain agreements where it succeeded in uncovering stolen money that had not already been declared by the informants. 'This could bring down a plea bargain because the person would have lied and could not therefore benefit from a reduction in sentence,' Motta told journalists. In reality, it would be a chance for the accused to question the nature of the accusations. Some legislators even raised suspicions about Kroll's work. 'What are Kroll's tasks? What is its objective?' asked Congressman Ivan Valente from São Paulo, in almost every session. Motta parried the accusations with the argument that the Kroll contract had been entered into in accordance with Brazilian law.

Kroll worked for the Petrobras congressional inquiry from 8 April to 10 June. It searched for real estate and financial assets owned by twelve of those being investigated by Operation Car Wash in thirty-three countries. The team tracked thirty-nine bank accounts, but the material was not even used by the congressional inquiry in its final report. Among those being investigated were three former directors of Petrobras, various construction bosses, Alberto Youssef and João Vaccari Neto. There were no elected politicians on the list. Kroll's report did not provide any new evidence against any individuals: it could not be certain whether those under investigation had money abroad, it merely indicated lines of enquiry that could lead to some assets arising from corruption and hidden abroad. For many congressmen, this preliminary finding was a disappointment. In the light of negative feedback, Kroll announced that it would not be entering into a new contract with the congressional inquiry because they had not reached an agreement, but added that 'the congressional inquiry was satisfied with the work undertaken'.

The congressional inquiry spluttered to a halt several months later without any major revelations or recovering any misappropriated funds, but exonerated Eduardo Cunha and attacked the plea bargains.

The congressional inquiry came to nothing, but federal prosecutors, assisted by tax authorities in other countries, were obtaining remarkable results in the task of recovering the stolen money. The US$97 million held offshore by Pedro Barusco, the former Petrobras manager, had been repatriated and was being held by the judicial authorities, a result that was unprecedented in the history of Brazil. Under Operation Car Wash, a lot of money was being recovered. This was one of Rodrigo Janot's triumphs in his campaign to be reappointed.

Janot's term of office as prosecutor-general was coming to an end, but he wanted to stay on for another two years. He had the ideal pitch. Under his leadership, the federal prosecutors had achieved tremendous results and he needed more time to consolidate this work. His name had received the most votes in the list of three names sent to President Dilma Rousseff by the National Association of Public Prosecutors, so that she could make the final selection. Despite pressure from the PMDB and her own Workers' Party, Rousseff nominated Janot to remain in post. The news was welcomed at the prosecution service's headquarters, but without much fanfare. There was still one further obstacle: Janot's nomination had to go to the Senate.

It fell to the senators to confirm Rousseff's nomination and approve Janot's appointment in two votes, first by the constitution and justice committee, and then by the full Senate. Would Janot get the necessary votes? After all, major figures in the Senate, such as the speaker Renan Calheiros and Senator Romero Jucá, were among those being investigated by Operation Car Wash.

Chapter 9

THE RULE OF LAW

22 August 2015

CHARGES AND ACCUSATIONS

As the end of August approached, five months after Operation Car Wash's first judicial investigations opened at the Supreme Court, Rodrigo Janot found himself facing a dilemma. In a few days he would be scrutinised by the Senate, with his reappointment needing to be approved in two separate votes. Meanwhile, his team of prosecutors had been working well – some of the cases were making quick progress and two sets of charges were ready. If the charges were presented immediately, this could slow down his reappointment as prosecutor general. If he waited to do them later, he would be criticised for having waited until after the confirmation hearings. Janot decided not to wait, and on 20 August he filed charges against the speaker of the Chamber, Eduardo Cunha, and Senator Fernando Collor de Mello, a former president of Brazil.

Suspicions against Congressmen Eduardo Cunha had first arisen from Alberto Youssef's testimony in 2014. Youssef had said that Cunha had used information requests in the Chamber of Deputies to apply pressure for the payment of kickbacks using money misappropriated from Petrobras. The facts had been investigated and the prosecutor general's office had obtained evidence that the information requests had indeed come from him. Then came Júlio Camargo's testimony, which added further information about the congressman's participation in the scheme being investigated by Operation Car Wash. This was the basis of the first set of charges from the federal prosecutors against the speaker of the Chamber for his involvement in the Petrobras scandal.

The prosecution's investigations pointed to sixty financial transactions linked to the laundering of money from kickbacks allegedly paid to Eduardo Cunha. These included various payments to bank accounts abroad, cash delivered by employees of Alberto Youssef and even payments to churches made on Cunha's instructions. Former congresswoman Solange Almeida was also accused of corruption for allegedly having helped in applying pressure for the payment of kickbacks. In addition to the accusation of corruption and money laundering, the prosecutor general also filed a claim for the return of the money taken, to the amount of US$40 million, and a claim for damages for the harm caused to Petrobras, also coming to US$40 million.

In a long statement to the press, Eduardo Cunha said he was absolutely unperturbed: 'I vehemently refute all the inferences being drawn from this charade coming from the prosecutor general. I am innocent and I am relieved that these charges have been brought, since the matter will now pass to the judicial authorities. As I have previously said, I was singled out for investigation and now, it would seem, I am also being singled out for prosecution. Indeed, I'm first on the list.' In another section of the statement, he stated:

> I have a clear conscience and will carry on my work as speaker of the Chamber of Deputies with the same sincerity and independence that have always guided my actions, honouring my campaign promise to uphold the independence of the Chamber. I emphasise that my lawyer will respond to the specific allegations raised in the charges. I was charged on other grounds by federal prosecutors in 2013. The Supreme Court accepted by majority vote to hear the charges and subsequently, in 2014, I was unanimously absolved. This confirms the federal constitution's provision upholding the principle of presumption of innocence. Finally, I have complete confidence in the independence and impartiality of the Federal Supreme Court to rein in this attempt at injustice.

Eduardo Cunha was expecting the charges. The day before, the whisperings in Brasília were so loud that the congressman himself viewed the filing of charges as inevitable. He became aware of the possibility shortly before lunch and met with around ten leaders of various political parties that afternoon. He was uneasy, but assured his allies that he was innocent and would be able to prove it. Before leaving to preside over the legislative session, he gave an interview commenting on the threat from some political parties that they would call for him to step down if he were actually charged: 'I will not step down under any circumstances, and will continue to carry out precisely the same functions for which I was elected by a majority of the Chamber. On this I am absolutely clear. I will perform my functions as speaker in precisely the way our institutions require me to do so. I will not seek retaliation, nor will I adopt a certain stance because of the behaviour of others,' said Cunha. The pressure on him would increase in the following weeks.

Senator Fernando Collor de Mello was accused in the Supreme Court – along with Pedro Paulo Leoni Ramos, who had been a minister in Collor's government in the 1990s, and three other officials – of crimes of corruption, money laundering and evasion of currency controls. According to the federal prosecutors, Collor had received R$26 million in kickbacks between 2010 and 2014, through contracts signed by Petrobras's subsidiary, BR Distribuidora. Rafael Angulo Lopez, one of Alberto Youssef's employees, said that Senator Collor had personally received R$60,000 in R$100 banknotes. The investigators said there were indications that some of the kickbacks may have been used to purchase, in the name of front companies, the luxury cars that had been seized by the Federal Police, such as the Ferrari and Lamborghini.

Senator Collor, who had been making speeches in the Senate stating his innocence and attacking the prosecutor general, released the following statement:

Senator Fernando Collor reiterates his position on these charges, which have been built on a succession of speculative attacks. Like a circus ringmaster, the prosecutor general has taken it upon himself to select the order of acts for his audience, without any regard for the principal victim of this charade, who has not been given any opportunity to tell his side of the story. The senator has on two occasions sought to provide evidence and, on both occasions, appointments to do so were strangely cancelled the day before the scheduled dates. If the senator's right to speak and to see the court documents had been respected, everything could have been cleared up long ago. Instead, they have opted for a media circus, to the detriment of the rights and safeguards of individuals.

Collor's lawyers said, 'It is symptomatic and worrying for charges to be filed against any citizen before he has been given the right to be heard. The situation is even more serious when the person being charged exercises a parliamentary mandate, confirmed at the ballot box.'

SCRUTINISING JANOT

Fernando Collor prepared to face Janot at the Senate confirmation hearings. It would be the perfect opportunity to question his accuser and attempt to undermine him. In a speech to the full Senate, Collor said that the federal prosecutors' accusations were lies and that Janot was trying to intimidate the Senate on the eve of his own confirmation hearing.

He wants to make the Federal Senate a house of eunuchs, but he will not succeed in this. He will have to respect the institutions and, above all, an upper chamber of the importance of this Federal Senate. I would like to say to you, ladies and gentlemen, that nothing Mr Rodrigo Janot has been doing in relation to myself will make any difference, because he will not silence me. Every minute of every day I will be dogging his heels, right behind him, listening and figuring out what he's up to, his scheming and mischief-making, so that from this very podium I can denounce him as a dupe and a fraud, someone who has been clothing himself as the high priest of morals and good practices, the sole owner of the truth, which he most certainly is not.

On the day of the confirmation hearing, Senator Collor was the first to arrive at the Senate's constitution and justice committee room. He sat in the front row, which was still completely empty, and calmly straightened his papers. From where he sat, he would be able to see Rodrigo Janot straight in front of him and could look the prosecutor general in the eye. Collor had already made several speeches against Janot in the preceding weeks. In one of them, soon after the presentation of the charges against him in the Supreme Court, the former president let slip a swearword – between clenched teeth, he called the prosecutor general a 'son-of-a-bitch'. In a session of the full Senate, surprised officials asked themselves, 'Can he say that?' An insult like that, spoken from the podium of the Federal Senate, would in itself be a serious breach of decorum, but no one took the trouble to raise the issue. By that point, Collor had presented four motions calling for Janot to be stopped.

When Rodrigo Janot arrived for the hearing, he noticed the senator but did not show any visible reaction. He began to answer the committee's questions. His entire team were watching the hearing, either there or at the prosecutors' headquarters. Most of those present stood at the back, watching Collor's movements. Several friends had joked with Janot in the days before the hearing, recalling the famous incident when Arnon Affonso de Farias Mello, Fernando Collor's father, had fired a gun at an adversary during a session of the full Senate. 'Be careful, with this family you're playing with fire. There is a precedent for violence in the Senate anterooms,' they said. The prosecutor general laughed. However, Janot's bodyguards warned him seriously that Collor might be armed that day and he had discussed the matter with the speaker of the Senate, Renan Calheiros.

'Look here, my security guys have put out an alert. But I believe in the republic, the Senate and in you, sir, that nothing like that will happen in Congress. I'm not going to wear a bullet proof vest,' said Janot.

'Don't worry, I'll talk to Collor, don't worry,' replied Calheiros.

The story ended up becoming a joke. Senator Aécio Neves told Janot's team not to be concerned because he would sit beside Collor and would grab his arm if anything happened. Neves really did sit in the front row, beside Collor. When it came to the senators' questions, Fernando Collor was not first on the list, but his questions were the most eagerly awaited by the journalists. He continued to stare pointedly at the prosecutor general, to the consternation of Janot's bodyguards.

Janot began by saying that he would 'stand firm in the fight against corruption' and went on answering the senators' questions one by one. He once again rejected the possibility of an overall deal to smother the investigations, and defended the use of plea bargains. When Collor's turn finally came, the senator made various accusations. He said that under Janot's leadership, the federal prosecution service had rented a house in the prestigious South Lake area of Brasília for meetings, and that the public purse had incurred losses as a result. He queried the employment of a press attaché, and stated that Janot had provided accommodation for a relative who was under police investigation. The prosecutor general did not waver and refuted the allegations one by one. At a certain point, when Collor began to make comments during his answers, Janot had to control himself. 'Do not interrupt me,' he said, looking sternly at the senator. He refused to reply to only one question, concerning his brother: 'In relation to the dead, I am not going to participate in the exhumation of someone who cannot defend themselves.'

Janot used a popular saying from his home state of Minas Gerais to explain how everyone deserved the same treatment from the courts: 'The rules of justice must apply equally to everyone, and its force must prevail over both the weak and the strong, the poor and the rich, without fear or favour. Translated into the straightforward language of the people, the saying "The stick that beats the son also beats the father" tells us all an essential message about equality, the values of our republic, the absence of privilege, impartiality and, above all, the proper functioning of the state.' The Senate listened in silence.

At the end of the hearing, after answering yet another round of questions from Collor, Janot said something that hit home: 'We will stay firm in the fight against corruption. There is no viable future if we give in to corruption. There is no country possible without law. We are all equal before the law.' After ten hours of questioning, Janot's reappointment was approved by senators on the committee and, that same night, by the full Senate. Sergio Moro was following the hearings from Curitiba, and he liked the prosecutor general's words. It was exactly what he was seeking: the rule of law for everyone.

THE FIRST JUDGMENTS

By the end of September 2015, eighteen months after the beginning of Operation Car Wash, Sergio Moro had already sent to prison a good number of the most important figures in the criminal organisation that had taken root in Petrobras. The trials had proceeded quickly; those convicted were already serving their sentences, determined in accordance with the weight of the evidence, and some had also lodged appeals against their sentences. Everything had followed a rhythm carefully determined by the judge. Out of all the criminal actions relating to the Petrobras scandal, the first that was ready for final judgment from Sergio Moro was that which had come from the initial suspicion of corruption discovered by Operation Car Wash: the case of misappropriation of funds in the construction of the Abreu & Lima oil refinery in Pernambuco. The construction of the refinery was originally budgeted at R\$2.5 billion, but by the time charges were filed, the costs on the still unfinished refinery had already exceeded R\$20 billion, according to federal prosecutors. The investigations revealed indications of corruption and money laundering.

Judgment was handed down on 22 April 2015. Of the ten people charged, eight were found guilty, among them Alberto Youssef and Paulo Roberto Costa. This was Costa's first conviction under Operation Car Wash, and he was the first Petrobras employee to be sentenced by Sergio Moro. He was given seven years and six months in a semi-open prison. On account of his plea bargain, and having already spent five months and seventeen days in police custody, he would serve one year of detention under house arrest, back-dated from 1 October 2014. After that, there would be one more year in which he could leave the house during the day, but had to be at home at night and during weekends and public holidays, and wear an electronic tag at all times.

In the same trial, Alberto Youssef was sentenced to nine years and two months in a closed-regime prison for the offence of money laundering – in this specific case, for the laundering of R$18.6 million split into many different transactions, one of which was for R$1.9 million. In passing sentence, Sergio Moro said that it had been proved that the misappropriation of funds from Petrobras took place through payments from Consórcio Nacional Camargo Corrêa, responsible for the construction of the refinery, to six front companies controlled by Youssef, including MO Consultoria e Laudos Estatísticos, RCI Software, GFD and Empreiteira Rigidez. However, in Youssef's plea bargain agreement, it had been agreed that he would only serve three years in a closed-regime prison, backdated with effect from 17 March 2014. In justifying the imposition of lighter sentences for those criminals that had cooperated, Sergio Moro cited Youssef's case: 'Despite Alberto Youssef's high level of culpability, cooperation requires the granting of legal benefits, for it is not possible to treat the cooperating criminal with excessive harshness, otherwise the plea bargain mechanism would cease to function.'

The others accused of helping Youssef to operate front companies were sentenced to various penalties, in accordance with the degree of guilt and level of cooperation of each one. The brothers Leandro and Leonardo Meirelles, Youssef's front men in the pharmaceutical firm Labogen that was used to make illegal payments of foreign currency to overseas accounts including in Hong Kong, voluntarily cooperated with the judicial authorities and even made themselves available to go to Hong Kong in order to bring back documents. For this, they received sentences of six and five years respectively in a semi-open prison for the offence of money laundering, and were soon released. However, where the judge considered that a defendant was more significantly involved in offences of money laundering and criminal organisation, such as Márcio Bonilho from Sanko Sider, one of Camargo Corrêa's suppliers, and Waldomiro de Oliveira, who had administered Alberto Youssef's companies, they received a harsher sentence. Sergio Moro gave both these individuals a sentence of eleven years and six months in a closed-regime prison. Two other defendants, both accountants at Sanko Sider, were acquitted. As he reflected on the case and prepared his judgment, Sergio Moro did not see it as a large-scale criminal operation with a rigid and hierarchical structure, since few were convicted of that kind of crime in the Abreu & Lima refinery case. The full extent of the criminal operation would only become clear in the following judgment, the first in which building contractors would be convicted.

BUILDING CONTRACTORS CONVICTED

The case involving Camargo Corrêa executives was dealt with even faster than the Abreu & Lima refinery trial. It was only seven months and nine days from initial charges to judgment, was issued on 20 July 2015. Six of the nine defendants were convicted, among them Dalton dos Santos Avancini, former chairman of the company; Eduardo Hermelino Leite, former vice chairman; and João Ricardo Auler, former chairman of the board of directors. Dalton Avancini and Eduardo Leite had spent just over four months in prison, having been released after providing the necessary testimony, leaving behind Auler – the only one of the three who had not made a plea bargain – in jail, with dim prospects. Around a month later, he benefited from a decision by the Supreme Court that allowed the various business executives under investigation to be held under house arrest.

Dalton Avancini and Eduardo Leite were each sentenced to fifteen years and ten months in a closed-regime prison for the offences of corruption, money laundering and participation in a criminal organisation. However, as they had made plea bargains and cooperated with the judicial authorities, the custodial part of their sentence was limited to the period they had already been held in Curitiba: four months and sixteen days. In addition to this, they would have to serve one further year under full house arrest with effect from 14 March 2015. After this, if everything went well, they could proceed to the more flexible regime of wearing an electronic tag and staying at home at nights and at weekends, for a period of between two and six years. The remainder of their sentence would be served on parole. Meanwhile, for João Ricardo Auler, who had not cooperated, the sentence was nine years and six months in a closed-regime prison, for the offences of corruption and participation in a criminal organisation.

According to the charges filed by the federal prosecutors, Camargo Corrêa had formed a cartel with other large Brazilian building contractors; these had coordinated, in order to systematically defraud Petrobras's tendering process for large construction projects from 2006 onwards, including the Abreu & Lima oil refinery in Pernambuco, the Presidente Getúlio Vargas refinery in Paraná, and the Rio de Janeiro Petrochemical Complex. The construction companies met in what they called the 'club', arranging their bids in advance to decide who would win each round of tendering, having bid the maximum price that Petrobras could possibly accept. To increase the success of the cartel, the contractors also corrupted various high-level employees at Petrobras, among them the former director, Paulo Roberto Costa, paying them a percentage of the contract value in exchange for invitations to participate in tender offers, together with privileged information about the bidding process. By virtue of this scheme, according to the prosecutors, Camargo Corrêa won the main contract for the Getúlio Vargas and Abreu & Lima refineries, which were carried out in consortium with other construction companies under its overall leadership. In exchange, the directors of Camargo Corrêa were accused of funnelling around 1 per cent of the contract value into the scheme, some of which was delivered directly to Petrobras's then-director of supply, Paulo Roberto Costa. After his retirement, he continued receiving kickback money under the guise of consulting contracts with his consultancy firm, Costa Global.

On 5 August 2015, OAS became the second building contractor to have its senior executives convicted. Of the nine individuals charged, seven were convicted for corruption, money laundering and participation in a criminal organisation. The OAS executives were found guilty of having defrauded the Petrobras tendering process as part of the cartel, from 2006 onwards. The chairman of OAS, José Aldemário Pinheiro, known as Léo Pinheiro, was sentenced to sixteen years and fourteen months in prison. During the investigation, the police found proof that Youssef had carried out transactions with OAS right up until a few days before Pinheiro was arrested. In its report, the Federal Police revealed that they had seized documents and text messages from directors of the construction firm, the content of which caused a lot of embarrassment. In more than one of them, Léo Pinheiro referred to former president Lula da Silva by the nickname 'Brahma', a reference to the brand of beer famous for its slogan 'the Number One'. It was another indication that Operation Car Wash was getting close to the Workers' Party's most senior figure. Various other executives from construction companies were also convicted. Sérgio Mendes from Mendes Júnior received a sentence of nineteen years and four months for corruption, money laundering and criminal organisation. Gerson Almada from Engevix was also sentenced to nineteen years in jail for the same offences. Erton Medeiros Fonseca from Galvão Engenharia was given a sentence of twelve years and five months. By May 2016, all of these sentences were being appealed.

A HEAVY SENTENCE FOR RENATO DUQUE

On 21 September 2015, the first of the cases against Petrobras's former director of services, Renato Duque, was ready for Sergio Moro to give his judgment. The charges were money laundering, corruption and criminal association for misappropriating funds from Petrobras and paying kickbacks to the Workers' Party. Ten individuals were convicted in all, including Renato Duque, João Vaccari Neto, Augusto Mendonça, Júlio Camargo and Pedro Barusco.

Renato Duque received the heaviest sentence of all: twenty years and eight months in a closed-regime prison for crimes of corruption, money laundering and criminal association. In his judgment, Sergio Moro spoke of the damage caused to democracy itself: 'The money laundering had an impact on the democratic political process, contaminating it with criminal resources, and I regard this as particularly reprehensible. It is perhaps this, more than the illegal enrichment of public officials, that is the most reprehensible element of the criminal scheme at Petrobras: the contamination of the political sphere through criminal influence, to the detriment of the democratic political process.'

The second major conviction in this trial was that of Pedro Barusco, manager in the Services Division and the person who administered Duque's bank accounts abroad. He was given eighteen years and four months for corruption, money laundering and criminal association. In his judgment, Sergio Moro cited the receipt of more than R$20 million in one single offence of corruption: 'Corruption involving the payment of kickbacks worth tens of millions of reais, with consequently an equivalent loss to the public purse, merits particular condemnation.' Moro, however, emphasised the record amount of money handed over by Barusco after making a plea bargain agreement: 'The agreement included a commitment to repay approximately US$98 million, which probably constitutes a record for criminal trials in Brazil, at least as regards individuals. The amounts have already been returned and for the most part repaid to Petrobras, which will ensure at least a partial recovery by the victim, Petrobras, of the public assets that were misappropriated.'

Since Barusco had made a plea bargain, the closed-regime prison would, despite the length of his sentence, be replaced by an open regime: he would serve his sentence at home and be allowed to leave the house between the hours of 6 a.m. and 8 p.m., other than over weekends and public holidays. In addition, he would have to wear an electronic tag for a period of two years and do community service. The rest of his sentence would be served on parole.

In the same trial, the Workers' Party's former treasurer João Vaccari Neto was sentenced to fifteen years and four months in a closed-regime prison for corruption, money laundering and criminal association. Sergio Moro highlighted the use of electoral donations to launder kickbacks: 'The laundering, in the present case, involved particular sophistication, with the use of criminal assets to make registered electoral donations, conferring upon them an appearance of legality in a way that is rather unusual and, at least to the knowledge of this court, unprecedented in Brazil.' In his judgment, Sérgio Moro referred explicitly to the institutionalisation of the scheme: 'In the understanding of this court, the criminal enterprise in question continued at least until the departure of Renato Duque from the Services Division of Petrobras in April 2012, payments of kickbacks having occurred the preceding month.'

Finally, Moro justified the need to impose jail sentences by virtue of the sheer size of the scheme: 'In a criminal scheme involving kickbacks and money laundering on such a scale, the imposition of a custodial sentence is indispensable in order to protect public order, whether on account of the gravity of the offences, or to prevent relapses, including the commission of further acts of laundering criminal proceeds that have not yet been recovered.' The judge cited the example of Renato Duque, arrested twice during Operation Car Wash: 'Between his first and second periods of arrest, it was discovered that he still held a large amount of money in secret accounts in the Principality of Monaco, which he continued to hide from the Brazilian authorities and had failed to disclose in his previous applications for habeas corpus. In 2014, while the investigation was ongoing, he went as far as clearing out his Swiss bank accounts, in an attempt to put the proceeds of crime beyond the reach of the Brazilian authorities, who were already cooperating closely with Switzerland.'

Noting that 'there are records of voluminous transfers to other bank accounts in the United States and Hong Kong, which may also be controlled by Renato Duque and still remain beyond the reach of the Brazilian authorities', Moro drew attention to an important detail: the value of Duque's money seized abroad was around €20 million, whereas the amount repaid by Pedro Barusco, Duque's subordinate, exceeded US$97 million. To the judge, this was an indication that Duque may still have other bank accounts hidden abroad. 'Releasing him, as with the others who were held on remand, before all the facts have been established and all the proceeds of crime recovered, puts at risk the chances of eventual sequestration and confiscation of such assets by the judicial authorities and the due application of criminal law, on account of the risk of the guilty party escaping the jurisdiction and holding on to the proceeds of his criminal activity,' warned the judge.

Finally, in relation to João Vaccari Neto, Sergio Moro held that even at the time of this judgment, new suspicions were still arising that Vaccari's activities in collecting kickbacks and laundering money extended well beyond the Petrobras scheme. In the most recent phases of Operation Car Wash, evidence had arisen that initially seemed to indicate Vaccari's involvement in the receipt of kickbacks from Consist Software in a scheme involving the ministry of planning. For Moro, in cases like this where the evidence pointed towards 'a professional and habitual tendency towards committing offences, detention on remand is a harsh but necessary remedy, in order to protect public order and safeguard the application of the criminal law'.

A BITTER PILL FOR CERVERÓ

Sergio Moro gave Nestor Cerveró a sentence of five years in jail for the offence of money laundering, committed in 2009 when he purchased an apartment on Rua Nascimento Silva in Ipanema, Rio de Janeiro, with money from the Petrobras corruption. According to Moro, there was a risk of flight: 'It is not acceptable to run the risk that those who have committed serious offences against the public administration can escape from justice and still enjoy, in exile, the multimillion-dollar proceeds of their criminal activity. In this case, such a risk is aggravated by the defendant's dual nationality, which casts doubt over the eventual success of any extradition request in the event of him, once released, seeking refuge in another country.' Moro added that Cerveró should remain in prison during any eventual appeals by his defence: 'In the opinion of this court, this should be the rule in cases of serious offences committed against the public administration, especially when the proceeds of the crime have not yet been recovered in full.'

Cerveró lost his apartment in Ipanema, which was auctioned to reimburse the public purse. In his decision, Moro highlighted something Justice Newton Trisotto had said in rejecting a writ of habeas corpus for one of the Operation Car Wash defendants: 'In the last twenty years, no instance of corruption and improbity in public administration, not even the infamous "Big Monthly" scandal, has caused such indignation, such "damaging and detrimental repercussions for the social environment", as those that have been investigated under Operation Car Wash – an investigation that each day reveals yet more scandals.'

This was not, however, Cerveró's only conviction under Operation Car Wash. He was also found guilty in the trial relating to the payment of kickbacks in two contracts for operating Petrobras drillships, signed in 2006 and 2007 respectively.

In the first case, according to the federal prosecutors, Júlio Camargo, representing the Korean shipbuilding company Samsung Heavy Industries, succeeded in winning for them a contract from Petrobras to supply a deep-sea drillship, the

Petrobras 10000. They did this by paying US$15 million in kick-backs to Petrobras's International Division, headed by Nestor Cerveró, using Fernando Baiano as middleman. In return for the money, Cerveró recommended that Petrobras's executive management award the contract to Samsung, which they duly did, at a price of US$586 million. Júlio Camargo paid the kick-back via thirty-four financial transactions that passed through bank accounts provided by Fernando Baiano.

The following year, they repeated the same transaction. Petrobras contracted Samsung to build another drillship, the *Vitória 10000.* This time they had to pay more: in fact, it was a settling of accounts. Júlio Camargo had promised US$20 million for the first drillship, but only US$15 million had actually been paid, so this time he had to pay US$25 million. Once again, Cerveró recommended to Petrobras's executive management that they award the contract to Samsung, and this was done for a total price of US$616 million. Júlio Camargo paid around US$5 million to Fernando Baiano, but then the payments stopped. Pressure was applied, demands were made, and Camargo had to dip into his own pocket to honour his commitments. In any event, according to Sergio Moro's ruling, it was proved that Cerveró and Baiano received more than R$54 million in kickbacks, converted at the rate of exchange at the time. For this, Nestor Cerveró, Júlio Camargo and Fernando Baiano were sentenced to twelve, fourteen and sixteen years in jail respectively. Cerveró still had one more charge to face. According to the Federal Police and federal prosecutors, he had received a Range Rover Evoque from Baiano, valued at R$220,000. According to the charges, the gift was purchased at the same dealership where Youssef had bought a similar car for Paulo Roberto Costa. In February 2016, Jorge Zelada,

Cerveró's successor at the International Division, was also found guilty of corruption and money laundering, and sentenced to twelve years and two months in jail.

CONVICTED POLITICIANS

The first politician to appear in Operation Car Wash was also the first to be convicted: he was given fourteen years and four months. André Vargas, former deputy speaker of the Chamber of Deputies, was found guilty by Sergio Moro of corruption in receiving kickbacks from Ricardo Hoffmann at the advertising agency Borghi/Lowe. Leon Vargas, his brother, was convicted of acting as middleman for the payment. The three of them were convicted of sixty-four offences of money laundering arising from sixty-four transfers of money siphoned off from advertising contracts entered into by Caixa Econômica Federal with the two Vargas front companies Limiar and LSI, between June 2010 and April 2014.

On determining André Vargas's sentence, Moro wrote:

> His level of culpability is high. He received kickbacks not merely in his capacity as a federal congressman, but also in his role as deputy speaker of the Chamber of Deputies during the period 2011 to 2014, the years in which he carried out the greater part of the criminal acts which are the subject of this trial (06/10 to 04/14). The responsibilities of a deputy speaker of the Chamber are great, and so consequently is his culpability when he commits a crime. His volatile personality also does him no favours. I am reminded of his insulting gesture on 4 February 2014, recorded in various photographs, when he raised a clenched fist while

sitting beside the eminent Justice Joaquim Barbosa, then president of the Federal Supreme Court, at the ceremony marking the beginning of the 2014 legislative year. The congressman, just like anyone else and perhaps even more than anyone else, has a right to freely express himself. Protesting against the judgment of the Federal Supreme Court in Criminal Action 470 [the Big Monthly trial] is therefore something that can and could be validly done by him or by anyone else for that matter, notwithstanding the Supreme Court having acted with its customary wisdom on the matter. Nevertheless, we now know that Congressman Vargas, at the time he made that gesture, was simultaneously receiving kickbacks on public contracts through the intermediation of Borghi/Lowe. In such circumstances, his gesture of protest is nothing more than hypocrisy and, with the benefit of hindsight, demonstrates a personality not only open to crime, but also disrespectful to the institutions of justice.

Moro ruled that André Vargas should begin his fourteen-year sentence in a closed-regime prison. If he wanted to move to the semi-open regime, Vargas would have to comply with the provisions of the Criminal Code, which state that a person found guilty of a crime against the public administration could be held under the semi-open regime, but only on condition that they provide redress for the harm caused or returned the proceeds of crime. In Vargas's case, this meant returning all the money which, according to the judicial authorities, he had laundered in successive operations, thereby hiding its public origin: R$1,103,950.12 exactly. 'The laundering of such a significant amount of money deserves particular censure,' concluded Moro.

Another politician convicted by Sergio Moro under Operation Car Wash was Pedro Corrêa from the Progressive Party, who had also been convicted in the Big Monthly trials. When he was arrested, on Moro's orders, Corrêa was serving a jail sentence in his home state of Pernambuco, so the Federal Police had an easy job collecting him from jail in Pernambuco and transferring him to Paraná. After months of legal proceedings, judgment time had come. By this stage, the judge knew that Pedro Corrêa was negotiating a plea bargain with the federal prosecutors, but he issued his ruling without waiting for the outcome of discussions between Corrêa and the prosecutors. If Corrêa later cooperated, he could review his decision. He therefore convicted the former congressman for corruption. In this trial alone, Corrêa was accused of receiving R$11.7 million in kickbacks. Sergio Moro ruled:

> Corruption through payment of tens of millions of reais in kickbacks, resulting in a corresponding loss to the public purse, deserves particular condemnation. However, the most disturbing aspect in relation to Pedro Corrêa consists of the fact that he received kickbacks even while he was being tried by the Federal Supreme Court under Criminal Action 470, since there are records of him receiving money as late as October 2012. Even a conviction by the highest court in the land failed to inhibit his criminal conduct, this time in another illegal scheme. He has therefore acted with extreme culpability, and this must also be taken into due consideration.

In this single trial, Corrêa was held to have committed seventy-two counts of corruption and 328 counts of money laundering, according to Sergio Moro's calculations. Due to the number of offences committed, he was given a sentence of twenty years, three months and ten days – one of the longest under Operation Car Wash. As with Vargas, Corrêa was ordered to begin his sentence in a closed-regime prison and could only request a transfer to the semi-open regime after returning what he had stolen from the public coffers.

Luiz Argôlo, one of the politicians closest to Alberto Youssef, had been sentenced to eleven years and eleven months for offences of corruption and money laundering. According to the judgment, he had received almost R$1.5 million from the scheme run by Youssef. In addition, Argôlo and Youssef had business dealings together. In his testimony, Youssef said he viewed Luiz Argôlo as an opportunity for him to 'grow' politically and had decided to help him financially for this reason. The judge decided to keep Argôlo in prison because, among other reasons, he was still a substitute congressman: 'If he were released, he could, in certain circumstances, come to exercise a congressional mandate, which would be intolerable. It is not possible that someone convicted of criminal offences can exercise a legislative mandate, and society should never run the risk of having criminals in its legislature.' The judgment also required that Argôlo return approximately R$1.5 million in damages to Petrobras and have his Robinson helicopter, which had been purchased with proceeds from the scheme, confiscated.

In the very first judgments under Operation Car Wash, given back in 2014, Sergio Moro had dealt with the four criminal groupings that had been identified right at the beginning of the operation, one of which was linked to money laundering and drug-trafficking. A leading black-market currency dealer

on São Paulo's 'parallel' foreign exchange markets, Nelma
Kodama and her group were convicted early on for having set
up and operated a veritable financial institution, moving up to
US$300,000 per day in black-market foreign exchange trans-
actions. She was in business for at least eight years, stopping
only when she was arrested. She was sentenced to eighteen
years in jail. In the judgment, Moro recalled that twelve
high-value works of art were found in her apartment. At the
end of the trial, these paintings were donated to the Oscar
Niemeyer Museum in Curitiba. The trial involving Hermes
Magnus's company – the one that began the whole process
of Operation Car Wash – also reached judgment in 2015 and
resulted in Alberto Youssef's first conviction under the operation. He was sentenced to three years, on account of his plea
bargain. Carlos Habib Chater, owner of the petrol station that
gave its name to the entire operation, received a four-year jail
sentence.

By November 2015, a year and eight months after the beginning of Operation Car Wash, Sergio Moro had already handed
down twelve judgments and convicted fifty-four individuals.
The investigations revealed that almost every major contract
between Petrobras and its suppliers contained a payment of
undue reward to the managers of the state-owned company. In
just five criminal actions, it had been proved that companies
such as Camargo Corrêa, OAS and Mendes Júnior had paid
tens of millions of reais in kickbacks to managers like Paulo
Roberto Costa, Nestor Cerveró, Renato Duque and Pedro
Barusco, using the money laundering and intermediation services of middlemen such as Alberto Youssef, Júlio Camargo and
Fernando Soares. The scheme had been broken up and some
of its ringleaders punished. Every step of the way, Sergio Moro

had needed to overcome a seemingly never-ending series of difficulties. There was nothing to indicate that things would be easier in the future.

PLEA BARGAINING CALLED INTO QUESTION

One day at the end of August, a highly unusual application from the defence came before the Supreme Court, indicating a new strategy: the lawyers representing Erton Medeiros Fonseca, from the engineering firm Galvão Engenharia, presented an application for habeas corpus with the aim of annulling Alberto Youssef's plea bargain agreement, one of the pillars of the Operation Car Wash investigation. Their argument was that Youssef had already breached a previous plea bargain agreement in the Banestado case, and that as a result he could not enter into a new one. The defence also stated that Youssef was an 'inveterate criminal' and that the information obtained from him was not reliable. The lawyer José Luís de Oliveira Lima, representing Erton Medeiros Fonseca, criticised the federal prosecutors' behaviour in the case. 'Federal prosecutors misled Justice Teori Zavascki by omitting to mention that seven days before the plea bargain was signed with Youssef, the previous plea bargain had been terminated by another judge. As a citizen and a lawyer, I want the facts to be investigated, and those who are guilty to pay the price for their actions. But as a defence lawyer, I must insist that matters are dealt with within the democratic rule of law.'

Deputy prosecutor general Ela Wiecko defended the agreement signed between federal prosecutors and Alberto Youssef: 'The cited circumstance – a breach of the previous agreement – was duly considered within the context of restricting the benefits the defendant would receive pursuant to his new plea

bargain agreement. Federal prosecutors proposed stricter conditions because of this. While other cooperating witnesses were
offered house arrest, Youssef is being held in a closed-regime
prison and will remain so.'

Dias Toffoli, the Supreme Court judge dealing with the
application, spoke for over two hours on the subject. Among
other things, he said that a judge approving a plea bargain cannot assess the credibility of the informant: 'On ratifying a plea
bargain agreement, the judge does not make an assessment of
the testimony provided before or after. It does not fall to the
judiciary to examine aspects such as suitability or conditions,
nor to test the veracity of information they are given.' Toffoli
highlighted that any cooperating informant necessarily forms
part of the criminal organisation, and that the argument that
he is criminal should not be taken into account: 'Given the very
nature of the legal concept of criminal association, it is only
normal that its members may display a personality that is
inimical to the wider social environment and inclined towards
the commission of serious crimes. The institution of plea bargains would be of little effect, and rarely used, if it were offered
only to individuals of a favourable psychological profile.' Toffoli ruled that Youssef's plea bargain was entirely valid, and his
decision was immediately followed by concurring judgments
from two other Supreme Court judges, Justice Gilmar Mendes
and Justice Luiz Edson Fachin. By then, it was the end of the
day and the hearing was adjourned.

When the hearing resumed the following day, the court
decided unanimously that Youssef's plea bargain was valid. It
was an important victory; Operation Car Wash had overcome yet
another obstacle and now no one could question the validity of
Youssef's evidence. The Supreme Court judges emphasised that

plea bargaining was just one way of obtaining evidence against criminals and that such evidence could not be the only method used to gain a conviction. However, some of them praised its effectiveness in the case of Youssef: 'His plea bargain enabled the penetration of this group that had usurped the functions of the state, promoting an immoral and criminal assault on the public exchequer and criminally diverting resources that were otherwise destined towards socially necessary and worthy ends. Using this individual's testimony as a means of obtaining evidence has shown itself to be an effective means of drawing back the veil that had protected this conspiracy of delinquents, who are now finding themselves in the sights of the public prosecutors,' said Justice Celso de Mello.

SWISS BANK ACCOUNTS

At the end of September 2015, investigations against the speaker of the Chamber, Eduardo Cunha, gained a new momentum when a middleman allegedly linked to the PMDB, the businessman João Augusto Henriques, said in evidence to the Federal Police that he had opened an account in Switzerland to pay kickbacks to the congressman. Suspicions increased when documents forwarded by the Swiss authorities arrived in Brazil. Cunha had denied for months that he had bank accounts abroad, but the evidence pointed the other way, and this was enough to start procedures against him in the Chamber of Deputies' ethics committee.

The strength of the congressman's denials became even stranger when the press published images of a Swiss bank account application form, in which a copy of his passport appeared. The address given was a P.O. Box in the United States, the explanation being that he lived in a country with an unreliable postal service. Cunha had filled out the form by hand, writing that he had decided to open the account because he wanted to work in Switzerland. The Central Bank undertook an investigation and sent its conclusion to the ethics committee, stating that it was beyond 'all reasonable doubt' that the speaker of the Chamber had bank accounts in Switzerland. Even so, Cunha continued to deny that he was the owner of the accounts, claiming that the accounts were in fact 'trusts', of which he was 'merely' the beneficiary. With the help of his political allies, he began a long campaign to defend himself against the ethics committee.

The Cunha family's expenditure abroad also caught the public's attention. On a trip to Paris in February 2015, the speaker of the Chamber had spent more than US$27,000 in five days, of which US$15,800 was spent on staying at the luxurious Hôtel Plaza Athénée and US$8,100 at the men's clothing shop Textiles Astrum France. On the same trip his wife, Cláudia Cruz, spent US$14,500 on shopping trips to Louis Vuitton, Chanel, Charvet Place Vendôme and Hermès.

During their 2013 New Year's holiday in Miami, the Cunha family spent US$42,000 on meals and hotels, equivalent to R$84,000 at the time, something of an extravagance for a man earning an official monthly salary of R$17,800. In his formal charges against Eduardo Cunha for the offences of corruption, money laundering, invasion of currency controls and electoral falsehood, the prosecutor general, Rodrigo Janot, considered that such expenditure was 'incompatible with the legitimate and declared assets of the accused'.

The investigations caused further consternation in political circles when detective Josélio de Sousa, from the Federal

Police's team in Brasília, applied to the Supreme Court for authorisation to interview former president Lula da Silva as part of the investigation into senators and congressmen involved in the corruption scheme. In his report, the detective recognised that there was no proof of Lula's direct involvement as yet, but defended his request on the basis that the investigation 'cannot avoid, in the light of facts already established', verifying whether or not the former president benefited from the 'scheme set up within Petrobras, thereby obtaining advantages for himself, his party (the Workers' Party), or even for his government, through the maintenance of a party political support base sustained at the expense of illegal transactions within the aforementioned state-owned company'.

The detective recalled that when commenting on Lula's potential role in the Petrobras scheme, Alberto Youssef and Paulo Roberto Costa had 'assumed that the former president of the republic had knowledge of the corruption scheme', bearing in mind 'its characteristics and dimension'. There was no proof, but Lula would have to give evidence to the Federal Police.

Chapter 10

THE FACTS, THE EVIDENCE, THE LAW – AND PUBLIC OPINION

30 October 2015

AN INCOMPLETE JIGSAW

Prosecutor Deltan Dallagnol sat down at a table in a hotel in Caucaia, near Fortaleza on the far north coast, with two glasses of coconut water – a healthy start to breakfast. At the table were two of his colleagues from the Operation Car Wash task force, Andrey Borges de Mendonça and Orlando Martello, along with Orlando's wife Letícia, herself a senior prosecutor in Curitiba. It was a sunny morning and the tropical palm-fringed beach at Cumbuco was a tempting prospect, but despite the relaxed atmosphere, they were not there for pleasure. They would be spending the next few hours in the auditorium of the XXXII National Conference of Public Prosecutors, whose theme that year was 'Public oversight in the fight against corruption', a subject that interested all four of them.

Later that morning, they would need to change the venue for Dallagnol's lecture quickly, in order to accommodate all those

wanting to attend. The audience would include former prosecutor general Roberto Gurgel and deputy prosecutor general
Raquel Dodge, along with colleagues from all over Brazil.

Over breakfast, the smile disappeared on Dallagnol's face
when Orlando Martello showed him his phone.

'Have you seen this?' asked Martello.

'No way. You're joking! I don't believe it!'

It was 30 October 2015, and Dallagnol had just seen that
Justice Teori Zavascki had decided to send yet another part of
the Car Wash trial to Rio de Janeiro, taking it away from the
Curitiba task force and the jurisdiction of Sergio Moro. What
they had feared most was now happening: the case was being
salami-sliced and shared out between different judges on the
Supreme Court and lower courts, and other prosecutors in
other cities. This time it was the Eletronuclear case, which was
investigating Vice Admiral Othon Pinheiro da Silva – the man
who had reacted to his arrest by yelling that he was a military
officer and threatening to shoot – and Edison Lobão, the former
minister of mines and energy.

The information about Eletronuclear had been obtained from
the same informants as the rest of Operation Car Wash and it
was the same companies that had been paying the kickbacks.
The scheme for misappropriating funds also followed an identical pattern: a percentage was deducted from the contractual
payments made by the state-owned company, and the money
was divided between politicians and those running the companies. The only difference was that the corruption had taken
place at Eletronuclear, the state-owned nuclear energy firm,
rather than at Petrobras.

'It's like a jigsaw puzzle with pieces missing. It's impossible to
complete,' muttered Dallagnol angrily.

'Don't worry, Deltan. We're going to appeal,' said Douglas Fischer, one of the leading members of the prosecutor general's team in Brasília, who was also staying at the hotel.

'How are we going to do that?'

'I'm already preparing something. Janot has instructed us to appeal to the full court.'

'You're going to write a memorandum to every Supreme Court judge?' asked Dallagnol.

'More than that. We're going to give them all the information. Leave it with me, I'm already on it.'

The sun was still tempting them towards the beach, but the prosecutors stayed huddled in a corner of the hotel restaurant, discussing what their next step should be at this delicate moment. Letícia Martello smiled and thought to herself that she had been absolutely right on that day, almost two years ago, when she had gone into Dallagnol's office and told him that he had to work on Operation Car Wash, because it would be a historic opportunity in the fight against corruption. He had been reluctant at first but had ended up accepting the role of coordinator of the task force.

This morning at the hotel near Fortaleza, Dallagnol seemed in low spirits for a moment, perhaps because he hadn't slept much the night before. 'This just can't happen. It weakens us. It's not that we are the only ones who know how to do things – it's just that a colleague in another state will have other priorities and won't be as familiar as we are with every detail of the investigation. What's more, it's all the same scheme.'

THE FIRST SLICE OF SALAMI

The first piece to be sliced off was the Consist Software case, which involved former ministers Paulo Bernardo and Gleisi

Hoffmann, the Workers' Party senator for Paraná. The case went to São Paulo, despite being part of the overall group of Car Wash trials and even though both politicians were from Curitiba. One of the prosecutors travelled to São Paulo to hand over the documents relating to the case and sensed that his colleagues there did not have the same sense of urgency. The São Paulo prosecutors had their own cases to deal with, and the deadlines they were used to dealing with might not follow the same breakneck pace as Operation Car Wash. With the Consist Software decision due on 23 September, this was now one of the investigators' main fears.

The prosecutors texted each other in the hours before the Supreme Court hearing that would decide whether Sergio Moro and Justice Teori Zavascki would be responsible for all the Car Wash trials, or just those connected to the fraud at Petrobras. They were clearly nervous about the possibility of important trials, such as the alleged frauds at the ministry of planning, the ministry of health, Eletronuclear and the Belo Monte hydroelectric power station, being taken away from Sergio Moro. Their worry was that elements of the most important corruption trial in Brazil could slip out of the hands of the people with the greatest knowledge of the scheme. These elements would then go to other judges, who would have to start from scratch. At the very least, time would be lost.

Prosecutor General Rodrigo Janot appeared calm on his way into the Supreme Court hearing. He arrived smiling, joking with the waiting journalists. 'Can we have a word, prosecutor? Just one minute of your time?' asked a reporter. Janot turned around, held up a finger and answered 'Yes, but just one!' and went into the room chuckling. But it was no ordinary day. Even Eduardo Pellela, Janot's right-hand man who had been heavily involved in the Operation Car Wash working group and didn't usually attend court hearings, went to the Supreme Court that day. He left shortly before the end once it was clear which way the decision would go.

The Supreme Court were discussing whether 'Pixuleco II', a trial that was already under way in Curitiba as part of phase eighteen of Operation Car Wash, should be divided. If it were, the charges against Senator Gleisi Hoffmann would remain with the Supreme Court, and the rest of the trial against Alexandre Romano (the former town councillor in Americana in São Paulo state), would go to the lower courts. Justice Teori Zavascki had declined jurisdiction over Hoffmann's case, saying that it was not for him to oversee the judicial investigation into her case, because it concerned fraud at the ministry of planning rather than at Petrobras. Where cases did not have an obvious connection to each other, it was necessary to redistribute them to the oversight of a different judge.

Justice Ricardo Lewandowski, the president of the Supreme Court, also ruled that there was no connection and ordered that the case be reallocated to one of the other judges. Justice Dias Toffoli was chosen. The prosecutor general appealed. If Teori Zavascki ceased to be the natural choice for any aspects of Operation Car Wash that did not concern Petrobras, Moro would automatically lose jurisdiction over such matters. Judgment of the appeal began with Justice Dias Toffoli, the court's lead judge on the matter, who simply gave a summary of the facts. The prosecutor general was then asked to speak, and strenuously defended the principle of keeping all the cases under a single judge:

'There is a single criminal operation that uses the same method, the same principals, the same middlemen, acting both in the case involving Consist (which had contacts with the ministry of planning) and that involving Petrobras. We are not investigating individual firms or individual informants, but rather a vast criminal organisation that extends throughout numerous branches of the public sector,' he stated.

Toffoli's vote came after Janot's submission, and was a setback for the Car Wash team: he was in favour of separating the cases. If the majority of the court followed his vote, Teori Zavascki would no longer oversee cases that did not involve Petrobras. Toffoli said that since the crime in this case had taken place in São Paulo, which was also where the headquarters of most of the companies involved were located, the relevant legislation indicated that the case should be tried there. Sergio Moro would therefore lose an important part of the case, albeit not the most important one. Furthermore, the decision opened the way for lawyers to start calling Moro's jurisdiction over various other cases into question, trying to take other bits of Operation Car Wash away from him.

Justice Gilmar Mendes and Justice Luís Roberto Barroso questioned Rodrigo Janot. If the prosecutor thought it was so important to maintain the unity of Operation Car Wash, then why, only a few days earlier, had he been in favour of removing Teori Zavascki from the investigations into the alleged accounting frauds concerning the president's chief of staff, Aloizio Mercadante, and Senator Aloysio Nunes Ferreira, of the PSDB? The accusations made by businessman Ricardo Pessoa of UTC, who had reported using dirty money to finance candidates in the 2010 election campaign, had ended up being dealt with by Justice Celso de Mello. Janot replied to this and a series of other questions. He argued, that two firms that had paid money to Gleisi Hoffmann were located in Curitiba and therefore that suspects who were subject to Supreme Court jurisdiction by virtue of their political rank should be tried by the Curitiba courts. Dias Toffoli rejected this argument, saying that in the charges it had filed against Alexandre Romano, the prosecutor general's office had clearly written that the crime was committed in São Paulo. And if the crime had been committed in São Paulo, the trial should go there. The debate continued until the prosecutor general had nothing more to say, at which point Dias Toffoli declared that the Curitiba judiciary could not be made the 'universal arbiter' of all corruption cases:

> No single court can assume the role of universal arbiter of all and any offence relating to the misappropriation of funds for party political purposes, in defiance of the normal rules of jurisdiction. Evidently, this is not intended to undermine or obstruct the investigations, which must proceed efficiently so as to uncover all unlawful conduct. But there are federal prosecutors, federal police officers and federal judges in every state of Brazil, with more than adequate available capacity. It cannot be said that there is only one arbiter with the skills or judgment to undertake such an investigation. Is there only one judge in Brazil? Are all the others relieved of their jurisdiction? Are we going to override all the normal rules of procedure?

Justice Teori Zavascki gave further force to the argument. For him, it was a technical issue. If there was no connection with Petrobras, the crux of the investigation, the cases should go to other courts. Justice Gilmar Mendes was the only dissenting voice: 'It is a matter of great importance, otherwise there would be no dispute before this court. To put it bluntly, what is feared is that cases will leave Curitiba and then not proceed as they ought to in other places.' Gilmar Mendes reminded the court yet again that this concerned 'the biggest corruption case in the world'. 'You can send a case to be tried in Cabrobó [a small town in Brazil's rural north-east]. It will simply not get the same level of support. Not to mention the risk of losing the thread of all the accumulated knowledge developed throughout the investigation.'

Losing the thread. That was the point. It wasn't about wanting to make Moro the 'universal arbiter', but that he had buried himself in the subject and teased out all the threads from that complex ball of wool. Even so, in the end the Supreme Court decided, by eight votes to two (Gilmar Mendes and Celso de Mello), that Teori Zavascki would not be the Supreme Court judge in charge of aspects that were not specifically related to the fraud at Petrobras. By seven votes to three, the court also decided to remove from Sergio Moro the investigation into frauds at the ministry of planning. As well as Gilmar Mendes and Celso de Mello, Luís Roberto Barroso was against, holding that it was for the Curitiba judge himself to declare himself incompetent or not to proceed, but they were outvoted.

While journalists rushed to file their reports on the judgment, Rodrigo Janot left the court in a hurry. Only one reporter, from the newspaper *O Estado de S. Paulo*, managed to catch him as he was getting into his official car. She asked him what he thought about the judgment, to which Janot replied with the Latin dictum: '*Roma locuta, causa finite.*' When Rome has spoken, the matter is finished. The prosecutor general closed his door and the car sped away.

TAKING STOCK OF OPERATION CAR WASH

By this time, Operation Car Wash had already produced evidence, information and suspects on a scale that surprised even the prosecutors. The operation had exceeded all normal expectations and provided Brazil with noble principles that seemed far removed from the actual experiences of its ordinary citizens. *Erga omnes* – 'To All' – is the very opposite of the rule of a privileged elite, such as had always held sway in Brazil. A country where those with power, influence and money had always been spared the severity of the law was finally showing its citizens that, yes, the law did indeed apply to everyone. Operation Car Wash strengthened the hand of the federal prosecutors, and for that reason the auditorium at the conference hotel near Fortaleza was packed for Deltan Dallagnol's joint lecture with prosecutor Diogo Castor de Mattos.

The theme of their talk was 'Federal prosecutors and the fight against corruption'. In the audience were prosecutors dealing with environmental issues, education and what was called 'transition justice', seeking punishment for crimes committed by the military dictatorship. Federal prosecutors pursue cases in many different areas, but in recent years the number of scandals, and mounting public indignation, showed that greater effort was needed in combating corruption. Among a wide range of other convicted individuals, the Big Monthly scandal had jailed a former minister and a former treasurer of the Workers' Party, but when the investigation started, many people were convinced that it would go nowhere. By that time, the scheme within Petrobras, which shared with Big Monthly the objective of extracting money from business deals with the state for the benefit of political parties and individuals, had already been set up. When the Big Monthly scandal erupted, this newer scheme continued to function. The seven years of Big Monthly trials had shocked the whole of Brazil, but as the investigation showed, it had not intimidated those involved in Car Wash. During all this time, they had continued to extract money from Petrobras. This sense of impunity had deep roots: *erga omnes* was not a principle Brazil had been accustomed to living by. Operation Car Wash was trying hard to break this tradition.

'I want to start by saying that this investigation is not partisan. We are not against party A, B or C. We are combating a very old practice in Brazil,' explained Dallagnol at the beginning of his talk. He spoke about how the investigation had managed to go further than others, but also emphasised that it was necessary to go even further, beyond Operation Car Wash, so that investigations like this would not be the exception but the rule. In light of this objective, Deltan Dallagnol had even become involved in the 'Ten Measures Against Corruption' campaign. Some of his colleagues disagreed and felt that this was not the role of federal prosecutors.

'We're public servants, Deltan. That's the job of wider society, not us,' Orlando Martello had said over breakfast that morning.

'If no one was interested, I'd let it go. But there are more than 400,000 signatures,' Dallagnol had replied.

The ten measures had grown out of studies undertaken by prosecutors on the Operation Car Wash task force. Working committees were then set up by the federal prosecutors' office to prepare proposals for legislative changes aimed at combatting corruption. Next, a campaign was launched to gather 1.5 million signatures and present the ten measures in the form of a citizens' initiative draft legislation. The number of signatures rose rapidly in the following weeks and months.

The objective of the measures was to attack corruption on various fronts at the same time and to turn it into a high-risk crime. The measures include more prevention, control and transparency within government and companies and, when a crime is committed, harsher penalties and the closure of legal loopholes that currently gave rise to effective impunity through endless appeals or retrials. The guilty would stay in prison for longer, so as to ensure that stolen money was recovered and returned to the public purse. The proposed measures include other changes, such as the introduction of integrity tests in public office and making the illicit enrichment of a public servant a criminal offence. High-value corruption would be placed in the most serious category of criminal offences, along with crimes such as murder or rape.

The campaign won immediate support from various public figures, artists and intellectuals and, as the months went by, it gradually headed towards its target: by Christmas 2015, it had reached one million signatures; by carnival time in February, it had reached 1.5 million, the minimum required by law; by the end of March 2016, when the signatures were delivered to Congress, they had reached the record number of 2,028,000. The proposals became a citizens' initiative draft law and began to make its way through Congress. 'We have to change this culture of some people being more equal before the law than others,' said Dallagnol in speech after speech, reviving old hopes for equality.

Sergio Moro shared the same conviction that the courts must be neutral and egalitarian, upholding the values of the republic. Throughout his cautious judgments and pronouncements, Moro had been consolidating these principles and emphasising the values that ought to determine the lives of Brazilian citizens, one of which is that justice is equal for everyone. By May 2016, Sergio Moro had passed eighteen judgments, convicting seventy-four people. Their combined sentences exceeded 1,000 years in jail. There were still thirty-three more criminal cases to be heard, as well as the two cases he had lost to other courts – the Consist case and the Eletronuclear case. But Moro was satisfied. If Operation Car Wash had stopped right then, it would already have left a legacy. Never had so many powerful people gone to jail, never had so much been revealed about the functioning of the corruption machine within the Brazilian state and never had so many people decided to tell what they knew, hand back stolen money and cooperate with the judicial authorities. The operation had its good days and bad days, its moments of alarm and of unprecedented success. Everything about Operation Car Wash was superlative. Between 17 March 2014 and the middle of April 2016, there had been twenty-eight phases of the operation, thirty-eight criminal cases had been started and thirteen cases divided.

Moro also strongly supported the principle of transparency, the idea that the trials should be public and everything that could be disclosed should be made available to citizens, because, as he said, 'the judiciary cannot be the keeper of dark secrets'. Moro is not the only judge who thinks like this or who is capable of conducting a trial of this magnitude, but he is the one who succeeded in doing it. He and the prosecutors were convinced that it was necessary to inform public opinion as much as possible. This belief unsettled those under investigation and their defence lawyers, who accused Moro and the prosecutors of 'selective leaks' throughout the trials. The work of journalists was always fraught: there was constant stiff competition between different media and much was published about various parts of the case. But almost all the material that reached the press came from a careful study of documents disclosed, perfectly legally, through the courts' own 'e-proc' electronic disclosure system. As Moro explained, public disclosure must be the rule in any trial. Only things that are subject to judicial reporting restrictions should be kept confidential, to protect an ongoing investigation, for example. Everything that is not subject to such restrictions should be accessible in its entirety. It was from their reading of this vast amount of information that the press obtained most of its information.

Some defence lawyers criticised the trials for having more informants than accused. It is true that Operation Car Wash had an unprecedented number of informants, but by the end of its first two years, more than 140 people were under investigation, using evidence from around sixty informants. During the first two years of the operation the Brazilian state trembled, twisted and took fright. There was a moment in which it really could be said that no one slept – 'Nessun Dorma', as Puccini's famous aria puts it – or at least, the judiciary didn't seem to sleep. There were many mornings that began with the surprise of yet another police operation taking to the streets, banging on doors that had never before received that kind of visit from police. Among criminal proceedings, judicial investigations, warrants to access tax records, banking records, wiretaps, search and seizure, detention, information-sharing requests, seizure of assets, evidential rulings and other procedural matters, there were more than 1,200 judicial decisions or proceedings.

Another important victory was that never before had it been possible to recover so much stolen money. Before Operation Car Wash, the largest amount the state had recovered in a single trial was R$45 million. By April 2016, Operation Car Wash had already recovered, under the various plea bargains, R$2.9 billion. Among those convicted, Pedro Barusco returned the most, a sum of US$97 million. The money was paid into an account controlled by the courts and then returned to the injured party. In 2015, Petrobras received two repayments reaching almost R$300 million.

It was not the first operation against corruption and would not be the last, but from then on it would be more difficult to repeat a scheme to rob the coffers of a state-owned company with the same ease. And it had not just been any old company, but the biggest state-owned company of them all. Petrobras lost market value, changed its senior management, spent months without an audited balance sheet, lost its investment grade and suffered unprecedented losses. The operation helped to stem the misappropriation of funds in almost all the firm's contracts – for this reason, it can't be blamed for the company's current problems. On the contrary, Petrobras's financial fragility was the result of the crimes uncovered. Operation Car Wash is, in fact, the company's hope of salvation.

Operation Car Wash's success is in part due to Moro's speed in dealing with the trials under his remit. But in a country where the courts have always been criticised for their slowness, the judge was accused of the opposite tendancy: taking decisions too quickly, rushing into things and doing all the work, taking on aspects that should have been done by other courts or states. Moro always worked with a small group – his office has only fifteen employees, one assistant and Sergio Moro himself. He had promised speed and that is what he delivered. But it came at a cost.

At a seminar in São Paulo organised by *The Economist* in October 2015, Moro admitted that he was tired. He was right:

things had been very intense since those first steps in July 2013. Officially, Operation Car Wash began on 17 March 2013, and between July 2013 and the seminar, a whirlwind had torn through the judge's life, all in less than two and half years – a short period of time for so many events and revelations. At the seminar, the organisers asked Moro to talk about the case. In his usual calm tone, he quickly took stock of where things stood:

> This case began, like all cases, in a small way. We were investigating, or rather the Federal Police and federal prosecutors were investigating, four alleged black-market currency dealers, and one in particular: Alberto Youssef. The deepening of investigations brought them to other activities, some of which involve Petrobras. In reality it was like pulling a thread and suddenly there is a whole ball of wool, and after that ball comes a ... I was going to say a cat, but in fact it was a monster. It was difficult. Of course, when the investigation began, no one had any real idea of the extent of the activities it would reveal. It is difficult to foresee what will happen, since it very much depends on the evidence that is thrown up. A criminal investigation often takes new directions, but on other occasions it reaches a dead end. It is all rather unpredictable. I would like to think, if only for personal reasons – I must confess I'm a little tired of the work – that we are approaching some kind of conclusion.

Moro carried on by talking about the parameters that should be followed in the trials: 'What determines the judge's actions are the facts, the evidence and the law. In trials involving complex crimes and individuals who are economically or politically powerful, public opinion is fundamental to enabling the judge to give due weight to the law, the evidence and the facts. I have no doubt that public opinion has overall been in favour of the work that has been done, and this has been fundamental to its success.'

On the panel, a representative from *The Economist* asked in a strong British accent if all this could be characterised as 'a fishing expedition', in which Moro was just waiting to see what might come out. His response drew laughter from the audience, showing once again that despite his serious expression, Moro had a sharp sense of humour: 'There's been a lot of fish.'

JUDGING BIG FISH

Some of the biggest businessmen in heavy construction sat facing Sergio Moro. They were the bosses of traditional companies like Odebrecht, Andrade Gutierrez and Camargo Corrêa, or newer groups like Engevix, with shorter histories but rapid growth in terms of government contracts. All demonstrated the same respect for the judge, who was so often said to be inflexible. Sitting directly in front of Moro, only Marcelo Odebrecht behaved as if he were still sitting at the head of the table, master of all he surveyed. Grandson of the founder of Brazil's largest construction company, he had handed Moro a document in which he had written sixty questions, along with his answers. He was a defendant facing the judge, but his words and gestures made clear that he would only deign to answer his own questions. Sergio Moro wasn't fazed by even the most irritating moments of the hearing, such as when the businessman asked to make an initial statement and refused to answer the judge's questions.

This hearing, on 30 October 2015, was an example of Odebrecht's line of defence. When Moro asked Marcelo Odebrecht the standard question of whether he would remain silent or speak, he replied that he would speak, but not answer questions. In what he called his 'initial statement', he accused federal prosecutors of not listening to him and the judiciary of not allowing his lawyers access to trial documents and of breaching the privacy of his daughters' telephone calls. Moro interrupted him to refute the breach of privacy, but Odebrecht told the judge to let him speak. Moro asked which documents his defence team had not been able to access. Odebrecht did not reply and once again asked to be able to continue with his initial statement. And so it went on. Only Odebrecht spoke, without permitting any objections to his assertions nor answering any of Moro's questions. He accused the judiciary of 'oppressive publicity' and of 'dangerous prejudging'. He said that he disagreed with the format of oral responses to questions, questions that were themselves full of assumptions. Moro listened to everything without losing his calm. The businessman was telling the judge that his questions contained assumptions and that he, Marcelo Odebrecht, disagreed with the trial format established by law. Odebrecht was taking on the roles of both judge and defendant.

'For this reason, I am providing you, in writing, with detailed replies to every line of questioning on absolutely all the events that are attributed to me.'

Moro merely repeated, 'Aha.' By now, ten minutes had passed while Marcelo Odebrecht gave his initial statement, and he had still not answered a single question from the judge. He claimed he was innocent of everything, lauded the Odebrecht group's business policies, and asserted that 150,000 families directly depended on the company and a further million families indirectly. When Moro asked him about his bank accounts abroad, he simply said that he would continue making his initial statement. After speaking for eleven minutes and thirty-five seconds, the businessman agreed to hear his first question from the judge. But he did not answer it, claiming that he had already provided all his answers in writing. Moro observed that oral replies carry a greater evidential weight, and asked the defence lawyer, 'Will he answer the questions or not? That is the issue.'

The lawyer reiterated the same line, saying that his client had already replied to everything, but the judge had not even asked his questions.

'Are you chairman of the Odebrecht holding company?' asked Moro.

'That is one of the questions I have already answered,' said Odebrecht.

'A query regarding timing: when did you take charge at Odebrecht?'

'That has also been answered.'

The judge also wanted to know about his bank accounts in Switzerland, and listed them by name. Marcelo Odebrecht said that he had already replied. After asking several more questions without obtaining answers, Moro handed over to the federal prosecutor, who also wanted to know about the accounts in Switzerland; once again, the businessman claimed he had already answered. In official documents, the Odebrecht group's construction subsidiary had denied ownership of the bank accounts, but the federal prosecutor had evidence that the company's bank accounts in the United States had sent money to the Swiss accounts. Asked about this, Marcelo Odebrecht replied that it was not for him to answer on behalf of the construction company. The construction company was a major subsidiary of the holding company chaired by him. All in all, after twenty-two minutes, in which the owner of the country's largest construction firm had shown himself completely oblivious to the clear wishes of the judiciary, the police and the prosecutors decided that it was necessary to put an end to the old Brazilian practice of impunity.

The curious thing was that Marcelo Odebrecht had begun by saying that the federal prosecutors had not listened to him, despite his wish to cooperate. Nevertheless, he was in front of the judge and the federal prosecutor, saying that he would only answer his own questions. A few months later, Marcelo Odebrecht was convicted and sentenced to nineteen years and fourteen months. In his judgment, Sergio Moro said, 'Although the judgment in this case is not directed against the Odebrecht group itself, I take the liberty of making several observations which I consider pertinent.' He then made several recommendations to the company: 'The Odebrecht group, by virtue of its size, has a political and social responsibility that it cannot escape: it is necessary, as a first step in putting this criminal scheme behind it and restoring its reputation, to assume responsibility for its past mistakes.' He concluded: 'Admission of responsibility does not eliminate wrongdoing, but it is the decent way of overcoming it, especially for a large company.' The defence appealed against Moro's judgment, on the basis that there had been manifest error by the judge, since all the informants and witnesses whose evidence had been heard during the trial had absolved Marcelo Odebrecht of any blame.

WHEN TALKING IS THE ONLY WAY

Others involved in Operation Car Wash, such as Ricardo Pessoa, UTC's boss, did not behave like Marcelo Odebrecht, and decided to cooperate with the judicial authorities. For this reason, they found themselves in a completely different situation – although their lives were restricted, they were much more comfortable.

The electronic tag worn by Ricardo Pessoa is almost unnoticeable. In the plea bargain agreement approved by the judicial authorities, Pessoa was authorised to work, but had to follow various rules. If he didn't obey them, he would find himself back in jail. For example, he was not allowed to meet with the other Car Wash defendants, nor leave his office for any reason whatsoever without the judge's permission. He arrives at the UTC/ Constran headquarters in the Chácara Santo Antônio neighbourhood of São Paulo at 8 a.m. and must be home by 10 p.m. He therefore leaves the office between 8 and 9 p.m. and has dinner at home with his wife and two daughters. He is banned from travelling, especially abroad, and has surrendered his passport to the courts. He makes the journey to and from work in his new bulletproof car. Until he was arrested on 14 November 2014, he had driven a Honda 2008, but upon his release in June 2015, the UTC directors bought him a brand-new bulletproof car, fearing that he might be a target. In the end, after winning his application for habeas corpus and being released from jail, sixty-three-year-old Ricardo Pessoa decided to cooperate with prosecutors, by providing incriminating information on politicians and business friends. Personally, he says, he would have carried on with the same old car. He doesn't like ostentation, so much so that he still hasn't had the cracked glass face of his wristwatch fixed.

Constantly chewing nicotine gum – he had been a heavy smoker before stopping during the six months he was held in the police cells in Curitiba – Pessoa lost fifteen kilos during his time in jail. He still has the same worried look. As vice chairman of UTC's board, he now focuses on studying how to save his company: UTC's annual revenues have fallen from R$5 billion to R$2 billion, and the firm is banned from entering into new contracts with Petrobras, which used to be its biggest client. Business is not going well, although it is not considering filing for insolvency protection, as OAS, Galvão and Alumini did. The company still has two major projects under way: Viracopos International Airport in Campinas, and the São Paulo metro's new Line 6. It is renegotiating some of its bank debts.

While worried about the future, especially for his company, Pessoa thinks he did the right thing in signing the plea bargain agreement. He felt 'tortured' in prison, having to share a tiny cell of twelve square metres and only a very basic latrine with four other prisoners.

'I'm relieved I did the plea deal,' Pessoa told friends at UTC, explaining that whatever sentence Sergio Moro imposes, the plea bargain means he will serve it under house arrest and the length will be significantly reduced. Without the plea bargain, he would have ended up with a jail sentence of at least twenty years.

In his plea bargain testimony, Pessoa explained how the 'club' of Petrobras's building contractors worked, but he becomes indignant when people say that he was the leader of the club, coordinating the construction companies. He told colleagues:

How can the boss of a R$5-billion construction company be the leader of a club alongside other companies with revenues of R$100 billion, like Odebrecht? I wasn't the leader of anything. It's true that I was the only company chairman at the meetings, while the others sent directors. As chairman of the Brazilian Association of Industrial Engineers,

I had a certain influence over the others, but I wasn't the leader. The best Petrobras contracts, the Abreu & Lima oil refinery in Pernambuco, valued at R$60 billion, doesn't have any UTC involvement at all. If I had as much control as they say, UTC would have been involved in Abreu & Lima.

One thing Pessoa deeply regrets is having set up a property development division. The company partnered with GFD, Alberto Youssef's firm, in building hotels in Porto Seguro (in Bahia state) and Aparecida, halfway between São Paulo and Rio de Janeiro. They also set up a property company in Lauro de Freitas, Bahia, together, whose building projects were still uncompleted at the time of writing. 'While the business was entirely legal, I stood accused of associating myself with Youssef in money laundering business projects. All the money invested in the project, including Youssef's money, was done through normal bank transfers, completely above board. But the business was still tainted,' Pessoa said regretfully.

Someone else who regrets not doing things differently is Paulo Roberto Costa. Even so, he reached the end of 2015 in a comfortable situation living in Itaipava, in the mountains just north of Rio de Janeiro. He was sentenced to remain under house arrest until 1 October 2016, and on parole thereafter with various restrictions. His daily routine is peaceful, other than his numerous trips to give evidence. One of the most tiring was to Curitiba, where he had to confront an old acquaintance: Fernando Baiano. It was a long confrontation. Costa and Baiano arrived at Curitiba at 2 p.m. on a Thursday and went straight from the airport to the Federal Police building without stopping for lunch, expecting they would at least be given a sandwich. There was only coffee, water and a few chocolates. Hours passed by. It was after 9 p.m. when the second part of the meeting began, which dealt specifically with former minister Antonio Palocci and the R$2-million donation to Dilma Rousseff's 2010 campaign. It went on for another three hours.

The tensest moment of the long day was when Baiano recounted that he had once gone to Brasília and been driven down the Esplanada dos Ministérios – the monumental line of modernist blocks that house all the federal government ministries – with Paulo Roberto Costa, in an official Petrobras car. Costa said categorically that he would never drive round Brasília with Fernando Baiano in an official car. The confrontation between the two witnesses ended only in the small hours of Friday morning. Since Costa had another meeting scheduled with them the following Tuesday, the Federal Police decided it would be better for him to stay in Curitiba. He spent the weekend locked in a hotel, under police guard.

Several times as the months passed by, usually when least expected, a new door would open in the investigation and yet another murky world would be revealed to the investigators. One day in the police jail in Curitiba, Pedro Corrêa, another important figure in the investigation, decided to make a plea bargain. The former federal congressmen and leader of the Progressive Party, who had jokingly admitted to friends that he had been committing illegal acts all his life, sat down with the prosecutors and made a long list of things he could tell them about. The list was long indeed – the longest so far of any person. Compared to Alberto Youssef's approximately sixty annexes of testimony (covering sixty subjects), it was said that Pedro Corrêa's testimony would take more than 200 annexes. The eventual definitive number was somewhat lower: seventy. The prosecutors said that he would point to an allegation published in the press and say: 'That's something I can talk about. I know about that.' Alberto Youssef made fun of him in jail. 'Next he'll be telling them stuff going back to General Figueiredo's time,' he would say referring to General João Baptista Figueiredo, the last president under the military dictatorship in the 1980s.

It wasn't all plain sailing. At certain points, Pedro Corrêa was reluctant to sign the deal, not wanting to inform on friends such as former congressman João Pizzolatti and Congressman Eduardo da Fonte. He finally signed it in March 2016, convincing himself that it was the best he could do under the circumstances. Older and wearier, he was facing the possibility of spending the rest of his life behind bars: at the end of October 2015 he had been sentenced to more than twenty years. He spoke to various defendants in jail, including José Dirceu, and they all told him there were no good outcomes for him. Even Alberto Youssef advised him to do a deal, and bet that if Pedro Corrêa signed a deal, federal prosecutors and judiciary would approve it. Corrêa was afraid because of the example of Ivan Vernon (another Operation Car Wash defendant), who had entered into negotiations and provided information, but in the end wasn't able to make a deal. Putting this unfortunate precedent aside, the former leader of the Progressive Party provided his long list of information and signed the agreement. His confession was of epic proportions. As far as the investigators were concerned, it could lead to a whole new operation.

Among the most important elements he promised the prosecutors were descriptions of events allegedly showing the direct interference of former president Lula da Silva in dubious management decisions by Petrobras. According to reports in the magazine *Veja*, on compiling his plea-bargain list, Corrêa cited a meeting between Lula and José Eduardo Dutra, who had been chairman of Petrobras at the time. In the meeting, Lula was said to have told Dutra to appoint Paulo Roberto Costa to a directorship at Petrobras, at the request of Congressman José Janene. According to Corrêa, Dutra argued that it wasn't usual practice to appoint someone in that way, especially since another new director had been appointed only a year earlier. Lula said that Janene's request had to be met and concluded: 'If we all followed usual practice, then you wouldn't be chairman of Petrobras, and I wouldn't be president of the republic. Appoint Paulo Roberto. It's decided.'

According to *Veja*, Pedro Corrêa also promised details of an event that supposedly happened in 2011, at the beginning of Dilma Rousseff's first term, when Paulo Roberto Costa stopped paying kickbacks to congressmen from the Progressive Party. Since Janene was already dead and Youssef had definitively taken over the 'treasury' aspects of the scheme on behalf of the party, Corrêa went to see Youssef and was told that Costa would only start to pay the kickbacks again if he received direct approval from the president's staff at the Palácio do Planalto. Youssef had made it clear that he would carry on with the scheme involving the construction companies, but would only release money to the Progressive Party if the president's office gave the green light. Pedro Corrêa said that he went to see the then-secretary general of the president's staff, Gilberto Carvalho, and Senator Ideli Salvatti, to explain the situation. According to Pedro Corrêa, after this conversation the Progressive Party started receiving its money once again. Corrêa did not have proof that authorisation had been given from higher up, but didn't think that either Gilberto Carvalho nor Ideli Salvatti had the power to act on their own. These stories were only a sample of what Pedro Corrêa had to tell; it was a confession with the potential to push the Brazilian political system to its very limit once more.

Who knows whether it was because of this or because of what would take place a few weeks later that, according to the newspaper *Folha de S.Paulo*, stories began circulating around the Supreme Court that Justice Teori Zavascki had told colleagues that with Operation Car Wash the worst was yet to come.

THE TURN OF LULA'S FRIEND

Just as it seemed that an intense year of Operation Car Wash was beginning to quieten down, it all flared up again. On the morning of Tuesday 24 November, the Federal Police arrested José Carlos Bumlai, the cattle breeder and close personal friend of former president Lula da Silva, who had had unlimited access to the Palácio do Planalto throughout Lula's government. As previously mentioned, there was a notice at the entrance to the presidential palace informing staff that Bumlai could enter whenever he wished. For this reason, phase twenty-one of Operation Car Wash was code-named 'Free Pass'. Bumlai was the principal target. The applications for search and arrest warrants were made by federal prosecutors who had been following his movements ever since he had first been mentioned in one of Paulo Roberto Costa's statements in 2014. On that Tuesday, in addition to arresting Bumlai in a Brasília hotel, the police brought in six other people to answer questions. Among them were two sons and a daughter-in-law of the well-connected businessman, as the investigation extended to his family.

Bumlai and the other individuals were suspected of participating in a complex corruption scheme that, according to the investigators, basically worked as follows: the Workers' Party had a debt; the businessman borrowed money to pay the debt; and the bank gave a loan which was discharged when the bank's engineering company won a contract without tendering from Petrobras. Other versions of the story that surfaced later would be even more shocking.

The investigators began by unravelling the complex web of contracts entered into by Schahin Engenharia to operate the drillship *Vitória 10000*. According to federal prosecutors, the contract was only signed by Petrobras because Banco Schahin had agreed to discharge, fraudulently, the loan for R\$12 million it had nominally extended to José Carlos Bumlai, but which was in fact destined for the Workers' Party. The granting of the drillship contract and the choice, by Nestor Cerveró at Petrobras's International Division, of Schahin as operator, was the subject of an internal audit at Petrobras. The audit report shows that every stage of the negotiation breached the company's own rules. The accusation was that Bumlai had put together the financial wizardry that discharged the Workers' Party debt, and that Petrobras then gave the multibillion-real contract to the engineering company owned by Banco Schahin. The Federal Police was also investigating Bumlai's involvement in other cases of suspected corruption and money laundering.

Sergio Moro considered Bumlai's detention necessary in order to 'staunch the potential for damage to the former president's reputation'. The suspicion was that Bumlai had used Lula's name for his own advantage. In this section of his ruling, Moro took the opportunity to say that there was no evidence against Lula: 'There is no evidence that the former president of the republic was actually involved in these illegal acts, but the repeated behaviour of José Carlos Bumlai raises the natural fear that the former president's name could in some way, without justification, be invoked to obstruct or interfere in the investigation or judicial process. Events of this kind could have the potential to cause harm not only to the trial, but also to the reputation of the former president, and therefore detention on remand is necessary in order to impede both such risks,' wrote the judge.

After his arrest, José Carlos Bumlai was taken to the Federal Police headquarters in Curitiba, like so many others before him. He was not questioned immediately. The days went by and he waited. Bumlai made an application to Sergio Moro that he be questioned before the court, in the hope of being released. Moro declined Bumlai's request and he was instead questioned by the Federal Police – but he wasted the opportunity. He gave a false version of events regarding the R$12-million loan, saying that he used the money as a down payment on the purchase of a ranch from the Bertin group, and denied transferring any money to the Workers' Party.

The evidence that had led to the arrest of Lula's friend was strong. It had been gathered through in-depth and detailed work by the Federal Revenue and reinforced by statements from cooperating witnesses such as Eduardo Musa, former manager at Petrobras's International Division. Musa was critical to the investigation, because he revealed that Schahin Engenharia had been chosen as the contracter for the *Vitória 10000* since the beginning of negotiations. Musa had heard this directly from his boss at the time, Nestor Cerveró, the former director of the International Division. Musa said the former director had told him that he had been given guidance 'from above' to do this, precisely because of the R$12-million loan taken out by Bumlai from the bank in order to discharge the Workers' Party's debts.

The lobbyist Fernando Baiano added further details to the story, when he said in his statement that since the end of 2004, Bumlai had been trying to get the Schahin project at Petrobras off the ground in order to discharge the loan, which he had taken out that same year. Fernando Baiano said there had been doubts within Petrobras's management regarding Schahin's financial resources, but that Bumlai had gone to see the chairman of Petrobras, José Sérgio Gabrielli, to overcome these difficulties. The Federal Police questioned the former chairman of Banco Schahin, Sandro Tordin, who said that former minister José Dirceu and former treasurer of the Workers' Party Delúbio Soares had also made requests to speed up the discharge of the loan. In the end, Salim Schahin himself, the patriarch of the family that owned the bank, decided to cooperate and provided the investigators with the final details they needed to confirm that the R$12-million loan to José Carlos Bumlai was indeed fraudulent. Only one question remained: what had the money been used for?

This thread of investigation seemed to stretch back a long way to a very old case indeed. Fernando Baiano and Eduardo Musa said that the money had been used to pay off debts from the presidential campaign. However, Marcos Valério, a public relations consultant who had been found guilty in the Big Monthly trial, gave a different version of events. In testimony that is not entirely clear, even today, given after his conviction in an attempt to reduce his forty-year jail sentence, Marcos Valério said that the money was used to pay off a businessman from Santo André on the outskirts of São Paulo, who was threatening to make sensational revelations about the death of the mayor of Santo André, Celso Daniel.

A complex scheme had been set up to discharge the loan, which the investigators carefully unpicked. In order to 'formally' pay the debt, Agro Caieiras, an inactive Bumlai family company run by Mauricio Bumlai, José Carlos's son, took out a second loan from Banco Schahin at the end of 2005, for R$18 million. This loan also remained unpaid and, in 2007, the bank had to transfer the debt to the group's securitisation vehicle, in order to avoid having to mark it down as a loss. But a solution to the impasse was being put together. At this point, the lobbying for Schahin to be awarded the *Vitória 10000* operating contract was in full swing. According to Salim Schahin, even the treasurer of the Workers' Party, João Vaccari Neto, was involved in the negotiations.

The agreement was a long time in the making. At the beginning of 2009, around five years after the interim loan from Bumlai to the Workers' Party, the contract with Petrobras was signed. On almost the same day, the loan to Bumlai was formally discharged in a complex series of financial transactions that involved promissory notes and a fictitious sale of livestock embryos to cattle ranches belonging to the Schahin family. The embryos were never delivered. If they had been, that in itself would have been illegal. The Schahin ranch named in the contract as receiving the supposed embryos, Agropecuária Alto do Turiaçu, was located in the indigenous territory of Awá-Guajá, in the state of Maranhão. Commercial occupation of land in an indigenous territory is a criminal offence. But according to the investigators, there was no delivery whatsoever: it was all an attempt to conceal the fraud. On 28 January 2009, Schahin was awarded the contract to operate the drillship for a duration of thirty years, at a value of US$1.6 billion. Once again, money began to flow from Petrobras every month and the kickbacks were distributed. It was said that Eduardo Musa, for example, received payments from Fernando Schahin in Swiss bank accounts.

The Federal Police were also able to obtain Bumlai's banking records, where they discovered a large number of loans from banks that were on the verge of insolvency and dozens of cash withdrawals of amounts exceeding R$100,000, with no obvious reason for the expenditure. As if that were not enough, despite his companies' financial difficulties, they had received loans from BNDES, the national development bank. The suspicion arose that Bumlai might be involved in various money laundering operations, or indeed that he might also be a middleman in the corruption scheme discovered by Operation Car Wash.

BNDES admitted that it had lent a total of R$395 million to São Fernando Açúcar e Álcool, a sugar and ethanol producer linked to Bumlai. The loans were guaranteed by other group companies and by the Bertin group. In 2012, a further R$101.5 million were lent by BNDES to São Fernando Energia, through Banco do Brasil and BTG Pactual. BNDES denied accusations of favourable treatment and of making loans to businesses that were in financial difficulties or not producing taxable income. But São Fernando went into judicial reorganisation and in 2015 BNDES itself petitioned for the company's insolvency.

In the light of the evidence revealing various irregularities, José Carlos Bumlai was questioned by the Federal Police on 14 December and gave a new version of the reasons behind the loan. The story he gave is full of strange assertions. Before being questioned, he was informed that charges had just been filed against him by federal prosecutors for offences of corruption and money laundering. The news was given to his lawyers by a police detective, which greatly irritated them. His lawyer

Arnaldo Malheiros Filho protested: 'It is most unusual, and could be termed audacious, to present formal charges against someone who has not yet been questioned, especially when further clarification could contribute to a fuller understanding of the truth.' But Bumlai knew he could do little more than answer the detective's questions. The interview lasted six and a half hours.

José Carlos Bumlai admitted during the interview that he took the R$12-million loan from Banco Schahin in order to pass money on to the Workers' Party. What's more, he said that two former treasurers of the party, Delúbio Soares and João Vaccari Neto, had been involved in the deal, although he made no reference to former president Lula da Silva. Delúbio Soares appears to have been his primary contact in these dealings, in which everyone behaved in a very unusual manner, as shown by Bumlai's version of events.

Bumlai said that on one night in October 2004, he was called to an urgent meeting in Campo Grande with Sandro Tordin, chairman of Banco Schahin. Delúbio Soares was already there with two election campaign officials. Bumlai told the police that when he arrived just before 9 p.m., he didn't know the purpose of the meeting. Tordin had explained that 'there was an urgent need to raise money from Banco Schahin'. Bumlai said to the police that no one told him categorically where the money was destined. The two campaign officials said that the second round of the municipal elections were starting and they needed to pay for some services, but they would return the money shortly afterwards. Delúbio said it was a 'matter of urgency' and assured Bumlai the loan would be repaid quickly. He did not reveal the reason for this urgent need of money. In the police interview, the detective asked Bumlai what any reasonable person would ask: why did he agree to this request and take out a loan of R$12 million with nothing in return? Bumlai replied that the Workers' Party had 'a lot of influence on the national stage' and that he did not want to get on the wrong side of its members. Also, he said, because he didn't believe the loan would actually go ahead. He eventually left that night without signing any papers.

However, the bank's chairman himself turned up at Bumlai's home in Campo Grande at lunchtime a few days later, with all the paperwork under his arm. Bumlai signed and so did his sons. During lunch, Tordin called Bumlai aside and suggested he transfer the money to the Workers' Party via the Bertin group, a company that Bumlai had some business dealings with and which might be able to help. It was a way of disguising the source of the money. Bumlai asked his old friend Natalino Bertin to let the money go through his bank account and made the deposits to the account number given to him by the chairman of Schahin. A few months later, when the first tranche of the loan matured in January 2005, Bumlai went to Banco Schahin to speak to its chairman. Sandro Tordin said that it would not be possible to discharge the debt, because Schahin Engenharia had obtained a contract with Petrobras, but with a value less than that required to cover the loan. According to Bumlai's version of events, it was only then that he found out that Schahin's compensation for granting the loan was a contract with Petrobras. Bumlai said that he went home that day thinking that he would end up paying the loan himself, but only looked into the matter again seven months later, when the Big Monthly scandal broke.

Bumlai says that in the light of Big Monthly, he called his sons and told them everything about the loan that they too had signed. The sons decided to redeem the loan using part of a family property, but the bank refused. It preferred to keep Bumlai as a 'hostage', according to him, because of his friendship with Lula. He then went to see João Vaccari Neto, who had taken over as treasurer of the Workers' Party. He told Vaccari everything, including the participation of his predecessor Delúbio Soares in the first meeting. Vaccari listened in silence and said he would see what he could do. Some time later, Vaccari returned with his response: Schahin was in negotiations for the *Vitória 10000* drillship operating contract, and the loan would be discharged when Schahin obtained the contract. That is indeed what happened. A day before the signature of Schahin's contract with Petrobras in 2009, Bumlai and the bank set up the fictitious delivery of livestock embryos as repayment of the loan. The amount lent by Banco Schahin was never actually repaid and was treated as 'discharged' without any payment of interest. In reality, the drillship contract was Schahin's compensation for the amount it had paid in 2004. In his statement to the police, however, José Carlos Bumlai ruled out any involvement of former president Lula in the episode. He confirmed that he was a friend of Lula's and often visited his home, but would never ask him to interfere in any of his business dealings. When the interview terminated, Bumlai went back to his cell. He would spend Christmas 2015 and New Year in jail.

His version of events is full of odd behaviour: a banker in a hurry to lend, who then doesn't want to be repaid; a businessman who agrees to lend money to a political party without asking questions; a loan of R$12 million which needs a US$1.6 billion contract with Petrobras in order for it to be discharged. And there remain doubts as to the reasons why the Workers' Party treasurer Delúbio Soares needed the money so urgently that he set up a meeting with the banker at night.

Hearings were arranged to reconcile the various accounts, at which conflicting witness statements could be heard and challenged in parallel. On 14 January 2016, one of these took place between Fernando Baiano and José Carlos Bumlai. Baiano said that Bumlai had set up a meeting between him, Paulo Roberto Costa and former minister Antonio Palocci, to discuss funds for President Dilma Rousseff's 2010 re-election campaign. According to Baiano, this meeting agreed on a campaign contribution of R$2 million and that Costa would stay on as director of supply at Petrobras, as indeed he did until the end of March 2012. The hearing was necessary because Bumlai was denying – and continues to deny – that this meeting took place. He did, however, admit discussing with Fernando Baiano whether Costa should stay in his directorship at Petrobras. Even this admission is highly irregular. What role could a lobbyist and a friend of the president, neither of whom were members of the government, possibly have in deciding whether a director of Petrobras remained in his post?

Bumlai's arrest caused enormous uproar. After all, for many years he had been a close friend of the former president. But on the day following his arrest something happened that would shake Brazil even more. As day broke, the Federal Police drew up outside the Senate. Until that day, 25 November 2015, a serving senator had never before been arrested in Brazil. This would be the first time.

Chapter 11

AN UNEXPECTED YEAR-END, AND A SURPRISING NEW YEAR

25 November 2015

A SERVING SENATOR ARRESTED

Senator Delcídio do Amaral had a shock when he went down for breakfast and came face to face with Federal Police officers wandering around the hotel where he was staying, near the president's official residence in Brasília. Not knowing the reason for the police presence, the Workers' Party senator for the state of Mato Grosso do Sul phoned the person he was due to meet that morning. An unfamiliar voice answered, saying that the owner of the mobile phone – Mauricio Bumlai, José Carlos Bumlai's son – was not available. Senator Amaral read on his tablet that José Carlos had just been arrested and Mauricio had been taken in for questioning. The senator, who had introduced Bumlai to Lula, had breakfast alone that morning, thinking about his various connections to these events.

Bumlai's arrest was a serious matter that had grave consequences within the ruling coalition. No one yet knew what those repercussions would be, but the inescapable fact was that someone with a direct link to the former president had just been arrested. Senator Amaral spent the day watching events unfold and, on account of his role as government leader, keeping an eye on votes taking place in the Senate. He was still in the Senate chamber at 10 p.m. and was one of the last to leave, along with Renan Calheiros, the speaker. It was then that he heard that Justice Teori Zavascki of the Supreme Court had convened an extraordinary meeting of his fellow judges for the following morning.

Diogo Ferreira, Senator Amaral's chief of staff, called him into a corner and asked him, 'Have you heard that Zavascki has asked for an emergency meeting?'

'No, I hadn't,' replied Amaral.

'Is that sort of thing normal?'

'No, it's not. If he's doing that, it's something serious.'

Before going to sleep, the senator posted on social media that the government had won a marathon series of votes in the Senate that day, and finished off with 'More tomorrow'. He went to bed at 1 a.m. after knocking back a whiskey and eating some prawns, with no inkling that the following day, in that very same hotel as Bumlai's arrest, yet another shocking event would unfold, and he would be the target. 'This time it would be me, and I had no idea,' said Senator Amaral in an interview for this book.

During the night the senator woke up with a splitting headache; not something that usually happened. At 6.10 a.m. the telephone rang.

'Could you open the door, Senator?' asked the hotel receptionist.

'Why?' asked Amaral.

The receptionist hung up. At the same moment, Senator Amaral heard a loud knock at the door. He opened it in his pyjamas. The police officers barged in, grabbed his mobile phone and tablet, searched the hotel room and found a locked black briefcase. They broke the lock but inside were only papers of no importance. The detective then approached the dazed senator, saying, 'I have another warrant here from Justice Zavascki. Would you like to sit down while I read it to you?'

Senator Amaral said he would prefer to stand while the arrest warrant was read out.

'Can you do that to a serving senator?' he asked.

The police answered that yes, they could. They considered that he had been caught 'red-handed', because there were indications that he was trying to obstruct the investigations and assist Nestor Cerveró, who had already been convicted, to flee the jurisdiction, which is one of the strongest justifications for arrest provided for in the Criminal Code. It was neither the time nor the place to protest, so he simply followed the detectives' orders. He was taken to a room at the Federal Police headquarters in Brasília, where he was detained. On leaving his hotel room, the senator asked the police only if they could divert the attention of the press. The detectives and prosecutors agreed, and Senator Amaral left the hotel in the prosecutors' car accompanied by the police officers, unnoticed by the waiting journalists. Meanwhile, the prosecutors travelled in the police car, alone. Even so, the senator was filmed from a helicopter arriving at police headquarters. It would be the last image of him for quite some time. His chief of staff, Diogo Ferreira, was also arrested.

Another shock was in store, this time for the financial markets. The prominent banker André Esteves was arrested at the same time as Senator Amaral, under the same charges, and a warrant was issued to arrest the lawyer Edson Ribeiro, who was in the United States. The Federal Police issued a Red Notice through Interpol, the global mechanism used by police forces to apprehend wanted persons. All three were accused of conspiring to interfere in the plea bargain of Nestor Cerveró, the former director of Petrobras's International Division, and to help him to flee the country. The police also searched Senator Amaral's house in Campo Grande, while eighteen police officers and prosecutors entered his office at the Senate, to the consternation of everyone. They arrived at 6 a.m. and tried to enter via the Chamber of Deputies, but the Legislative Police would not allow them; they had to wait until the Senate staff arrived.

The morning of 25 November 2015 completely overshadowed the previous day's events. This time the targets were a serving senator and a very senior banker. André Esteves was almost legendary in the financial markets and was frequently held up by business schools as a case study in success: a young man from a humble background in Rio de Janeiro, who had joined the investment bank Banco Pactual as a trainee in the 1980s, later becoming a partner in the firm and eventually its owner. He had then sold Banco Pactual to the Swiss bank UBS and set up a new firm, BTG. During the 2009 financial crisis, he had seized the opportunity to buy Banco Pactual back from the Swiss and merged it with BTG to form BTG Pactual, which expanded its operations to eighteen countries. The company became the eighth largest financial institution in Brazil, with R$154 billion in assets, and André Esteves joined the list of Brazil's richest men. Young, daring and assertive, he was the very definition of all the qualities admired in business and financial circles. His firm continued to grow, expanding into new areas. No one would ever have imagined him being arrested by the Federal Police in Rio, as he was that morning.

The sequence of events leading to these arrests began with the negotiations over Nestor Cerveró's plea bargain. His son,

Bernardo Cerveró, who was actively participating in the plea bargain negotiations, began to suspect that the lawyer, Edson Ribeiro, was not properly defending his father's interests. Cerveró junior pretended to take part in a deal between the lawyer and Senator Amaral, who was offering to 'help' the family. Senator Amaral was an old acquaintance of his father's, having been his boss at Petrobras's Oil and Gas Division. The prosecutors were consulted and gave their go-ahead. Bernardo Cerveró, an actor by profession, set up the scene. First he called Diogo Ferreira, Senator Amaral's chief of staff, asking for a meeting. It would be their second encounter. The first had been at the beginning of the year, a few weeks after his father had been arrested. Now things were different: his father was trying to negotiate a deal with federal prosecutors. A meeting was arranged for 4 November 2015 in Bernardo Cerveró's hotel room in Brasília.

THE RECORDING

Bernardo Cerveró had hidden four devices in the hotel room to record his conversation with the senator. He had taken these precautions because he knew that at these types of meetings mobile phones were handed over and locked securely away. He had everything prepared but, while waiting for the other participants to arrive, he dozed off. He woke to find Senator Amaral, Diogo Ferreira and Edson Ribeiro knocking at the door, giving him time to turn on only two of the recording devices, one of which was his spare mobile phone, hidden in his pocket. As soon as the others entered, they went through the ritual of handing over their mobile phones. Diogo Ferreira took Bernardo's and put it in the wardrobe. They began to talk, but as Bernardo Cerveró later recounted, Ferreira suspected that something was up and nearly discovered that the meeting was being recorded. Ferreira glanced at Bernardo Cerveró's backpack and spotted a key fob with a recording device hidden inside it. Luckily, it was switched off, but even so, Ferreira placed himself between the backpack and the senator, switched on the TV and turned up the volume. Bernardo Cerveró picked up the backpack and put it in the wardrobe. No problem – he still had another recording device hidden and switched on, and was able to record an hour and thirty-four minutes of conversation, enough to reveal the nature of their meeting. André Esteves was not in the room, but he was mentioned by Senator Amaral as an interested party and an alleged financier of the scheme.

As soon as the meeting began, Edson Ribeiro, Cerveró's lawyer, made it clear what was being agreed.

'Just to get things started, what I've agreed with Nestor is that he'll deny everything relating to you and everything relating to [...] Everything. Isn't that right?' said Ribeiro, looking to Nestor Cerveró's son for confirmation.

'Yes,' confirmed Bernardo Cerveró.

'So that's agreed. If there's no deal, that's how it'll be. That's agreed. If there's no deal. OK? And if there is a deal, he'll also leave it all out. Isn't that right?' Edson asked once again.

'That's right,' replied Senator Amaral.

The group was offering Nestor Cerveró R$50,000 per month not to sign a plea bargain, or if he did, not to name either Senator Amaral or the banker André Esteves. A further R$4 million would be transferred via the lawyer Edson Ribeiro. To complete the package, the group was to put pressure on the Supreme Court to try to release Cerveró, who had been held in Curitiba for nearly a year by then, and had already been convicted. Mentioning the Supreme Court judges was a fatal mistake for Senator Amaral.

'Now then Edson, Bernardo, I think we have to concentrate our fire on the Supreme Court now. I've spoken to Teori and Toffoli. I've asked Toffoli to speak to Gilmar. Michel spoke to Gilmar as well, because Michel is very worried about Zelada, and I'm going to speak to Gilmar myself. Because Gilmar is wavering all over the place – one moment he's fine, next moment he's not, and I'm one of the few people ...' said Senator Amaral.

The senator even said that he would speak to Justice Edson Fachin, the lead judge on an application for habeas corpus that was seeking to overturn Paulo Roberto Costa's plea bargain, which had the potential to bring down a number of cooperation agreements.

'Diogo, we really need to set this up quickly with Fachin, OK?' said Senator Amaral.

'Uhuh.'

'Speak to Tarísco about it.'

'OK.'

'To see if I need to pay a visit to Fachin,' said Senator Amaral.

'This [habeas corpus] is what everyone should be going for – it solves everything,' said Edson Ribeiro, the lawyer.

'It kills everything ... I mean, from a legal point of view, depending on how the habeas corpus goes. We're only missing Gilmar,' agreed Senator Amaral.

The senator, his chief of staff and Cerveró's lawyer carried on talking, completely at ease, about how to influence a ruling by the judges of the Supreme Court. Ribeiro asked if he should also ask Renan Calheiros to help.

'I'll talk to him.'

'There's a Senate leaders' meeting today,' Ferreira reminded him.

'I'll speak to Renan today,' said Senator Amaral.

'OK,' agreed Ribeiro.

'I'll do it today, because I think the focus has to be on the get-away. Whenever he gets out, he has to go straight away,' added Senator Amaral, referring to the plan for Cerveró to flee the country.

The plan was that as soon as Cerveró was transferred to house arrest, they would help him get out of Brazil. The route had already been decided and the plane chosen – a Falcon 50 private jet, which has enough range to fly directly to Spain without stopping to refuel. Spain had been suggested because Cerveró had dual citizenship that would protect him from being extradited. The worst-case scenario was that he would serve his sentence in Europe. Behind the scenes at the Supreme Court, the 'plan' was considered risible. Even Senator Amaral later acknowledged that it made no sense: 'It was complete bollocks. A crazy, irrational conversation.'

By the time the meeting ended, Bernardo Cerveró had ample proof of the plot. He had recorded the conversation between a senator from the ruling party, his chief of staff and his own father's lawyer – a conversation that was deeply compromising. The family, who feared that Nestor Cerveró might be given a very lengthy sentence and who had been trying to negotiate a plea bargain for months, had another chance. One of the prosecutors from the Operation Car Wash task force received a phone call from a lawyer speaking on behalf of Cerveró's son and other family members. After the call, the prosecutor turned to her colleague and said, 'You know that son of Cerveró's?'

'Yes.'

'Well, he recorded the senator.'

The news fell like a bombshell in the prosecutors' office; everyone stopped what they were doing and listened. From then on, this would be the investigation's number one priority. The lawyer who made the call travelled to Brasília to play the recording to prosecutors – the evidence was compelling. Two prosecutors immediately left for Curitiba to sign Nestor Cerveró's plea bargain agreement and start taking his evidence. Another two went to Rio de Janeiro to take a statement from Bernardo Cerveró. Meanwhile, a transcript was made of the recording.

Bernardo Cerveró told prosecutors that Senator Amaral said he had even been to see President Dilma Rousseff in an attempt to help his father. Earlier that year, on 1 February 2015, Senator Amaral had held an initial meeting with Bernardo Cerveró at a luxury hotel in São Paulo. At the meeting, he had promised to make some political moves to help Bernardo's father and had also suggested the family approach Renan Calheiros and Edison Lobão, because Nestor would have 'worked with these people'. According to Bernardo, Senator Amaral said that he 'had contacts at the Supreme Court', that he had 'been to see Dilma' and 'the leadership', in each case trying to convince Bernardo that using these political contacts could help improve his father's situation. Bernardo Cerveró had been hoping that the senator, either on his own or with the help of other politicians, could convince one or more of the judges to grant his father's application for habeas corpus. His father's lawyer, Edson Ribeiro, had always said that a habeas corpus was viable from a legal point of view. He had considered getting a legal opinion from a highly respected jurist on the subject, but in addition to the purely legal aspects, they needed 'goodwill' on the part of the Supreme Court judges.

On the return flight to Brasília, after taking Bernardo Cerveró's statement in Rio, the two prosecutors discussed what should be done next. The idea of seeking the arrest of a serving

senator was highly controversial. Everyone said it was impossible. However, one of these two prosecutors had previously
been involved in an arrest that had also been unprecedented:
that of the then-governor of the Federal District of Brasília, José
Roberto Arruda, in 2009. Arruda had been arrested for interfering in an investigation – he had allegedly tried to buy a witness. When the prosecutor, Sérgio Bruno, asked his colleague
Marcelo Miller what he thought about trying to get an arrest
warrant for Amaral, Miller replied, 'I already have something
in mind.' They were determined to give it a go.

When they arrived at the prosecutor general's office, the two
of them asked Eduardo Pellela, Janot's chief of staff, to study the
matter and they discussed making an arrest. Pellela's first reaction
was to say that it wouldn't fly, but he took the audio file home with
him, listened to it and changed his mind. There was no doubt:
it was an arrestable offence. The next morning, he discussed it
with Janot. The prosecutor general said he thought the chance of
getting a warrant was slim, but he followed Pellela's suggestion
and also listened to the audio file at home. The next day Janot
went straight to see his chief of staff. After listening again to the
recording and reading the transcript, Janot kept repeating: 'I
have to file for arrest; I'm going to have to file for arrest.' And
he went to talk to Justice Teori Zavascki at the Supreme Court.

As soon as Janot began speaking, Zavascki immediately
interrupted: 'You're not going to ask me to arrest a senator,
right?'

They were. In their application for a warrant, the prosecutors wrote: 'The scheme contains an intricate mechanism for
impeding the investigation: once the financial agreement is
finalised, Nestor Cerveró would face almost insurmountable
difficulties in telling the truth. His silence would buy him the

financial security and upkeep of his family, in an almost mafia-like way.' Justifying their application for an arrest warrant, the prosecutors continued: 'Other less onerous precautionary measures would be demonstrably insufficient: Senator Delcídio do Amaral and the banker André Esteves are powerful and influential individuals in their respective spheres and have a common interest in ensuring that Operation Car Wash leaves them alone. There is no doubt that outside of police custody, the two would continue to have at their disposal a multiplicity of means to influence the results of the investigation and the application of criminal law, as they explicitly and demonstrably tried to do in relation to Nestor Cerveró.' The application reached Teori Zavascki's office that same Sunday.

THE SUPREME COURT'S DECISION

Marcio Schiffer, the judge assisting Teori Zavascki, had already read the audio transcript provided by the prosecutors and seemed convinced. The team just had to persuade Zavascki. Sérgio Bruno reminded Schiffer that in the case of Arruda's arrest, the lead judge had taken the case to the full court, in order to endorse his decision. The assistant judge had some reservations about whether to go to the full court in this instance; he thought it would be better to present the matter to the panel of judges specifically allocated to Operation Car Wash.

On Tuesday 24 November, the day before Senator Amaral's arrest, Teori Zavascki called each of the five judges on the panel, as well as the president of the Supreme Court, informing them that something very serious had occurred. The decision fell to him alone, as lead judge, but he considered it important to keep them informed, so he arranged a meeting in his office. They all turned up and were astonished when Zavascki began to speak. One of the judges asked the question they were all thinking: 'But he's a senator. Is he really going to be arrested?' Zavascki then played the recording for the other judges to hear: it came as a monumental shock. Cármen Lúcia was outraged, as was Celso de Mello. The senator's fate was sealed and they decided that there was no alternative but to arrest Senator Delcídio do Amaral for obstructing the investigations. The evidence was all there in the recording. A panel session was scheduled for the following day in order to endorse Zavascki's decision officially. The Federal Police were on standby to carry out the operation on Thursday, but after Zavascki's meeting with the other judges, they had no choice but to bring it forward to Wednesday. After all the to-ing and fro-ing when José Carlos Bumlai had been arrested, the police team found themselves back at the same hotel the very next day, this time to arrest Senator Amaral.

At 9 a.m., Justice Teori Zavascki presented the case to the panel of Supreme Court judges responsible for hearing all the Operation Car Wash cases, in order to confirm his decision to arrest a federal senator. He had ordered solitary detention but wanted to hear the views of the other judges, since it concerned the arrest of a legislator and a search within the confines of the Senate building itself. Zavascki began by setting out the reasons that had led him to take such an unprecedented decision. He explained that Senator Amaral, the banker André Esteves and the lawyer Edson Ribeiro were technically in flagrante delicto – caught red-handed in the act of committing an offence – in their hampering of the Car Wash investigations, which justified Amaral's arrest, despite his status as a senator. 'The grave facts set out herein leave no doubt that Senator Delcídio do Amaral, his aide Diogo Ferreira and the lawyer Edson Ribeiro form part of the criminal organisation being investigated by Operation Car Wash,' said Zavascki. He made a point of emphasising that the investigation revealed that Senator Amaral implied in the conversation that he had influence over the judges of the Supreme Court.

André Esteves, the banker, was arrested on suspicion of corruption and of leaking confidential documents. He had obtained access to the draft of Nestor Cerveró's plea bargain agreement, which, according to the investigators, showed there was a 'back-channel of leaks within Operation Car Wash that was providing people in positions of power with information relating to the investigation'. In the plan outlined by the senator, the banker would deal with the financial cost of the agreement, so that Cerveró would either not make a plea bargain at all, or that he would omit information relating to Amaral and Esteves if he did. The lawyer Edson Ribeiro was charged with the offence of dishonestly failing to defend his client's interests, since at that moment Edson was effectively protecting the interests of Delcídio do Amaral rather than Nestor Cerveró, his client. Diogo Ferreira was charged with being an accessory to their plan by setting up the meetings with Bernardo Cerveró and trying to prevent Bernardo from recording the conversation during the meeting. In summary, Teori Zavascki made clear that he considered there to be sufficient grounds for such an unprecedented step:

The application for detention on remand robustly shows, based on the evidence gathered so far, and indicates with a sufficient margin, the potential occurrence of serious offences against the administration of justice, against the public administration, of criminal organisation and even of money laundering, concerning the alleged involvement of those named in the application. The principal grounds are, as they must necessarily be, the upholding of due process in the criminal justice system, bearing in mind the apparent attempt to bribe a cooperating defendant via the payment of financial inducements to prevent information being provided in relation to certain persons and events. The aforementioned individuals were thus attempting to obstruct a criminal investigation. This clearly demonstrates the need to ensure the integrity of the investigatory process and that of any resulting criminal proceedings, bearing in mind what has occurred and the potential for further interference in obtaining witness statements and other evidence. Such circumstances therefore authorise the imposition of precautionary detention.

The other judges made clear, in unambiguous terms, the indignation of the Brazilian Supreme Court: 'Anyone who transgresses such fundamental commandments [of democracy], irrespective of their position, whether patrician or plebeian, exposes themselves to the full force of the criminal law: such acts must be punished according to the law. No one, not even the government leader in the Senate, is above the laws that govern this country. Parliamentary immunity is not a mantle to protect senators from the consequences of criminal behaviour,' said Celso de Mello.

Cármen Lúcia also spoke out, and her speech reverberated on social media throughout the day, as a warning to corrupt politicians and businessmen that the law was finally going to triumph in Brazil:

In our country's recent history, there was a moment when many of us believed in the saying that 'hope had overcome fear'. Then we were faced with Criminal Action 470 [the Big Monthly trial] and we discovered that cynicism had overcome hope. It now seems that derision has overcome cynicism. Crime will not overcome justice. I give this warning to those navigating these muddy waters of iniquity and corruption: criminals will not prevail in confusing immunity with impunity. They will not prevail over the judges of Brazil. They will not prevail over the new hopes of the Brazilian people, because deception cannot hold back our determination to rectify matters in public life. They will not prevail over the constitution of Brazil.

The judges on the Supreme Court panel unanimously upheld the detention of Senator Amaral. During the course of the day they said how shocked they had been at what they had heard. Justice Edson Fachin commented that he considered it deplorable that the names of Supreme Court judges had been used in an attempt to peddle influence. In an official letter, the senator's defence team said that it did not accept the panel's decision and was convinced that the initial decision would be reversed. Signed by the lawyer Maurício Silva Leite, the letter questioned the arrest and detention of a federal senator against whom no formal charges had been made: 'The federal constitution does not authorise judicial detention in respect of a holder of a congressional mandate and this must be respected as a mainstay of the Democratic Rule of Law.' Delcídio do Amaral's last hope was now in the hands of his Senate colleagues.

CONGRESS REACHES BREAKING POINT

The atmosphere in Congress that morning was one of agitation and fear. Rodrigo Janot had telephoned Renan Calheiros, the speaker of the Senate, shortly after the arrests, to inform him formally of the Supreme Court's decision and the investigations relating to Senator Amaral. Janot reminded him that, in accordance with article 53 of the federal constitution, in the event of a senator being arrested, a sitting of the full Senate is convened to vote on the matter, either confirming or overturning the arrest of the senator in question. Delcídio do Amaral still had a chance of getting out of jail. All he needed was for his Senate colleagues to overturn the order for his arrest and he would be free. Renan Calheiros asked Rodrigo Janot to send him the audio file so he could listen to it. The prosecutor general did so and, as a courtesy, also sent a copy to the minister of justice, José Eduardo Cardozo. The speaker said he would await the delivery of the documents relating to the proceedings, and informed the party leaders and presiding officers that there would be an emergency sitting of the Senate that day.

Calheiros wanted to put the order for Senator Amaral's detention to the full Senate as soon as it arrived. By 9 a.m., congressmen were coming in and out of the Workers' Party offices at the Chamber of Deputies, trying to get information from the party leader, Sibá Machado. They were puzzled and apprehensive, some of them questioning the way in which the arrest had been carried out. Others offered support for their friend. 'It is clear that it is impossible not to be upset following an event like this. Especially because it concerns a friend, a serving senator and everyone is asking: "What happens now?"' explained José Guimarães, the government leader in the Chamber of Deputies.

At the offices of the opposition, Congressman Rubens Bueno, leader of the Popular Socialist Party, was giving statements to the press, calling on the Senate to confirm the Supreme Court's decision. 'If they have an ounce of responsibility and decency, the senators will confirm Delcídio do Amaral's detention. Any other course of action, such as ordering the senator's release, would be completely demoralising,' said the congressman. Journalists also asked Eduardo Cunha, the speaker of the Chamber of Deputies, what he thought of the senator's arrest. He replied laconically, 'It would be ungracious on my part to comment on documents I have not seen.' A reporter asked whether he was afraid of being arrested himself. 'I am not going to comment on that,' he said, curtly.

A sitting of Congress was scheduled for that day to deal with budgetary matters, but it was postponed because of the distractions. The arrival of documents from the Supreme Court was keenly awaited. By law, they needed to be sent within twenty-four hours, and Renan Calheiros had been advised that they would arrive well before the deadline. The Senate was called into session to consider this single issue, and to decide whether to confirm or suspend the Supreme Court's decision. It was Senate against Supreme Court.

'Did the arrest take the Senate by surprise?' a journalist asked Calheiros.

'Yes it did, because there was no formal investigation against Senator Delcídio do Amaral. But we don't yet have the information relating to the investigations. We will wait for the information, then we will listen to the party leaders and presiding officers, and the Senate will decide by majority vote what needs to be done,' replied Calheiros.

There was no deadline for deciding about Senator Amaral's detention, but the decision needed to be made quickly. Somebody asked whether it would be an open vote or behind closed doors. Calheiros avoided giving an opinion at that point, 'I don't know if it will be an open or closed vote. I will look into the matter now.'

As Calheiros was leaving, a reporter asked him, 'Are you worried about Delcídio's arrest?'

The speaker of the Senate did not like the question. He scowled at the journalist and said, 'Well, thank you, all of you, for such an agreeable interview ...'

Apprehension hung heavily in the air.

Maurício Leite, Senator Amaral's lawyer, landed in Brasília at around 12.30 p.m. and went straight to the Supreme Court to petition for his client's release. After all, the constitution did not authorise the arrest of a serving federal legislator, still less a senator who had not been formally accused of anything. He began by attacking on Cerveró, saying that the accusations came from a convicted informant who was trying to curry favour for himself by attacking others. Shortly before 1 p.m., news began to circulate that behind the scenes the Workers' Party was arranging with Calheiros to ensure that the vote on Senator Amaral's arrest would be secret. This was what Calheiros wanted, but there was resistance: Ronaldo Caiado, an opposition senator, sought an injunction from the Supreme Court that the voting should be public.

Blogs, online newspapers and news channels provided intense coverage of the events, bringing information from behind the scenes and gathering statements on the unfolding drama. The well-known blog Noblat posted a transcript of the recording made by Bernardo Cerveró, and the journalist Matheus Leitão posted the audio file itself on his blog. Anyone who listened to it was shocked by the ease with which the senator talked about putting pressure on the Supreme Court, obstructing Cerveró's plea bargain and even giving details of how to flee the country using the Falcon 50 private jet.

At 4 p.m. came the news that the documents from the Supreme Court had been officially received by the Senate. The speaker immediately scheduled a special sitting at 5 p.m. with a single item on the agenda: Delcídio do Amaral's arrest. The senator, who was by then in police custody, was speaking with his lawyer about the accusations while watching developments on TV. His fate was about to be decided. His wife, Maika do Amaral, said that the speaker of the Senate had called her, promising his full support. She had one request for him: 'Help to free my husband.' According to Maika do Amaral, Calheiros replied: 'I'll do what I can.' There was still hope.

The clock in the Senate chamber showed 5.45 p.m. when the session began. The face of the speaker, Senator Renan Calheiros, who had also been involved in the Operation Car Wash investigations, did not hide his profound embarrassment. Everyone knew that what was being discussed was how to protect various members of the Senate, including the speaker himself, from facing the same fate. Calheiros indicated that his intention was to go for a closed session and a secret vote, which provoked uproar and an intense debate. The afternoon's events in the Senate were being watched across the nation as if they were the climax of a TV soap opera. If the session were behind closed doors, with a secret vote, Senator Amaral might well be saved, but then how would the decision go down with the general population?

Senator Cássio Cunha Lima of the PSDB raised a point of order and called for an open vote. Calheiros promised an immediate reply. Another senator, Randolfe Rodrigues, made the same point and reiterated the arguments Cássio Cunha Lima had made. The two justified an open vote on the basis that the word 'secret' had been removed from the constitution, and that the Senate's own internal rules could not take precedence over the constitution.

Senator Jader Barbalho asked to speak and made an impassioned speech defending a secret vote:

What is now at stake isn't the drama facing our colleague, Delcídio. What is at stake is the life of this institution, it's the life of the Federal Senate. May God spare the Senate and Congress from going through other episodes like this. And if He doesn't? Let's hope to God that we will not have the difficulty and embarrassment of examining other such episodes. With apologies to those who disagree with me, I refuse to interpret the constitution by removing a power that I believe to be part of the Senate and the responsibility of each senator. After so many years of public office, I have no inhibitions, not least because no one owns me. I am here by virtue of the secret ballot of the people of my state, as are each and every one of you. I do not need to be shackled or corralled. What is at stake today is not Senator Amaral, even if, as I think we do, we all deeply regret the events concerning him. What is at stake is the Senate itself.

As the debate wore on, it gradually turned in favour of an open vote. Senator Cristovam Buarque went up to the microphone and said that he would open his vote, because he wanted it to be known. Senator Ricardo Ferraço said the same thing; this meant that two senators from the government's support base were calling for the whole country to be able to witness the dramatic vote in which senators would decide the fate of one of their own.

Courteous and gregarious in manner, Senator Amaral had always been able to work with all parties and factions. His personal qualities were praised as much in the speeches calling for an open vote as in those calling for a secret one. They had nothing against him, said those asking for an open vote. It was not for the senator but in defence of the Senate, said those asking for a closed session and secret vote. The two sides battled on and tensions rose. Those who wanted an open vote reminded their colleagues that Brazil was watching. The debate on social media was even more intense, calling for transparency in the Senate. Those who wanted a secret vote recalled that a sitting senator was under arrest, an unprecedented situation in the history of Brazil, and that the Senate had to assert its prerogatives. Other senators under investigation by Operation Car Wash could be seen in the TV coverage of the debate. Fernando Collor sat in silence, his face tense and attentive, while Senator Gleisi Hoffmann was whispering in the ear of government senators.

It was almost 8 p.m. by the time Calheiros announced that he had listened carefully to all the points of order raised and had decided that the vote would be secret. However, he submitted his decision for approval by a majority the Senate as a whole:

Before we begin the vote, I would like to remind senators that it is one thing for us to discuss this decision of the Federal Supreme Court, approved today by the panel of judges presided over by Justice Toffoli, and to discuss the merits, as some here have done, of whether or not the recordings made public today contain evidence of a criminal offence. But that judgment is not for us to make. The Federal Supreme Court cannot be substituted in its judgment, and if we were to make that judgment, we would be infringing on the functions of the judiciary and of the Federal Supreme Court. It does not fall to us to make that judgment of whether or not the recordings contain any criminal offence or impropriety. It is not within our domain to make a judgment. The judgment that is in our domain is whether the Federal Supreme Court can, as it has done today by decision of a panel of its judges, order the arrest and detention of a serving senator who has not been charged with a non-bailable offence. It is this decision that we are facing, for the first time in the history of this republic. I repeat: the first time in the history of this republic. We must equally uphold the right of the Supreme Court to judge the offence which the recording may contain. It is the Supreme Court that will judge it, but the Senate should not lightly give up its prerogatives under every single constitution of Brazil, including the current one, which has been in force for almost thirty years, longer than any previous constitution: the issue of whether the Federal Supreme Court can arrest a serving senator or congressman or woman. That is the decision which this Senate must take. That Senator Amaral will be judged by the Federal Supreme Court is something we must all uphold. To try to argue against that here, ladies and gentlemen, is to attempt to infringe the constitutional role of the Federal Supreme Court. I know that this is a very sad day for all of us, very sad indeed, since it must mean that we either overturn an arrest, or allow that arrest to continue. We would not merely be making tomorrow's morning news. We would be giving up a prerogative of the Legislature that I have no doubt will cause great damage to democracy and the separation of powers, which is of fundamental importance.

At the same time, over at the Supreme Court, they were dealing with applications for preliminary rulings requiring an open vote. It was a moment of extreme tension between the different institutions of state. The applications were allocated to Justice Teori Zavascki, but he declared that he could not rule on them and so they ended up being dealt with by Justice Edson Fachin. He granted a preliminary ruling requiring an open vote, on the basis that the constitution did not expressly state that the vote had to be secret and the Senate was not at liberty to choose, since the constitution requires the acts of public institutions to be public. It was a difficult and risky decision, which could well have inflamed tensions between the institutions. However, no one found out what the Senate's reaction would have been, because while Fachin was preparing his judgment, it was reaching its own decision.

When Renan Calheiros put to the Senate his own decision in favour of a closed session and a secret vote, he lost by fifty-two votes to twenty, with one abstention. The Senate had decided that the vote would not be secret. Perhaps Senator Amaral's fate was already sealed. Many consider that this moment determined the result of the substantive vote that followed. If the session had been secret, the result might have gone the senator's way, releasing him to face whatever charges may follow. But with an open vote, he himself knew that he had little chance: 'I'd be skewered one way or another,' he said. In the second vote, on whether or not to uphold Senator Amaral's detention, the result followed more or less the same pattern. By fifty-nine votes in favour and thirteen against, Delcídio do Amaral's detention was upheld. It was an unprecedented decision. Among those who voted against his detention were some who were under investigation as part of Operation Car Wash themselves, such as Gleisi Hoffmann, Fernando Collor and Humberto Costa. Among those who voted in favour were some who Senator Amaral considered personal friends, such as Aécio Neves. When the result was announced, there was silence in the Senate chamber. In general, after heated debates and votes, everyone leaves talking loudly. That night, the senators left in silence. The Senate had just confirmed the arrest and detention of a serving senator. The atmosphere was one of despondency, even among the victorious.

THE SAD REALITY OF ARREST

The result of the vote was a further blow for Senator Amaral. He was now facing the reality of police custody. He would be sleeping between chairs, tables and office shelving in the meeting room where he had been taken at the Federal Police's headquarters in Brasília. In one corner, the police had cobbled together a place for him to sleep. There were no bathroom facilities in the room. He had to use the employees' facilities down the corridor, always escorted by two police officers even when going to the toilet. He was given the same food as other detainees. Outside the front of the building, protesters spent the day celebrating the senator's arrest. They let off fireworks, congratulated police officers going in and out of the building, shouted slogans and waved placards.

Early the following morning, Eduardo Marzagão, Senator Amaral's press assistant, went to visit him at the police headquarters. He took him a milky coffee, orange juice, a toasted ham and cheese sandwich, an apple and a pear. Senator Amaral had already eaten the breakfast provided by the police, but he was grateful for his long-standing friend's kindness. Marzagão managed to have a brief conversation with him, one of the guards allowed the senator to come to the door of the room where he was being held, close to the reception desk. He looked less dejected than he had the day before. It was a very brief encounter, less than a minute, just enough time for the assistant to ask how his boss was feeling. The senator replied that he was fine, that he had slept well and that he was confident and serene. 'God bless,' the assistant said as he left.

Senator Amaral gave a statement to a group of detectives and prosecutors that same day. The interview went smoothly, with the senator being repeatedly confronted with the recording of his conversation but always denying involvement, until a stressful moment when he objected to the way in which the interview was being conducted. This irritated the prosecutors. 'This is a police interview, not a public appearance,' one of them said curtly. Voices were raised and an argument almost ensued. Amaral's lawyer asked for a moment with his client, and also said he wanted to withdraw some of what his client had said, but this was not permitted. The lawyer asked to speak with his client separately for a moment and the interview was suspended.

While they were waiting, a prosecutor and detective chatted about the case. A police officer in the room next door overheard their conversation and decided to show them something he had printed off the internet: former president Lula da Silva had called Amaral an idiot on hearing of the senator's arrest. The detective and prosecutor were surprised when the police officer came into the interview room, but they read the news story he handed them and then left it to one side. When Amaral and his lawyer returned, the senator noticed the piece of paper on the table. He picked it up, read it and allowed his deep irritation to show: 'He's afraid of BTG,' he commented.

The investigators decided to provoke him further: 'What do you think of the Workers' Party's statement, Senator?'

On the day of his arrest, the Workers' Party had released a statement criticising Senator Amaral. Signed by Rui Falcão, it left no doubt that the party had chosen to abandon one of its principal figures:

The national chairman of the Worker's Party, deeply concerned at the events which have given rise to the Federal Supreme Court's decision to order the arrest of Senator Delcídio do Amaral, wishes to state the following:

1. None of the dealings attributed to the senator have any connection whatsoever with his party activities, whether as legislator or party member;
2. For this reason, the Workers' Party does not feel obliged to offer any gesture of solidarity;
3. The chairman's office will be shortly be calling a meeting of the party's National Executive Committee, in order to adopt whatever measures the party leadership considers appropriate.

Brasília, 25 November 2015.
Rui Falcão, Workers' Party National Chairman.

Senator Amaral scowled and said, 'That lot are shit, but they don't know who they're messing with.' He asked once again to adjourn the interview, which had been going on for around four hours by this point. The detectives complained that some of their questions hadn't yet been answered. The senator and his lawyer said they needed to discuss some matters and insisted that the interview be continued another day. The investigators acquiesced.

On leaving the police headquarters, lawyer Maurício Leite said that Senator Amaral had confirmed that the voice on the recording was his but had denied trying to hinder Nestor

Cerveró's plea bargain or interfering in the investigations. The lawyer said that the recorded conversation had been taken out of context and that further details would be provided later. But he confirmed that Senator Amaral had only agreed to meet Bernardo Cerveró as a 'humanitarian matter', in order to 'say some words of comfort', and that he denied having committed any wrongful acts.

That same night, the banker André Esteves was transferred from the Federal Police headquarters in downtown Rio de Janeiro to the vast Bangu 8 prison complex in the hardscrabble western outskirts of the city. The Supreme Court had denied his lawyers' application to revoke his temporary detention and had authorised his transfer.

BTG Pactual's share price had plunged 20 per cent the previous day. The investment bank acted quickly, announcing that André Esteves had temporarily stepped down as chairman of the bank. The economist Pérsio Arida, a partner at the bank and one of the authors of Brazil's successful plan to overcome hyperinflation in the 1990s, took over the chairmanship. The bank also announced a share buyback programme, under which BTG would purchase its own shares in the open market, thereby helping to support its share price. It was a way of showing the market that the bank was solid and confident of its future. When questioned by police, Esteves admitted meeting Delcídio do Amaral five times in the preceding months, but he denied involvement in the attempt to interfere with Cerveró. The lawyer Edson Ribeiro was arrested at 8 a.m. the following day as he disembarked at the main airport in Rio de Janeiro on his return from the United States. His US visa had been revoked and the only reason he was not arrested in Miami was because the Brazilian police, who were monitoring his movements, saw that he had bought a return ticket to Rio de Janeiro, and therefore preferred to wait and arrest him themselves on Brazilian soil. He was ultimately acquitted.

Senator Amaral remained in prison, visited by relatives and aides who did their best to reduce his discomfort. On one occasion an aide brought him a McDonald's Big Mac and Coca-Cola; another time they brought homemade cake and milky coffee. By then, Delcídio do Amaral, like many other Operation Car Wash inmates, had taken up reading and was finishing *The Rise of Islamic State* by Patrick Cockburn. But despite the best efforts of his family and friends, he was very dejected. In the first two days, he had faced a succession of bad news – his arrest, the Senate decision, Lula's comment and the Workers' Party's statement.

The impact on him was all the greater because he could see his political support collapsing, and as the weeks continued it disintegrated completely. Years of work were lost. He was a public figure, a national leader ever since he had been appointed chairman of the joint congressional inquiry into the post office corruption scandal, which had gone on to investigate Big Monthly. As the government's leader in the Senate, he had been one of President Rousseff's closest colleagues. A graduate in electrical engineering, he was married with three daughters. He had been director of gas and energy at Petrobras in the 1990s. In 2002, already a politician, he was elected senator with around 500,000 votes, making him one of the most important public figures in his home state of Mato Grosso do Sul. Now, following his arrest, no one could predict his future. There were persistent rumours that he might cooperate with the judicial authorities. There was no doubt that he knew a lot, and that his information would be of great interest to federal prosecutors.

According to the information he provided in his eventual plea bargain, before he was arrested Delcídio do Amaral was part of a select group of people who spoke to former president Lula da Silva about Operation Car Wash. They would meet almost every week in Brasília or São Paulo, with Senator Amaral acting as a sort of behind-the-scenes firefighter, containing the damage from the scandal that was engulfing his party. Indeed, one of his principal tasks was to monitor Nestor Cerveró, the former director of Petrobras, who had been his subordinate back when Amaral himself had been a director at the company. In his last meeting with Lula on 12 November, the former president had been worried about the news that businessman Salim Schahin had signed a plea bargain and pointed to Bumlai's involvement in the R$12-million loan. When Bumlai was arrested, Senator Amaral had arranged a further conversation with Lula but was unable to attend, for obvious reasons.

There was more than enough pressure on Senator Amaral to confess. A few days before Amaral's arrest, Nestor Cerveró had signed his plea bargain agreement with federal prosecutors. One of the first pieces of information he had given was about a case of corruption involving Delcídio do Amaral, relating to Petrobras's purchases of drillships and the Pasadena oil refinery in Texas. Cerveró also accused André Esteves of paying kickbacks to Senator Fernando Collor in the contract to rebrand 120 São Paulo petrol stations belonging to BTG.

Delcídio frightened the government by hiring Alberto Youssef's lawyer, Antonio Figueiredo Basto, who was an expert in plea bargains. The senator decided, at least initially, not to use that particular weapon – but his choice of lawyer sent out a warning that he could decide to tell investigators what he knew at any point.

André Esteves's life was not much easier. The BTG Pactual share price was R$30.89 on 24 November, the day before the banker's arrest. On 25 November it fell to R$24.40, and by 10 December it was at R$12.10, a fall of 60 per cent in twelve trading days. His lawyers sought a ruling that his temporary detention be revoked, but the application was refused. Even worse, on Sunday 29 November, Justice Teori Zavascki changed Esteves's temporary detention to indefinite remand. It was the signal the other shareholders were waiting for, allowing them to trigger a provision in the shareholders' agreement that Esteves's shares should be converted in the event of an 'impediment' preventing him from performing his functions. They had provided for almost every eventuality when they negotiated the shareholders' agreement: death, serious illness or any kind of incapacity, but never arrest. However, once his detention became indefinite, the seven other major shareholders met and agreed that that this was indeed an 'impediment'. And so they triggered the clause, with the result that Esteves lost control of the company from that moment onwards. He owned 29 per cent of the ordinary shares, but he also held a golden share that gave him a veto on strategic decisions. In reality it was even more significant than this – he had previously exercised complete control over the sprawling conglomerate the bank had become. In the event of an 'impediment', the seven other shareholders could seize control, and that is exactly what happened. From his prison cell, Esteves resigned from his posts as chairman and CEO. At the bank's headquarters in São Paulo, under the leadership of its new chairman, Pérsio Arida, the shareholders carried out the share exchange and Esteves lost control of the company. The new management put up assets for sale in order to recapitalise the bank, and on 4 December they requested a loan of R$6 billion from the banking industry's deposit insurance fund. Their strategy was to have enough cash available to see it through whatever turbulence might arise and ensure the bank's survival.

André Esteves's arrest and detention would also have repercussions abroad, since the financial health of BTG Pactual affected financial institutions outside Brazil. Following Esteves's arrest, the chairman of the Swiss central bank telephoned the president of the Central Bank of Brazil, Alexandre Tombini, to ask what was going on and whether there was any risk of BTG Pactual collapsing. This was not mere curiosity, since BTG owned a bank in Switzerland. The chairmen of the central banks of Peru and Mexico also telephoned Tombini, each deeply concerned. Tombini told all of them that the Central Bank was monitoring the situation closely and that BTG had enough liquidity to ride out the storm.

Meanwhile Esteves's position eased, thanks to Delcídio do Amaral. The senator made a deposition saying that André Esteves was worried about his name being mentioned and that, although he had initially agreed to the scheme to hinder Cerveró's plea bargain, he had then dropped out and had not made any payments to Cerveró's family. On 17 December, Justice Zavascki ordered Esteves to be released.

Shortly before Christmas, Delcídio do Amaral's lawyers applied for his release. Janot said there was no justification for doing so. The Supreme Court agreed, and kept Senator Amaral in jail even after freeing André Esteves. In the prosecutors' submission to the court, Rodrigo Janot wrote that 'it must be understood that this type of criminal intermediary, committing an extremely serious breach of the crucially important functions entrusted to him by popular vote, has taken every opportunity (and will certainly continue to do so, given the modus operandi he has already clearly demonstrated), to pursue unlawful ends available to him through greed for assets misappropriated from the public purse towards exclusively private interests'. This was enough to seal his fate and ensure that the senator would spend Christmas and New Year in jail.

When 2016 began with no sign of any release from custody, not least because of the judicial recess over the holiday period, Delcídio do Amaral set himself the task of studying his own trial in detail. He had few visitors during those rainy January afternoons in Brasília – just family, close friends and lawyers. To everyone else he sent word that once he was released in February, he would agree to talk, but would not before then. His priority was to come up with a way of getting out of jail. One of the things he did in prison was to write letters to the judges of the Supreme Court, apologising for what he had said in the recording and claiming that it had all been boastful bragging. He needed to wipe out the terrible impression he had created in the recording in saying that he would apply pressure to some of the Supreme Court judges. After all, they might well be judging him in the near future. André Esteves had already been released, so Delcídio do Amaral had high hopes that once the judicial recess was over, he would be freed too. According to his calculations, he reckoned it would be three votes to two when it came to the judges on the Supreme Court's second panel: Gilmar Mendes, Dias Toffoli and Celso de Mello against Teori Zavascki and Cármen Lúcia.

The government was also in favour of such a scenario, for one obvious reason: it would avoid a plea bargain from Amaral. He had enough ammunition to bring the government down if he so wanted. The main argument in support of a relaxation of his conditions of detention was that there was no clear criminal organisation in operation. In their formal charges, even the federal prosecutors had concentrated on showing how he was obstructing justice by attempting to destroy and falsify evidence. But to Delcídio do Amaral's lawyers, the prosecutors had not proved the element of criminal organisation.

EDUARDO CUNHA REVEALS HIS WEAPON: IMPEACHMENT

The speaker of the Chamber of Deputies spent all of 2016 under the spotlight, whether as a target of Operation Car Wash or as the person threatening to trigger the impeachment of President Dilma Rousseff. He had been saying that he would make his decision in November on the various petitions he had received to initiate the process of impeachment. In the days following Senator Amaral's arrest, with November drawing to a close, journalists began to press him on his decision. Eduardo Cunha had already rejected several of the impeachment petitions, but he left the most important one to the end: that filed by the jurists Hélio Bicudo, Miguel Reale Júnior and Janaína Paschoal. When they asked him whether the specialist reports from the Chamber's advisory services had been delivered, he replied that they had, adding that his decision had almost been finalised. He did not, however, go into details: 'November doesn't end until Monday. I'm not yet in default on my promise. You can pursue me after Monday.' December would bring major surprises, especially for Eduardo Cunha.

When December began, the speaker of the Chamber was making headlines again. Contrary to what he might have wished, this time he was in the newspapers as a target. He was accused of manoeuvring, through his allies on the Chamber's ethics committee, to hold up the proceedings that could lead to his own removal from office. And he was succeeding – the committee was going round and round in circles and had reached no decision; the efforts of Cunha's 'shock troops', as they were called, had reached a point where he only needed three more votes to ensure that the charges against him would be shelved. There was just one problem: those votes needed to come from the Workers' Party's representatives on the committee.

Eduardo Cunha tried to negotiate with the president's staff at the Palácio do Planalto for a month. After all, the government wanted to unblock the legislative process and get congressional approval for a range of measures to help deal with the economic crisis. In an interview for this book, Delcídio do Amaral stated that he advised the president: 'Dilma, call Eduardo. Invite him over for coffee at the official residence.' Rousseff decided not to, saying that she would keep things strictly institutional with Cunha. According to Cunha, Jaques Wagner, Dilma Rousseff's chief of staff, had promised to help him in exchange for supporting the government, but when the time came for the Workers' Party to help, this did not happen. Quite the contrary: the party's representatives on the ethics committee announced that they would vote in favour of the proceedings against Cunha. This was the last straw. The same day, 2 December, Cunha went to meet reporters in the journalists' lobby at Congress and announced that he had decided to accept the petition to initiate the process to impeach President Dilma Rousseff, sending a nuclear weapon right into the very heart of Brazilian politics.

The president immediately summoned her chief political adviser. In an interview, her chief of staff, Jaques Wagner, reacted: 'Now the knives are out, things will become clearer.

We have received a huge number of expressions of support. People know that you don't mess with democracy. The election isn't over. People who didn't like the result are trying to change it. We're going to fight for democracy and I think that this sentiment will prevail.' In Congress, the political parties had already begun negotiating the composition of the special committee that would analyse the impeachment petition and report back to the full chamber. Under the rules of impeachment, the petition would be read out in the following session, and a committee would then be selected.

The following day, Congressman Beto Mansur, first secretary of the Chamber, read out the petition for the removal of President Dilma Rousseff from office, on the grounds that that she had issued presidential decrees increasing public spending without congressional approval, and had approved the use of 'fiscal pedaling' and other dubious accounting practices in the federal budget. The petition also included various extracts from the Operation Car Wash investigations. The reading took more than three hours, and towards the end Congressman Mansur became quite emotional as he read out several verses from the national anthem. Choosing the members of the special committee was set for the following week. The whole of Brazil spent the weekend in a state of extreme suspense.

The session appointing members of the special committee was the most heated in a long time. Brawls broke out in the chamber. Congressmen clashed with their opponents. The speaker ruled that the vote would be secret and installed voting booths. Government supporters contested this angrily and the chamber descended into chaos. The session ended by approving an alternative slate of nominees, containing a majority of opposition members. The decision was so controversial that it ended up in the Supreme Court. The lead judge on the case, Justice Edson Fachin, confirmed most of the decisions taken by the Chamber of Deputies, but among the other judges on the panel, Justice Luís Roberto Barroso cast his vote in the opposing direction, arguing that there should not be a secret vote and that the precedent of former president Fernando Collor's impeachment should be followed. Barroso's view won the day when matters reached the full court, which angered Eduardo Cunha and led him to announce yet another appeal to the Supreme Court. This had the effect of pushing the matter into 2016, which somewhat reduced the tension that had reached boiling point in December.

It looked as if nothing more would happen relating to Operation Car Wash in 2015, but that was not to be. On 16 December 2015, former president Lula da Silva attended the headquarters of the Federal Police in Brasília to give his first statement in relation to Operation Car Wash. Lula answered the detectives' questions. He said that he had not been involved in nominating the directors of Petrobras, but rather that names had been proposed by the various political parties to the presidential chief of staff. 'He placed the job of receiving requests from the parties, selecting a name and endorsing the decision, squarely on José Direcu's shoulders,' recounted one of the detectives who participated in the investigation. Lula also said that he didn't know anything about the instances of corruption revealed by the operation, and that he had no knowledge of illegal donations to the Workers' Party. He ended by telling detectives that one of the reasons why people linked to the government were being investigated was a 'process of criminalising the Workers' Party'.

At around the same time, the homes of various politicians were searched. This phase of the operation was code-named 'Catiline', a reference to the famous speeches given by Cicero in the Roman Senate, in which he accused another senator, Catiline, of leading a plot to overthrow the Roman republic. Fifty-three warrants of search and seizure were issued. Among the locations visited by the Federal Police were Eduardo Cunha's official speaker's residence as speaker of the Chamber, along with addresses linked to other important PMDB politicians including Renan Calheiros, speaker of the Senate, Senator Edison Lobão, Celso Pansera, minister of science and technology, and Henrique Eduardo Alves, minister of tourism.

POLICE SEARCH THE SPEAKER'S OFFICIAL RESIDENCE

Eduardo Cunha was just waking up when the Federal Police turned up at his front door. Still smarting from the confrontation with the Senate Police during Operation Politeia, the Federal Police brought along its elite squad, the Tactical Operations Unit, to assist with a forced entry in case the Chamber of Deputies' security personnel attempted any resistance or hindered the investigators' access. This time they were fully prepared. They stopped the traffic throughout the surrounding area and approached the house. There was only one guard, from an outsourced security firm, who was startled by the Federal Police's arrival and allowed them in. He said that the Chamber of Deputies' security officer was asleep and that it was necessary to tell him what was going on. The Federal Police officers told the guard to call the security officer, but carried on entering the premises. The security officer came running and said he needed to inform his superior. The

Federal Police officers agreed, but by then they were already inside the building. There was no one around. They found the door to the private wing and knocked. There was no answer. Eduardo Cunha's bedroom was in the furthest part of the private wing. The police threatened to enter by force, but one of the domestic staff knocked on the bedroom window and Cunha answered.

He opened the door angrily, half-dressed, with his shirt tails hanging out. He asked what was going on but was ignored. The police officers seized his mobile phones. Cunha looked worried. Soon after, a detective pulled a piece of paper from the inside pocket of the jacket Cunha had been wearing the night before. He tried to stop the police from taking it, saying that it was nothing important, just a police incident report. The detective insisted on looking at the document and read aloud the name of the person named in the report: Fausto Pinato – the very same federal congressmen who was dealing with allegations against Cunha in the Chamber's ethics committee. The incident report described threats Pinato had received on account of his actions in the Chamber of Deputies, where he had indicated that he intended to present a report in favour of opening an investigation that could lead to Eduardo Cunha's removal from office. What was a copy of an incident report made by Fausto Pinato to police in São Paulo doing in Eduardo Cunha's jacket pocket? The speaker was unwilling to answer this question, and the investigators did not insist. After all, Eduardo Cunha had many things to explain – this would only be one of them.

The speaker's residence is not very big, and the investigators spent 80 per cent of their time in the office studying documents. As Cunha had moved in only the year before and had brought many documents with him, there were still some boxes stacked in the living room that would need to be searched. In the middle of their search, the police officers heard a ringing sound coming from the trouser pocket of the congressman, who quickened his step in an attempt to disguise the sound of the concealed mobile phone. Caught red-handed, he apologetically handed it over to police. Other than this, Eduardo Cunha accompanied the officers throughout their work without causing them any problems. Perhaps he was afraid they might have a warrant to arrest him as well as search the house. He knew that, in such cases, the police carry out the house search first and only then deliver the arrest warrant, which is what had happened with Senator Amaral. However, Cunha did not allow his fears to show. His only irritation seemed to be at the helicopters from TV news stations hovering over his house trying to get pictures of him. This restricted his movement around the building so much that one of the few people he telephoned, other than his lawyers and his wife, was his press officer.

THE PETITION TO REMOVE CUNHA

The investigators had to work quickly, for one simple reason: the following day, 16 December 2015, the prosecutor general's office applied for Eduardo Cunha's removal from office as both speaker of the Chamber and as congressman. The result of the searches at his house had convinced all the prosecutors that such a move was necessary. The allegations were serious: promoting and being a member of a criminal organisation, as well as obstructing and hindering the investigations. According to Rodrigo Janot, the prosecutor general, Eduardo Cunha had improperly used his electoral mandate both as congressman and as the office of speaker of the Chamber, to inhibit and intimidate witnesses, informants, lawyers and public officials.

All, allegedly, in order to hinder and impede the investigation against him and his fellow criminals.

In the application, the prosecutor general's office said that the speaker of the Chamber had used his office 'solely with the purpose of protecting himself using improper actions', and stated that there was not a 'sliver of doubt' that he had overstepped 'all acceptable limits'.

The list of acts attributed to Eduardo Cunha began with his use of formal requests from the Chamber of Deputies' public accounts committee to put pressure on one of the middlemen in the scheme, Júlio Camargo, who had delayed payment of kickbacks to him. According to the investigation, which gave rise to the first of the charges against Cunha, the congressman had asked one of his allies, Solange Almeida, to file a congressional information request about Mitsui, a Japanese multinational represented in Brazil by Júlio Camargo.

The second allegation listed on the prosecutors' application was electrifying. A black-market currency trader by the name of Lúcio Bolonha Funaro had been involved in a legal dispute with the Schahin group, resulting from the collapse of the Apertadinho hydroelectric dam in Rondônia. Funaro was the owner of the hydroelectric power station, which had been built by Schahin. After the dam burst, causing widespread social and environmental damage, Funaro and Schahin had gone to court over responsibility for the accident. Following this dispute, the Schahin group found itself being singled out by the Chamber of Deputies. There were more than thirty information requests, along with onerous audit and inspection requests and invitations to appear at committee hearings, according to the Chamber's own records. In 2010, statistics from the public accounts committee revealed that twelve out of forty meetings had been to discuss matters relating to Schahin: 30 per cent of its work was devoted to a single company.

The pattern continued with the Petrobras congressional inquiry, in which the Schahin group was the subject of seven further summonses. During the session scheduled to hear evidence from members of the Schahin family, a congressman linked to Eduardo Cunha brandished a dossier listing 107 overseas bank accounts belonging to the family, which allegedly contained deposits of US$500 million. Milton Schahin blamed Funaro for the pressure from Congress on his company. 'I see it as pure malice coming from Funaro. Now you're asking me: "How can someone like Funaro have so much influence?" Because Eduardo Cunha is behind him. We have a major dispute with Funaro, and Cunha's links with him are very well known. What is bizarre is that the Chamber is getting involved in a quarrel between two companies. What do congressmen have to do with a legal dispute between private companies?' he said to *O Globo* newspaper. Milton Schahin also said, in a statement to the Federal Police, that he had already received death threats from Funaro, as had his brother Salim.

Milton Schahin even wrote to the prosecutor general's office alleging that new death threats had come from Lúcio Bolonha Funaro. In an interview with *piauí* magazine in August 2015, Funaro said the following about Milton Schahin: 'Does he think he's not going to get fucked with any more? Well, he's wrong. I've only just begun to mess with him. He doesn't realise that he's buggered.' Eduardo Cunha denied any close relationship with Funaro, but the prosecutors cited evidence that Funaro purchased two cars registered in the name of C3 Produções Artísticas e Jornalísticas, a company owned by Eduardo Cunha and his wife. Furthermore, the passenger list of an aircraft belonging to Júlio Camargo, one of the middlemen in the Petrobras corruption scheme, reveals that Cunha travelled with Funaro between São Paulo and Brasília.

The third justification presented by prosecutors in their application was the issuing of a summons to Beatriz Catta Preta, the lawyer responsible for negotiating various plea bargains under Operation Car Wash, requiring her to appear before the Petrobras congressional inquiry. The application was made by one of Edward Cunha's allies, the PMDB Congressman Celso Pansera, who later became a minister in Dilma Rousseff's government. Curiously, the request that she be subpoenaed was approved shortly after Júlio Camargo, one of Beatriz Catta Preta's clients at the time, provided new evidence to the prosecutor general, in which he revealed that Eduardo Cunha had received part of the kickback relating to the drill-ships sold by Samsung Heavy Industries to Petrobras. When news surfaced that Catta Preta's summons had been issued, it caused surprise; other summonses that had been requested several months earlier, such as that of Júlio Camargo himself, had still not been decided upon. Catta Preta didn't, in the end, appear before the congressional inquiry, due to the furious reaction her summons provoked. The Brazilian Bar Association filed an application with the Supreme Court against her being required to give testimony, but her summonsing weighed heavily against Cunha.

There were further allegations in the prosecutor general's list justifying Cunha's removal from office, such as hiring Kroll, the international investigation agency, to work on the Petrobras congressional inquiry. The contract, which cost R\$1 million, was vague about the purpose of Kroll's investigation, but for the prosecutors there could be only one reason: to find evidence that would undermine the plea bargains on which so much of

Operation Car Wash was based. Behind the scenes, people were saying that the targets of Kroll's investigation were those who had cooperated most with the prosecutors in bringing events to light.

Another allegation stated that Eduardo Cunha made use of Congressman Celso Pansera to intimidate Alberto Youssef. He filed a series of twelve formal requests seeking, among other things, to compel Youssef's ex-wife, sister and daughters to testify to Congress. Youssef had been the first person to cooperate under Operation Car Wash and to mention the name of Edward Cunha. In his own testimony, Youssef complained bitterly about his family being subjected to this kind of pressure.

The prosecutor said that Cunha was also suspected of using his position to approve executive decrees benefiting certain banks and companies, and that he was charging them for this. Various executive decrees under investigation were the subject of messages exchanged between businessman such as Léo Pinheiro from OAS and Otávio Azevedo from Andrade Gutierrez.

Finally, prosecutors listed the manoeuvres undertaken within the Chamber's ethics committee, where Cunha's 'shock troops' acted openly to ensure that he would not face censure.

New suspicions against the speaker of the Chamber continued to surface. At the end of December, in another police operation in Rio de Janeiro, a document was found containing a reference to Eduardo Cunha and Fábio Cleto, who had been appointed by Cunha as vice chairman of Caixa Econômica Federal, a large state-owned bank. The document indicated to the investigators that Cunha and Cleto had charged kickbacks in exchange for approving financing from the state-run investment fund used to guarantee workers' statutory severance pay in the event of unfair dismissal. The situation appeared similar to that described by two new cooperating witnesses, Ricardo Pernambuco and his son, Ricardo Pernambuco Júnior, from the construction company Carioca. In their testimony, both father and son said they had paid a kickback to Eduardo Cunha in order to release funds for the Porto Maravilha construction works, one of the infrastructure projects for the 2016 Rio Olympics. The construction works were the responsibility of a consortium composed of OAS, Odebrecht and Carioca, in which Carioca accounted for only 25 per cent of the project. The two businessmen said they had paid more than R$50 million to Cunha and provided the numbers of various overseas bank accounts where the deposits had been made. These were different to the secret bank accounts that had already been uncovered with other banks such as Israel Discount Bank – Cunha had, once again, failed to declare their existence in Brazil. Text messages exchanged between Cunha and Léo Pinheiro of OAS also discussed releasing payments from the workers' indemnity investment fund.

For all of these reasons, the prosecutor general's office lodged a formal application for the speaker of the Chamber to be removed from office: 'It is a matter of urgency that Eduardo Cunha be stripped of his powers as federal congressman and as speaker of the Chamber.' He resisted nevertheless, convinced that his position would protect him.

A SEA OF MUD

The serious allegations of corruption came in the wake of other tragedies that left the people of Brazil deeply demoralised towards the end of 2015. On 5 November, the Fundão dam owned by the mining company Samarco burst, dumping thirty-five million cubic metres of mud and mining waste on the village of Bento Rodrigues, near Mariana in the state of Minas Gerais. It was an environmental disaster unprecedented in the history of Brazilian mining, leaving seventeen people dead, more than 1,200 homeless, and a trail of pollution and destruction all the way down the Doce River to the Atlantic Ocean, more than 600 kilometres away. To make matters worse, Brazil also found itself facing an outbreak of microcephaly – a medical condition in which a baby's brain does not develop properly – linked, according to initial findings, with the Zika virus transmitted by the *Aedes aegypti* mosquito, which is also responsible for the frequent outbreaks of dengue fever in many parts of Brazil. The year also ended with the federal and state governments still in financial difficulties, due to a fall in tax receipts.

The only glimmer of hope in the traditional year-end retrospectives was Operation Car Wash, which would pick up the same frenetic level of activity in 2016, with new names appearing in the evidence cited before the courts. In the first ten days of the new year came two bombshells. Firstly, the text messages of Léo Pinheiro, former chairman of OAS, were disclosed, implicating Jaques Wagner, presidential chief of staff, and Edinho Silva, the government's communications director, among others. Secondly, Nestor Cerveró revealed that a gigantic building had been constructed in the northern state of Bahia in order to house Petrobras's Financial Division, despite there being space available in the company's headquarters in Rio de Janeiro.

In response to renewed suspicions against politicians and members of the government, President Dilma Rousseff spoke about Operation Car Wash in her first interview of 2016: 'They can poke around as much as they like. There's no shadow hanging over my conduct.'

On 8 January, the journalist and writer Nelson Motta published an article in *O Globo* newspaper calling Operation Car Wash the best TV series around. He began the article by asking provocatively, 'What team of scriptwriters could possibly create a better plotline than this, packed with more emotions, surprises and mysteries?' Motta went on to say:

> In the near future Operation Car Wash will certainly be turned into a television series, where reality surpasses fiction in the sensational story of a police operation that changed Brazil, led by a fair and courageous judge and a band of young and brave prosecutors working with a Federal Police that is honest and efficient – albeit with its own traitors and corrupt officers – revealing the full trajectory of heroes and villains, bigwigs, informants, powerful businessmen and their families, each with their own individual dramas, a vast criminal conspiracy at the heart of the state, and the web of interests that bind together politicians, political parties and corrupt professionals in their plunder of the nation.

The article ended with: 'Meanwhile in Curitiba ...', inviting the reader to expect yet more twists and turns in this real-life drama.

Meanwhile in Curitiba, indeed, powerful businessmen remained behind bars, spending New Year in jail. Sergio Moro had taken advantage of the judicial recess to take his whole family on holiday to Spain. The Federal Police had strengthened its Operation Car Wash team, which was already considered the largest one ever dedicated to a single set of investigations. The federal prosecutors' task force, including the eleven prosecutors working on the case and their support staff, now numbered fifty people.

In Brasília, the federal government passed an executive decree permitting leniency agreements with companies involved in corruption trials, which was interpreted as a way of weakening the federal prosecutors and the Federal Audit Office. This was the understanding of prosecutor Carlos Fernando dos Santos Lima, and Júlio Marcelo de Oliveira at the audit office. Luís Adams, the government's attorney general, said that those opposed to the measure were 'prophets of chaos'.

Operation Car Wash was being both praised and severely criticised. In the middle of January, more than a hundred lawyers signed an 'Open letter repudiating the selective suppression of rights and entitlements witnessed under Operation Car Wash'. One of the signatories, Antônio Carlos de Almeida Castro, said that their objective was to provoke reflection: 'This manifesto is not merely intended to catch the judiciary's attention. It is much more about inviting society to reflect as a whole on why, suddenly, Brazil has become a country with a single dominating theme, where only accusations are given a voice.' The author of the letter was Nabor Bulhões, Marcelo Odebrecht's lawyer in the Operation Car Wash proceedings. 'We had to react, because Moro had begun authorising a whole series of arrests and police operations in order to compel the group to seek leniency and plea bargains,' said Bulhões in an interview for this book. The letter said that 'there had never been a criminal case in which violations of the minimum standards for a fair trial were occurring with so large a number of defendants and in such a systematic manner'. In another section, the letter attacked the use of arrest warrants: 'It is completely unacceptable, in a judicial system that claims to be democratic, for temporary detention to be used in a naked attempt to force suspects to sign plea bargains.'

The text criticised Sergio Moro's 'judicial activism', although without actually naming him: 'It is difficult to imagine legal proceedings being conducted by a judge acting in a less impartial manner, behaving in fact in a more accusatory manner than the actual prosecution.' The letter ended by saying: 'It is fundamentally important that we stand up against these abuses. The rule of law is under threat and the actions of the judiciary must not be influenced by the oppressive publicity which has been launched against the accused.' Sergio Moro replied to the criticism, saying that his objective was simply to follow the trail of the money stolen from Petrobras.

The open letter had a strong impact, and an equally strong reaction. Both the associations of judges and of prosecutors refuted the lawyers' criticisms in writing, robustly defending Operation Car Wash and calling attention to the fact that many of the signatories of the manifesto were representing defendants in Operation Car Wash proceedings.

DELCÍDIO DO AMARAL'S PLEA BARGAIN

In his cell, Delcídio do Amaral was hatching a plan that seemed perfect. He knew he posed a nightmare to both the government and numerous other politicians. The question almost everyone in Brasília was asking was whether the senator would talk.

He began to tell the prosecutor general's office what he knew immediately after carnival finished, providing the first in a series of devastating depositions starting on Thursday 11 February and continuing through to the Sunday. At several points he showed regret at having begun talking. He asked to stop, then started again. But he kept going and was eventually released on 19 February. Fear spread when the senator came out of custody. Why had he been released? Doubts increased even more when he requested fifteen days' leave from the Senate. Politicians and journalists began to phone his wife, Maika. She implied that he wouldn't make a plea bargain: 'No, you must be mad. I'm against all that, it's against my principles.'

O Globo reported that he had signed a plea bargain, but everyone was denying it vehemently, including his lawyer. It was all part of the plan. He had negotiated with the prosecutor general's office that he would become an informant, but that it should remain confidential for six months. This would allow him to go through the Senate's disciplinary hearings without being removed from office, thereby maintaining his rights of privileged forum, the right to be tried by the Supreme Court rather than the ordinary courts. These terms would have to be accepted by the Supreme Court, which could well reject the confidentiality clause. In any event, confidentiality began to crumble when the first of two reports were published in *IstoÉ* magazine containing extracts of his testimony, despite it still being protected by judicial confidentiality. In the extracts, Senator Amaral attacked President Dilma Rousseff, former president Lula da Silva and the principal leader of the opposition, Aécio Neves.

While the senator was in custody, Aloizio Mercadante, the minister of education and a key figure in Dilma Rousseff's government, invited Delcídio do Amaral's aide, Eduardo Marzagão, to his office. He offered to help Marzagão's boss, while also advising the senator not to talk. He also warned Amaral's aide that the situation was going to get worse: 'Next it'll be

Andrade Gutierrez, maybe Zelada, the fucking piece of shit. There's going to be all kinds of crap flying everywhere.'

Mercadante suggested that Amaral sit tight and wait until everything cooled down. He offered to help pay the lawyer, to talk to the speaker of the Senate and the president of the Supreme Court to 'work on a solution' and asked Marzagão to let him know how he could help. But he also warned: 'I think he should wait, and not make any hasty moves.'

The conversation was being recorded. Delcídio do Amaral suspected that Aloizio Mercadante was acting as an emissary of President Dilma Rousseff and handed over the recording made by his aide to the prosecutor general's office. The release of the audio file on Tuesday 15 March was another shock for the government. Rousseff released a statement saying that the minister had been acting on his 'own initiative'. Mercadante defended himself and said that he was just trying to show solidarity with a former colleague. He highlighted parts of the recording in which he had said: 'He should defend himself whatever way he thinks best ... I'm not getting involved in that, the decision's up to him ... It's none of my business if he wants to turn informant.'

The recording seemed as though it would be the biggest scandal that day, but by the afternoon, the headlines had moved on to a different story. Justice Teori Zavascki had approved Delcídio do Amaral's plea bargain and had suspended the confidentiality clause; in the plea bargain, Senator Amaral had cited former president Lula da Silva several times. He said that he had been approached by Lula at the time of Paulo Roberto Costa's arrest, soon after the beginning of Operation Car Wash. Delcídio do Amaral had agreed that they needed to follow the case closely because the former director of Petrobras knew so much, but that nothing had been done to block the operation. 'In fact, the government underestimated the situation with Costa. It allowed things to carry on,' said Senator Amaral in an interview for this book. According to Amaral, when the first senior businessmen were arrested at the end of 2014, Lula tried to convince the government to create a 'crisis cabinet' to follow events, but Rousseff didn't buy the idea.

'He felt, as I did, that this thing was going to explode. When it reached phase seven of the operation, Lula became even more insistent. But Rousseff got it into her head that it was nothing to do with her, and that the legacy she would leave behind was one of having combated corruption,' said the senator. Amaral even revealed that the former president approached him in May 2015 and asked him to help protect his friend José Carlos Bumlai and to prevent Nestor Cerveró becoming an informant. The senator asserted that Lula da Silva knew everything and was in charge of the whole scheme. He also said he had attended a meeting in São Paulo with Lula, Senator Renan Calheiros and Senator Edison Lobão to deal with the political crisis triggered by Operation Car Wash. Lula denied these allegations and accused Senator Amaral of lying.

In his statements to prosecutors, Delcídio do Amaral also claimed that President Rousseff had nominated Marcelo Navarro Ribeiro Dantas to the Superior Court of Justice with the aim of interfering in the direction of Operation Car Wash, and revealed that he had met with Ricardo Lewandowski, the president of the Supreme Court, with the same objective. He also claimed that the construction firms involved in the Belo Monte hydroelectric dam paid kickbacks to finance Dilma Rousseff's presidential election campaigns in 2010 and 2014. Furthermore, he accused the vice president, Michel Temer of the PMDB, of having links with João Augusto Henriques, one of the arrested middlemen in the scheme, and with Jorge Zelada, former director of Petrobras. He also implicated Senator Aécio Neves of the PSDB in a scheme for receiving kickbacks from Furnas, the state-run energy company, and said that data provided by the now-defunct Banco Rural to the post office congressional inquiry – chaired by Senator Amaral – would have implicated Senator Aécio Neves, if that data had not been 'tampered with' by the bank.

Delcídio do Amaral said in his statements that when the post office congressional inquiry authorised the lifting of banking confidentiality in relation to Banco Rural, among others, Aécio Neves sent representatives to the inquiry asking that the lifting of the bank's confidentiality obligations be delayed, on the basis that there was insufficient time for the bank to prepare the necessary responses. Senator Amaral said that when he finally received the material, he noticed 'with surprise' that 'the time had been used to tamper with the data sent by Banco Rural', and that the data 'fully implicated Aécio Neves and Clésio Andrade, respectively governor and vice governor of the state of Minas Gerais'. The two of them denied everything. Aécio Neves's office issued a statement saying that he 'never had any kind of relationship with Banco Rural', and that he had 'never had any dealings with Delcídio do Amaral on any matter relating to the post office congressional inquiry', nor had he asked anyone else to do so. Delcídio Amaral's plea bargain testimony had made the political atmosphere even more inflammatory.

Chapter 12

ALETHEIA – THE SEARCH FOR THE TRUTH

4 March 2016

LULA IN THE EYE OF THE STORM

At 6 a.m. on Friday 4 March, three detectives, two notaries and ten police officers knocked at the door of Apartment 122 of Block 1, 1501 Avenida Prestes Maia, São Bernardo do Campo, São Paulo. The atmosphere was tense. The door was opened by the former president of the republic himself, Luiz Inácio Lula da Silva. Wearing a tracksuit, he looked at the police officers and greeted them with a brisk 'Good morning'.

Detective Luciano Flores de Lima, who was leading the team, had taken every possible precaution in preparing for the operation. He had already commanded important missions for Operation Car Wash, including the arrest of former minister José Dirceu, but this one was different; they were dealing with a former president of the republic. More than ever, everything had been planned down to the last detail. There would be two armed police officers at the apartment, who were trained to defend the former president. What if they reacted with force? This was one of the many scenarios they had thought through, and was why one team knocked at Lula's door, while eight men from the Federal Police's elite squad, the Tactical Operations Unit, waited inside a white van on the street outside, ready to swing into action at the slightest sign of trouble. Helicopters were ready to take off from São Paulo's Congonhas Airport nearby.

Detective Lima was the first to enter Lula's apartment. 'Good morning,' replied the detective, and then risked something somewhat friendlier: 'It's a pleasure to meet you in person, sir.' After introducing himself, he announced in the calmest voice he could muster, 'Look, we have a warrant to carry out a search here in your home.' Lula nodded and told the police officers to come in.

The only people in the apartment were Lula, his wife Marisa Letícia, and his two official bodyguards. The fear that they might resist the search and seizure warrant or get in the way of the police's work proved unfounded; they allowed the detectives to enter. Even stranger, they did not appear surprised. It was as if they had already been alerted to the possibility of this happening. Nevertheless, the detectives were relieved.

Lula, meanwhile, was visibly annoyed. As the officers entered, he looked at them one by one, as if looking for someone. 'So, you didn't bring the Japanese guy then?' he asked. Despite the tension, the officers nearly laughed. Newton Ishii, the police officer of Japanese-Brazilian heritage who had become famous because he was always the one seen on national TV leading away those arrested under Operation Car Wash, was on holiday and wasn't part of that day's operation. Images, masks and even life-size puppets in homage to Ishii had already become popular at carnival parades throughout Brazil. But it wasn't a time for jokes. Detective Lima had the task of telling the former president that he was to be formally interviewed and that it would be necessary to take him to a quiet place where this could be done without causing a disturbance.

When the detective explained the situation, Lula raised his voice: 'I will only leave here in handcuffs. If you want to take me ... If you want to interview me, you'll have to interview me here.' Detective Lima said that he could not interview him in his home, it wasn't a suitable location. It was a question of security – there would be protests outside which were certain to hinder the interview and the search of the apartment. A room in the presidential suite at Congonhas Airport where the interview could take place had already been prepared. They would not be going to the Federal Police headquarters, and the cars they would be travelling in were unmarked, with tinted side windows. The detective also assured Lula that they would not allow any photographs or video footage to be taken of him during the journey. It would be better to leave straight away, before the press arrived. Lula listened, but did not reply.

The detective then used his final argument, telling Lula that he had a warrant to take him in for questioning and making it clear that if the former president refused to go with him voluntarily, he would carry out the warrant to compel him. Lula did not have much choice. He asked his head of security, Lieutenant Valmir Moraes da Silva, to call his lawyer Roberto Teixeira. He told Teixeira that the Federal Police wanted to take him to the airport for questioning and that they had a warrant to compel him. After listening to his lawyer's advice, he said that he would change clothes and go with the police officers to answer their questions. Lula had enough political experience and instinct to know how to handle the situation.

At 6.30 a.m., seven police officers went with Lula to the airport, while eight remained in the apartment to carry out the search, in the presence of Marisa Letícia. Lula sat in the back seat of the police car. He was advised not to look out from between the front seats, to avoid being photographed through the windscreen. The strategy worked. As the convoy of police cars made its way to the airport followed by the Tactical Operations Unit van, Lula did not say much. He merely commented in a pleasant tone of voice on the day's news, the changes at the ministry of justice, and President Rousseff's various dilemmas.

In many ways, everyone who was following Operation Car Wash had either hoped or feared that something like this might occur. Nevertheless, Lula being required to attend a police interview came as a shock to the nation. The news hit Brazil just as it was reeling from the revelations published in *IstoÉ* magazine the previous day, including extracts from Senator Delcídio do Amaral's proposed plea bargain. The government had been stunned by Amaral's declarations, which directly implicated President Rousseff and former president Lula. According to what Senator Amaral had promised to reveal, Rousseff knew more than she had ever admitted about the controversial purchase of the Pasadena oil refinery in Texas and had nominated a judge to the Superior Court of Justice with the mission of granting habeas corpus to various imprisoned businessmen. What's more, Lula may have been behind the offer to buy Nestor Cerveró's silence. As if the crisis provoked by Delcídio do Amaral's scattergun allegations were not enough, Brazil was facing its worst recession in twenty-five years, with GDP falling by 3.8 per cent in 2015.

With phase twenty-four now in full swing, Operation Car Wash, which had begun two years earlier by targeting the black-market currency trader Alberto Youssef, was now getting close to the most senior political figure of all. In choosing a code name for phase twenty-four, the Federal Police had symbolically picked the Greek word 'Aletheia', meaning truth. According to the German philosopher Martin Heidegger, the could be understood as 'unconcealment'. For the Federal Police, the purpose of Operation Aletheia was to seek the truth. And to reveal it, 200 police officers and thirty tax inspectors were carrying out forty-four judicial warrants: thirty-three for search and seizure and eleven to compel people to attend police interviews, throughout the three states of São Paulo, Rio de Janeiro and Bahia.

Among the locations visited by the Federal Police were Lula's apartment in São Bernardo, the home of his son Fábio Luís in the upmarket Moema district of São Paulo, a country retreat in Atibaia, a seaside apartment in Guarujá and the Lula Institute's headquarters in São Paulo. Other companies and individuals were also being investigated that day, but the principal target of phase twenty-four was by now already on his way for questioning at Congonhas Airport. As the police convoy made its way through the traffic, the news that former president Luiz Inácio Lula da Silva was being taken in for questioning flashed around Brazil and the world, and was the top story on news websites around the globe.

THE POLICE INTERVIEW IN THE PRESIDENTIAL SUITE

It was 8 a.m. when Lula began to answer questions in the presidential suite at Congonhas Airport. His journey there had been uneventful and he had waited patiently for his lawyers to arrive at 7.45 a.m. After speaking privately with them for fifteen minutes, the former president was ready. He asked his bodyguard for a tissue, wiped his face and prepared himself.

The news that Lula was at Congonhas spread quickly by word of mouth, and many people decided to go to the airport. In the room set aside for the police interview were two detectives, three police officers and two prosecutors, along with Lula, one of his bodyguards, three lawyers and Paulo Teixeira, a Workers' Party congressman who managed to get into the room uninvited. When the detectives discovered that Teixeira's registration with the Brazilian Bar Association was currently suspended, they reached an agreement that he could stay, but that no one else would get in. The police knew that other politicians and legislators would soon appear, along with various supporters.

The detectives had prepared more than 120 questions and needed to get Lula's answers to them all, despite repeated interruptions. The police recorded the interview using both audio and video, and one of Lula's lawyers recorded everything on his mobile phone. Throughout the long interview, Lula denied all the accusations. He said he didn't know anything about the Lula Institute's financial dealings, and that he had never personally sought donations. The former president wasn't able to say exactly who dealt with donations: 'You'll have to ask somebody who knows about that.' The person in question was Paulo Okamotto, chairman of the Lula Institute. The former president referred to Okamotto several times as being the person who would be able to answer the detective's questions, including those about the payment made by the institute to the company

owned by his son, Fábio Luís. Paulo Okamotto was also interviewed by police that day.

Lula talked about the lectures he gave, the principal
source of income of LILS Palestras, Eventos e Publicações
Ltda, of which he was a shareholder. He said that he charged
US$200,000 per lecture, based on the amounts received by
former US president Bill Clinton: 'We do more than he does,
so we deserve at least the same.' Regarding the activities of the
Lula Institute, a non-profit-making organisation, he explained
that his aim was to explain what he had done in government
and develop ideas, such as the 'My House, My Life' social
housing programme. When asked more detailed questions
about payments from the institute, he said he didn't know the
answers. He couldn't say, for example, why the company G4,
owned by his son Fábio Luís, had received more than R$1.3
million from the Lula Institute in 2014. When he was asked
for a second time about G4, he said, 'If G4 provided services to
the institute, then the institute correctly pays for the services
provided.' He added that he had already provided all the information to the tax authorities, who had been 'poking around' at
the institute. The detective reminded him of the amount of tax
paid and persisted: 'Have you any idea, sir, what services might
have been provided by G4 to the Lula Institute in order for G4
to receive such an amount of money?'

'Listen, if my memory serves me well, it must have been the
Memorial to Democracy, because we did the Memorial website together that's now online. We did the Memorial and we
did Public Policy – those are two online programs to spread
the word about what happened in Brazil. All of that involves
making films, carrying out research. It must've been that.

But as you're, you're ... Are you going to interview Paulo Okamotto or not?' answered Lula.

'He's on our list. I've no idea if ...' said the detective.

'Well, if he is, he ought to tell you, because it's him who does the hiring,' said Lula.

At that point in the interview, Lula talked about Brazil and corruption:

> Over the years, one of the things that has fostered corruption in Brazil is that a ministry or public authority pretends to commission work, pretends to pay, then the company pretends to do the work, and everything carries on as before. Before I became president, a public official pretended to work, the government pretended to pay, and Brazil got screwed, if you'll excuse my language. We decided to raise the moral standard. I adopted the following policy: first of all pay the day it's due. I only have credibility with people if I pay when it's due. If I pretend to pay and the person pretends to receive, someone's going to swindle someone. So I opted for integrity, and that also goes for the institute.

The former president couldn't say precisely who at the Lula Institute had a close relationship with the businessmen and companies being investigated under Operation Car Wash, to the extent of asking for donations. But he agreed that he was a friend of Léo Pinheiro, former chairman of OAS, who had been sentenced to more than sixteen years for involvement in the Petrobras corruption scheme, and also of José Carlos Bumlai, the cattle breeder arrested during phase twenty-one of the operation. Lula vehemently denied being the owner of the seaside apartment in

Guarujá and the house in Atibaia, that were also being searched. He claimed that he had been sucked into the most convoluted set of legal proceedings in Brazil because someone had accused him of owning properties that weren't his, but that other people said belonged to him. According to Lula, the whole story of the triplex apartment had been invented by the Federal Police, and he called it 'pure malice of epic proportions'.

At one point, Lula recalled a visit he had made to the apartment in Guarujá accompanied by Léo Pinheiro, saying that the property was too small for him: 'When I went the first time, I said to Léo that the building wasn't suitable. As well as being small, a triplex of 215 square metres is a "My House, My Life" social housing size of triplex – it's small.'

'Is that good or bad?' asked the detective.

'Huh?'

'Is that good or bad?' repeated the detective.

'It was very small, the bedrooms, the staircase was very, very … I said: "Léo, it's not suitable, for an old man like me, it's just not suitable",' replied Lula.

The lawyer Roberto Teixeira interrupted the interview several times, complaining about the questions or other aspects he considered irrelevant to the interview. The detectives rejected his interruptions each time, saying that it was an opportunity for Lula to give his explanation. During the three hours of interviews, water and coffee were passed around the room and the former president's bodyguard brought in some food, which he graciously offered to everyone. From time to time they could hear the noise outside.

At one point, a group of Workers' Party congressmen managed to reach the door of the room where the interview was taking place. When one of the police officers opened the door, the politicians tried to force their way in. It was one of the most bizarre scenes of the day: congressmen trying to push the door open and police officers trying to close it. Other politicians were firing up the protesters outside the building through a glass wall that faced onto the pavement. Inside the interview room, the noise got steadily louder, increasing the tension.

The defence lawyers requested that the interview be adjourned. With the pressure and risk of conflict rising, the detectives decided to terminate the interview quickly; after all, the most important questions had already been asked. Furthermore, they were under the impression that when it came to the issues of most interest to the investigation, Lula would simply repeat that he didn't know, that he didn't remember or that it wasn't a matter for him.

As soon as the former president had signed the transcript of the interview, the police officers let the congressmen enter the room and greet Lula, which they did enthusiastically. This gave rise to a further impasse. The congressmen wanted to take Lula outside to where his supporters were protesting, whereas the detectives preferred to take him away from the airport as quickly as possible. They had absolutely no wish to leave him there, especially as the atmosphere was beginning to turn hostile. As for Lula himself, he simply wanted to leave with his colleagues, but the detectives insisted that they should take him away themselves. The argument lasted almost an hour, and once again Lula got annoyed. He talked loudly with the congressmen and his lawyers and seemed very indignant. The police officers overheard the group saying things like: 'This is a declaration of war!' and 'After today we're going to set the country alight!'

While all this was going on, the detectives were trying to find a discreet way out of the stand-off. After a tense negotiation, followed at a distance by the Federal Police's senior command, they agreed that Lula would get into a car belonging to one of his lawyers and leave within the airport perimeter, which would be more secure. As Lula's supporters didn't want the officers to accompany the former president back to his home, the whole charade ended there and then. Despite everything, Lula said a friendly goodbye, shaking the officers' hands and asking them to return the things they had taken from his apartment. When one of the police officers wished him good luck, he replied warmly, and left.

Operation Aletheia would be the biggest test of Operation Car Wash, engulfing Brazil in controversy and rekindling divisions and conflicts that had barely been resolved after the 2014 election campaign. While Lula was leaving Congonhas Airport, protestors were piling into the Federal Police building within the airport, even occupying the escalator lobby. Groups for and against Lula each shouted slogans. The Federal Police had thought that interviewing the former president at the airport would avoid disturbances and protests. It didn't. There were confrontations on the streets of the city, and outside the apartment building in São Bernardo where Lula lived.

PROPERTY DEALINGS UNDER INVESTIGATION

The tension reflected the escalation of events over the preceding months. Before Operation Car Wash began closing in on Lula, he had already been on the radar of the São Paulo state prosecutors. Back in 2010, they had opened an investigation into the disappearance of funds from Cooperativa Habitacional dos Bancários de São Paulo (Bancoop, a large cooperative property developer). The investigation had resulted in charges against the then-chairman, João Vaccari Neto, who was subsequently arrested under Operation Car Wash. During the investigations, suspicion arose that Lula might be the real owner of the triplex apartment in the Solaris condominium in Guarujá, which had originally been one of Bancoop's developments. When Bancoop found itself in financial difficulties, completion of the development was transferred to OAS, one of the companies involved in the Petrobras corruption scandal.

The Bancoop case had been back in the news in December 2014. Each time claims were made that he was the owner of the apartment in Guarujá (and later of the Santa Bárbara country retreat in Atibaia), Lula would put out a statement from his institute, denying everything. His appearances and statements became more and more frequent.

Faced with rumours that he was to be the next target of Operation Car Wash, Lula had decided to clarify that he was not being investigated. On 20 January 2016, in a breakfast meeting with bloggers sympathetic to his views, the former president spoke about his superiority when it came to moral issues. 'If there's one thing that I'm proud of, it's that there isn't a living soul in this country more honest than I am. Not even within the Federal Police, the federal prosecutors, the Catholic church, or the evangelical church for that matter. Some might be just as honest, but I doubt it,' said Lula. 'I doubt there's a prosecutor, detective or businessman who would have the nerve to claim that I'd been involved in something illegal,' he challenged. 'There is not a single criminal case against me, and Moro himself has said that I am not under investigation.'

A few days later, on 27 January, the Federal Police launched phase twenty-two of Operation Car Wash, the first of the new year. Its code name, 'Triple X', was a clear reference to the triplex in Guarujá that Lula claimed he didn't own. That day, the police were looking into OAS's apartments in the Solaris condominium. Their investigations suggested that the apartments might be being used to launder money misappropriated from state-owned companies, and there were suspicions that assets were being concealed. In a press interview given that day, the prosecutor Carlos Fernando dos Santos Lima said that 'all the apartments in the condominium' were being investigated. Six people were arrested and searches took place in four cities, including São Bernardo do Campo.

Phase twenty-two also had the objective of investigating a scheme to set up offshore companies and bank accounts to conceal kickbacks. One of the targets was the Panamanian law firm Mossack Fonseca – which would later surface at the centre of the 'Panama Papers' scandal that revealed, among many other things, that the law firm had set up offshore shell companies for Brazilian politicians of various parties. The task force had information that Mossack had set up an offshore company called Murray, which owned a triplex in the Solaris condominium. Other individuals investigated under Operation Car Wash, such as Renato Duque and Pedro Barusco, may have used offshore companies set up by Mossack in order to transfer money outside of Brazil. Now there were suspicions that relatives of João Vaccari Neto may have been given apartments in the Solaris condominium as kickbacks.

To confuse matters further, on 29 January 2016, Lula and his wife Marisa Letícia received a formal summons from the São Paulo state prosecutors to answer questions the following month regarding the triplex in Guarujá. According to the São Paulo prosecutors, building work had been carried out by OAS at triplex 164-A. The improvements to the property, which even included the installation of a private lift, had cost R$770,000. The São Paulo prosecutors were seeking an explanation for why OAS had invested in an apartment that, in theory, did not yet have a purchaser. Another piece of the puzzle was that OAS had paid for a fitted kitchen in the apartment, which had been purchased in a shop on the prestigious Avenida Brigadeiro Faria Lima in São Paulo, and installed at the end of the building work.

On 30 January, the Lula Institute published a long statement entitled 'The Guarujá Documents: Dismantling the Farce', containing detailed explanations about the apartment. The statement said that Marisa Letícia, Lula's wife, had become a member of the Bancoop housing cooperative in April 2005, acquiring a share in Unit 141, a three-bedroomed apartment. For four and a half years, she had paid monthly and one-off contributions to a total of R$286,000. In September 2009, when Bancoop transferred the development to OAS, the payments were suspended because Marisa Letícia did not become a party to the contract with the new developer. Even so, according to the statement, Lula da Silva's family retained the right to seek the redemption of their share in the development at any time, but no longer specifically in relation to Unit 141, which was subsequently sold to another purchaser.

As Marisa Letícia's spouse, the former president regularly declared on his tax return the share in the development owned by his wife. The statement said that one year after the works at the Solaris condominium had finished, Lula and Marisa had gone there with the then-chairman of OAS, Léo Pinheiro, to visit another unit that was for sale: triplex apartment 164-A. According to the statement, this was the only time Lula visited the apartment. Marisa and their son Fábio Luís came back on other occasions while work was going on there, but 'at no time did Lula or his family use the apartment for any purpose'. In November 2015, because of the controversy, Marisa officially withdrew from the deal and requested the redemption of her share. According to the statement, 'even after the building works and modifications were carried out to the property (the cost of which would naturally have been reflected in the final purchase price), the unfounded reports, rumours and press speculation had destroyed the privacy necessary for the family's use of the apartment'.

The Lula Institute criticised the investigations by the São Paulo state prosecutors and by Operation Car Wash into the apartment, claiming that the big discovery of Operation Triple X, the existence of triplex apartments in the Solaris building that were registered in the name of the offshore shell company Murray, with links to Mossack Fonseca, had been publicly known for months. 'These facts have nothing to do with former president Lula, his family's or his activities, before, during or after his period in government,' said the statement. The institute finished by stating that 'the pettiness of these "charges", which will lie buried in court documents to be judged by historians, is the inglorious ending of the biggest campaign of persecution that has ever been inflicted on a political leader in this country'.

NO REST AT HIS FRIENDS' HOUSE IN THE COUNTRY

The Guarujá penthouse, however, was not the former president's only problem. Other doubts fell on the Santa Bárbara country retreat in Atibaia, a couple of hours north of São Paulo, where he was a frequent visitor. The land, which extended to around 170,000 square metres, the equivalent of twenty-four football pitches, was owned, on paper, by Fernando Bittar, the son of one of Lula's oldest and closest friends, Jacó Bittar, and Jonas Suassuna, a business associate of Lula's son, Fábio Luís. Each of them owned part of the site. A survey carried out at the federal government's Transparency Portal showed that Lula may have visited the property 111 times between 2012 and January 2016. This was the number of times that the bodyguards provided by the government, to which Lula is entitled as former president, were listed as being on duty at the house in Atibaia. They spent the night there 283 times during this period, including over New Year 2016.

The house frequented by the former president and his family became the subject of repeated newspaper reports. On 29 January, the *Folha de S.Paulo* newspaper published a lengthy article in which the former owner of a shop selling building materials stated that the construction firm Odebrecht had carried out most of the refurbishments at the property; Patrícia Fabiana Melo Nunes told *Folha* that Odebrecht had spent R$500,000 just purchasing building materials. Nunes explained that Odebrecht engineer Frederico Barbosa, who was coordinating the building works, would telephone a man, who would then pay her weekly. 'I don't have the phone number, the address or anything else relating to this gentleman. I only know that at 3 p.m. every Friday, he would pass by my shop to pay. The payments varied between R$75,000 and R$90,000 a week, in cash,' said Nunes. At the time, Frederico Barbosa told *Folha* that he had indeed worked on the project, but that he had done it as a personal favour while on holiday and that he didn't know about the link with former president Lula. Odebrecht responded that 'after initial verification, it had not identified any involvement by the company with the project'.

Later on, both engineer and construction company would change their stories.

In the light of the news reports, some of the former president's allies gave interviews, trying to explain the expenses paid by the construction company. Gilberto Carvalho, who had worked at a senior level in both Lula's presidency and that of his successor Dilma Rousseff, said to *Folha* in an article published on 4 February, that it was 'the most natural thing in the world that you could have companies making contributions to this or that person. In most of these instances, Lula was no longer president. Suppliers contribute to the Fernando Henrique Cardoso Institute,[6] and also to the Lula Institute. Since he is no longer president, Lula can receive these things. People can give him anything they like. What is criminal is to insinuate a relationship of cause and effect when there is, in fact, no such link.'

Several days later, another defender appeared. Luiz Marinho, the mayor of São Bernardo do Campo and a close ally of Lula's, gave an interview published in *O Globo* newspaper on 7 February, in which he said: 'As far as I know, two individuals bought the house between them and made it available for his use, with proof of source of funds. There is therefore no problem whatsoever. Strictly speaking, today the place belongs to friends and not to him.' The reporter persisted: 'But he uses it regularly.' Marinho replied: 'Let's imagine that I have a beach house and I make it available for you to use every weekend. What business is it of anyone else's? This is the same thing.'

---

[6] Note to English edition: Fernando Henrique Cardoso, one of the founders of the centrist PSDB party, was Lula's precedessor as president of Brazil, and a leading critic of his government.

The journalist from *O Globo* wanted to know what he meant by 'make available' – did he mean giving a house key? Marinho's answer was: 'Take it [gesturing handing over a key]. Put your furniture in, it's yours. If one day you decide to buy it, I'll sell it to you. If not, then one day my son will inherit it.' The interviewer wanted to know why someone would do something like that for the former president, to which Marinho replied: 'You'll have to ask the people who did it. The problem is that they're not trying to find the truth. They're trying to find some gimmick to show that Lula was involved in Car Wash.'

At the end of the interview, the mayor of São Bernardo also spoke about the triplex in Guarujá. 'What he bought, and fully declared, was a share in a property. When he went to see it, he said: "I don't want it – it's got three floors and a really awful staircase. I'm getting old." He told me this and joked: "For Christ's sake, it's a hovel. It's nothing like I imagined, and now I'm in a real bind – I don't know if I should keep it or not." Curiously, after the visit, they started to paint it, and then he decided to get rid of it. What's the problem?' asked Marinho.

Sergio Moro did not see the situation in the same light as Lula's friends. On 9 February, he authorised the opening of a separate investigation into the building works at the house in Atibaia, which had begun in October 2010 when Lula was reaching the end of his second term in office. The Federal Police were already analysing the case as part of their investigation into OAS, but as new evidence came to light involving other companies and individuals, they needed to open a separate, confidential investigation. Various professionals who had worked on the project were interviewed and indications emerged that José Carlos Bumlai, Odebrecht and OAS had all been involved in the building works.

In the space of a few months, the property, which had previously amounted to an old house with an access road and a small lake, gained a new building with four en suite bedrooms and an open-plan living area with an outdoor barbecue. The lake was enlarged and became one of Lula's favourite places to relax. Marisa Letícia bought a little boat that could be used for fishing, one of her husband's favourite hobbies. An employee at the president's office purchased two pedalos, named after Lula's grandchildren. At the end of his term of office, some of his personal belongings were moved from his official residence to the address in Atibaia.

Another important revelation was that the fitted kitchen in the house had been paid for by OAS and purchased from the same shop that had supplied the kitchen furniture for the triplex in Guarujá. The Federal Police found out that the order for cupboards, worktops and appliances such as a dishwasher and electric oven, had been placed on 13 March 2014, a couple of days before the beginning of Operation Car Wash, at a cost of R$130,000. The invoice, which gave the Atibaia house as the delivery address, was in the name of Fernando Bittar. This strengthened the investigators' suspicions that ownership of assets was being concealed.

The São Paulo prosecutors invited Lula and Marisa to answer questions regarding this and other matters on 17 February, but the interview was delayed by a member of the National Council of Public Prosecutors, at the request of Congressman Paulo Teixeira, from the Workers' Party. Even so, demonstrators for and against the former president clashed outside the sprawling state court complex in Barra Funda, São Paulo. Stones and bottles of water flew, fights broke out and the police had to use tear gas to disperse the crowds.

THE INVESTIGATIONS DEEPEN

As if the atmosphere of confrontation wasn't tense enough already, a new bombshell landed with the arrest of marketing executive João Santana and his wife, Monica Moura. The couple were the target of phase twenty-three, launched on 22 February 2016 under the code name 'Acarajé' – the traditional Bahian dish whose name had been used by some of the suspects to refer to kickbacks. Santana and Moura were in the Dominican Republic and had to return to Brazil in order to hand themselves in the following day. This line of enquiry had begun when a note from Monica Moura with numbers of bank accounts in London and New York was found in the house of middleman Zwi Skornicki during phase nine of Operation Car Wash. In authorising the arrest, Sergio Moro cited that the Operation Car Wash task force had identified payments of US$4.5 million made by Zwi Skornicki to the couple via overseas bank accounts between September 2013 and November 2014, as well as payments of US$3 million from Odebrecht between April 2012 and March 2013.

'The most likely hypothesis from an evidential point of view is that such payments were intended to remunerate public relations services provided by João Santana and Monica Moura to the Workers' Party,' wrote Moro, stressing that he saw this as a serious indication of corruption in Brazil's party political system. 'There is a well-founded suspicion that the surreptitious transactions carried out by Zwi Skornicki on behalf of a company called Shellbill, through accounts used by Odebrecht, represent payments of undue benefits arising from Petrobras contracts. It is opportune to recall that, according to the statements of a number of criminals who are cooperating with the judicial authorities, there was a sharing of kickbacks, of which part was directed towards Petrobras employees and part towards political representatives or the parties to which they belonged,' stated Moro. This brought the operation ever closer to the Rousseff government, since it related to the 2014 presidential campaign.

Moro also sent the following message to his opponents: 'What is exceptional in the present case is not the use of precautionary detention, but the degree of degradation in public affairs revealed by the Operation Car Wash legal proceedings, with damages of around R$6 billion already identified in relation to Petrobras alone, and the possibility, currently being investigated by the Supreme Court, that the misappropriated funds may have been used to pay kickbacks to dozens of legislators, thereby compromising the very essence of our democracy.' In concluding his judgment, the judge once again defended the operation and the necessity of the arrests: 'While the precautionary detentions ordered as part of Operation Car Wash have received frequent criticism, the fact is that where corruption is systematic and deep, preventive detention is required in order to extinguish it and to avoid a progressive worsening of the criminal environment. If the costs of dealing with this are large today, they will certainly be even larger in the future. The country is already paying a high price, with a variety of individuals in public office either charged with corruption or under investigation in relation to such schemes, thereby undermining confidence in the rule of law and democracy.'

At this stage, Lula's lawyers appealed to the Supreme Court, on the basis that Operation Car Wash and the São Paulo state prosecutors were both investigating the same thing, and asked that the investigations be suspended on account of this duplication. On Saturday 27 February, at a rally held to mark the thirty-sixth anniversary of the foundation of the Workers' Party, Lula made an impassioned speech fiercely defending himself against the allegations being levelled against him. Controversially, President Rousseff had decided not to attend the rally and the crowd was not as big as expected. But Lula was in his element, surrounded by his faithful Workers' Party comrades-in-arms, for whom he would always be their undisputed leader. He let rip, holding back neither in his fierce criticisms of the media, nor in his choice of words. He said he was 'pissed off' and that the days of 'Little Lula peace and love' (a popular slogan from his 2002 election campaign) were over. The party couldn't just 'turn the other cheek every time they talk shit about us'. He went on to say that he had heard the courts were going to make public his confidential tax and banking records, and he spoke about the two properties under investigation: the apartment in Guarujá and the house in Atibaia.

He told his audience that the house was a present from his friend Jacó Bittar and other old comrades, and attacked the behaviour of the public prosecutors and police. '[Jacó Bittar] got it into his head to buy a place in the country that I could use once I stepped down from the presidency. They kept it a secret until my last day in office. The house isn't mine,' said Lula. He repeated that the apartment also wasn't his and accused the public prosecutors of playing to the media: 'People who abase themselves like this don't deserve the positions they hold in this country, chosen by public examination to provide justice and to investigate.' Lula's speech was the high point of the rally.

That same weekend, research by the polling company Datafolha indicated that 62 per cent of those interviewed believed that Lula had benefited from the improvements to the two properties carried out by OAS and Odebrecht. By that time, Odebrecht had already admitted its involvement in the building works at the house in Atibaia. The Odebrecht engineer, Frederico Barbosa – more accustomed to working on large projects like the Corinthians football stadium in São Paulo – had also confirmed his involvement in the refurbishment. In an application to the Supreme Court, Lula's own defence had spoken about the building works, saying that they were a gift from Lula's friend José Carlos Bumlai. Bumlai's defence team, however, played down his involvement, claiming that he had paid only 10 per cent of the total amount. Some people saw this detail as an indication of a coolness between the two friends. There was more to come.

On 29 February, the Lula Institute announced that the former president and his wife Marisa would not be appearing at the deposition hearing with the São Paulo prosecutors scheduled for 3 March. Instead, the couple's lawyers provided written explanations to the state prosecutors and filed an application for habeas corpus at the São Paulo state courts, so that their clients could not be forcibly required to attend. However, the habeas corpus related only to São Paulo state proceedings and did not cover federal orders coming from Curitiba. And on that very same day, in response to an application from federal prosecutors in Curitiba, Sergio Moro had signed a warrant compelling Lula to attend an interview with the Federal Police. The application had been made separately by federal prosecutors, unconnected to events in São Paulo. A few days earlier, on 24 February, Moro had authorised a warrant for search and seizure at various addresses linked to the former president, his sons, the Lula Institute, its chairman Paulo Okamotto and various other people.

The warrants would only be executed on Friday 4 March, with the launching of phase twenty-four of Operation Car Wash. On that day, as well as Lula, some of his long-time allies would be required to answer police questions, such as Clara Ant, his former secretary and special assistant during his presidency. Moro's ruling gathered together all the suspicions relating to Lula: 'Federal prosecutors have indicated evidential support for a well-founded suspicion that the former president may have covertly received material financial benefits from building contractors involved in Operation Car Wash, specifically relating to refurbishments and improvements to properties whose usage he enjoyed. There are also suspicions that the former president may be the real owner of two properties registered in the name of third parties.'

Sergio Moro set out a simple proposition: if the house in Atibaia genuinely belonged to Jonas Suassuna and Fernando Bittar, then the generosity of the building contractors and José Carlos Bumlai in spending money on the improvements did not make any sense. It would only make sense if the property did, in fact, belong to Lula. Similarly, Moro viewed OAS's behaviour in relation to the Guarujá apartment as highly unusual. The construction firm had spent R$750,000 renovating the property and a further R$320,000 installing kitchen and bedroom furniture. 'Lula's public statements regarding ownership of the triplex in Guarujá are not logically coherent with the business structures set up by OAS at the Solaris condominium,' stated Moro in his ruling.

The judge concluded by saying that 'deeper investigation may perhaps clarify the relationship between the former president and the building contractors, together with the motives for both the apparent concealment of assets and the improvements paid

for by the building contractors in relation to those two properties, as well as confirming or not the legality of the payments by
them to the Lula Institute and to LILS Palestras'.

The press conference to discuss phase twenty-four began
promptly at 10 a.m. on 4 March. Facing the cameras in the
Federal Police auditorium in Curitiba were prosecutor Carlos Fernando dos Santos Lima, detective Igor Romário de
Paula and his boss, superintendent Rosalvo Ferreira Franco,
as well as a representative from the Federal Revenue, Roberto
Leonel Lima. However, the atmosphere was very different to
previous such occasions: tenser and more subdued. The auditorium was packed with journalists and those who were there
simply out of curiosity. Members of the public, queuing in
the large waiting room next door to get their passports issued
by the police, tried to catch a glimpse of what the detectives
and prosecutors were saying about the investigations into the
former president.

Straight after the routine introductions, Roberto Lima from
the Federal Revenue began by showing some numbers: five
of the largest contractors involved in Operation Car Wash had
made 60 per cent of the donations received by the Lula Institute and were responsible for 47 per cent of payments to LILS
Palestras for lectures given by the former president. He added
that the Federal Revenue had discovered numerous indications
of operational irregularities in the Lula Institute's accounting.
According to Lima, the institute was tax-exempt, but paid the
expenses of LILS Palestras, the firm set up to run Lula's lectur-
ing activities, which was profit-making and had no staff of its
own. The institute also made payments to companies owned
by all of the former president's children, including paying R$1.3
million to G4, owned by Lula's son Fábio Luís.

Outside, the TV companies' broadcasting vans were squeezed into the narrow streets around the Curitiba Federal Police headquarters. As a precaution, only the main gate was open, which was unusual. The Federal Police knew that many Workers' Party supporters, as well as those who had come out in support of the investigations, would be outside. There was soon quite a commotion, with hundreds of people protesting both for and against the former president. The Military Police were called in to calm things down and set up a security cordon separating the two groups. Around ten men from the Paraná Military Police elite squad were stationed inside the Federal Police building, ready to intervene, although this ultimately proved to be unnecessary.

The prosecutor Carlos Fernando Lima began his address with these words:

Good morning everyone. This is simply a further stage in Operation Car Wash, a stage that is necessary in the light of evidence gathered during the investigations. In this case I am talking about a criminal organisation situated within the federal government, which was using Petrobras and other companies both for political financing and for personal enrichment. This criminal organisation clearly possessed a leadership structure. It has been verified, and we have already filed charges in relation to this, that former minister José Dirceu was part of this leadership structure, together with former party treasurer João Vaccari Neto, among others. However, this criminal organisation remained in place even after the arrest of the former minister. We therefore needed to carry out an investigation into the continued existence of this chain of command. We are now analysing evidence that the former president and his family received benefits potentially linked to actions carried out while in government. This is still an investigative hypothesis, in the sense that evidence exists of the payment of benefits and we have no plausible motive for such payments. As Roberto Leonel Lima has stated, we have these five largest donors to the Lula Institute, with 60 per cent of all donations coming from the five largest building contractors involved in Operation Car Wash. In addition, 47 per cent of fees paid for lectures were paid by the five largest building contractors involved in Operation Car Wash. There are these favours granted by the construction firms OAS and Odebrecht, and a piece of land whose ownership we are still trying to ascertain, but which we currently believe belongs, in fact, to Mr Luiz Inácio da Silva. And it is also clear to us that there were payments for improvements to the triplex apartment in Guarujá.

The prosecutor took a deep breath and carried on: 'This is the moment to uphold the values of our republic. No one is exempt from investigation in this country.' Carlos Fernando Lima went on to explain that OAS had shouldered the costs of storing the personal possessions of the former president when they were shipped from Brasília at the end of his term in office and stored in ten containers belonging to the removals firm Granero.

The reporters at the press conference had many questions, directed primarily at the prosecutor. They wanted to know more details, such as whether prosecutors were also seeking the arrest of the former president, whether the former first lady was implicated, and whether Lula would be brought to Curitiba.

Carlos Fernando Lima replied calmly to all of them. Detective Igor Romário de Paula confirmed that the confidentiality of Lula's tax and banking records had been lifted. Brazil virtually ground to a standstill watching these events unfold on TV. According to the investigators, most of the money received by the Lula Institute and LILS Palestras between 2011 and 2014, came from companies that were part of the Petrobras corruption scheme: Camargo Corrêa, OAS, Odebrecht, Andrade Gutierrez, Queiroz Galvão and UTC. These construction firms contributed R$20 million of the R$35 million raised in total by the institute, and they paid more than R$10 million to LILS Palestras. The alleged offences being investigated were those of corruption and money laundering.

While the press conference was going on in Curitiba, Lula was still answering police questions at Congonhas Airport in São Paulo, where crowds were growing ever larger. There were two sets of protesters. On one side, a group was shouting: 'Lula, warrior of the Brazilian people!' The other side shouted back: 'Our flag will never be red!' On one side: 'Down with the coup!' On the other: 'Lula is a thief!' The two groups spent the morning separated by a security cordon. The Federal Police's senior command remained in close contact throughout by phone. In Curitiba, Igor Romário de Paula was explaining that the location for Lula's interview had been chosen in order to avoid protests and ensure everyone's safety, but the reality at Congonhas was very different, with police officers struggling to separate the two factions who looked likely to come to blows, and eventually did so. In addition to the scuffles, at least eight journalists were threatened or attacked. Lula being compelled to answer police questions was given widespread coverage in the national and international press.

Back at the press conference, the investigators tried to antic-
ipate some of the criticisms they would later receive. They said
that the warrant compelling Lula to attend a police interview
was necessary, and that there were indications of evidence being
destroyed. They also claimed that they had not singled out their
target, contrary to what Lula's lawyers were saying, merely that
'events led them to certain individuals'. It didn't help much. The
Workers' Party released a message to a WhatsApp group of supporters and allies with talking points to be followed by those
speaking in support Lula, such as being on permanent mobili-
sation and denouncing the 'coup and media manipulation'.

'THE VIPER IS ALIVE'

On leaving Congonhas, Lula went straight to the Workers' Party
headquarters in downtown São Paulo and unleashed a volley of
criticism. In a video that Communist Party Congresswoman
Jandira Feghali accidentally posted on her Facebook page, it is
easy to see the former president's agitated state of mind, even
though Feghali's aim was to show how calm he was on leaving the police interview. During the recording, Lula is heard
saying in the background, in a telephone conversation with
President Dilma Rousseff, 'They can stick it up their arse and
"take account" of that,' referring to the eleven container-loads
of official gifts he had received in his capacity of president. The
video went viral and the congresswoman reacted by saying that
it was inappropriate to draw 'conclusions or suppositions about
the contents' of the recording. Lula's phrase, however, could be
clearly heard.

On speaking publicly at the Workers' Party headquarters shortly afterwards, the former president did not reply

to reporters' questions. He addressed his supporters, complaining vehemently about having been compelled to attend a police interview. Had he been asked, he said, he would have gone to Curitiba on a flight paid for by the Workers' Party. 'It was completely unnecessary. I felt outraged and affronted, like a prisoner, despite the courteous treatment from the Federal Police detectives,' he said. He went on to criticise Sergio Moro, the federal prosecutors and the media, and said that he was minded to travel round the whole of Brazil, indicating that he would be a candidate in the 2018 presidential elections. 'If they want to kill the viper, well, they should have hit it on the head. They hit it on the tail and it is very much alive,' he concluded, to loud applause from his supporters.

The former president spoke several more times throughout the day. His crowning glory was at a meeting of the trade union for banking employees that night, when he wept, made threats and said he had been 'kidnapped' by the Federal Police. 'Moro had no need to do that thing called … What's it called again? Compulsory attendance, that's it. It was as if I'd been arrested. Today was the last straw for me. It was offensive to me personally, to my party, to democracy and to the rule of law,' Lula railed. 'You can take the prosecutor general, Mr Moro, the Federal Police detective and stick them all together. If together they are even one cent more honest than me, I will withdraw from public life,' he challenged, alternating between playing the victim and the conquering hero.

In a statement, the Lula Institute said that 'the force used against former president Lula and his family, against Paulo Okamotto, chairman of the Lula Institute, and against former congresswoman Clara Ant and other citizens linked to the former president is an attack on the rule of law which strikes at the whole of Brazilian society. The actions of Operation Car Wash's so-called task force are arbitrary, illegal and unjustifiable, as well as constituting a serious affront to the Federal Supreme Court'. After using the words 'completely unjustifiable' around five times to criticise the operation's motives, the institute reaffirmed that 'Lula never concealed assets or received undue benefits before, during or after his time in government. He was never directly or indirectly involved in any illegalities, whether those being investigated in the scope of Operation Car Wash or any others.'

Lula's lawyers filed an application at the Supreme Court to halt Operation Aletheia, but it was later rejected. However, the compulsory questioning of a former president became the subject of intense debate in legal circles. Various legal experts criticised the measure; their main argument was that Lula ought first to have been invited to answer questions, and could only have been compelled to attend in the event of having failed to do so without good cause. President Rousseff made an announcement that Friday, saying that the compulsory attendance was 'unjustifiable'. The following day she went to Lula's apartment in São Bernardo, to show her support for the former president. Marco Aurélio Mello, one of the judges on the Supreme Court, said that it made no sense whatsoever for the former president to be taken to ask questions 'under duress'. But a former judge on the same court, Ayres Britto, saw nothing wrong in the measure.

The federal prosecutors released a statement emphasising that prior to the warrant compelling Lula's attendance at a police interview, 116 similar warrants had been executed as part of Operation Car Wash. The statement also claimed that criticisms of the former president's treatment were a 'smokescreen'. The Association of Federal Judges of Brazil said that there was no political aspect to the operation, merely the proper fulfilment of public duties: 'The facts revealed by the investigation are in line and coherent with all the preceding developments of Operation Car Wash, an operation that has been repeatedly upheld by the Regional Federal Court for the 4th district, the Superior Court of Justice and the Federal Supreme Court itself.'

On Saturday morning, Sergio Moro released a statement saying that he repudiated 'acts of violence of any nature, origin and direction, as well as incitement to violence, insults or threats to anyone, whether those under investigation, political parties, state institutions or any other person. Democracy in a free society calls for tolerance in relation to different opinions, respect for the law and for the institutions of the state, and understanding towards one another.' His also reaffirmed the principle that being compelled to attend a police interview did not signify a 'predetermination of guilt'. His statement deplored the fact that that 'the investigations have led to a number of confrontations in heated political demonstrations with attacks on innocent persons, which is exactly what the authorities had tried to avoid'. But it was too late. Brazil was in uproar, with the internet being the main forum for insults exchanged between the two opposing groups into which the country had divided since the 2014 presidential elections. Whether he wanted it or not, Moro found himself in the eye of the political storm.

Lula presented himself as a possible presidential candidate for 2018, because this would reinvigorate his support base and give him the allure of a man who could once again be hailed as a hero of the people. The main opposition, along with various other organisations opposed to the government, got ready for the demonstration that had already been called for 13 March 2016. Workers' Party supporters kept a vigil outside Lula's apartment building and his supporters attacked anyone who tried to defend Operation Car Wash. The film director José Padilha wrote an article in *O Globo* in which he questioned the reluctance of some sectors of society to face up to the reality revealed by Operation Car Wash and used Freudian theories to diagnose the Brazilian left: 'They have invested their lives and reputations in pro-Lula and pro-Workers' Party positions. Now, they cannot bear to recognise the mistake they made, as a matter of saving face. Freud and his daughter Anna called this phenomenon "denial".' The actor Wagner Moura, who had starred in the film *Elite Squad* and the Netflix series *Narcos*, both directed by Padilha, wrote an article a few days later in the *Folha de S.Paulo*, criticising Operation Car Wash: 'The country is living in a sinister police state motivated by political hatred. Sergio Moro is a judge who behaves like a prosecutor. The investigations display blatant disregard for rights of privacy and the presumption of innocence.'

One solitary voice in the Workers' Party did not deny what had happened. This was Olívio Dutra, former governor of the southern state of Rio Grande do Sul and minister of cities during Lula's first term of office. In an interview with the newspaper *O Estado de S. Paulo*, he criticised the party and stated that 'the people who changed were not our adversaries. It was we who changed – and, in my view, we changed for the worse.'

Like some sort of allegory of the temperature that the Petrobras scandal had reached, Petrobras's Pasadena oil refinery in Texas caught fire the day following Lula's police interview. The blaze destroyed part of the installations. Meanwhile, in Curitiba, police officers and prosecutors pored over all the information that had been gathered during the latest phase of Operation Car Wash. They now carried the hefty responsibility of presenting Sergio Moro with a solid dossier of evidence and a set of formal charges in relation to the crimes allegedly committed.

The searches at addresses linked to Lula had borne some fruit. Nothing was seized at the house in Atibaia, but the investigators identified personal objects of the former president and his wife, including clothing, towels and medication marked with their names. The investigators were therefore able to confirm that the couple had indeed been using the house, and they did not find anything belonging to the official owners, Fernando Bittar and Jonas Leite Suassuna Filho. At Lula's apartment in São Bernardo do Campo, the police discovered that the apartment next door was connected to the former president's and had been used by him and his family. The Granero storage facilities in São Bernardo do Campo were sealed by the Federal Police over the weekend. On Monday, police officers and tax inspectors began to open the crates of Lula's belongings that had been brought from Brasília at the end of his presidency, among which were gifts, some made of gold, received during his period of office.

Far away in Brasília, the political crisis was escalating. The Supreme Court had accepted one of the federal prosecutors' charges against Congressman Eduardo Cunha, and the Chamber of Deputies found itself in the strange situation of being presided over by a defendant in criminal proceedings. Cunha announced that he would not resign, which created an unprecedented institutional impasse. Meanwhile, Lula's lawyers were once again applying to the Supreme Court to suspend the Operation Car Wash investigations against the former president, on the grounds that the task force was using 'arbitrary and invasive measures'. Lula said he was a victim of political persecution. He was reported by the *Estado de S. Paulo* to have said to several people, 'From now on, if they arrest me I'll be a hero. If they kill me I'll be a hero. And, if they give me liberty, I'll be president again.'

The risk of Lula being arrested was very real. On 9 March, the São Paulo state prosecutors charged the former president with money laundering in the case relating to the Guarujá apartment, and applied for him to be taken into custody and held on remand. The case would be dealt with by judge Maria Priscilla Ernandes Veiga of the São Paulo 4th criminal circuit. One of Lula's lawyers, Cristiano Zanin Martins, released a statement saying that the São Paulo prosecutors were seeking to silence a political leader, to prevent him from expressing his opinions and exercising his rights. The application for Lula's arrest and detention caused uproar in Congress. By then, everyone was very worried about the demonstration scheduled for Sunday.

THE BIGGEST DEMONSTRATION IN BRAZIL'S HISTORY

Stormy conditions, in all senses, preceded the events of Sunday 13 March 2016. Brasília had several days of torrential rain that week. In São Paulo, a big storm broke out on the Friday. On Saturday night, many neighbourhoods in the southern part of Rio de Janeiro were completely flooded, seriously restricting movement around the city. Sunday, however, began with a more stable outlook.

One of the earliest protests was in Brasília, scheduled for 10 a.m. Starting early that morning, a large crowd dressed in the national colours of green and yellow began to arrive at the Esplanada dos Ministérios. By 11 a.m. there was already a sea of people filling the wide spaces between the federal government buildings. There were 100,000 people, the largest demonstration the federal capital had ever seen. On the

Copacabana seafront in Rio de Janeiro, there were one million people, according to the organisers. On Avenida Paulista in São Paulo, 1.4 million. The government had feared that the protest might be as big as the one that took place in March 2015, but it was much bigger. According to TV Globo's G1 website, there were demonstrations in a total of 326 cities involving, according to the organisers, 6.8 million people. The Military Police estimated 3.6 million, but this did not include the demonstration in Rio de Janeiro. Whatever the exact number, by the end of the day it was clear that it had been Brazil's largest ever political demonstration. It was a historic day.

The crowds in the streets shouted slogans condemning corruption, President Rousseff, former president Lula and the Workers' Party. But it wasn't a demonstration in favour of any other political party – Senator Aécio Neves and Geraldo Alckmin, the governor of São Paulo, both from the PSDB, were jeered when they appeared at the demonstration in Avenida Paulista. The heroes of the day were Sergio Moro, the public prosecutors and the Federal Police. Masks of the judge, enormous placards of his face and banners carrying slogans like WE ARE MORO left no doubt of that. In Rio de Janeiro choruses of 'Mooroo!' were sung with the same fervour as football chants. Moro watched it all on TV from Curitiba and released a statement at the end of the day saying that he had been 'touched by the support for the Operation Car Wash investigations'. Despite the references to his name, he praised the goodwill of the Brazilian people for the success of 'the hard work of the Federal Police, the federal prosecutors and all levels of the judiciary, as institutions'. He asked politicians to 'listen to the voices from the streets' and concluded, 'There is no future for the systematic corruption that is destroying our democracy, our economic well-being and the dignity of our country.'

The following day, 14 March, another weighty responsibility fell on Sergio Moro's shoulders. The São Paulo judge Maria Priscilla Ernandes Veiga decided to send the charges against Lula to Moro to investigate whether the alleged offences were a federal matter that would sit within the scope of the investigation already under way at the Curitiba federal courts. It would fall to him to rule on the application for the former president to be held on remand. A few days earlier, Moro had taken a decision that would have enormous impact on Brazil: he had authorised the Federal Police to wiretap the former president, Luiz Inácio Lula da Silva.

LULA'S PHONE TAPPED

Breathtaking: this was the word used by several journalists to explain the sequence of events on 16 March, the eve of the second anniversary of Operation Car Wash. It was a Thursday, and Lula was in Brasília to work out the details of his return to government. This alone was a reason for uproar. Reports had circulated since the preceding week that the former president's allies had been applying pressure for him to be given a ministerial rank in Dilma Rousseff's government, since this would grant him 'privileged forum', the right to be tried only by the Supreme Court, thereby avoiding being judged by Sergio Moro at first instance. Lula had initially appeared resistant to the idea, fearing that it might give the impression of an admission of guilt. The first announcement that he had accepted the invitation was posted on social media by José Guimarães, the government leader in the Chamber of Deputies. His post also said that his appointment would take place the following Tuesday, 22 March. The news and the date were quickly confirmed by Rui Falcão, chairman of the Workers' Party, who hailed Lula as 'minister of hope'.

The nomination of the former president as Rousseff's new chief of staff – a post that carries ministerial rank – provoked indignation among those who had taken to the streets three days earlier to demand the end of corruption; it was taken as a cynical manoeuvre to remove him from the jurisdiction of Sergio Moro, who could at any moment take a decision regarding the prosecutors' application for him to be held on remand. On the internet, a comment made by Lula in 1988 went viral: 'In Brazil, when a poor man steals, he goes to jail. When a rich man steals, he becomes a minister.' The government denied that removing him from Moro's jurisdiction was the intention. President Rousseff gave an interview that afternoon stating that the former president had been chosen to strengthen the government, and not for reasons of obtaining legal privilege. Pointing out that appointment as a minister merely changed the location of any investigation to a higher court, Rousseff queried, 'Am I really going to consider that Sergio Moro's investigation is better than the Supreme Court's?'

The announcement that Lula was joining the government seemed to be the biggest headline that day, and journalists set to work reporting it. In the late afternoon, some protesters made their way to the Palácio do Planalto to demonstrate against his nomination. Then another bombshell fell. Sergio Moro had released recordings of conversations recorded by the wiretap he had authorised on the telephones of Lula, his wife Marisa Letícia, his son Fábio Luís, the Lula Institute and LILS Palestras. Globo News was the first to broadcast the news.

Soon, the transcripts and audio recordings became available to journalists on the 'e-proc' online platform, used by the Curitiba courts to disclose all public documents relating to the trial. In a conversation that had taken place that same day, President Dilma Rousseff was recorded talking to former president Lula. She too had been recorded. The phone call took place at 1.32 p.m.:

'Hello,' said Rousseff.

'Hello,' replied Lula.

'Lula, I just want to tell you something.'

'Go on, love, tell me.'

'Look, I'm sending over "Bessias" with the letter, just so you have it. Now, only use it if you really have to – it's the appointment letter, OK?' says Rousseff.

'Uhuh. OK, OK,' replies Lula.

'That's all – just you wait there, because he's on his way.'

'OK, I'm here, I'll hold on.'

'OK?'

'OK.'

'Bye.'

'Bye-bye, dear,' ended the former president.

The release of this conversation was enough to bring huge crowds onto the streets. One of the many questions it raised was whether the president was obstructing justice. Why had she sent her deputy head of legal affairs, Jorge Messias (referred to as 'Bessias' in the transcript), to take the appointment letter over to Lula at the airport? On the streets of Brasília, the protest quickly grew. After hearing the conversation on radio, TV or the internet, people left work and headed towards the Palácio do Planalto. As night began to fall, there were more than 5,000 people chanting in front of the seat of government for the president to resign. In Congress, the opposition repeated the same calls. Beyond the federal capital, protests spread through nineteen states. In São Paulo, Avenida Paulista, the stage for the largest demonstrations against corruption and in favour of impeachment, was once again thronged with demonstrators.

But that was not the only shocking conversation. There were others. Many others. With the release of the recordings, newspapers worked frenetically to update their morning editions; astonished presenters delivered the evening news on TV. In another conversation with President Rousseff, just after being taken in for questioning on 4 March, Lula had not minced his words in talking about Brazilian institutions:

> We have a Supreme Court that's completely cowed, a Superior Court of Justice that's completely cowed, a Congress that's completely cowed; only recently has the Workers' Party and Communist Party woken up and started to fight back. We have a speaker of the Chamber who's totally fucked, a speaker of the Senate who's totally fucked, I don't know how many members of Congress under threat, and everyone just waiting around for a miracle to happen and save everyone. Quite frankly I'm shocked at this 'Republic of Curitiba'. Just because of one judge in the lower courts, anything could happen in this country.

Shortly afterwards, when Rousseff passed the phone to her chief of staff, Jaques Wagner, Lula suggested that Wagner should ask the president if he, Wagner, could speak to Supreme Court Justice Rosa Weber, who was analysing the application made by Lula's defence to paralyse the investigations:

'Oh, Wagner, I want you to have a look at it, talk to *her*, while she's there, talk to her about that Rosa Weber business ...'

'OK.'

'The decision's in her hands ...'

'Sure!'

'If a man doesn't have the balls, well, then maybe a brave woman can do what the men can't.'

'OK, sure thing! Understood. Cheers, mate. Give Marisa and the kids a hug,' replied the chief of staff.

Talking to lawyer Sigmaringa Seixas, Lula complained about the ingratitude of the prosecutor general, Rodrigo Janot, who was not behaving as he had hoped.

'He refuses four requests to investigate Aécio, and then accepts the very first request from some gangster up in Acre to investigate me.'

'Yes, but if you file an application ...' commented Seixas.

'Well that's some gratitude from him for being made prosecutor general,' finished Lula.

Rodrigo Janot, who was in Europe meeting with Swiss public prosecutors, was indignant on hearing the former president's comment: 'All I can say is that I took up my position through an open selection process. I have been in this profession for thirty-two years. I have had a long career and am now reaching the end of it, and if I owe my position and my career to anyone, it is to my family.' Janot added: 'Public prosecutors need to have a thick skin. They have an impact on people's liberty and wealth, and it is normal that people react badly. The public prosecution service must always act calmly and professionally, but fearlessly.'

A phone call between Lula and the mayor of Rio de Janeiro, Eduardo Paes, was also given widespread coverage by the media because of some unfortunate comments by Paes, who poked fun at President Rousseff and the governor of Rio de Janeiro state, Luiz Fernando Pezão, and made ill-judged jokes about Lula's 'common touch': 'I'm with you there, my friend. You have my support; we'll get through this business. Now, next time, cut out all this man-of-the-people crap, this common touch of yours buying those "miserable little boats" and "crappy little plot of land". For Christ's sake!'

Lula laughed and the mayor carried on: 'Well, man, you've still got the common touch. To all those who go on and on about it, I tell them this: "Imagine if this plot of his was here in Rio. Well, it's not in Petrópolis and it's certainly not in Itaipava. It's the same as if it was in Maricá! It's a fucking shithole!"'

The day after the release of their conversation, the mayor of Rio de Janeiro apologised for his words, especially to the inhabitants of Maricá. 'I realised that, because of all the difficulties, I should give him a friendly call. This led me to make jokes in extremely bad taste, but they were only jokes, comments that are not part of my character. They make me feel ashamed and regretful, and they don't reflect what I think,' he claimed. But the damage was already done.

In various recordings, Lula clearly showed an intention to interfere in matters of state. On 7 March, when the finance minister Nelson Barbosa called to show his solidarity, Lula asked him to rein in the tax inspectors who were investigating the Lula Institute.

'Oh, Nelson, just wanted to tell you something by phone, this line here. The thing is the Federal Police might be recording the other one. We need to look into what the Revenue is doing along with the Federal Police, my friend!' said Lula.

'No, it's …' stammered Nelson Barbosa. 'They're part of it.'

'Yes, but you need to look into what they're doing at the institute. If they did this sort of thing with half a dozen big companies, it would wipe out the whole government deficit.'

'Uhuh. I know,' said the minister.

'Know what I mean? They're taking the piss,' complained Lula.

'OK,' replied Barbosa.

'It's just bloody nitpicking. I think ... I'm going to ask Paulo Okamotto to try and put everything down on paper, because you might need to call whoever's in charge and ask them, "What the hell's going on? Are you doing the same thing to Globo, the same thing to the Fernando Henrique Cardoso Institute, the same thing to Gerdau, to SBT, or even to Record?! Or only to Lula, for fuck's sake?" They can go fuck themselves.'

'OK, get Paulo to put it in writing,' said the minister.

'I'll get Paulo to write it down and send it to you. Because, you see, there's no problem in them investigating, no ...'

'It has to be the same for everyone,' interrupted Barbosa.

When all of these recordings emerged, the government was caught completely off-guard. An emergency meeting was held at the president's official residence to try to decide how to react. A statement was then issued saying that there had been a 'flagrant violation of the law and the constitution committed by the judge responsible for the leak'. What the government referred to as a 'leak' was the judge's decision to lift the judicial confidentiality of audio recordings and transcripts of conversations between Lula and persons who were entitled to 'privileged forum' – the right to be tried by the Supreme Court rather than in the ordinary courts.

In his ruling, Sergio Moro said he was acting in Lula's case exactly as he had done in all the others, lifting confidentiality and making the court documents public in order to enable 'not only the exercise by those under investigation of their rights of defence, but also the healthy public scrutiny of the actions of public bodies and of the criminal justice system itself'. And he concluded: 'Democracy in a free society requires that those being governed know what those in authority are doing, even when the latter seem to act in the shadows.'

However, a fierce battle of legal interpretation ensued over whether Moro could legally disclose the recording of a conversation with the president of the republic. In order to refute the argument that Rousseff had sent the appointment letter to Lula so that he could avoid being arrested by Sergio Moro before becoming entitled to 'privileged forum', late that night the president's office released the appointment letter signed by Lula but not by Rousseff, explaining that without Rousseff's signature the document had no legal effect to exempt Lula from arrest. The government's justification for taking the unusual step of sending the appointment letter to be signed at the airport was that the swearing-in was due to take place the following day, and that Lula might not be able to attend because his wife was unwell. It was all simply a procedural matter. However, the law relating to holding public office says that an appointment must be made with the person physically present. Or, at the very least, they must send someone in their place with a power of attorney to sign on their behalf. There were other irregularities. Why had the swearing-in, initially scheduled for 22 March, been brought forward to 17 March, particularly if there were doubts as to whether Lula could attend that day? Why the rush in publishing, on the night of 16 March, a special edition of the government's official gazette containing the required legal announcement of the forthcoming appointment?

THE SWEARING-IN

On 17 March 2016, former president Luiz Inácio Lula da Silva was sworn in as Dilma Rousseff's new presidential chief of staff in a ceremony at the Palácio do Planalto that was more reminiscent of a political rally. The audience was made up of ministers, senators and congressmen and women from the government benches, as well as representatives from social organisations and trade unions, who started up a chorus of 'Down with the coup!' and chanted 'Olê, olê, olê, olá, Lula!' Vice President Michel Temer, Renan Calheiros, speaker of the Senate, and Eduardo Cunha, speaker of the Chamber, did not attend the event. Outside in the streets, the atmosphere was tense, with protests both for and against the government.

During the swearing-in ceremony, President Rousseff made a long speech justifying her decision to appoint her predecessor to her government, and denying that his appointment had the objective of granting him privileged forum. The president also showed the appointment letter signed only by Lula, which she said was proof that there had been no attempt to obstruct justice, since without her signature the document had no legal effect. Without mentioning the names of either Sergio Moro or Operation Car Wash, she harshly criticised both. 'There is no justice when evidence from informants is made public, in a selective manner, in order to denigrate some of those under investigation, and when police interviews are turned into public spectacles. There is no justice when laws are disrespected and, I repeat, the constitution debased. There is no justice for citizens when the constitutional rights of the presidency itself are violated.'

One important detail strengthened the government's argument. Moro had given an order to suspend Lula's telephone surveillance shortly after 11 a.m. The public prosecutors duly informed the Federal Police, who passed the order to the telecom operator, Claro. The conversation regarding Lula's ministerial appointment took place at 1.32 p.m. The order suspending surveillance had already been given, but the wiretap was still in place, with the result that a further conversation was recorded – the conversation with the president.

As well as the specific matter of whether a recording intercepted after the suspension of a surveillance operation could be included as evidence, the larger issue was whether a judge could disclose the president of the republic's private conversation, as they have the right of 'privileged forum'. Or had Moro usurped the jurisdiction of the Supreme Court and infringed an important principle of national sovereignty, as Rousseff claimed in her application to the Supreme Court? Moro's reply was that the phone being tapped was Lula's, not the president's, and that it was Rousseff who had called Lula's number. The controversy did not go away and the matter would only eventually be resolved by the Supreme Court.

In the end, Lula was not able to take up the post of chief of staff. Shortly after being sworn in at the Palácio do Planalto, his appointment was suspended by the courts and he took himself to a hotel to carry on working, trying to build up his support base. That afternoon, the Chamber of Deputies selected a special committee for impeachment, and the following day (a Friday, on which Congress never normally sits), Eduardo Cunha, the speaker of the Chamber, it held its first meeting in order to accelerate the process. After ten meetings, President Rousseff would be called to present her defence.

The day of that first impeachment committee meeting, 18 March, government supporters took to the streets to defend

President Rousseff, former president Lula and the Workers' Party. In total, the demonstrations included 1.3 million people according to the organisers, although the Military Police estimated the numbers at 275,000. Lula made a speech at the demonstration on São Paulo's Avenida Paulista, trying to repair the damage done by the recordings, with their swearing and attacks on Brazilian institutions. To those protesting against impeachment, Sergio Moro was the villain rather than hero, and was even compared to Hitler. Another target of the protesters' anger was Eduardo Cunha, speaker of the Chamber and arch-rival of Rousseff and Lula.

That day, Moro was also the subject of harsh criticism from the Supreme Court's lead judge on Operation Car Wash. At a ceremony where he was receiving the freedom of the city of Ribeirão Preto, Justice Teori Zavascki used the opportunity, without citing names, to give a robust speech about how judges should behave: 'At a time like this, a time of difficulties for the country, a time when emotions are running high – it is precisely at times like this, more than ever, that the judicial authorities must exercise their role with prudence, calmness and rationality, and without any sense of ego, because that is what society expects from a judge. The role of a judge is to resolve conflicts, not to create them.'

That night, another Supreme Court judge took a decision that would end the government's plans to make Lula chief of staff. Justice Gilmar Mendes suspended Lula's appointment and ruled that there had been an intention on the part of the former president to obtain privileged forum, sending the investigations regarding Lula back to Sergio Moro. The following week, however, there was yet another volte-face. In one of his harshest decisions, Justice Teori Zavascki ruled that

Moro should send all the investigations involving the former president back to the Supreme Court, and re-imposed judicial confidentiality on the conversations of the former president, sternly criticising the arguments used by Moro to justify his decision. 'It is improper to invoke public interest, or the public status of those participating in such conversations, as justification for releasing such conversations, as if such persons, or their interlocutors, were entirely without rights to the protection of their personal privacy.'

In reply to Teori Zavascki, Moro sent a thirty-one-page letter, in which he apologised to the Supreme Court and tried to explain his motives: 'The lifting of judicial confidentiality did not have the objective of generating political disputes or controversies, which are matters beyond the scope of the judicial authorities; but, in response to a request from federal prosecutors, to inform the public of the proceedings and, in particular, of aspects of former president Luiz Inácio Lula da Silva's conduct that are relevant from a criminal and juridical point of view and which could amount to obstruction of justice or attempts to obstruct justice.' Moro went on to conclude: 'Even though I might have erred in my legal understanding and admit, in light of the ensuing controversy, that this may have occurred, it was never my intention in reaching the aforementioned decision 16/03, to provoke controversy, conflict or embarrassment, and for these I once again reiterate my respectful apologies to this most distinguished Federal Supreme Court.' Lawyers acting for Lula's wife Marisa Letícia, his son Fabío Luís and daughter-in-law Renata, who had also had their conversations intercepted, started legal proceedings against the state for damages arising from the release of their private telephone conversations.

All in all, it was a breathtaking week, with news stories developing so quickly that they were difficult to take in at times. It began with the whirlwind caused by the approval of Senator Delcídio do Amaral's plea bargain and the decision of Justice Teori Zavascki to remove the judicial confidentiality of Amaral's statements in which he made accusations against Rousseff, Lula, Temer and the leader of the PSDB, Aécio Neves. The most damaging and unexpected revelation was the recording of a conversation between the minister of education, Aloizio Mercadante, and Senator Amaral's aide, in which the minister offered to help Amaral and suggested that he should not cooperate with the judicial authorities – a suggestion which investigators viewed as an attempt to obstruct justice. President Rousseff released a statement denying any responsibility for the personal actions of an individual minister, even one who had previously been close to her. This all happened on Tuesday 15 March. By Wednesday, the matter had been forgotten, since the spotlight had turned back to Lula and a much bigger crisis. Then came Lula's appointment as chief of staff, the suspension of that appointment, the election of the impeachment committee, and the demonstrations for and against the government.

On Sunday 20 March, the *Folha de S.Paulo* published the results of an opinion poll with devastating implications for the government: 68 per cent of those interviewed said they were in favour of President Rousseff's impeachment, 8 per cent more than a month earlier. Support for her removal from office had grown across all sectors of the population. Fifty-seven per cent said they would not vote for Lula in a presidential election under any circumstances, the worst ratings of any potential candidate. However, when asked the question of who the best ever president of Brazil was, he came out with the highest score of 35 per cent.

Regarding his rejoining the government, 68 per cent said he had done it to escape the clutches of Sergio Moro. When asked whether Moro had done the right thing in compelling the former president to attend a police interview, 82 percent said yes and only 13 per cent said that Moro had acted wrongly, with 5 per cent saying that they didn't know.

LULA CHARGED, ROUSSEFF UNDER INVESTIGATION

Operation Car Wash carried on making steady progress. Late on the afternoon of Tuesday, 3 May 2016, the prosecutor general Rodrigo Janot filed an application to add twenty-nine further individuals to the existing Operation Car Wash case before the Supreme Court. Among them were former president Lula da Silva, government ministers Jaques Wagner, Ricardo Berzoini and Edinho Silva, President Rousseff's senior aide Giles Azevedo and the former chairman of Petrobras, José Sérgio Gabrielli. It was a very significant document. Janot stated, 'The conversations intercepted under judicial authority leave no doubt that, although no longer formally in government, former president Lula maintains control over most significant decisions, including those relating to underhand dealings intended to influence the progress of Operation Car Wash, his own appointment to the senior echelons of government and the Workers' Party's relations with the PMDB, bypassing the normal dealings between members of those parties in furtherance of the criminal organisation now under investigation.'

Further on, in a strongly worded section, the prosecutor general stated that 'in view of the evidence collected here and described herein, this criminal organisation could not have functioned within the federal government for so many years and in so extensive and aggressive a manner without the participation of former president Lula'. Or, to put it another way, in Janot's eyes, the evidence gathered and the testimonies of cooperating witnesses – among them Delcídio do Amaral, Nestor Cerveró and executives from Andrade Gutierrez – indicated the existence of a criminal organisation within the Workers' Party that had a much wider reach than initially imagined and 'an enormous concentration of power in the hands of the organisation's leaders'. According to the prosecutor general, 'within the inner nucleus of the Workers' Party, the organisation was, according to the evidence, specifically focused on the raising of illegal funds through official donations to the National Executive, which, later on, made transfers in the interests of the criminal organisation. This exercise of power is evident in various statements made by cooperating witnesses'.

The document contained other sensational material. A single sentence in the text revealed that Lula had been accused before the Supreme Court of attempting to hinder Nestor Cerveró's plea bargain. Delcídio do Amaral and his chief of staff Diogo Ferreira stated that Lula was the person with the most interest in silencing Cerveró, and that the family of Lula's friend José Carlos Bumlai had been given the task of paying for Cerveró's silence. The prosecutor general indicated that Lula, Bumlai and Bumlai's son Maurício paid R$250,000 to Cerveró's family in five instalments. The first instalment of R$50,000 was paid by Delcídio do Amaral in May 2015. The lifting of Maurício Bumlai's banking confidentiality revealed that two withdrawals of R$25,000 had been made at a branch of Banco Bradesco in São Paulo. The other instalments were delivered by Diogo Ferreira between June and September 2015. Janot said that Lula had met with Delcídio do Amaral in the period preceding the payments, and that their meetings and conversations in April and May 2015 were confirmed by emails and telephone records obtained by court order. 'From then on the investigations took on a new dimension, and it became apparent that Luiz Inácio Lula da Silva, José Carlos Bumlai and Maurício Bumlai had been actively attempting to buy Nestor Cerveró's silence in order to protect other interests, as well as interests linked to Delcídio do Amaral and André Esteves, which has therefore given rise to the additional charges set out herein,' wrote Janot.

So there it was: Lula had been formally charged at the Supreme Court. And, unbelievable as it may seem, the prosecutor general's office was about to present yet another surprise that same day. One week before the Senate was due to vote on President Rousseff's impeachment, Janot requested the opening of a judicial inquiry into President Rousseff, former president Lula, the former minister of justice José Eduardo Cardozo and the former minister of education, Aloizio Mercadante, for obstruction of justice in relation to Operation Car Wash. Among the evidence presented was Lula's recorded conversation with Rousseff, in which she talked about the appointment letter she was sending Lula to use if the need arose. In Janot's view, the group had also tried to hinder the investigation at the time of Marcelo Navarro Ribeiro Dantas's nomination to the Superior Court of Justice. The government was alleged to have approached Dantas, who would later handle some of the Operation Car Wash cases, to ask for his assistance in releasing the arrested businessmen. In his plea bargain, Delcídio do Amaral said that Cardozo, while minister of justice, had made several attempts to try to bring about the release of Operation Car Wash detainees.

Rousseff, Lula, Dantas and Cardozo denied all the allegations. The former minister of justice called Amaral's accusations 'dishonest and baseless'. The Lula Institute released a statement saying that the only offence evident in the whole episode was the 'clandestine recording and illegal disclosure of a telephone call made by the president of the republic'. It also lambasted Sergio Moro: 'Graver still, this offence was committed by a federal judge, in an affront not only to the law but to a decision of the Federal Supreme Court.' According to the Lula Institute, the former president's telephone conversations intercepted by Operation Car Wash were 'conclusive proof that there was neither illegality nor obstruction of justice in his governmental appointment by President Dilma Rousseff'. The investigations would follow their course. The prosecutor general's application would be studied by the Supreme Court. The intercepted conversations were held to be valid evidence in the trial. Operation Car Wash was coming ever closer to Lula.

THE FUTURE IS OPEN

On Sunday 17 April 2016, Brazil stopped in its tracks to watch the lengthy session in which the Chamber of Deputies authorised the opening of impeachment proceedings against President Dilma Rousseff. Whole families gathered together to watch the decision, and the atmosphere felt almost like a football cup final. After a series of speeches that seemed almost surreal at times, the final tally of 367 votes in favour and 137 against showed that the government's support had evaporated. The crisis continued to worsen. The Senate set up its own committee and began analysing the charges. Events were happening so quickly that Brazil did not know where to look next.

In the first week of May, while the impeachment process was advancing quickly through the Senate, Operation Car Wash was also closing in on President Rousseff, as there were suspicions that she had tried to interfere in the operation. Congressmen Eduardo Cunha, who had played a key role in the opening of impeachment proceedings, was suspended from office by Justice Teori Zavascki for hindering the investigation into his own activities, among other reasons. The Supreme Court judges met as a full court to confirm Zavascki's decision unanimously. In the four months that had elapsed between the prosecutor general's application and the Supreme Court's decision, the reasons for Cunha's removal from office had grown stronger. He faced an investigation by the Senate's ethics committee, which proceeded slowly, thanks to various manoeuvres by his allies, and he was also facing criminal charges based on allegations that he had benefited from the Petrobras corruption scheme. Now he was both removed from office as speaker and suspended from the Chamber itself. Meanwhile, Renan Calheiros, the speaker of the Senate, was facing more than ten investigations and, as with many other politicians, was facing charges from federal prosecutors. By May 2016, the prosecutor general had filed ten sets of charges with the Supreme Court against politicians linked to Operation Car Wash. More were on the way and many months of investigations lay ahead. Brasília had never seen a political crisis of such proportions.

On the morning of Monday 9 May, Brazil found itself once again in a state of shock. Senator Antonio Anastasia was getting ready to present his report to the full Senate in favour of impeachment, when the interim speaker of the Chamber, Waldir Maranhão, took a highly controversial decision: with a stroke of his pen, he annulled the hearings in the Chamber that had triggered impeachment, and asked the Senate to return the proceedings to the Chamber. This resulted in hours of turmoil in Brasília and on the financial markets, until Renan Calheiros decided to ignore this attempt by government supporters to gain time, and allowed the impeachment proceedings to go ahead. 'Allowing this kind of messing around with democracy would implicate me personally in delaying the proceedings,' said Calheiros. By the end of the day, Maranhão had backed down and revoked his own decision. The marathon of speeches in the Senate discussing the president's removal from office began two days later. There was a clear majority in favour of impeachment, but those who were against reacted with long and impassioned speeches. In the face of criticisms that the government was obstructing a vote, Senator Jorge Viana from the Workers' Party retorted: 'If they want to speed things up, they should make shorter speeches, because there are fewer of us on the government's side.' On the morning of Thursday 12 May the results were displayed on the Senate's electronic voting screen: fifty-five votes in favour of the president's impeachment, twenty-two against. Many in Brasília awoke to the sound of fireworks. Dilma Rousseff's fate seemed to be sealed.

It was a day of contrasts at the Palácio do Planalto. In the morning, the Workers' Party bid its farewells. In her final speech, President Rousseff said she was a victim of injustice and betrayal. Various mistakes had brought her to a position where she was unable to govern, but the final straw was the earthquake caused by Operation Car Wash. As she left the seat of government, she once again addressed her supporters outside. She was still in a combative mood, but Lula, standing silently beside her, appeared tired and dejected. Rousseff withdrew to the president's official residence. It fell to the Senate to decide which of the trappings of office she would retain while suspended during the impeachment trial, and Calheiros informed the senators that he would grant her 'humane treatment'. She could remain in the official residence and retained the use of military aircraft, along with aides paid for by the federal government. Rousseff indicated that she would contest the charges and continue to fight to return to government.

By the afternoon, the Palácio do Planalto was a completely different place. The PMDB was now in power. At the entrance, while a small group of diehard protesters continued to chant abuse, the Workers' Party's former allies arrived smiling, ready for the collective swearing-in of ministers in the new government of the interim president, Michel Temer. They were all men. The atmosphere was festive. In his speech, Temer defended Operation Car Wash, despite the glaring contradiction that his new government included many who were under investigation or named in the investigations themselves. This would bring problems for him in the first few days of government.

As this political whirlwind swept through the federal capital, Brazil was going through one of the most serious economic crises in its history. The wider context could not have been more difficult. The economy had slumped into recession in the second quarter of 2014, just as Operation Car Wash was beginning, and the situation had worsened throughout the investigations. According to the Getúlio Vargas Foundation, Brazil was going through its longest ever recession. Forecasts predicted eleven quarters of falling output, until the end of 2016. The road ahead would be even more treacherous because inflation had reached double digits for the first time in thirteen years. Unemployment rose during these months, frightening workers and forcing wages down. In the first quarter of 2016, the ranks of the jobless swelled by two million, to over eleven million people. The Brazilian Institute of Geography and Statistics revealed that GDP had fallen by 3.8 per cent in 2015, the country's worst performance in twenty-five years. The economic crisis, which had its own causes, worsened with the decline in investment by Petrobras, both directly and through the contracts with the companies involved in the corruption scheme. In addition, Petrobras was facing various lawsuits in the United States. Three of the principal informants in Operation

Car Wash, Augusto Ribeiro de Mendonça Neto, Júlio Camargo and Pedro Barusco, had signed agreements to provide information to the United States authorities regarding the corruption scheme at Petrobras. The case would be heard by the US federal court in New York, which had agreed to hear claims from foreign investors that the state-owned company had provided false information and misleading public statements, and had failed to disclose a culture of corruption within the company.

During 2014 and 2015, the largest construction firms in Brazil saw their senior executives and chairmen sent to jail. In 2016, battling for their survival, they had tried to re-negotiate their debts. The banks agreed to reschedule the debt because the companies formed such a large portion of their loan portfolio, but the companies had to make profound changes. Marcelo Odebrecht's office at the company headquarters still had his nameplate on the door, but it was already obvious that he would have difficulty returning to take up his old position. The company decided that it needed to completely restructure if it were to return to its former prominence in the national economy. In the corporate world, many companies were discussing how to protect their business activities from corruption: the conclusion they reached was that they needed to give more powers and independence to their control and compliance functions, increasing the transparency of their internal procedures.

There was much to be done in this area. On 22 March 2016, phase twenty-six of Operation Car Wash, code-named 'Leftovers', had discovered that the Odebrecht group had a department responsible for parallel accounting, essentially a specific section dedicated to paying and accounting for kickbacks. Consisting of a small team of trusted, well-paid and long-serving employees, it operated out of São Paulo and

Salvador and was called the Department of Structured Operations. In her plea bargain testimony, a secretary in the department said that the payments had continued even after Marcelo
Odebrecht's arrest in June 2015 and the department only closed
in August of that year. The money remained in the accounts of
various black-market currency traders. The kickbacks were paid
both overseas and within Brazil, with transfers to bank accounts
and deliveries in cash, always with the authorisation of company
executives. At the home of one such executive, Benedicto Barbosa
da Silva Júnior, chairman of Odebrecht's construction subsidiary,
investigators found a number of lists containing the names of 300
politicians from more than twenty political parties. Amounts of
money were recorded beside each name. Many were identified
by code names such as Caranguejo ('Crab' – Eduardo Cunha);
Atleta ('Athlete' – Renan Calheiros); Nervosinho ('Twitchy' –
Eduardo Paes); and Lindinho ('Cutie' – Lindbergh Farias). The
firm's influence throughout Brazilian politics was evident. Sergio
Moro sent the list to the Supreme Court.

On the same day that phase twenty-six began, the Odebrecht
group issued a press announcement declaring that it would
change its stance and begin cooperating fully with the Operation
Car Wash investigations: 'We hope that greater clarity resulting
from our cooperation will significantly contribute to Brazilian
justice and the building of a better country.' Full cooperation,
however, was not unconditional. Negotiations dragged on for
months, with both sides demanding costly concessions that
would be difficult to accept. For example, the investigators
wanted Odebrecht's management to acknowledge having participated in attempts to snuff out Operation Car Wash in its
early days. One of the contentious issues was the bugging device
found in Alberto Youssef's cell. Another was a press report about

political statements made by Operation Car Wash detectives on Facebook. The information in the report had apparently been gathered in a dossier with the participation of Car Wash defence lawyers, including a lawyer from Odebrecht. In April 2016, the Federal Police's disciplinary body initiated proceedings against two lawyers, one detective and two police officers from the Federal Police. Even so, Marcos Josegrei da Silva, the federal judge in Curitiba responsible for this particular part of the investigation, accepted the prosecutors' application, instructing the Federal Police to investigate the matter further. Odebrecht said that its chairman had nothing to do with these matters and that he would not admit to offences he had not committed. The company's executives would also make their own plea bargains, where they had relevant information. An entire team of lawyers was set up to organise this complex collaboration.

Other construction firms that had already signed cooperation agreements and accepted various accusations of corruption adopted a different strategy. In May 2016, Andrade Gutierrez published a statement in Brazil's leading newspapers retracting its previous defence. The company did not repeat the same formula as other companies who had, particularly at the beginning of the investigations, claimed they were innocent and victims of arbitrary behaviour. Andrade Gutierrez announced that it was paying R$1 billion to the government: 'It is the moment for the company to come forward and transparently admit, to the whole of Brazilian society, its mistakes and make good the damage caused to the country and to its own reputation.' It went on to offer 'its sincere apologies to the Brazilian people'. After sixty-seven years of existence and operations in twenty countries, the company recalled its role in the creation of thousands of jobs and displayed its willingness to change, in order to continue its activities in Brazil. The end of the crisis, however, was nowhere near.

Politics had plunged into the abyss. Each day brought something new that increased the tension between the various state institutions and made the political landscape ever hazier and more difficult to predict. The investigation went on with its work, revealing more and more details of the depth and extent of corruption in Brazil. Many of those involved were now in prison or serving sentences at home as the result of their plea bargain agreements. Others were still being investigated, and yet more names were continually surfacing. The new president himself, Michel Temer of the PMDB, had already been named by informants such as Delcídio do Amaral. Amaral also accused the main leader of the opposition, Senator Aécio Neves from the PSDB, of involvement in corruption schemes and of having participated in an operation to tamper with data provided by Banco Rural to the post office congressional inquiry. This led to the opening of an investigation into Senator Neves by the Supreme Court. New informants came forward to clarify aspects that had been murky until then. One of these informants was Pedro Corrêa, who offered to provide information relating to previous governments going back a very long way, since he had been involved in politics since the days of military rule.

Time and time again, Operation Car Wash had to go back in time to pick up yet another loose thread. One instance of this took place on 1 April 2016 with phase twenty-seven, codenamed 'Carbon-14', when Ronan Maria Pinto, owner of the São Paulo newspaper *Diário do Grande ABC*, was arrested. Pinto was from Santo André, an urban municipality on the outskirts of São Paulo, and the media immediately connected his arrest with the assassination of Celso Daniel, the Workers'

Party mayor of Santo André, in 2002. Silvio Pereira, the former secretary general of the Workers' Party was also arrested, and Delúbio Soares, former treasurer of the party, was taken in for questioning. Pereira and Soares had been connected with the Big Monthly scandal. This re-excavation of other scandals was necessary because the investigators had discovered that half the loan of R\$12 million lent by Banco Schahin to the Workers' Party had ended up in Ronan Maria Pinto's bank account. This seemed to connect three cases involving the Workers' Party: the death of Celso Daniel, the Big Monthly scandal and now 'Big Oil', as Operation Car Wash was sometimes called.

In the following phase of Operation Car Wash, phase twenty-eight, Gim Argello, the former Brazilian Labour Party senator for the Federal District who was still a major figure in Brazilian politics, was arrested. This phase was code-named 'Pyrrhic Victory', because it investigated the payment of kickbacks to avoid construction firms being summoned by congressional inquiries into Petrobras. In 2014, Argello was a member of the Senate inquiry and vice chairman of the joint inquiry of both Senate and Chamber. The former senator was arrested at his home in Brasília, taken to the Federal Police's cells in Curitiba and, from there, to the prison hospital unit in Pinhais, where other Operation Car Wash detainees were also being held.

In phase twenty-nine, the main target was João Cláudio Genu, the former treasurer of the Progressive Party, who was arrested in Brasília after being named by three informants as a recipient of kickbacks in Petrobras contracts. It was said he had received R\$2 million in cash. In Alberto Youssef's tables of payments, Genu was variously identified as Mercedão ('Mercedes Truck'), Gordo ('Fatty'), João and Ronaldo. Phase twenty-nine was code-named 'Second Chance', because Genu was another of the names investigated under Operation Car Wash who had also been involved in Big Monthly.

Meanwhile in Curitiba, as Operation Car Wash had become the largest investigation in Brazil's history, the team had grown correspondingly: at the Federal Police, there were almost sixty police officers directly assigned to the operation. In the rooms allocated to the team at the police headquarters, one group was investigating these new leads, while another was analysing the material gathered from searches and seizures throughout the operation. This meant poring over computer hard drives, mobile phone apps and documents obtained from banking and tax authorities, as well as transcripts from telephone surveillance operations. New data was being added almost every day to 'e-proc'. A room was set aside for meetings between detectives, those under investigation and their lawyers. There had never been a structure like this for a Federal Police investigation.

The scene was the same over at the federal prosecutors' offices. By May 2016, more than fifty people were almost continuously analysing data and wading through documents. The task force that had begun with six prosecutors now had thirteen. 'We will go on to the very end, to wherever the investigation takes us,' the prosecutors said resolutely. The fear that dividing Operation Car Wash into separate proceedings might weaken the operation turned out to be unfounded. Some parts of the proceedings were taken away from Curitiba, but this allowed the team to concentrate on the central theme of their investigation: Petrobras. If Operation Car Wash were a tree, an image that Deltan Dallagnol liked to use in some of his lectures, you could say that once it had been pruned, it grew back even stronger.

In the federal courts, trials were processed within a relatively short space of time at a speed dictated by Sergio Moro. Many of those found guilty were serving heavy sentences by now. And the appeal courts confirmed Moro's decisions in 95 per cent of cases. In little over two years of Operation Car Wash, 432 applications for habeas corpus were filed with the higher courts in attempts to overturn Moro's initial verdicts. Of these only seventeen, 3.9 per cent, were successful. In November 2014, at a hearing of the Fifth Panel of the Superior Court of Justice, Judge Newton Trisotto – the lead judge for Operation Car Wash at that court – and the other judges of the Fifth Panel severely criticised the criminal scheme uncovered by the investigation. Newton Trisotto said that corruption was one of the greatest disgraces of humanity and Judge Felix Fischer, former president of the Superior Court of Justice, said that he had never witnessed 'thievery on such a scale' anywhere in the world.

The difference now is that all this thievery is and will continue to be investigated. At the Supreme Court, Justice Teori Zavascki, the lead judge on Operation Car Wash, is in the habit of saying that on this case, all the decisions are difficult and, most of the time, unprecedented. Experienced and meticulous, Zavascki has in front of him one of the greatest challenges ever faced by the Brazilian judiciary. In the calm stillness of his office, he seeks always to do the right thing, weighs the pros and cons carefully and studies the details of every case in order to take the right decision. 'Often the judge does not know what to do. He has to think, stop and reflect, and study – most of all study,' he says to colleagues and friends. For Zavascki, going for a walk is the best way of reaching a decision. By the time he returns to his office, his mind is clear. This is how Zavascki intends to deal with Operation Car Wash. To the very end. On account of some of the rigorous positions he has taken, his home in Porto Alegre has been the target of protests. Security was reinforced and he changed some of his habits. He now walks outdoors less often.[7]

Many people said that it was the beginning of a new era in Brazil, and there have been various signs of this. The once all-powerful former minister and presidential chief of staff, José Dirceu, was now in a cell at the prison hospital unit in Pinhais. Sergio Moro had given him the longest prison sentence handed down under Operation Car Wash: twenty-three years. His lawyers protested that the judge's decision amounted to a life sentence, since Dirceu was seventy years old. The former minister wanted to return to the sentence of house arrest he had been serving in Brasília for his part in the Big Monthly scandal when Operation Car Wash came knocking at his door. Shortly after his verdict, Moro recognised Dirceu's age as a mitigating circumstance and reduced the sentence to twenty years and ten months in a closed-regime prison. Other politicians were also behind bars. The former congressman and former deputy speaker of the Chamber André Vargas had been found guilty and was serving a sentence in a Curitiba prison, as was former congressman Luiz Argôlo.

Paulo Roberto Costa, the first public-sector employee arrested under Operation Car Wash and the first to make a plea bargain, was wearing an electronic tag. He could leave home

---

[7]   Note to English edition: Justice Teori Zavascki died in January 2017 (after the original publication of this book in Brazil), when the light aircraft he was travelling in ditched into the sea near Rio de Janeiro while trying to land during bad weather. All five people on board were killed. Investigators have ruled out both mechanical failure and foul play, but there has been inevitable speculation surrounding the cause of the crash.

during the day, but had to return at night and stay there over the whole weekend. Locked into his routine as a cooperating witness, Costa had already provided more than 180 statements. At the end of 2016, he would regain his freedom. In testimony to the court, one of his daughters, Arianna, said that her father was remorseful: 'I know that my father made a mistake, a big mistake, and that he is paying very dearly for everything he did. Not just him, but the whole family.'

Alberto Youssef, another key player in this story, remained incarcerated in the Federal Police jail in Curitiba, which he left at the end of 2016. He spent the days talking to his new friends in jail, thinking about what he would do to earn his living once he was released. 'Money? I have no attachment to money. Money comes and goes, and the more you get attached to it, the more it slips through your fingers. If I have to start again, I'll start again. I can go back to selling snacks in the street, no problem,' Youssef said confidently. He said that most of the politicians he knew had got involved in corruption in order to win elections. 'Brazil has to change its way of financing election campaigns. Brazil has to change. If it doesn't change this, pal, then there's no way out,' he said philosophically. Youssef did not seem bitter or thirsty for revenge: 'I'm not sore at Moro. I even admire the guy. I don't hold grudges against anyone. I messed up, they took me in and brought me here. It's part of the game. I messed up. Anyone in this game knows it can happen.' Youssef didn't hide his admiration for Operation Car Wash: 'For all that it was me they were after, the guys did a good job. They went in there and dealt with the problem. I have to give them that.'

At the end of a court hearing in May 2016, Youssef made a point of complimenting Sergio Moro for being selected by *Time* magazine as one of the hundred most influential people in the world. The judge had just returned from the award ceremony in New York, which he had attended with his wife Rosângela. On that night, so different from anything he had previously experienced, Moro thought about the path that had brought him there and of the changes that Operation Car Wash had made to his life. His son Vinícius could not hide his pride in his father, while his daughter Julia, shyer than her brother, felt rather awkward talking about him at school. Faced with the sudden fame of her husband, Rosângela tried to overcome her worries with humour, joking that she would write her own book about him.

Whenever anyone asks him how he feels about being famous, Moro shrugs his shoulders, bows his head and says in Latin that all fame is fleeting. He has modest plans for the future. He dreams, when Operation Car Wash comes to an end, of taking a sabbatical year outside Brazil, if he manages to convince the kids. A few years ago he applied for a Fulbright scholarship – he met all the criteria but ended up being rejected in favour of another candidate. In the short term, he wants to go to Italy to find out more about the anti-corruption and anti-Mafia cases that so inspired him.

The study of what happened in Italy after Operation Clean Hands, when setbacks in the fight against corruption may have led to the rise of a controversial leader like Silvio Berlusconi, has given Moro doubts as to whether Operation Car Wash will improve the quality of political life in Brazil. Not every process of purification leads to a virtuous outcome, but the unsuccessful example of the Italians may help Brazil to identify what to avoid. Sergio Moro is convinced, however, that his role as judge is simply to judge. His Facebook profile picture shows him in judicial robes and a long white wig to make clear his role in this story. His WhatsApp profile picture is of one crocodile fighting another, the bigger one devouring the smaller. His friends say that this reminds them of the challenges facing Moro and to which he has dedicated himself, even at the expense of personal sacrifices. Moro has had to give up the small pleasures in life, such as cycling to work or walking the streets alone without worrying. He still runs and plays tennis for exercise, but even going out for dinner with his wife requires security measures. He can't go out in his own car or take a taxi. He travels in a car with bodyguards provided by the judicial authorities. At an event in São Paulo in March 2016, he had a police escort of twelve officers. There is good reason for this: he has displeased many people, and he has received threats.

They are all still trying to escape Sergio Moro. This was evident at the end of May 2016 in another twist of the scandal: Sérgio Machado, former chairman of Transpetro, made recordings of various conversations, in order to negotiate a plea bargain. This new revelation provoked the first crisis in Michel Temer's new government. The minister of planning, Romero Jucá, lost his job when conversations were disclosed in which he appeared to be hatching a plot to bring an end to Operation Car Wash. 'We have to change the government so as to stop all this bleeding,' said Jucá in one call, referring to the effects of the operation. Machado responded threateningly: 'We have to set up a structure to stop me from going down. If I go down …' By 'going down' he meant falling under Moro's jurisdiction. Machado also made recordings of Renan Calheiros and former president José Sarney. They were all trying to find ways of stopping the operation. The government was still in its first twenty days when a second minister fell, and soon after him came another, Fabiano Silveira, the minister of transparency, supervision and control. Machado had recorded a conversation in which Silveira guided Calheiros on what he should hide when talking to the prosecutor general's office. The whole of Brasília was plotting against Operation Car Wash. Politicians from various parties were involved, showing that the operation was aimed not just at the Workers' Party, but at all corruption. The moment was coming when Operation Car Wash would begin to focus on politicians from more traditional parties such as the PMDB. There was a long road ahead.

Operation Car Wash uncovered a framework of systematic corruption in Brazil and brought the criminal justice system to bear on everyone, regardless of wealth or power. An operation of this scale, in which every thread brings unforeseeable revelations, will not be easily forgotten. The first two years were breathtaking and mould-breaking, and forced new patterns of behaviour to be established in both politics and the economy. In the phase named after Catiline, which targeted Eduardo Cunha and other politicians, it was necessary to delve into ancient history and Cicero's speeches to the Roman Senate to understand the current situation in Brazil: 'How long, O Catiline, will you abuse our patience? How much longer is that madness of yours still to mock us? To what extremes will you push your unbridled audacity? ... Do you not realise your plans have been exposed?' The feeling in Brazil was indeed that they were mocking us and abusing our patience. The question 'How long?' continues to echo in the ears of many Brazilians.

The answer can only be found in strengthening Brazil's institutions. In the interviews given for each new phase of the operation, Federal Police officers and prosecutors spoke of the 'republic', its values and principles. Prosecutor Carlos Fernando dos Santos Lima emphasised that in a republic, everyone is equal before the law. In coordinating Operation

Car Wash, the young prosecutor Deltan Dallagnol resolved to lead a movement calling for changes in anti-corruption legislation. In his Master's dissertation, prosecutor Diogo Castor de Mattos warned of the distorted use of habeas corpus to slow down trials and facilitate impunity. 'Brazil is living through a unique historical moment. The biggest corruption scandal in the country's history is bleeding the coffers of our biggest state-owned company, and is, yet again, testing the effectiveness of a criminal justice system of questionable efficiency and chronic leniency towards financial crimes that shame us all. On the other hand, it is in times of crisis and difficulty that the courage arises for change and innovation, giving the whole country a chance to renew confidence in its public institutions,' he wrote in his conclusion.

Perhaps to prove that courage does indeed arise in the most troubled of times, the Supreme Court handed down a historic restatement of the principle of presumption of innocence in March 2016, when it decided that a person found guilty at second instance should remain in detention and begin to serve their sentence while pursuing their right of appeal to the higher courts. There were criticisms from lawyers and jurists, although in making this change Brazil was simply following the same practice as many other countries where the justice system has fewer delays than in Brazil. Along with the Association of Federal Judges, Moro had tried to propose this change to Congress, but the Supreme Court got there first. The decision shocked those being investigated under Operation Car Wash. They could no longer use the old trick of appealing again and again in order to delay going to prison.

Whenever he spoke publicly during this period, Sergio Moro always took the opportunity to defend certain values. This was the case, for example, during the tumultuous beginning of March 2016, when he was under fierce criticism from Lula, the Workers' Party and a large number of prominent lawyers. At the events he attended during that period, he preferred not to speak about the case itself, but rebuffed those who criticised him for having party political motivations: 'I have absolutely no, zero, zero connection with any party or person connected to a party. The judge works with the facts, the evidence and the law. If charges are filed and criminal responsibility is proven – categorically and above all reasonable doubt – the judge can pass a guilty sentence. If it is not proven, he must find the accused not guilty. Issues of political party, interests or other such matters are not the business of my profession.'[8]

As for the criticisms of Operation Car Wash, Moro's response was to remind people that the alternative was to leave things as they had always been in Brazil: 'We have two alternatives. We can, as has often been done, brush these problems under the carpet, forget that they exist and carry on as before. Or we can face up to these problems, seriously and in the way these things ought to be dealt with. Once we do face up to the problem, we are going to find that it is much bigger than we thought.'

The day will never come when all theft is stopped. No police operation will ever bring corruption to an end, but Operation Car Wash has created templates that can help to break the cycle of exchanges of favours, improper use of public resources and payments of kickbacks in the form of overpricing in government contracts. It has created a new consensus in Brazilian

---

[8]   Note to English edition: Following the October 2018 presidential election, Sergio Moro has, controversially, been appointed minister of justice and public security in President Jair Bolsonaro's new government.

society that we must stamp out corruption. Other cases will be uncovered, but what has been achieved is the diagnosis of an evil that was metastasising within the Brazilian state, and this could lead to a rebuilding of the political system. Operation Car Wash was not the work of one man alone, as Sergio Moro so often repeats. But the judge's face, splashed across the front pages of newspapers and magazines, became the symbol of the fight against corruption. There are faces and voices in the Federal Police and the federal prosecutors that history will also record as an important part of this process, but the figure of Moro has always been central. What Brazil will do with the results produced by the police, prosecutors and Sergio Moro is not yet known. Operation Car Wash is an opportunity to improve the quality of our democracy. The changes may or may not happen. The choice is in the hands of Brazilians.

Acknowledgements

I chose not to write this story in the first person. Ironic perhaps, since the name of the imprint that first published it means precisely that: 'First Person'. Marcos da Veiga Pereira, editor and partner at my Brazilian publishers Editora Sextante, asked me over lunch why I had made that choice. I did not want to include myself as a character, despite being deeply involved with the events I have described. It was a personal decision, based perhaps on one of the very first professional lessons I learned: that the journalist is not the news. In these acknowledgements, however, I want to explain a little about how this book was made and thank the people who helped me make it. As with Operation Car Wash, this book is not the work of one man on his own.

It all began with a lunch in Ipanema with Hélio Sussekind, who was at the time partner in Editoria Sextante's Primeira Pessoa imprint. That day, he and Débora Thomé threw down the challenge of my writing this book. It was they who gave me this opportunity and I am very grateful for that; it has changed my life. I started working on this project on 1 January 2015, after returning from covering Dilma Rousseff's swearing-in ceremony for her second term as president. When I got home that night, the first thing I did was call some sources. Without them, none of this would have been possible. I explained that they would need to tell me everything that had happened since the beginning of Operation Car Wash, and continue doing so as things developed. My sources generously accepted, and this made all the difference. It was one of the most important moments in my personal involvement with Operation Car Wash. I asked my sources where I should begin. One of them gave me an important piece of advice: 'Keep on writing as events unfold. This story is just beginning.' So that is what I did.

For seventeen months, from January 2015 to May 2016, I set about gathering information from behind the scenes, picking out the most important conversations and profiling the key characters to tell their side of the story. I lost count of how many interviews I did, how many messages I sent and received, how many people I spoke to and how many coffees, lunches and dinners I had in connection with Operation Car Wash. My talented editor, Virginie Leite, whom I deeply thank for her patience and generosity, asked me to record all these meetings in minute detail. Apologies, Virginie – if I had done that it would have delayed the book. The only thing I managed to collate was that there were more than 132 hours of interviews, not to mention all the time taken reading court transcripts and cross-checking information from the Federal Police, federal prosecutors, judiciary, lawyers and those under investigation. During that whole period, there was not one single day when I did not talk to someone about Operation Car Wash.

Working as a journalist for TV Globo was a great help to me. For many years I have been based in Brasília working on investigative reporting, and as Operation Car Wash became such an important news item, I found that almost all my time was spent covering various aspects of the operation and the political crisis it generated – reporting endeavours that received TV Globo's 2015 prize for major news coverage. At this point I would like to express my gratitude for the great support given to me by my managers, including allowing me to take time off to research and write. Daniel Martins, Maria Fernanda Erdelyi, Marlon Herath, Ricardo Villela, Mariano Boni, Silvia Faria, Ali Kamel, many thanks to you all.

Faced with the scale of the undertaking, I quickly realised that I would also need my own 'task force'. As my friends at Globo well know, I am very keen on working in a team. I therefore invited Mariana Oliveira and José Vianna to help me on this project, and they generously set aside much of their free time for this book. Mariana, based in Brasília, and José, in Curitiba, were both loyal allies throughout the whole project, contributing with comments, fact-checking and verification. Without them I would not have been able to carry out the task. I would also like to highlight the work of Germano Oliveira, who greatly helped me for months on end, and I also thank all the professionals who helped me at one time or another, including James Alberti, Thaís Skodowski, João Pedro Netto, Luiza Garonce, Diego Schutt, Alvaro Gribel and Marcelo Loureiro. I would also like to thank Paulo Roberto Gomes da Silva, Renata Martinelli, Débora Santos and Christianne Machiavelli, press officers at the Federal Police, federal prosecutors' office, Supreme Court and Paraná federal courts respectively. I pay a special tribute to all of them. They are professionals whom I already held in high regard and admire even more today. They know a lot and they taught me a lot. Thank you, my friends; it was an honour to work with you. I also thank all the aides, assistants and civil servants who were invariably attentive and courteous towards me in my endless scurrying between offices, departments and meeting rooms. And I would also like to thank Antônia Cristina Magalhães. Without your perceptive observations, it would be very difficult for me to find myself amid this sea of information and sentiments.

In the last two years, in there is no city I have been to more often than Curitiba. I had never been there before Operation Car Wash, but today it is a place I love dearly. I remember when I arrived there during the second week of November 2014 – the 12th to be more precise. I had done a piece for the national evening news about the works of art that had been seized from the home of Nelma Kodama and were now being exhibited in the Oscar Niemeyer Museum. I took the following day off to meet with some sources and find out about new developments in Operation Car Wash. One of these sources, a person I have a great deal of trust in, made a discreet suggestion: 'Stay until tomorrow. We'll be able to talk more then.' They were words I will never forget. I followed the advice, called my boss and requested permission to stay another day. I then changed my flight and went to bed early. The following day, 14 November, phase seven of Operation Car Wash began, when the first senior executives of the construction firms were arrested. I can't say how grateful I was to have stayed and witnessed that day in Curitiba with my own eyes. Because of that phase of the operation, which awoke public interest in the case, I spent the next three weeks in the city. My wife had to pack a suitcase with two more suits and a variety of shirts, and ask a friend from Globo News – the reporter Marcelo Cosme, who was going to Curitiba to reinforce the team – to bring it to me.

From then on, I was constantly travelling to and from Curitiba. The pace only slowed when the developments began to take off back in Brasília, for which I needed to remain in the federal capital. During all these months, one thing was crucial in ensuring that things went well: accurate information from trustworthy sources. It was these sources who guided me through the immense sea of data being churned out by

Operation Car Wash. For this, above all, I would like to thank my sources, on all sides of this multifaceted story. In the interests of protecting my sources, I won't name you, but I would like to say a big thank you to you all. Thank you for trusting in my work, thank you for giving me your time, thank you for sharing the stories which most affected you personally and which gave this book its guiding light.

Finally, I would like to thank my family, because I love you all and because I was away from home so much on account of this book. I want to thank my beloved wife, Giselly, who had to adapt her routine to my absences, both when I was travelling and when I was writing, while at the same time being with our children and helping me with the book. I want also to thank my daughters, Manuela and Isabel, who don't yet know how to read, but will one day see here my gratitude for their patience in putting up with daddy's book. My two little princesses, I love you both. I love my family and would like to thank my mother Miriam Leitão, my stepfather Sérgio Abranches, my father Marcelo Netto, my brothers Matheus Leitão and João Pedro Netto, my stepbrothers Rodrigo Abranches and Frederico Leitão, my cousins, aunts and uncles, among them my beloved aunt Beth, and my friends, for all the help and support they have given me in life, and in this project in particular.

To the reader, I would like to thank you for accompanying me throughout these pages. Operation Car Wash is so vast that it can hold many different points of view. This is mine. My aim has been to provide a faithful account of events, trying to see the various sides of the story. I wanted to enable people to understand why this operation was longer than any other in Brazil's history, and why it became an unparalleled success.

Legal Status of Those Investigated under Operation Car Wash

Name	Status under Operation Car Wash at 1 January 2019
Alexandrino de Alencar	He was convicted under Operation Car Wash, and is serving a sentence under house arrest on account of having provided information.
Gerson Almada	He was convicted under Operation Car Wash, and is serving a sentence at the prison hospital unit near Curitiba.
Solange Almeida	Released.
Henrique Eduardo Alves	He has been convicted, but has been released while appealing his conviction.
Ednaldo Alves da Silva	He was investigated under Operation Car Wash, but was never charged.
Delcídio do Amaral	He is under house arrest after making a plea bargain.
Antonio Anastasia	He is being investigated.
Clara Ant	She was investigated but never charged.
Rogério Araújo	He was convicted under Operation Car Wash, and is serving a non-prison sentence on account of having provided information.
Gim Argello	Convicted under Operation Car Wash, he is serving a sentence at the prison hospital unit near Curitiba.
Luiz Argólo	Convicted under Operation Car Wash.
José Roberto Arruda	Released, but awaiting lawsuits in the Federal District Court.
João Ricardo Auler	He was convicted under Operation Car Wash, and is serving a non-prison sentence on account of having provided information.
Dalton dos Santos Avancini	He was convicted under Operation Car Wash, and is serving a non-prison sentence on account of having provided information.
Otávio Azevedo	He was convicted under Operation Car Wash, and is serving a non-prison sentence on account of having provided information.

Giles Azevedo	He is being investigated.
Arianna Azevedo Costa Bachmann	He was convicted under Operation Car Wash, and is serving a non-prison sentence on account of having provided information.
Fernando 'Baiano' Soares	Sentenced, released, turned informant.
Roberto Egídio Balestra	All investigations against him have been dropped.
Marcelo Barboza	He was investigated on suspicion of money laundering but was never charged.
Pedro Barusco	He was convicted under Operation Car Wash, and is serving a non-prison sentence on account of having provided information.
Márcio Thomaz Bastos	Deceased.
Fernandinho Beira-Mar	Convicted, imprisoned.
João Antônio Bernardi Filho	He was convicted under Operation Car Wash, and is serving a non-prison sentence on account of having provided information.
Paulo Bernardo	He was accused and is answering charges at liberty, while on bail.
Ricardo Berzoini	He is under preliminary investigation.
Márcio Bonilho	Sentenced under Operation Car Wash.
José Ricardo Nogueira Breghirolli	Sentenced under Operation Car Wash.
Roberto Britto	He is under preliminary investigation.
José Carlos Bumlai	Sentenced under Operation Car Wash.
Maurício Bumlai	Investigated, turned defendant but acquitted in Operation Car Wash
Renan Calheiros	He is the subject of a preliminary investigation and has already been formally charged by the Public Prosecutor's Office, but has not yet responded to criminal proceedings and remains at liberty.
Júlio Camargo	He was convicted under Operation Car Wash, and is serving a non-prison sentence on account of having provided information.
Gladson Cameli	All investigations against him under Operation Car Wash have been dropped.
Eduardo Campos	Deceased.
Waldir Maranhão Cardoso	All investigations against him have been dropped.
José Eduardo Cardozo	All investigations against him have been dropped.
Tiago Cedraz	He was recently formally charged by the Public Prosecutor's Office, but has not yet become a defendant.
Nestor Cerveró	He was convicted under Operation Car Wash, and is serving a non-prison sentence on account of having provided information.

Carlos Habib Chater	Convicted under Operation Car Wash.
Fernando Bezerra Coelho	He is under preliminary investigation.
Fernando Collor de Mello	He is defending himself against criminal charges, but remains at liberty.
Pedro Corrêa	Informant, released.
Aline Corrêa	She is subject to a preliminary investigation.
Paulo Roberto Costa	He was convicted under Operation Car Wash, and is serving a non-prison sentence on account of having provided information.
Shanni Costa	He was convicted under Operation Car Wash, and is serving a non-prison sentence on account of having provided information.
Humberto Costa	He is under preliminary investigation.
Vilson Covatti	He is under preliminary investigation.
Eduardo Cunha	Convicted, imprisoned.
Paulo Roberto Dalmazzo	Convicted under Operation Car Wash.
José Dirceu	Convicted, released by decision of the Federal Supreme Court.
Renato Duque	Convicted under Operation Car Wash, imprisoned.
'Edson'	He was never officially identified.
André Esteves	All investigations against him have been dropped.
Julio Faerman	Convicted under Operation Car Wash, he became a informant.
Márcio Faria	He was convicted under Operation Car Wash, and is serving a non-prison sentence on account of having provided information.
Luiz Fernando Faria	He is defending himself against criminal charges, but remains at liberty.
Lindbergh Farias	He is under preliminary investigation.
Diogo Ferreira	Informant, released.
Ildefonso Colares Filho	He is defending himself against criminal charges, but remains at liberty.
Eduardo da Fonte	He is defending himself against criminal charges, but remains at liberty.
Graça Foster	She was subject to a civil (non-criminal) lawsuit for improbity, but has been released.
Agenor Franklin	Convicted under Operation Car Wash, imprisoned by the Federal Police in Curitiba.
Bernardo Freiburghaus	He was the subject of a preliminary investigation and was formally charged, but the actions against him have not gone any further on account of his dual Swiss nationality.

Lúcio Bolonha Funaro	Convicted, arrested, turned informant.
José Sérgio Gabrielli	He was subject to a civil (non-criminal) lawsuit for improbity, but has been released.
João Cláudio Genu	Convicted under Operation Car Wash, however, he is not imprisoned
José Otávio Germano	He is defending himself against criminal charges, but remains at liberty.
Jerônimo Goergen	Charges dropped by the Federal Supreme Court for lack of evidence.
Mario Goes	He was convicted under Operation Car Wash, and is serving a non-prison sentence on account of having provided information.
Aníbal Gomes	He is defending himself against criminal charges, but remains at liberty.
Guilherme Gonçalves	He is defending himself against criminal charges, but remains at liberty.
Afonso Hamm	He was not arrested and accusations were dropped for lack of evidence.
Luis Carlos Heinze	He was not arrested and accusations were dropped for lack of evidence.
João Augusto Henriques	Convicted under Operation Car Wash, he is serving a sentence at the prison hospital unit near Curitiba.
Pedro Henry	He has been formally charged but has not yet responded to criminal charges, and remains at liberty.
Gleisi Hoffmann	She was acquitted in relation to the payment of R$1 million to her election campaign (referenced on p. 205) but formally charged in relation to two other cases. She has not yet responded to these criminal charges and remains at liberty.
Ricardo Hoffmann	Convicted under Operation Car Wash.
Jose Janene	Deceased.
Romero Jucá	He's a defendant, responding to a criminal lawsuit, but at liberty.
Sandes Júnior	He is under preliminary investigation.
Pablo Alejandro Kipersmit	He is defending himself against criminal charges, but remains at liberty.
Nelma Kodama	She was convicted under Operation Car Wash but later became an informant and is now serving a non-prison sentence.
João Leão	The investigation against him was dropped.
Eduardo Leite	Convicted under Operation Car Wash, he turned informant and remains at liberty.
Marcio Lewkowicz	Convicted under Operation Car Wash, he turned informant and remains at liberty.
Marice Corrêa de Lima	He is under preliminary investigation and could be criminally charged, if there is enough evidence.

Giselda Rousie de Lima	She was investigated in 2015 but has not yet been formally charged.
Arthur Lira	He has been formally charged but has not yet responded to criminal charges, and remains at liberty.
Benedito de Lira	He has been formally charged but has not yet responded to criminal charges, and remains at liberty.
Edison Lobão	He has been formally charged but has not yet responded to criminal charges, and remains at liberty.
Rafael Angulo Lopez	He was convicted under Operation Car Wash, and is serving a non-prison sentence on account of having provided information.
Vander Loubet	He is defending himself against criminal charges, but remains at liberty.
Luiz Inácio Lula da Silva	Convicted, imprisoned.
Sérgio Machado	Turned informant, released.
Carlos Magno	He is under preliminary investigation.
Hermes Magnus	He has never been charged, and there is no suspicion of involvement. He assisted law enforcement and is currently living in hiding.
Lázaro Botelho Martins	The investigation against him was dropped for lack of evidence.
Erton Medeiros Fonseca	Convicted under Operation Car Wash.
Leonardo Meirelles	Convicted under Operation Car Wash.
Leandro Meirelles	Convicted under Operation Car Wash.
Sérgio Mendes	Convicted under Operation Car Wash.
Augusto Mendonça	He was convicted under Operation Car Wash, and is serving a non-prison sentence on account of having provided information.
José Mentor	The investigation against him was dropped for lack of evidence.
Aloizio Mercadante	He is under preliminary investigation.
Humberto Mesquita	Deceased.
Nelson Meurer	Convicted, released.
Renato Molling	The investigation against him was dropped for lack of evidence.
Othon Zanoide de Moraes Filho	He is defending himself against criminal charges, but remains at liberty.
Monica Moura	She was convicted under Operation Car Wash, and is serving a non-prison sentence on account of having provided information.
Fernando Moura	He was convicted under Operation Car Wash, and is serving a non-prison sentence on account of having provided information.

Elton Negrão	He was convicted under Operation Car Wash, and is serving a non-prison sentence on account of having provided information.
Mário Negromonte	He is under preliminary investigation.
Adarico Negromonte Filho	He was accused only once, and was acquitted in Operation Car Wash. There are no further investigations against him.
Aécio Neves	He is defending himself against criminal charges, but remains at liberty.
Ciro Nogueira	He has been formally charged but has not yet responded to criminal charges, and remains at liberty.
Marcelo Odebrecht	He was convicted under Operation Car Wash, and is serving a non-prison sentence on account of having provided information.
Paulo Okamotto	He was acquitted in the only case in which he was charged. There are no other investigations against him.
Missionário José Olímpio	The investigation against him was dropped for lack of evidence.
Waldomiro de Oliveira	Convicted under Operation Car Wash.
Mateus Coutinho de Sa Oliveira	Convicted under Operation Car Wash.
Rogério Cunha de Oliveira	Convicted under Operation Car Wash.
Eduardo Paes	He is being investigated and is the target in a judicial inquiry. He has not yet been formally charged and therefore has not responded to a criminal lawsuit.
Antonio Palocci	Convicted, under house arrest, turned informant.
Milton Pascowitch	She was convicted under Operation Car Wash, and is serving a non-prison sentence on account of having provided information.
Silvio Pereira	He is the subject of an ongoing lawsuit. He is defending his case but remains at liberty.
Ricardo Pernambuco	Informant, released.
Ricardo Pernambuco Junior	Informant, released.
Ricardo Pessoa	He was convicted under Operation Car Wash, and is serving a non-prison sentence on account of having provided information.
Léo (José Aldemário) Pinheiro	Convicted under Operation Car Wash and imprisoned.
Ronan Maria Pinto	Convicted under Operation Car Wash.
João Pizzolatti	He is defending himself in ongoing legal proceedings and remains at liberty.
José Linhares Ponte	He is being investigated but is not yet the subject of criminal charges and remains at liberty.

Meire Poza	Convicted under Operation Car Wash.
João Procópio	He is no longer being investigated. He is defending himself against criminal charges and remains at liberty.
Pedro Paulo Leoni Ramos	He is defending himself in ongoing legal proceedings and remains at liberty.
Valdir Raupp	He has already been formally charged but has not yet gone to court, and remains at liberty.
Aguinaldo Ribeiro	He has already been formally charged but has not yet gone to court, and remains at liberty.
Edson Ribeiro	Acquitted.
César Rocha	He was convicted under Operation Car Wash, and is serving a non-prison sentence on account of having provided information.
Alexandre Romano	Informant.
Dilma Rousseff	She is defending herself against criminal charges and remains at liberty.
Walmir Pinheiro Santana	He was convicted under Operation Car Wash, and is serving a non-prison sentence on account of having provided information.
João Santana	He was convicted under Operation Car Wash, and is serving a non-prison sentence on account of having provided information.
Alexandre Santos	He is under preliminary investigation.
José Sarney	He has already been formally charged but has not yet gone to court, and remains at liberty.
Roseana Sarney	The investigation was dropped for lack of evidence.
Fernando Schahin	Convicted under Operation Car Wash and turned informant.
Salim Schahin	Convicted under Operation Car Wash and turned informant.
Simão Sessim	The investigation was dropped for lack of evidence.
Edinho Silva	He is under a preliminary investigation that could lead to criminal charges, if there is enough evidence.
Vice Admiral Othon Pinheiro da Silva	Convicted under Operation Car Wash, he remains at liberty.
Luiz Eduardo de Oliveira e Silva	Convicted under Operation Car Wash.
Fabiano Silveira	He has never been investigated, only cited. He remains at liberty.
Zwi Skornicki	He was convicted under Operation Car Wash, and is serving a non-prison sentence on account of having provided information.
Edilaira Soares	Acquitted under Operation Car Wash.
Delúbio Soares	Convicted under Operation Car Wash.

José Antunes Sobrinho	Investigated, subsequently became an informant.
Dilceu Sperafico	The investigation was dropped for lack of evidence.
Roberto Teixeira	He is defending himself against criminal charges, and remains at liberty.
Michel Temer	He has been formally charged but has not filed a plea.
Cândido Vaccarezza	He is defending himself against criminal charges under Operation Car Wash, and remains at liberty.
Nayara de Lima Vaccari	She has already been investigated and has not been formally charged.
João Vaccari Neto	He was convicted under Operation Car Wash, and is serving a sentence at the prison hospital unit near Curitiba.
Marcos Valério	Imprisoned under the 'Big Monthly' trial, he is now an informant.
Leon Vargas	He was convicted under Operation Car Wash, and is serving a sentence at the prison hospital unit near Curitiba.
André Vargas	Convicted, on parole.
Ivan Vernon	Convicted under Operation Car Wash.
Jaques Wagner	He is under preliminary investigation.
Alberto Youssef	He was convicted under Operation Car Wash, and is serving a non-prison sentence on account of having provided information.
Jorge Luiz Zelada	He was convicted under Operation Car Wash, and is serving a sentence at the prison hospital unit near Curitiba.
Marco Antonio de Campos Ziegert	Acquitted.